Governing Through Crime

Recent Titles in STUDIES IN CRIME AND PUBLIC POLICY

Michael Tonry and Norval Morris, General Editors

Governing Through Crime

*How the War on Crime
Transformed American Democracy
and Created a Culture of Fear*

Jonathan Simon

OXFORD
UNIVERSITY PRESS

2007

OXFORD
UNIVERSITY PRESS

Oxford University Press, Inc., publishes works that further
Oxford University's objective of excellence
in research, scholarship, and education.

Oxford   New York
Auckland   Cape Town   Dar es Salaam   Hong Kong   Karachi
Kuala Lumpur   Madrid   Melbourne   Mexico City   Nairobi
New Delhi   Shanghai   Taipei   Toronto

With offices in
Argentina   Austria   Brazil   Chile   Czech   Republic   France   Greece
Guatemala   Hungary   Italy   Japan   Poland   Portugal   Singapore
South Korea   Switzerland   Thailand   Turkey   Ukraine   Vietnam

Published by Oxford University Press, Inc.
198 Madison Avenue, New York, New York 10016

www.oup.com

Oxford is a registered trademark of Oxford University Press

Library of Congress Cataloging-in-Publication Data

Simon, Jonathan.
Governing through crime: how the war on crime transformed
American democracy and created a culture of fear / Jonathan Simon.
p. cm.—(Studies in crime and public policy)
Includes bibliographical references and index.
ISBN-13 978-0-19-518108-1
1. Crime—Political aspects—United States—History—20th century.
2. Criminal justice, Administration of—Political aspects—United States—
History—20th century.   3. Crime prevention—Political aspects—
United States—History—20th century.   I. Title.   II. Series.
HV6789.S57 2006
364.40973'09045—dc22   2006006732

5 7 9 8 6 4
Printed in the United States of America
on acid-free paper

This book is dedicated to the memory of

My father
William Simon
1930–2000

and

My brother
Marc David Simon
1951–2002

Acknowledgments

I am indebted to three institutions for support during the research phases of this book. In 1999, I was awarded a Soros Senior Justice Fellowship by the Open Society Institute, which funded a semester off from teaching to begin work on this book. The Open Society Institute and George Soros, its founder and benefactor, have recognized crime and crime control as one of the fundamental challenges to democratic governance that the developed world faces. Their staff and fellows have made tremendous progress in bringing the problem of governing through crime before the world public. I hope this book can contribute to that process.

This book has also been nurtured by the collegiality and financial support of the University of Miami School of Law, which has provided numerous summer research grants, a semester of public interest leave, and lots of collegial encouragement. I would like to thank Deans Sam Thompson, Mary Doyle, and Dennis Lynch for their support. The revisions of the manuscript took place after my arrival at the University of California at Berkeley. The book might have been done more quickly if not for the move, but it has been enriched by the interactions here. I am especially indebted to my colleagues at Boalt Hall, School of Law, led by Dean Bob Berring and Dean Christopher Edley, for their financial and intellectual support of my work.

During the decade in which these ideas have developed into the present volume the debt owed to many colleagues for their criticism and encouragement has become vast and unnamable (and inevitably unrepayable). Thanks to David Abraham, Tony Alfieri, Tom Baker, Ian Boal,

Marianne Constable, John Ely, Angelina Godoy, Henry Green, Rosann Greenspan, Pat Gudridge, Susan Haack, Don Herzog, David Kirp, Rob MacCoun, Frank Munger, Pat O'Malley, Richard W. Perry, Judith Randle, Robert Rosen, David Sklansky, Adam Simon, William Simon, Richard Sparks, Christina Spaulding, Nikolas Rose, Michael Tonry, Susan Tucker, and Marianna Valverde. The work was assisted by a number of extraordinary research assistants. Thanks to Ashley Aubuchon, Kellie Bryant, Jessica Gabel, Santhi Leon, Ariel Meyerstein, and Viktoriya Safris.

For their critical reading of the entire manuscript, I would like to thank David Caploe, Malcolm Feeley, David Garland, Mona Lynch, Stuart Scheingold, Marlene Simon, Lucia Zedner, Franklin Zimring, and several anonymous reviewers for Oxford University Press. I would also like to thank Dedi Felman and James Cook, my Oxford editors, for their confidence and patience.

The views expressed in this book, and any errors of fact or interpretation, are, of course, exclusively mine.

Contents

Governing Through Crime

Introduction

Crime and American Governance

> For a long time before that in the United States it had not been
> safe to walk in the big cities at night: sometimes in certain areas
> not in the day. For years they had moved about by the grace
> of paternal or brutal police; or under the protection of some
> gang. (It was in the mid-seventies that it came out for how
> long the United States had been run by an only partly
> concealed conspiracy linking crime, the military machine, the
> industries to do with war, and government.) Whether he chose
> to be protected by the bully men of the gangster groups, or by
> the police, or by the deliberate choice of a living area that was
> safe and respectable and inside which he lived as once the Jews
> had lived in ghettoes, in America the citizen had long since
> become used to an organized barbarism.
>
> —Doris Lessing, *The Four-Gated City*

In her 1969 book *The Four-Gated City*, Doris Lessing writes of the 1970s from the perspective of someone looking back at the end of the twentieth century.[1] Her imagined observations of the United States, presumably based on the tumult and civil violence of the late 1960s, remind us that fear of sudden and terrible violence was a major feature of American life long before September 11, 2001. The collapsing towers were only the latest—and most lethal—of a series of spectacular scenes of violence that have unfolded at the centers of our largest cities since President Kennedy was shot to death in Dallas with a mail-order rifle in 1963.[2] By the end of that decade, many Americans from all walks of life had come to believe that a personal confrontation with armed violence—robbery, riot, police deadly force—was a distinct possibility.

In the intervening decades, much as Lessing predicted, Americans have built a new civil and political order structured around the problem of violent crime. In this new order, values like freedom and equality have been revised in ways that would have been shocking, if obviously imaginable—in

3

the late 1960s, and new forms of power institutionalized and embraced—all in the name of repressing seemingly endless waves of violent crime. Though Lessing condemned this new order as an "organized barbarism," many Americans have come to tolerate it as a necessary response to unacceptable risks of violence in everyday life.

Criminologists and sociologists have long sought to document that this fear of crime and violence is irrational in its scope and priority. But even if the public were to seriously consider the empirical evidence for this position, there would be little reason to expect the civil order built around crime in America to disappear anytime soon. Nor should we expect the current decline in crime rates, should it continue, to produce a commensurately dramatic shift. Crime has become so central to the exercise of authority in America, by everyone from the president of the United States to the classroom teacher, that it will take a concerted effort by Americans themselves to dislodge it. They will have to find ways to disrupt the flow of information, discourse, and debate tied to crime while creating new pathways to knowing and acting on the people and relationships that are their responsibility to foster and protect. This book is intended as a start in that direction.

The title claim—that the American elite are "governing through crime"—is polemical, and perhaps overstated. But it has at its core a key insight into a central feature of contemporary American law and society that generates three specific and important corollaries.

First, crime has now become a significant strategic issue. Across all kinds of institutional settings, people are seen as acting legitimately when they act to prevent crimes or other troubling behaviors that can be closely analogized to crimes. Thus, in chapter 2 we will explore how political executives, especially governors, have sought to expand their role on issues ranging from the death penalty to restoring voting rights for felons.

Second, we can expect people to deploy the category of crime to legitimate interventions that have other motivations. Recent legislation (state and federal) making an assault on a pregnant woman that causes death or harm to the fetus a distinct federal crime has more to do with the politics of abortion rights than crime (Sanger 2006), but because it is about crime and directed at criminals it can achieve majority support despite polarization on the choice issue.

Third, the technologies, discourses, and metaphors of crime and criminal justice have become more visible features of all kinds of institutions, where they can easily gravitate into new opportunities for governance. In this way, it is not a great jump to go from (a) concerns about juvenile crime through (b) measures in schools that treat students primarily as potential criminals or victims, and, (c) later still, to attacks on academic failure as a kind of crime *someone* must be held accountable for, whether it be the student (no more "social passing"), teachers (pay tied to test scores), or whole schools (closure as a result of failing test scores).

It is essential to distinguish "governing through crime" from "governing crime." Any institution or organization that is not in deep crisis has to respond when subjects under their jurisdiction suffer threats to their persons or property. Some institutions, namely those of criminal justice, are dedicated to addressing those threats across society, but other institutions, including families, schools, and businesses, are also mobilized to act when crime threatens, though that action may be limited to securing the intervention of professional criminal justice agents. When institutions suffer repeated or destructive criminal threats, they will develop strategies that go beyond that intervention, however. These efforts to employ their own forms of governance or bring in new approaches from outside can be distinguished from governing through crime to the extent that they are proximate and proportionate to the crime threat experienced.

When institutions govern crime in this sense, they are not necessarily governing through crime, but it can be difficult to draw that distinction, particularly in times when high levels of reported crime make it difficult to discern which institutions are genuinely threatened by crime and which institutions are using crime to promote governance by legitimizing and/or providing content for the exercise of power. This book will offer interpretations of numerous particular examples, but the characterization of any particular practice will inevitably be open to argument.

Though these assertions are difficult to test decisively in ways social scientists prefer, they offer an interpretation of contemporary practices and discourses that can be evaluated by Americans themselves as to how well they provide insight into their own experience of governing and being governed at work, or school, or in the family, as well as their experience of the state. To this end, much of the book is descriptive, seeking to provide a thick account of the ways that crime as a problem influences the way we know and act on our selves, our families, and our communities.

The Consequences

But my intentions in writing the book are also normative. Governing through crime is making America less democratic and more racially polarized; it is exhausting our social capital and repressing our capacity for innovation. For all that, governing through crime does not, and I believe, cannot make us more secure; indeed it fuels a culture of fear and control that inevitably lowers the threshold of fear even as it places greater and greater burdens on ordinary Americans.

The consequences of the problem of crime gaining such status have been enormous. Whether one values American democracy for its liberty or its equality-enhancing features, governing through crime has been bad. First, the vast reorienting of fiscal and administrative resources toward the criminal justice system at both the federal and state level, has resulted in a shift aptly described as a transformation from "welfare state" to "penal state."[3] The result has not been less government, but a more authoritarian executive, a more passive legislature, and a more defensive judiciary than even the welfare state itself was accused of producing.

Second, the portion of the population held in custody for crimes has grown well beyond historic norms.[4] At the end of the twentieth century, more Americans than ever before were confined in prisons, jails, detention centers, and in detention spaces within schools.[5] The racial skewing of this incarceration has visibly reversed key aspects of the civil rights revolution. Indeed, for the first time since the abolition of slavery, a definable group of Americans lives, on a more or less permanent basis, in a state of legal nonfreedom—either because of a single life sentence, repeated incarcerations, or the long-term consequences of criminal conviction—a shocking percentage of them descendants of those freed slaves. Governing this population through the criminal justice system has not provided the guarantees of security that might inspire greater investment in inner cities, but instead has further stigmatized communities already beset by concentrated poverty.

Predictably, the poor, overrepresented in both groups, share this fate, but the everyday lives of middle-class families have also been transformed, not so much by crime itself, as by "fear of crime." For middle class families, choices such as where to live, where to work, and where to send children to school are made with increasing reference to the perceived risk of crime. As institutions which serve the middle class focus on addressing crime fears, those we have of others, and those that others have of us, the effects are multiplied. The point is not that the middle class are more affected by governing through crime than the poor, but to consider both the criminal justice system that is concentrated on poor communities and the private sector of middle-class securitized environments as class-specific modes of governing through crime that interact with each other.

The emergence of the gated community style of subdivision and the oversized sport utility vehicles (SUVs) both reflect a priority on security and on reinforcing the distance that middle class families seek from crime risks they associate with the urban poor. Yet as critics of sprawl have begun to document, this heavy emphasis on fortification makes these communities even more reliant on a command-and-control police and penal state to enforce norms of civility. Indeed, the new securitized environment tends to facilitate certain narrow routines, but when novel situations arise it tends to create what economists call (appropriately for us) a "prisoner's dilemma", i.e., a game where the players cannot cooperate and can prevail only by turning predatory first. The person outside last loses (even if she is on her way back to her own SUV or gated community). In such an environment, litigation and prosecution can both be expected to rise in order to establish social control in the absence of trust.

American democracy is also threatened by the emergence of crime victims as a dominant model of the citizen as representative of the common person whose needs and capacities define the mission of representative government (Garland 2001a, 144). A range of new forms of knowledge now bring the "truth" of crime victims into the criminal justice system and beyond (Simon 2004; 2005). These victims' truths are powerful, often overwhelming the emotional significance of other issues. They undermine the forms of solidarity and responsibility necessary for democratic institutions.

Plan of the Book

The thesis of governing through crime and its departures from the main sociological analyses of contemporary penal excess will be the focus of chapter 1. Readers who want to get right to the substantive explication should skip ahead to chapter 2, which begins an examination of how the war on crime has reshaped key aspects of the American state beginning with the executive. Presidents and governors have moved from their post–New Deal role as maestros of a complex ensemble of regulatory and service agencies, to be judged by the social results of their performance, to a set of lonely crime fighters, measured only in how much they seem to share the community's outrage at crime.

Chapter 3 looks at crime's influence on lawmaking. The crime-related output of state legislatures and Congress since the 1970s is not only prodigious in quantity, but represents a distinctive style of lawmaking that has forged a new circuit between the people and their representatives, in which the crime victim emerges as an idealized political subject. I will take a close look at the Omnibus Safe Streets and Crime Control Act of 1968, which can be fairly called the "mother of all contemporary crime legislation." That legislation and the metaphoric mapping of American society it promoted remain, I would argue, the dominant interpretive grid on which governable America is known and acted upon by government officials at all levels.

Chapter 4 examines the courts. Though executives and legislatures have found new purchase on the body politic through crime, courts by contrast have suffered a largely unmediated decline in power and prestige as crime has become a central public concern. Indeed, this development represents a great yet telling irony. Criminal law as schema of government would seem to place a high value on adjudication. The criminal trial remains the popular paradigm of justice. But during the war on crime, these same adjudicatory values have been delegitimized as unacceptably weak in combating crime.

Chapter 5 rejoins the subject of mass imprisonment that has recently concerned the sociologists of punishment. Rather than treat this as a political effect of social causes, I will build on previous chapters to show how mass incarceration is an inevitable effect of reshaping political authority around crime.

Part II moves beyond the core of the state to examine the institutions that govern the everyday life most of us experience—our families, schools, and workplaces. If the institutions that operate in this world also govern through crime, it is not because they are legally bound to follow the official institutions of government. While the law often does create pressures in that direction, we find a variety of less obvious forms of influence primarily responsible for their voluntary compliance.

Chapter 6 examines the family as a locus of crime. The legal status of the family has come full circle in the last generation, from that part of society most insulated from the force of the criminal law, whether instrumentally or ideologically, to one of the areas most subjected to it. Today, criminal accusations have replaced the traditional normative standards of marital dissolution law as key elements in divorce, especially when the custody of children is contested. The family is treated as a locus of suspicions about crime that requires surveillance and intervention by criminal law institutions. Parents are drafted as an extension of law enforcement. At the same time, a criminal conviction leading to imprisonment is an increasingly acceptable reason for terminating parental rights. This chapter charts the pathways along which the struggle for power in the family—and between the family and the state—has increasingly come to be regulated by criminal law, with its distinct methods and metaphors.

Chapter 7 examines a similar dynamic in relation to public schools. A generation ago, racial inequality was the pivot around which the federal government mandated a vast reworking in the way schools were governed at the state and local levels. Today, crime plays a similar role. The merging of school and penal system has speeded the collapse of the progressive project of education and tilted the administration of schools toward a highly authoritarian and mechanistic model. This model collapses all the normal / expected / predictable vulnerabilities of youth into variations of the categories of criminal violence. This transformation is especially problematic since when the generally preferred "solution"—the tight policing of everyone—fails, as it inevitably will, the response is to shift responsibility onto everyone but the incumbent regime, primarily through such emotionally satisfying, but substantively empty, slogans as "accountability" and "zero tolerance."

Chapter 8 examines the role that crime and crime control play in the workplace. The decline of collective bargaining and the general loss of bargaining power by American workers in the face of global competition for low-cost labor have opened a space for the return of crime as a central axis of regulation and resistance in the workplace. This takes multiple forms. There is a new emphasis on screening potential employees for illegal behavior of almost any sort. Fraud has become a pervasive concern for large information and financial services companies. In all workplaces, there is a heightened concern about violent crime, a concern that leads in turn to yet more efforts at surveillance. There is also a tendency to define workplace conflicts—say, between two employees or a subordinate and more managerial employee—into categories of misbehavior that have crime-like terms and structure, e.g. malice, harm, victim. Sanctions, including dismissal, once thought of as the capital punishment of labor relations, are again becoming an increasingly important part of workplace governance.

Chapter 9, the concluding chapter, imagines pathways of governing open societies beyond crime. To look forward, we look back. As President Richard Nixon struggled with themes to bring together a domestic agenda that would reinforce the "silent majority" he believed was responsible for his narrow victory in 1968, he settled on two wars: one on crime, in the form of a war on drugs, the other on cancer. Thirty years later, it is apparent that the war on crime has produced a major reorientation of governance, while the impact of the war on cancer has been barely noticed. It need not be so; an aging population is also one fearful of disease. As baby boomers watch their parents die and prepare to consider their own mortality, cancer looms as large as crime may have when they and their children were younger. How would a war on cancer in the present decade compare to the war on crime as a way of governing? What do both wars offer a society facing a possibly decades-long "war on terror"?

Thinking About Crime and Government

By describing, the ways that governing through crime has distorted American institutional priorities across a wide variety of domains, this book invites discussion of the real social costs of investing so much in crime as a model problem. Does producing large numbers of prisoners who after experiencing the social lessons of incarceration are discharged to many of America's most hard pressed cities improve the long-term governability of American families, communities, and states? Do prison resources invested in the prisoners who are removed and eventually returned to communities, raise or lower the costs of social coordination? Do leadership programs emphasizing punitiveness make power more or less accountable? Does fortifying the nuclear family by wrapping it in technological armor designed to exclude intolerable risks of violence, viruses, and drugs lend itself to collective acknowledgment of irreducible risks in late modernity? Or does governing through crime erode democratic capacity by destroying social trust and capital?

In my view, a movement to restore crime to its rightful place as *one* "social" problem among many should win assent from both Left and Right within contemporary American political ideology. In discussing crime, both sides typically prefer to emphasize a cluster of treasured values in the always symbolically rich territory of crime and punishment. Once they confront the effects of governing through crime on the governability of the public, both liberals and conservatives will recognize the danger to their preferred visions of governance. The Left will find most disturbing the hardening of inequality formed by governing through crime, whether in its racially concentrated prisons or gated communities. The Right will find that across a whole range of dimensions, governing through crime subverts the Right's mandate of responsible independence at the level of the firm and family.

The terror attacks of 9/11 have created a kind of amnesia wherein a quarter century of fearing crime and securing social spaces has been suddenly recognized, but misidentified as a response to an astounding act of terrorism, rather than a generation-long pattern of political and social change. Just as we now see the war on terrorism as requiring a fundamental recasting of American governance, the war on crime has already wrought such a transformation—one which may now be relegitimized as a "tough" response to terrorism. Failing to recognize this disturbing dynamic could not only delay a much needed rethinking of our commitment to governing through crime, but also, as I suggest in the conclusion, lead to an equally problematic approach to the so-called "war on terrorism."

This social amnesia is particularly crucial today, as we witness what may well be a fast-disappearing window of opportunity to question our commitment to governing through crime. Recent polling data suggest Americans are increasingly skeptical of harsh prison sentences, preferring a return to greater emphasis on rehabilitation of offenders in particular and social reform generally as a way to ameliorate crime (Hart Associates 2002). Part of that may be demographic. As baby boomers age beyond their parenting years—when crime may have loomed as especially threatening to their children—other issues, including education, retirement security, and health care, begin to loom larger. We will perhaps have arrived at the "tipping point" when baby boomers are more anxious about access to medical marijuana for their chemotherapy than if their kids are lighting up after school.

But even if crime becomes less central as a public obsession, it may not change the entrenched dynamic of governing through crime. The ways in which institutions know and act on their subjects are subtle and pervasive, and tend to remain largely beneath the surface of political controversy. Only by recognizing how these pathways of knowledge and power have been set by crime and fear of crime, and challenging them in their own terms can we come to grips with this sea change in our self-government.

Freedom Is Messy: Crime and Late Modern Democracy

After the looting of Baghdad in the spring of 2003 and the imagined crime wave in New Orleans after Hurricane Katrina in 2005, it became common for pundits and others to pronounce that the first task of government is necessarily providing security for body and property. Of course, as a historical matter, nothing could be more wrong. Families and clans were the prime units of security and retained substantial control over the resolution of interpersonal violence until the early modern period of European history. As a fact of historical development, the state only gradually laid claim to the power to punish crimes and secure civic order, and the "monopoly" of legitimate violence so often proclaimed on behalf of the state was the sheerest of fictions even in the most advanced countries before the twentieth century. Even the supposedly "logical" priority of "law and order" granted by classical political philosophers is best seen in terms of the struggles to renegotiate political life associated with political liberalism (Herzog 1989). Indeed, the emergence of criminology as a positive science of criminal behavior and an expert adjunct of state power in the late nineteenth century constituted a major revision of the liberal idea, recognizing that crime was best regulated by modern techniques of social governance rather than through punitive criminal justice (Horn 2003).

Still, if the oft-cited priority of law and order fails to reflect *deep* history, or logical necessity, it does in its own way reflect our *recent* history in the United States, in which crime has been framed as a, if not the, defining problem for government. In this time period, roughly from 1960 to the present, crime became a model problem for government. This does not mean that government did not recognize and seek to act on many other social problems (even at its inflated size contemporary crime control is only a small fraction of overall public spending), but that often it is crime through which other problems are recognized, defined, and acted upon.

It is a truism well worth remembering that behind all forms of law, public or private, lurks a background threat of violence within the law, generally embodied in the penal or criminal law. So if you refuse to perform on a binding contract, the other party may bring a civil law suit against you. If your adversary prevails and obtains a monetary judgment against you, your failure to honor it will ultimately result in a forcible taking of your assets, any resistance to which will generally constitute a criminal act. In this sense governing through crime might seem to state a rather unsurprising syllogism. Since all governance, public or private, in American society takes places within a structure of legal authority (of public officers but also parents, employers, property owners, and so on), and since all legal authority ultimately rests on the threat of lawful violence within the criminal law, all governance is "through" the implied threat of making resistance at some stage a "crime." This is a useful balance to the frequent celebration of liberal capitalist societies as ones governed by consent and through the instruments of free exchange (Cover 1986). The distinction I wish to draw with the way that American democracy has been deformed by the war on crime is one of priority. In the conventional syllogism, crime (and the violence it authorizes) is generally a last response, the end point of a pathway of resistance to lawful governance. What is visibly different about the way we govern since the 1960s is the degree to which crime is a first response.

To be sure, history is replete with political regimes that mobilize around crime, use the criminal law to cover up the asymmetrical effects of power, bolster the elimination of political dissidents, and terrorize and deter organized resistance by systematically exploited classes. The case of the use of criminal law by England's Whig ruling elite in the early eighteenth century, closely studied by E. P. Thompson and his students, provides a good example. Reluctant to consolidate their hegemony through a standing army—yet faced with popular discontent at the rapid economic dislocations being produced by Whig legal policy—England's elites turned to the criminal law to produce a highly flexible system of terror and mercy that managed political risk and improved the regime's legitimacy (Thompson 1975; Hay et al. 1975). Stuart Hall and his colleagues (1978) suggested something very similar was going on during England's "mugging crisis" in the 1970s. Media-stoked popular panic about crime helped make foreign immigrants the most visible targets of conflict unleashed by Britain's sustained economic bust of the period and did so in ways favoring police and punitive policies.

In other cases, such as Haiti under the Duvaliers, an entire political regime came to be based on organized crime, in the form of mass violence to terrorize the population and theft through corruption (Tilley 1985). In a somewhat broader sense, fascist states of all kinds govern through crime in multiple ways, using the tactics of crime, using existing criminal networks to exercise political power, and declaring its political opponents to be criminal enemies of the people.

It would be fascinating to look across the many historical examples in which crime and government have been in some deep sense intertwined. Here I only intend to call attention to the relationship between crime and governance that has emerged in the United States since the 1960s. Unlike some of these other examples, governing through crime of the type that has unfolded in this context belongs to the history of liberal political orders rather than to the self conscious exceptions associated with Fascisms and other modern authoritarian regimes.

To treat governing through crime as "liberal," in this sense, is not to suppose that it is determined by responsiveness to popular anxieties about crime, justified or not by objective factors. Instead, it is appropriate to treat governing through crime in the contemporary United States as liberal because for the most part it operates upon, rather than simply against, the freedom of its subjects (Rose 1999). Though criminal laws often speak in terms of prohibitions, and penal sanctions demand greater degrees of submission to authority, the work of governing through crime, seen in its larger totality, involves the effort of responsible actors of all kinds in contemporary American society who struggle to provide security for their families, their students, their customers, their employees, and others.

A great deal of the recent literature on the growth of punishment in the United States emphasizes the authoritarian character of prisons and the role of criminal justice in enforcing conditions of growing economic inequality (Currie 1998; Parenti 1999; Wacquant forthcoming). I do not wish to be read as denying this characteristic of mass imprisonment but instead to insist that it be analyzed politically in the same frame as the myriad of ways in which crime regulates the self-governing activity of people who are not targets of criminal justice repression but instead eager consumers of public and private governmental tools against crime risk. Indeed, it is the relationship between these two faces of governing through crime, the penal state and the security state, "the criminology of the other" and the "criminology of the self" (Garland 2001a, 137) that in the end we must map if we are to disentangle American democracy from its late modern relationship to crime. Mass imprisonment and the girding of public and private space against crime reflect an ongoing struggle by Americans and their public and private organizations to manage the relationship between security and liberty. Recognizing that does not mean accepting the current terms of this relationship as inevitable responses of a democratic society. This book attempts to be critical as well as descriptive. A crucial starting point for criticism is the growing gap between the way our political leaders talk about crime and the vision of government they otherwise promote, which is one of increasing diffusion of responsibility for managing risk. Ultimately, neither contemporary liberal nor conservative principles extol the kind of penal state and gated civil society we are building by governing through crime. For example, in considering health care, retirement, and most aspects of employment, both American political parties preach a greater assumption of risk and responsibility. But in the framework of governing through crime, a very different vision of risk and responsibility is in play. A zero-risk environment is treated as a reasonable expectation, even a right.

Crime as a Governmental Rationality

The late historian and philosopher Michel Foucault (2000a) noted that the word government, in the political debates of the sixteenth century, referred not only to "political structures or to the management of states":

> Rather, it designated the way in which the conduct of individuals
> or of groups might be directed—the government of children, of
> souls, of communities, of families, of the sick. It covered not only
> the legitimately constituted forms of political or economic sub-
> jection but also modes of action, more or less considered and
> calculated, that were destined to act upon the possibilities of

action of other people. To govern in this sense, is to structure the possible field of action of others. (341)

In reviving interest in this broader sense of government, Foucault was seeking to draw us away from our usual focus on the state and the priority we give typically to the problems of sovereignty, but he was also inviting empirical study of the broader array of actors operating in parallel fields of civil society, including academia, philanthropy, religious ministries, corporations and the like. These actors have always played a role in the exercise of state power and seem destined to do so all the more so in the post-1989 world which Foucault never lived to see (but anticipated in many respects).

The forms of knowledge through which the field of action is structured in the broadest sense, according to Foucault, constitute a kind of rationality of government. When we govern through crime, we make crime and the forms of knowledge historically associated with it—criminal law, popular crime narrative, and criminology—available outside their limited original subject domains as powerful tools with which to interpret and frame all forms of social action as a problem for governance.

The Oklahoma high school drug testing policy upheld by the Supreme Court in *Board of Education of Independent School District No. 92 of Pottawatomie County v. Earls* (2002)[1] provides an example of how crime can interpret and frame even social action seemingly far away from any real examples of crime. In the fall of 1998, the school adopted one of the most comprehensive drug testing policies in the nation. The more common approach nationally involved drug tests of athletes, a practice upheld by the Supreme Court in 1995.[2] School District No. 92, in contrast, required all middle and high school students to consent to drug testing to participate in any extracurricular activity. Unlike others districts, including the one whose policies had been earlier upheld by the Supreme Court, District No. 92 acknowledged that it had discovered no evidence of serious drug use or resulting problems in school.[3] The Supreme Court upheld the policy notwithstanding the lack of an actual drug threat in District No. 92, noting that "the nationwide drug epidemic makes the war against drugs a pressing concern in every school."[4] In a sense, the Court has it just right. A nationally constructed understanding of drugs as a threat has made it incumbent on school officials who wish to be perceived as doing a competent job in governing their schools to implement strategies drawn from the war on crime.

This is visibly the case in District 92, despite the absence of any significant local experience with drugs as a threat to the school, and the fact that these power strategies are far from cost free in their potential effects on the educational experience for students and teachers. Something of the effect of governing through crime on schools may be gauged by the way schools themselves are represented as institutions of confinement in the *Earls* majority opinion. For example, Justice Thomas describes public school teachers as "already tasked with the difficult job of maintaining order and discipline." Not once does the opinion acknowledge that schools might have a mission of educating their students rather than simply maintaining custody against a range of risks colored above all by crime.

Assumptions to Avoid

Keeping open this wider window of analysis is not easy, and we must struggle self-consciously against three assumptions that tend to pervade the general discussion of crime and governance in America (by both Left and Right): (1) that it is primarily about the poor and minorities; (2) that it is primarily about repression; (3) that it is primarily about the exercising of power from the center out to the periphery.

Not Just for the Poor/Not Just for African Americans

Some of the most insightful analyses of American crime politics argue that, rather than being seen in isolation, penal policy should be seen along with welfare policies as part of a larger body of governance aimed at addressing the problems and the threats of the poor (Simon 1993; Beckett & Western 2001; Garland 2001). Along with welfare, crime policy is taken to reflect how American political leaders consider the poor to be a problem of governance.

No doubt we do govern the poor through crime, but they are far from the only subjects of this practice. Crime does not govern only those on one end of structures of inequality, but actively reshapes how power is exercised throughout hierarchies of class, race, ethnicity, and gender. That crime and punishment now seem to rule the lives of those trapped in zones of hardened urban poverty, such as some of our mass public housing projects, is now taken for granted by America's political classes. As a nation, we have grown accustomed to this rule without noticing the spread of its logic to the spatial sites where middle-class life is performed on an everyday basis: office buildings, universities, day-care centers, medical complexes, apartment buildings, factories, and airports.

Schools today provide a striking example of this. Ethnographer John Devine titled his book on high schools at the academic bottom of the New York Public School system *Maximum Security* (1996). Frequent acts of violence and a massive security apparatus built up to respond to that threat have coated the surface of everyday life in those schools. The very architecture of the school has been given over to metal detectors and auxiliary technologies. The corridors are treated as drug courier routes, with a full-fledged security force. Teachers, withdrawn from the business of informal norm shaping, call on these guards regularly when the sullen boredom of the classroom is disrupted by overt defiance. At the same time, the schools higher up the hierarchy work hard to screen out students with a profile suggestive of violent acts, and striving families all over the city berate their student children to study harder lest they end up in the boot camp-like settings of the worst schools. Indeed, since the mid-1990s, even suburban schools are now covered with a plethora of crime-focused "official graffiti" (Hunt and Hermer 1996) warning that you are entering a "drug-free school zone" with a "youth crime watch" and the like (discussed in chapter 7).

Middle- and upper-class residential developments also speak to the pervasive regulative presence of crime. Who would guess that subdivisions built to reflect the every desire and whim of very affluent consumers would prioritize security against crime in both instrument and look (Garreau 1991)? The same has increasingly become true of new housing built for middle classes. Perhaps the increasingly ubiquitous gated community is for civil society what the prison has become for the state: the most concentrated and active nexus of a broad constellation of practices, mentalities, strategies, and rationalities that seem to be growing as the shadow side of the new technologies and rationalities of freedom.

Race is an even more tempting global explanation for America's growing penal state (Wacquant 2000a,b; 2006 forthcoming). Young African American males who reside in the centers of our nation's largest cities are the primary targets of the unprecedented expansion of criminal law and incarceration (Mauer 1999). It is also clear that blaming African Americans for high levels of city crime was a convenient riposte for both liberal and conservative whites to growing demands for substantial social reform in the name of racial justice in the late 1960s (Scheingold 1991; Beckett 1997). Perhaps more than any other population in a peacetime society, young African American men in cities have been subjected to mass confinement. Moreover, minority communities absolutely suffer the greatest concentration of overlapping dimensions of governing through crime as defined here. They experience the power of the punitive state through the removal of healthy working-age adults from the population. They experience the power of criminal organizations to shape the norms of the population both directly (through organizing parts of the population), and indirectly (through behavioral responses of the population at large, e.g., carrying weapons for self-defense). They experience fear of crime as a daily affair, and the identity of crime victim is one of the few valorized identities widely available.

While all of these empirical realities are undeniable, they do not tell the whole story. White Americans are not immune to the attention of the criminal justice system. In 2004, 465 white males were in prison for every 100,000 of their number in the free population, less than 1/7 of the 3,405 rate for black males, but more than twice the total rate of male confinement in prison in 1970. To be sure, one can provide a convincing interpretation of the contemporary "ghetto" and the contemporary prison as an integrated whole (Wacquant 2000a,b). But one can also trace the very visible outlines of fear of crime, and valorization of victims, in middle- and upper-class suburban neighborhoods (Davis 1998). This does not mean that ghetto and suburb are now the same. The inner city twelve-year-old confined to his or her apartment by parental fears of encounters with armed drug dealers and armed police officers—or literally imprisoned in a juvenile detention center—is not the same as the suburban twelve-year-old penned in by cul de sacs, malls, and fast food restaurants by parental fears of pedophiles and mass murderers. But there is an undeniable structural similarity across the boundaries of class and ethnicity in the ways of thinking, knowing, and acting that both conceive and justify these practices.

Enabling and Empowering

The most visible and discussed features of governing through crime involve practices of punishing, repressing, and confining people.[5] But much of the work of governing through crime involves equipping and guiding subjects in the socially valorized pursuit of security and justice. Here we are no longer talking primarily about the work of imposing discipline or punishment over a resentful mind and resistant body. Scholars have already noticed the rise of "fear of crime" as a distinct target for government efforts; less noted is the relative advantage of attacking "fear of crime" as against "crime" itself. Police and prisons focus on people who are by socialization or social construction highly recalcitrant to these efforts at governance. By contrast, the population of those managed by fear of crime and valorization of victims includes mostly those highly motivated to conform.

Multiple Centers of Power

Perhaps more than any other form of public law, criminal law is associated with sovereignty and the state's monopoly on the legitimate means of violence,[6] and usually only particular agencies of the state. This is true enough for the large and growing criminal justice system, but the effects of governing through crime are not limited to the formal political leaders of the state in its most sovereign formations. Rather, these effects also reach broadly to those in positions of "responsibility" for others, including high school principals, corporate executives, and parents. Conduct described as criminal produces powerful incentives for strategic action by subjects of power across a range of institutional contexts. Chapters 6, 7 and 8 provide a set of examples of how crime shapes the struggle for control and power in families, schools, and firms.

It is tempting to treat this as a story of crime control emanating from the sovereign, and being extended further and further out into the everydayness of life through the intermediaries of private governors of all kinds. In other instances, however, crime is brought into play in a more horizontal framework, as when a threat or a claim of victimization by one person against another in an employment dispute has the objective of influencing management. In still other instances, the initiative may come from the state, but may be used by management to extend its own control needs.

The state remains a very influential site of governing through crime, and we devote the first part of the book (chapters 2 through 5) to describing how crime has in some sense captured the imagination of those exercising state power. Yet the story is less one of extending state power through crime than it is one in which the importance the state has assigned to crime nudges out other kinds of opportunities that a different hierarchy of public problems might produce—e.g., a government obsessed with governing by educating would produce all kinds of incentives to define various people as efficient or deficient in education, capable or incapable, and so on (Zimring and Hawkins 1997).

War on Crime and the Crisis of New Deal Liberalism

In asking how the war on crime has transformed government, I pursue a path well forged by others. One can point to a number of important works in the 1970s and 1980s (Hall et al. 1978; Feeley & Sarat 1980; Scheingold 1984; Cohen 1985). Stuart Scheingold's 1991 book *The Politics of Street Crime* suggested that the politicization of crime was a response largely to the governmental crisis of the 1970s and 1980s, when the national government seemed to stumble in its ability to manage an economy that had produced reliably growing affluence in the 1950s and 1960s. Politicians competing for support in such dangerous times had powerful incentives to reframe American anxieties about the decline of civility and the economy into volitional narratives about street crime—and, at least in those terms, to lower expectations of what government could actually do about the problem.

Scheingold also offered a critical insight about how crime politics works by contrasting the far more extremist discourse about crime at the national level to the more moderate discourse at the state level. State politicians have even more occasion to politicize crime, but in Scheingold's account, they also have a closer level of accountability for the actual implementation of policies, and this makes it harder to give full vent to the political appeal of volitional narratives about crime and evil. The national political field, in contrast (and perhaps states like California, so huge as to be proto-national in scope), provide so much distance between top executive and legislative leaders and the people they represent that they constitute an essentially "imaginary community" in which crime fears can be mobilized with little accountability for producing results (Anderson 1983).

Katherine Beckett's 1997 book *Making Crime Pay: Law and Order in Contemporary American Politics* closely examined public opinion surveys and political speeches to track the progression of public sentiment and political mobilization about crime. Her data convincingly suggest—at least for the 1960s, '70s, and '80s—that public opinion followed, rather than led, political mobilizations. In explaining the motivation of politicians, Beckett makes a convincing case that the politics of race was a dominant factor.

Crime was first exploited by white southern politicians seeking firmer ground for resisting the Civil Rights movement and its demands than the alleged benefits of segregation. Later, Republican politicians seeking to appeal to disaffected southern Democrats could use crime to implicitly signal sympathy with the resentments of those voters.

David Garland's book *The Culture of Control: Crime and Social Order in Contemporary Society* offers both a reading of contemporary criminal justice practice and discourse, and a theory of how political order in the United States and the United Kingdom has been reshaped by fear of crime. According to Garland, the emergence of mass incarceration and the politicization of crime both reflect a fundamental transformation in what we might call the political experience of life in modern societies. In this view, the social crises of the 1960s and 1970s, inflation, civil disorders, political and trade union strife (the latter in the United Kingdom only; American unions were moribund far earlier), and, above all, sustained high crime rates combined to undermine the dominant post–World War II political order. In the United States this political order was associated with the New Deal and its successors, and in both societies with a welfarist outlook that sought collective security arrangements, what Garland calls the "solidarity project."

The old penal policies that had dominated in both countries before the 1980s were part of this broader strategy of welfarist governance. Rehabilitative penal policies promoted a kind of solidarity project by legitimizing a balance of risks between convicted criminals and society. Institutions like parole, probation, and juvenile justice all reflected a willingness to take a risk on offenders, and reduce the risk that adult imprisonment would do them more harm. The new penal policies that emerged during the 1980s, combining pragmatic risk management of presumptively dangerous populations with populist punitiveness belong to, and in many respects anchor, a new political order. This new order stresses personal responsibility, rather than collective risk spreading, and minimal protections against economic harm, with a harshly enforced, highly moralistic criminal law promising almost total protection against crime, while emphasizing how dangerous the world is despite these much-needed measures. What Garland calls a "crime complex"—a set of criminal justice principles that embody this mentality—determines not only crime policy and practice, but influences the broader tone and direction of government, especially when it comes to other policies for managing the poor.

This complex is, in turn, shaped by cultural, social, and demographic changes. Garland stresses the important role of changing social patterns, especially in urban formation / hyper-suburbanization, and the fragmentation of the family, with women in the workforce and children in professionally managed spaces. But for Garland, crime itself, real crime, ends up being the driving social force that creates the crime complex. Economic, geographic, and demographic changes actually fuel the crime increase that began in the 1960s, which was already overdetermined by the large postwar birth cohort and the growing material affluence of both the United States and the United Kingdom. But because of the distance between and fragmentation of work and family life, these changes simultaneously created greater independent levels of anxiety about crime. The crime complex is a response—although one not unmediated by politics or the mass media—to the new realities of lived experience in what Garland calls "high-crime societies (2001a, 139)."

American crime rates went up in the 1960s, including rates for the kinds of crime that most matter to ordinary people, such as robberies and stranger murders, and, more important, the *experience* of crime increased as well, sometimes directly, but more usually from the media, politicians, and local knowledge within communities.[7] Those forms of crime knowledge helped undermine the New Deal political order, and became an important feature of the landscape on which new approaches to governing operated. But crime knowledge competed with other kinds of risk knowledge in the 1960s that had much the same effect on the established New Deal political order, including knowledge about cancer in the environment, knowledge about dangerous defects manufactured into automobiles, and knowledge about government lies and cover-ups. As in Europe, the American political order in the 1960s was challenged by the rise of new social movements—"postmaterialist" groups formed around ideals and identities rather than classic twentieth-century economic interests, and many formed around these new risk issues, of which the victims' rights movement may be seen as only the most successful.

But why was crime so much more successful than other emerging hazards in the 1960s and 1970s that might have become the anchor for retooling the New Deal model for a postindustrial age? Competitors included cancer (and other environmental hazards); consumer safety; violence; and mental health. As Garland (2001a) shows, the "experience" of high crime rates is not in any sense prior to or independent of political strategies, but is rather interacting with them. Politicians began to turn to crime as a vehicle for constructing a new political order before the crime boom was recognized. Some, especially white southern politicians, found crime a convenient line of retreat from explicit support for legal racial segregation in education and other public accommodations (Beckett 1997). Others, like Bobby Kennedy, were liberals looking for social problems against which to form innovative government strategies that would be less tied to centralized bureaucracies than traditional New Deal governance. In his first years as attorney general, Kennedy identified juvenile delinquency as a critical focus of federal intervention, and launched an early form of the kind of local strategies that anticipated the Great Society strategies of the Johnson administration.

Most of the work on America's "war on crime" and the associated set of developments reflect the American state and society as a function of some combination of social, economic, and political factors that have also changed during the period. This is, of course, a familiar stance for social science, following the natural sciences, presumes that human affairs can be explained by relationships among variables that (while understandably and perhaps fatally complex) should in principle produce the same account in a different time or place if they could be precisely reproduced. Even if not explicitly committed to this scientific model, most studies adopt the view that the causes of our "war on crime" are crucial to any effort to reverse or even modify this development.

The question of causation is fascinating but ultimately less important than the question of what the "war on crime" actually does to American democracy, our government and legal system, and the open society we have historically enjoyed. In seeking to answer the "why" question, students of the "war on crime" have offered us rich accounts of the mechanisms that link that war to changes in state and society. By reviewing the major themes of these accounts, while relaxing the causal assumptions, we will frame the descriptive account in the next chapter.

Indeed, it was the crisis of the New Deal political order, both politically and in its capacity to exercise power effectively, that forms the actual problem to which the crime "problem" was, in a sense, a solution. In turning to crime to redefine the style and ambitions of government, political leaders were able to take advantage of existing cultural preference in America for political narratives emphasizing personal responsibility and will over social context and structural constraints on freedom and that could be enacted without fundamental changes in the status quo of wealth and power (Scheingold 1991). These advantages, however, are less determinative than the fact that crime, for a variety of largely independent and accidental reasons, was far less disabled as a pathway for government innovation than most of the available competing programs, especially those that could address the new risks and new social movements at work in the 1960s.

We should begin with the recognition that America's constitutional structure clearly prevented the formation of a fully developed welfare state as came to exist in even the most culturally conservative European societies (Caplow & Simon 1998). The complex strategic problems formed by the separation of executive and legislative branches, and by the separation of state and federal governments, have made the fashioning of a full-fledged welfare state, along the lines of those created in most Western European countries after World War II, virtually impossible in the United States. Those forms of welfarism that have been enacted, including Medicare and Medicaid, are disabled by constitutional structures that make any large program susceptible to the demands of well-funded minorities, that require duplicated administrations and agendas, and that invite adverse selection tactics by states competing to attract employers and repel dependent citizens.

The most direct way to revitalize the New Deal political order in the 1950s and 1960s would have been to restore the power of the organized labor movement, largely broken by the Taft-Hartley Act, which, under the auspices of fighting communism, dramatically limited the power of unions to organize (Geoghegan 1991). Opposition to labor from Republicans and southern Democrats doomed any such strategy for the Kennedy and Johnson administrations. Indeed, organized labor itself was relatively indifferent to the decline of unionized industrial jobs, so long as its ability to raise wages for remaining members stayed in place. In the absence of a labor movement capable of organizing the antilabor states of the South, deindustrialization rapidly eroded the economies of the very cities where the New Deal had built its political base, including Detroit, Cleveland, St. Louis, and Seattle.

Another strategy for building on the New Deal was to expand social insurance programs for the working and middle classes. The Medicare program, proposed by President Lyndon Johnson and enacted by Congress in 1965, is a good example. The last major piece of New Deal legislation and the last major governmental initiative before the launch of the war on crime in 1968, Medicare was over budget from its birth because it compensated physicians at something quite close to the private market rates they had enjoyed, and it built inflation in by allowing insurance companies with no financial stake to regulate the pricing of physician services (Beschloss 2001, 240). In any European welfare state, the medical profession would have been compelled to accept a significant reduction in its fees in exchange for assured compensation, or risk significant government oversight of medical choices and pricing. The high cost of Medicare ended any hope that President Johnson might have had to follow up with comprehensive national health care and has continued to haunt any substantial effort to expand health care coverage in recent years. In effect, the ability of a small group of senators to stop virtually any legislation (which still is a problem) assured that powerful interest groups would always get their major needs taken care of, virtually precluding sweeping reform of any important social service, whether health care, education, or pensions.

Another major alternative to crime as a locus of governance in the 1960s was environmentalism. Already in the 1950s, fears of cancer had led Congress to enact tough laws banning carcinogens in the food supply. But by the time of the enactment of the Environmental Protection Act in 1970, under Republican President Richard Nixon—itself a sign of the governmental potential of environmentalism—industry had already demonstrated its ability to use the courts to delay any prohibition of chemicals for years and raise enormously the cost of regulation. The Administrative Procedures Act, adopted by the first Republican majority in the House of Representatives after the peak years of the New Deal, opened the decisions of regulatory agencies to repeated review in federal courts, where top-grade law firms (whose own business expanded) could keep cases in litigation for years without resolution. Though expectations of government continued to rise until installation of the antiregulatory Reagan administration in 1980, as a practical vehicle for governing, environmentalism was dead.

The growth of due process in the 1960s and 1970s set major constitutional obstacles to expanding other pathways of twentieth-century domestic governance. The mental health system—which in the 1950s held almost as many people as prisons did in the 1990s—had been emptied by the 1970s. In part, the impetus was the pull of new policies favoring community-based treatment of the mentally ill made possible by the availability of new drugs to control psychotic symptoms. The expansion of constitutional due process protections against civil commitment also made it increasingly difficult to secure the long-term involuntary confinement of the mentally ill. Not only did this make it impossible to reverse the deinstitutionalization process once it became apparent that the promised community treatment model was not going to be forthcoming, it eliminated any possibility of using expanded mental health programs to address issues like drug addiction, family violence, and sexual crimes.

The expansion of due process rights had a similar effect on Aid to Families with Dependent Children (AFDC), the federal program that most people associated with the term "welfare" in America. AFDC was well on its way to being demonized as a subsidy to the undeserving poor by much of the white working and middle classes by the 1970s. But if an administration of either party had sought in the 1960s to requalify cash assistance to the poor on paternalistic grounds, while coupling it with much more demanding behavioral features, such a program would have faced both bitter political charges of racism and substantial challenges in court on due process grounds.

Perhaps the most promising program for recasting New Deal governance in the 1960s was the Civil Rights movement itself. Race had clearly been the most glaring defect in the New Deal. In a concession to the unique role of the South as a guaranteed base for the Democratic Party, Franklin Roosevelt had deliberately excluded most African American workers from the major labor protections of the New Deal, and they had been discriminated against again in the wave of post–World War II benefits for veterans and others (Cohen 2003). By the mid-1960s, the movement, whose public spokesperson became the articulate visionary Martin Luther King, Jr., of the Southern Christian Leadership Conference, had won major victories in the Supreme Court and in Congress with the enactment of the Civil Rights Act of 1964. Moreover, Lyndon Johnson, who won the White House by a landslide in 1964, embraced the movement and made clear that he would strive to implement its agenda in the second half of the 1960s. Civil rights appeared to be a highly promising pathway to reconstructing governance in the second half of the twentieth century, and it has been far from a failure. Yet its pathways were stymied easily when the crime agenda decisively sprinted ahead in the mid-1970s.

In the late 1960s, the major reforms demanded by the Civil Rights movement were real implementation of school desegregation and enforcement of housing and employment discrimination laws. But beginning in the 1970s, court decisions undermined the practical achievement of any of these goals. None cast a longer shadow than *Milliken v. Bradley* (1974)[8] which stopped busing across district lines for desegregation purposes. *Milliken* left the desegregation imperative of *Brown v. Board of Education* (1954)[9] a dead letter in the large urban core cities, which now found themselves alone in carrying the burdens of impossible desegregation objectives, while suburban municipalities built on white flight were permitted to set up virtually all-white enclaves operating as if 1954 had never happened. Decisions like *Milliken* punished desegregation's advocates and rewarded those who had defied the social objective of integration. Ironically, when the effort collapsed altogether a few years later, critics would point to the inevitability of popular resistance rather than legal decisions that rendered the desegregation campaign a case study in failure.

But it was not only liberals seeking to succeed the New Deal model who failed to provide viable alternatives to governing through crime. These were the years in which conservatives were rebuilding themselves and shaping a new agenda around the themes of the Goldwater campaign, including anticommunism, states' rights, mistrust of New Deal–style government, support for public enforcement of majority morality, and, already, the rise of street crime. Other than crime, the major objectives on the conservative agenda were constitutionally out of reach, or obstructed by the difficulty of changing settled policy in the American legislative system. A good example is public morality. Even before the present ascendance of the Christian Right, social conservatives advocated stronger protections for public morality through censorship, school prayer, criminal punishment of public moral offenses, and the criminalization of sexuality outside of wedlock. But virtually all of these objectives were blocked by the Supreme Court beginning in the 1950s, continuing even under the right-leaning Rehnquist Court.

Crime has provided a precious wedge for government. Because the power of the state to criminalize conduct and severely punish violations was one unquestioned in the Constitution, the ability of the state to take drastic action against convicted wrongdoers provides an unparalleled constitutional avenue of action. It was an avenue both conservatives and liberals would take with vigor. This thesis may seem counterintuitive for two reasons, both of which call for explanation.

First, the power to police crime is broad for state governments but is far more limited for the federal government, which has never been held to enjoy a plenary police power but only specific police powers arising out of federal jurisdiction (e.g., mail, banking, federal reservations, and so forth). Second, the "due process" revolution was thought to have severely hampered crime control by impeding police and placing high costs on the imposition of punishment.

The first of these constraints is quite real and helps explain why the states themselves moved forward as innovators in using criminal law to govern, especially in the 1970s and 1980s. But the lack of federal jurisdiction over the crimes Americans fear most, violent street encounters with strangers, did not hamper the ability of federal administrations to govern through crime. The war on drugs launched by President Nixon in 1971 and escalated by almost every president since, belonged to federal jurisdiction because it involves interstate or international commerce. By promoting the belief that illegal drug commerce was an underlying cause of violent street crime, the federal drug war has become an integral part of American life even in those local communities most sheltered from it (see the discussion of the *Pottawatamie* case above). Another method that federal administrations have increasingly used to escalate the state and local war on crime is through legislation providing federal revenue support to state and local programs provided they adopt particular federal initiatives, e.g., the so called truth-in-sentencing rules that condition federal prison funds on the state's adoption of laws and regulations requiring prison inmates to serve 85% or more of their nominal sentence.

A steady line of argument since the 1960s has asserted that constitutional burdens on police investigative methods has stymied the effectiveness of police and thus of the criminal sanction. If this were true it would operate as a substantial disincentive to govern through crime. But empirical research suggests that the "handcuffing of the police" complaint leveled at the Supreme Court after the expansion of due process protections for criminal suspects in the 1960s never happened. Few cases are lost to search-and-seizure limitations or the requirement of Miranda warnings before a custodial interrogation (Davies 1983). The limited Eighth Amendment restrictions on punishment have mainly involved prison conditions. There is good evidence that increased judicial enforcement on prison conditions did cause states to update prisons and establish modern bureaucratic controls (Feeley and Rubin 1996). But the result has largely been to make state prison systems more governable and easier to operate at ever-higher levels of incarceration. Virtually no constitutional limitations have been found on the amount of prison time as punishment. In short, alone among the major social problems haunting America in the 1970s and 1980s, crime offered the least political or legal resistance to government action.

Although society has shifted towards the rehab of offender, the role of the prosecutor never ceases to exist, esp as ineffective. When the program is reinforced as seeker of vengeance they are viewed as incapacitation

The Prosecutor

2

"Prosecutor-in-Chief"

Executive Authority and the War on Crime

The executive as law enforcer is surely not a new story. Historical rulers in European societies made their jurisdiction over felonies a critical part of their local presence from the beginning of the nation-state. Even before this, small territorial rulers claimed the power to punish as defining features of their rule. Indeed, the very meaning of territorial power, or dominion, derives from the notion of danger. To enter a dominion is to place oneself under the protection of the violent power that is the prince. It is tempting to assimilate the current tendency of politicians to champion their toughness on crime in contemporary democratic polities as a throwback or at least a gesture toward that older model of executive power. We acknowledge this when we speak of "drug czars" and when politicians openly compete to name the highest penalty that should be exacted for a crime. Yet these monarchical echoes miss the deeply liberal and democratic tone of the war on crime. If the expansive role of the executive in the era of the war on crime can be traced to anything in our political genealogy, it is less the image of the sovereign as vengeance taker than the imminently American and democratic institution of the local prosecutor.

The prosecutor has long been a unique and important officeholder within the American systems of justice and government, with deep but limited powers and a special claim to represent the local community as a whole. In the last decades of the twentieth century, however, the war on crime reshaped the American prosecutor into an important model for political authority while also giving real prosecutors enormous jurisdiction over the welfare of communities with little attention to the lack of democratic accountability.

In large part, this is a product of the crisis of the New Deal model of modern political leadership in America as described in chapter 1. Presidents from Roosevelt to Reagan presented themselves as wielders of economic and diplomatic/military expertise and technology capable of achieving prosperity and security for each and every willing American. This system of expertise was communicated and propounded through the expansion and use of mass communication. Governors and mayors all the way down the stream of governance took their cue from this New Deal model, most famously from Franklin D. Roosevelt in his various manifestations from "Dr. New Deal," to "Dr. Win the War." Administrators of private and public institutions were also shaped in varying degrees by this New Deal model.

The period since the assassination of John F. Kennedy has been one of growing crisis for the New Deal political leader. Kennedy's murder stood above all for executive failure of the most dramatic kind, a federal government that could not even see to the physical survival of its chief executive. In the wake of the Vietnam War, with U.S. involvement escalated by Kennedy, the problem of executive failure was exacerbated by repeated revelations of executive lies. The problem of scandal and deception has remained a kind of endemic disease of contemporary political leadership. The New Deal chief has also suffered from the broad softening of public confidence in the various forms of expertise that at one time epitomized New Deal leadership, including economics, psychology, criminology, and sociology.

In the vacuum created by the various crises, political and discursive, of the New Deal style of governance, crime has pointed to the prosecutor as offering a new model of leadership. Becoming a prosecutorial executive does not entail literally seeking the legal conviction and punishment of wrongdoers, although it can include a strong symbol of the public as seeker of vengeance and incapacitation.

This prosecutorial shift of executive leadership can be traced in a number of ways. It operates at the level of political rhetoric. Campaigns for the office of mayor, governor, attorney general, and especially president of the United States have become, to an important extent, a contest of prosecutorial resolve. Executives must show that they identify with the experience of criminal victimization and with the resulting desire for vengeance (Scammons and Wattenburg 1969; Dionne 1991). This is usually done by supporting the death penalty or some other severe punishment for offenders who personify the kind of monsters most feared by the public. In their exercise of authority, executives are at their strongest when they isolate wrongdoing and demand accountability. Political leaders take in the crime story whether through identification with the police, as did Mayor Rudolph Giuliani of New York during the 1990s, or with tough sanctions such as the death penalty (championed by George Deukmejian of California and by George Pataki of New York) or mandatory minimum prison terms for armed offenders. At times they find themselves in direct competition, as when Giuliani forced out successful police commissioner Benjamin Bratton, or when Pataki removed a prosecutor he thought to be soft on the death penalty from control over the case of an alleged cop killer.

It also operates at the level of knowledge and power at which political leaders link themselves to their publics through the media and other institutions. Mayors, governors, and presidents are limited in their ability to directly prosecute criminals, but they have a wider political capacity to define their objectives in prosecutorial terms and to frame other kinds of political issues in the language shaped by public insecurity and outrage about crime.[1] A clear example is President George W. Bush, a leader who misses few chances to define threats to the public—whether illiteracy or weapons of mass destruction—as forms of personal victimization wrought by willful and sinful wrongdoers. Political executives of this sort, particularly governors and attorney generals, have promised to back the effectiveness of prosecutors by meting out more severe punishments, restricting procedures advantageous to the defense, and overcoming judicial obstacles to enforcement of severe punishment, especially the death penalty. If recent election cycles have seen little overt debate about crime, it is because candidates have generally already been selected to maximize their prosecutorial bearing.[2] Less noted is the way this prosecutorial turn has transformed the organization of executive government. At both the state and federal levels, the office of the attorney general has risen in influence over policy and over the chief executive.

The enormous expansion of criminal sanctions and the new style of crime legislation (see chapter 3) is also transforming the traditional role of the prosecutor (Walker 1993; Humes 1999; Stuntz 2001, 2006). Perhaps the most important feature of this change has been an enormous expansion of power at the expense of judges, paroling authorities, and defense lawyers. On the critical question of how much punishment defendants will receive if convicted, prosecutors have garnered so much power that in a real sense even the role of judge and jury as fact finder has been nullified. For example, various forms of mandatory sentencing schemes have made the prosecutors' determinations of criminal charges the dominant influence on the ultimate prison sentence. Whether younger offenders will be kept in juvenile court, where they receive rehabilitative sanctions and relatively short prison sentences, or go to regular felony court, where they may face extremely long prison sentences, is determined in most states by prosecutors. Insofar as these decisions are matters of discretion rather than law in the conventional sense, it can fairly be asked whether the substantive criminal law taught in American law schools is even meaningful.

By turning the prosecutor into a far more powerful agent in the war on crime, these legal shifts have also turned the political prosecutor into one of the most important officials in local government with tremendous potential to affect the lives of citizens. This is especially true for those living in urban areas where high levels of violent crime, intensive police presence, and increasing rates of imprisonment are reshaping the community demographically, socially, and economically. In many of the poorest sections of American cities, the imprisonment of people (usually young men) who would otherwise be residents of the communities constitutes the largest form of public or private investment, and this spending is controlled most clearly by prosecutors. One signal of this increasingly broad government role for the prosecutor is the growing interest among prosecutors in claming a broad mandate to be involved in public policy under the banner of "community prosecution." A wide range of specific practices are collected under this term, ranging from a role in paying for social services that are not directly law enforcement–related to targeting particular offenders for "exile" using tough federal laws against armed criminals.[3]

Between the movement of executives toward the prosecutorial and the expansion of the prosecutor's role, executive power has become tightly bound up with crime and the political technologies available to confront it. The resulting politics is harsh. As successful politicians work to redefine public policy as crime policy, we have begun to see a variety of figures, including special prosecutors and crusading attorney generals, who have openly competed to assume the mantle of prosecutor-in-chief. Real prosecutors exert extraordinary power but over what is or should be a narrow jurisdiction and a limited set of government functions. But the influence of the prosecutor over American politics and culture extends beyond even its currently distended jurisdiction through the construction of a prosecutorial model of leadership, one promoted by popular culture as much as by real news let alone actual practice. This model consists of a number of elements that pervade the popular image of the prosecutor:

1. Prosecutors champion victims.
2. Victims seek only that the truth of their violation be recognized and validated by the degree of punishment imposed on their violators.
3. Prosecutors alone can help victims realize these objectives, and they do so only by seeking to increase the social isolation and moral distance of those accused or suspected of crimes.

The following section describes some of the institutional features that make the American prosecutor a powerful model for governing. I will examine this model in practice by looking more closely at three examples of the prosecutorial ascendance in American politics. Much of the political analysis of the war on crime has focused on such presidents as Richard Nixon and Ronald Reagan, who emphasized tough stances toward crime in their speeches. My first example looks beyond the presidents to the attorney general, a figure whose growing stature within the executive branch from the 1930s on presages and perhaps explains the prosecutorial presidency. My second example looks at the role of the death penalty in reenergizing the role of the nation's governors (a position once thought to be doomed to a secondary role in the modern state by the New Deal political order), which in turn led many governors to become champions of the death penalty. My final example draws a line between the first and second by examining the rise of governor as the predominant pathway to the presidency since the end of the 1970s.

Peculiar Institution: The American Prosecutor From Bureaucratic Professionalism to the Prosecutorial Complex

The institution of the American prosecutor appears to have borrowed traits from a variety of European and colonial offices including the English "attorney general," the Dutch "*Schout*," and the French "*procureur publique*." By the middle of the nineteenth century, however, these variable roots had coalesced into a distinctively American institution with features widely shared among the states and differentiated virtually all of them from similar roles in other societies. Historian Joan Jacoby summarizes the distinctive structure of the office as it is most commonly found in four traits: it is (1) public rather than private, (2) executive in nature rather than judicial, (3) local rather than statewide, and (4) elected directly by the eligible voters of the district (Jacoby 1980).

Each of these gives the prosecutor distinct advantages and incentives. The American prosecutor was a public official, in contrast to the private prosecutor that predominated in England until at least the late nineteenth century.[4] The private prosecutor, like most private litigants, is not necessarily committed to enforcing the letter of the law. He may be most inclined to settle for substantial compensation. The problem of who the "client" is for the American prosecutor has long been viewed as a conundrum, but it is clear that the American prosecutor is not her own client. She serves the public and must rationalize her decision making accordingly.

As an executive, the prosecutor belongs to the branch of modern sovereignty most directly descended from the monarch. Along with mayors, governors, and presidents, prosecutors stand authorized within their domain to represent the people completely. They are checked by the other branches of divided government but not (as legislatures are) by an internal principle of division or (as courts are) by a hierarchy of abstract authority. In that sense, each executive enjoys a kind of plenary authority. Under the U.S. Constitution and practice, for example, governors recognize that the president may hold superior authority in a face-off, but the governor is not an agent of the president; she is an independent vessel of popular sovereignty.

With some notable exceptions, the American prosecutor is a local actor with a specific territorial jurisdiction, typically equivalent to the county or municipality. The great exception to this is the prosecutorial power of the federal government, which is exercised through locally based U.S. attorneys who are subordinate to the attorney general. There is nothing in principle that would prevent a state from reorganizing its prosecutors along such lines, but almost nowhere is this done. American prosecutors answer to a very specific electorate, a public they generally share with a variety of local law enforcement agencies, judges, and defense attorneys. This means that rather than Texas law or Florida law, one really has to talk about Houston and Dallas law, Miami and Jacksonville law.

Since the spread of the electoral franchise in the early nineteenth century, American prosecutors have typically been elected, which is the overwhelming pattern today. Elections have traditionally been seen as compromising the autonomy necessary for professional prosecutors to exercise their wide discretion.[5] Though prosecutors can be brought down over particularly unpopular decisions, election also goes a long way toward establishing the autonomy of the American prosecutor. She is not a subordinate of the mayor or governor.

The combination of these features has long given American justice a distinctive character. Whereas criminal justice policies in most societies are set at the national or provincial level, nearly every county in the United States has its own criminal justice policy based on which charges the prosecutor chooses to bring or not bring. These features also made the prosecutor a potentially powerful but traditionally limited office. The political power of the office stems from its distinctive monopoly on the power to charge others with criminal offenses. In a society of private prosecution, this is potentially open to any litigant who feels himself or herself a victim of a crime by an identifiable wrongdoer. Almost everywhere, this power to charge is a public monopoly today, but few societies place so exclusive a control over this power in the hands of a singular executive official. The American prosecutor is empowered both by being an executive and one elected directly by the voters of a district (and thus not beholden to either the courts or a higher executive official for their lawful authority). Because this is almost everywhere a local office, it carries with it the distinctive power to decide which of the state's various criminal statutes is given priority, through the nearly total discretion of the officeholder to charge or not charge a particular defendant.[6]

It is well recognized that American prosecutors have comparatively extraordinary discretion to choose whether or not to bring charges against an individual. It is also well known that prosecutors are among the most political of offices, and often a steppingstone to higher office in state or federal governments. Less appreciated, however, is the great extent to which prosecutors have been exempted from the modern regime of restraints and reviews on administrative discretion that applies to other government actors. When exercising their powerful functions, including deciding whether to bring a prosecution and for what charge, prosecutors have virtually unlimited discretion.

The war on crime has transformed the status of prosecutors within American government through several parallel developments. The hardening of criminal sanctions that began in the 1980s, what some have called the severity revolution, has expanded the classic power of the prosecutor to select individuals to be exposed to criminal trial and the possibility of punishment.

The formal length of sentence is probably less important than the elimination, in many states and the federal system, of a substantial role for "administrative" release mechanisms such as parole boards capable of adjusting the differences in sentences created by the choices made by prosecutors. The growth of extreme sentences with no possibility of parole also deepens the significance of the prosecutor's charging role. By charging a suspect with any of the many forms of enhancements, such as using a gun during the primary offense or having a previous serious or violent conviction, the prosecutor today can effectively eliminate a person from the community for a generation. Just as the death penalty has established itself as a crucial part of the prosecutor's new power, the proliferation of crimes with extremely enhanced prison terms has created a wide range of "lesser" death penalties.

Legislative changes have also given prosecutors a larger role in choosing the fate of juvenile offenders. At the high tide of the juvenile justice movement, in the 1970s, only judges could waive a juvenile's right to be dealt with in a juvenile court with its then-dominant rehabilitative narrative and its much more limited prison sentences. Today, virtually all states allow prosecutors to place juveniles who are charged with serious or violent crimes in adult court, and states require them to do so for a range of violent crimes. The prosecutor now acts as a gatekeeper determining access to the juvenile process itself. Indeed, this gatekeeping function, once given largely to judges in the criminal justice system, now ends with the prosecutors. For example, successive habeas petitions, the means by which long-term prisoners and death row inmates are able to seek judicial review of new issues that earlier lawyers failed to pursue (or did not appreciate the relevance of) have now been barred by judicial decisions and statutes. This leaves prosecutors largely in control of whether new issues or new evidence will get a hearing.

These legislative changes, outgrowths of the war on crime (more on this in chapter 3), have expanded the traditional power of the American prosecutor by raising the stakes of the criminal sanction. The urban criminal court of the 1960s was overwhelmingly bureaucratic. Such practices as plea-bargaining and the bail bond system embodied a professionally oriented, teamwork approach to processing cases, one respected by prosecutors, defense lawyers, and judges alike. The growth of the traditional power of the prosecutor has increasingly strained the capacity of this bureaucratic model to do even the rough justice it once did. At the same time, it has invited prosecutors to look beyond their traditional perspective as players in an adversarial process to a perspective more commensurate with that of elected political executives such as mayors, county executives, or governors.

In some communities, this shift in perspective has earned its own name and narrative: community prosecution (Alfieri 2002). In one sense this means simply expanding the consideration of community effects in making classic criminal prosecution decisions. To do so requires the creation of new links that run between the prosecutor's office and the community beyond the classic roles of victims and witnesses. It also includes developing new narratives and new relationships linking prosecutors to the well-being of the community and its key components including markets, social and charitable organizations, and moralizing institutions such as schools and churches.

Starting in the Johnson administration, the Department of Justice began promoting federal/state task forces headed by the local U.S. attorney and including local prosecutors and state and federal law enforcement officials. These task forces coordinate the availability of federal charges, which often carry especially severe sanctions, potent procedural advantages for the prosecution, and federal resources. This approach has been continued and intensified through administrations of both parties. An even broader reach was added during the administration of President George H. W. Bush (1989–1993) in the form of a "weed and seed" program, combining the previous coordination of law enforcement with broader efforts to encourage investment in inner-city communities. State and local prosecutorial officials have also initiated similar programs that tie crime control to other governmental goals and place prosecutors in coordinating positions. The sheer size of the correctional population means that prosecutorial power has a large, even if unintended, effect on the maintenance of social order in local communities.

The emergence of the prosecutor as a more important locus of governing power has taken place broadly across the United States during the war on crime. More selectively, these more powerful prosecutors have begun to evolve a very different style and conception of the prosecutor, one defined by the war on crime. Because of the local nature of prosecution, the national picture remains extraordinarily variegated. In many American communities, particularly those angered by publicized instances of violent crime, some prosecutors have responded directly to the potent fear of crime and passion for punishment they can arouse. In these communities, the reciprocity underlying the old courtroom "work team" (e.g., Sudnow 1965) is replaced with a new model in which the prosecutor is clearly a dominant

[handwritten margin notes: Plea-Bargaining / shift to / prosecution / complex. / problem]

force. Plea-bargaining and similar modes of cooperation are replaced by a "prosecution complex" in which convictions are produced when needed through the application of police pressure and the ever-growing incarcerated population (Frisbie and Garrett 1998). Backed up by a sentencing system in which the possibility of substantial punishment may be available through a whole range of options to the prosecutor, this is a system that can convict the guilty at an ever-speedier rate but also can convict an unknown but not insignificant number of innocent persons (Dwyer et al. 2000).

Journalist Edward Humes closely studied one such community, Kern County, California, and an elected district attorney, Ed Jagels, who became the most powerful political figure in his community by using his office to respond to and stoke fears of crime with dramatic prosecutions (Humes 1999). Hume's description of Kern County suggests that it is an extreme place even in extreme California (which has one of the world's largest prison populations), but in broad strokes could also characterize America as nation.

> The region clings to its frontier legacy, a rough-hewn place built
> by gold and oil fever, where gunfights and lynchings continued
> well into the twentieth century, and where a fierce desire for law
> and order still competes with an intense distaste for government,
> regulations and outside interference in local affairs. (22)

Whatever its history, Kern County in the 1980s and 1990s shared with America a terrifying sense that unholy forms of violence surrounded them. One particularly acute wave of fear that ran through the country in these years concerned child molestation rings, especially in day care centers and involving satanic elements. Kern County prosecuted 83 people for such crimes in the 1980s and convicted 40; all received severe prison terms (Humes 1999, 451). These kinds of crime did more than frighten people. They confirmed to large portions of the public a new sense of reality when it came to understanding the depth and depravity of crime itself. If the world is really filled with satanic cults looking for human prey, and day care centers are filled with group molesters, it only makes sense to allow the control of crime to shape the governance of everything else. Something similar seemed to have happened in New York City in 1990 when a group of young African American youths from Harlem were convicted in a series of assaults on people enjoying Central Park on a spring evening, including a jogger who was raped. The age of the youths, the brutality of the rape, and the very notion that the youths were "wilding," as police claimed the youths called their activity,[7] demonstrably moved New York toward leaders with a strong prosecutorial emphasis. In 1991, Rudolph Giuliani, a high-profile U.S. attorney under President Reagan, won a rematch with David Dinkins, New York City's first black mayor, with a promise to crack down on crime. In 1994, New Yorkers statewide rejected incumbent Mario Cuomo in favor of a much lesser known Republican politician from upstate New York named George Pataki, mainly on the latter's support for a death penalty.

This fear of crime has been fertile ground for ambitious prosecutors who understand its unique political power. This new prosecutorial complex has a number of distinctive features that differentiate it from the traditional-modern bureaucratic professionalism model. These traits also help explain why the prosecutor is today such a powerful template for executive power generally.

One trait is hostility toward judges. In the twentieth century, judges loomed large, not just in criminal sentencing, but as model governmental actors. The war on crime has already shifted a great deal of power from judges to prosecutors, but there is an aspect of contempt here as well (Humes 1999, 343). Insofar as the new prosecutor bases her legitimacy on her advocacy of crime victims, judges are easily seen as biased by their neutrality (75). The traditional prosecutorial model called for deference to judges, but the new prosecutor understands that she has replaced judges as the more trusted agent of the public interest. This also includes an increasing willingness by prosecutors to use the media and speak as a voice for the crime victims of the community and to advocate politically for tougher sentences, more prisons, and getting rid of judges who are not sufficiently tough on crime (77).

A second trait is what appears to be a historically unprecedented willingness on the part of contemporary prosecutors to violate rules of professional conduct. As documented in cases of exoneration, prosecutors in many communities engage in routine violations of rules requiring them to turn over exculpatory evidence to the defense (Scheck, Neufield, & Dwyer 2001). Many of the rules always ignored the powerful incentives to win, but the war on crime has helped degrade the presumptive standing of the ethical duties to begin with. Prosecutorial misconduct is not surveyed in any comprehensive sense and becomes public only on occasion, and then rarely with lack of ambiguity. Although it is not possible to prove that misconduct is becoming more common than it was in the past, it is clear that the war on crime has helped shape a rationale for prosecutorial misconduct in the very metaphor of war and its premise of extraordinary circumstances. Viewing themselves as frontline operatives in the war on crime, prosecutors in this era sometimes see themselves as having a mandate to go to the very limits of the law to address forces they view as evil.

Though the projection of prosecutors into broader governmental questions makes them competitors with other elected political leaders, the development of a new prosecutorial model has exerted an influence on those leaders. Governmental actors who have traditionally been seen as responsible for the overall well-being of the population—mayors, governors, and presidents—have sought to project themselves in a prosecutorial light as champions of a vengeful and defensive community set upon by willful wrongdoers, and to project the nature of their power as largely punishing. This was most visibly exemplified by the successful 1988 presidential campaign of George H. W. Bush and in President Bush's governing style. Since then, virtually all candidates for executive office have adopted themselves in large part to this model.

The Nation's Prosecutor: The Attorney General and the War on Crime

Most of those who have studied the war on crime for its effects on American politics and government have focused, understandably, on the president. Republican Barry Goldwater found his most effective campaign theme in railing against the increasing level of "crime in the streets" in 1964. Democrat Lyndon Johnson beat Goldwater handily but wasted no time in declaring "war on crime" as part of his Great Society. Ever since, most chief executives have carefully honed their reputation for aggressively confronting crime. Richard Nixon ran in 1968 on the thesis, since taken for granted, that the Great Society (or social welfare programs, more generally) was a major source of the crime problem. Ronald Reagan touted his support for the death penalty in California, and George Bush, Sr., promised to bring drug dealers to their knees, pledging his commitment to the justness of the death penalty as a punishment for intentional murder. Even those campaigns that have not visibly focused on crime (the campaigns of 1976, 1992, and 2000) often reflect a crime control stalemate between the parties, in which each candidate has staked out similar enough positions to make significant gains difficult.

It is tempting to view the U.S. president as a kind of "commander in chief" in the war on crime, but recent history suggests that even tough-on-crime presidents have often found their crime policies overshadowed by economic conditions and international relations. The pattern of the presidencies since Roosevelt suggests that the enduring influence of the crime issue over the executive branch of the federal government, including the presidency itself, has generally been anchored in an axis running between the president and the attorney general—an axis in which law and, especially, crime have been influential. In a dynamic that begins in the early days of the New Deal, the attorney general has moved from being a relative outsider in the to one of the most politicized cabinet offices and departments within the whole executive branch.

With the criminal prosecution functions stationed front and center, the attorney general has also been repositioned. Attorney generals today are routinely dubbed "the nation's prosecutors" in newspapers, but this wasn't always so. Throughout the twentieth century, through the accumulation of crime- and criminal justice–related functions—including the FBI, the Immigration and Naturalization Service,[8] the Federal Bureau of Prisons, and the United States Marshal's Service—the Department of Justice has swollen into a planetary giant within the executive solar system. The war on crime began there and led to an even greater influence of the Department over state and local government as well as other federal agencies. It has become what the Department of Defense was in many respects during the Cold War: the agency within the executive branch of the federal government that most naturally provided a dominant rationale of government through which other efforts must be articulated and coordinated.

As the Department of Justice has expanded in size and become more colored by its crime-oriented functions, it has also risen in its political importance to the president. Most historians consider the attorney general's office to have been of only minor importance until Homer Cummings, Roosevelt's first attorney general, who saw the New Deal through its crisis of judicial review. That crisis helped place law at the center of executive authority and drove the function of the attorney general from being a bridge between the president and the Supreme Court to one of being the president's chief strategist in getting his policies validated by the Supreme Court. Committed to FDR's New Deal agenda, Cummings led the fight to discredit the Court, and carried the legislative initiative for Roosevelt's "Court-packing plan."

Since FDR, a number of highly regarded presidents chose to appoint their most trusted political advisors, in some cases their actual campaign managers, notably Robert Kennedy for his brother President John Kennedy, John Mitchell for President Richard Nixon, and Edwin Meese for the second term of President Ronald Reagan (N. Baker 1992). Like most of the other players in the cabinet of the modern U.S. president, the attorney general is not mentioned in the Constitution, but is a creation of Congress's broad authority to make all laws necessary to the enactment of the federal government, in this case a functioning executive limited by law. In the first law organizing the executive branch, an attorney general was allowed for, but had a subcabinet rank—his attendance at cabinet meetings would presumably depend on the relevance of a legal question—and was accordingly granted a lower salary. Perhaps more demeaning, no office space was provided for the attorney general, who would presumably have to devote a large portion of his or her private practice to keeping the federal government's legal counsel (N. Baker 1992).

The growth of the attorney general's role from a minor to major player in a federal power that was itself increasing, can be traced to three historical moments: Reconstruction, 1865–1875; the New Deal, 1932–1952; and, I would argue, the war on crime, 1965 to the present. During the short decade following the Civil War, the federal government enacted a dramatic series of statutes and constitutional amendments that set the stage constitutionally for the birth of the twentieth-century administrative state. Although much of this authority was stillborn, this outpouring of "higher law making" elevated the place of law itself in American political development (Ackerman 1998). Expansion of the attorney general's powers followed as a matter of course. In 1870, the Reconstruction Congress acceded to a longtime goal of attorney generals by placing them at the head of a Department of Justice, which was granted primary authority over the legal representation of the government in both criminal and civil matters.

Homer Cummings and the New Deal's War on Crime

The crime control role of the federal government grew appreciably with the adoption of Prohibition in 1920. Prohibition may have succeeded in its explicit aim of eliminating the legal trade in alcohol, as well as the network of legal saloons. But it also led to the creation of a lucrative black market in alcohol that promoted the growth of organized crime and resulted in

widespread popular participation in illegal enterprises, mainly as customers but also as employees. Faced with the perception that legal authority itself was being endangered by failures to enforce Prohibition, President Hoover appointed a commission under a former attorney general,
George Wickersham, to study the problem of enforcing Prohibition and
criminal justice more broadly. By the time the report was published in
1931, the beginnings of the Depression had moved crime somewhat lower
in order of national priorities, but the body of knowledge about crime as a
national problem that the commission created would influence the next
administration's effort to expand the role of federal governance.

The epic battle between the Roosevelt administration and the
Supreme Court over economic recovery legislation made constitutional
law, and law in general, a major issue for the executive branch, as issues long
part of the attorney general's role now came to the fore. By focusing on the
criminal law matters within the jurisdiction of the Department of Justice and
its FBI, the Roosevelt administration could bolster the department's popular
legitimacy against a long, hard battle with the Supreme Court, while simultaneously projecting in popular form a model of federal government power
(Potter 1998). The same period saw considerable growth in the criminal role
of the federal government, as Prohibition crime, largely prosecuted at the
state level, gave way to a new federal interest in "big crime" (Huston 1967, 191).

Big crime
from
Prohibition.

The major focus was on a group of mostly rural bandits, including John
Dillinger, Bonnie and Clyde, and the Barker family, who robbed small-town
banks while moving across state lines on routes laid out in the previous decade by bootleggers. Though this war on crime is not remembered as a key
feature of the New Deal, the fact that we remember those names even today
testifies to the popular media success of these "big crime" initiatives.

A crime conference organized by Cummings in 1934 introduced a
much broader agenda of reforms, many anchored in the practices and
knowledge highlighted by the Wickersham commission. In his welcoming
remarks, Roosevelt (1934, 17) began by offering a broad reminder of the
major problems that America faced and the commitment of the New Deal
to finding practical solutions. Chief among those problems were:

- subsistence of the population
- the security of the economic structures of society
- the release and direction of the vital forces that make for a healthy
  national life

To the president, the fight against crime was a part of all three. "As a component part of the large objective we include our constant struggle to safeguard ourselves against the attacks of the lawless and the criminal elements of our population," he said (Roosevelt 1934, 17). Using the war metaphor quite explicitly, Roosevelt called on conference participants to help launch a "major offensive" against crime (ibid.). Roosevelt went further in suggesting the direction for a New Deal crime control agenda. The contribution of the federal government was both important and limited, not to replace local law enforcement and state criminal law, but to bolster the national capacity for law enforcement in a whole host of ways.

The parallels between crime and the economic Depression in Roosevelt's imagery were hard to miss. Both were "national problems against which primitive forms of law enforcement [or economic intervention, one might add] are relatively powerless" (18). The New Deal proposal was to improve the organization and rationality of existing crime control institutions while using the enormous intellectual and media clout of an activist federal government to turn public opinion away from a Prohibition-era approval of gangsters.

This crime-based federalism was exemplified in Roosevelt's mention of "roving criminals" as a key area of federal interest (ibid.). The President was referencing the famous bandit gangs that had become the focus of the FBI's highly publicized and bloody efforts to eliminate crime. The public of the early 1930s saw these criminals as bold bank robbers who used the high-speed automobiles produced in the roaring 1920s, along with an intimate knowledge of back roads forged in bootlegging to outrun and outgun local and state law enforcement officers (Burrough 2004).

As President Roosevelt and others at the conference noted, these bandits operated in a distinctive spatial domain identified as the "crime corridor," which included the states of Kansas, Missouri, and Oklahoma, as the center of a line of crime running from Texas through Minnesota (Potter 1998, 65, 69). The administration's focus on the highway bandits primarily served to describe a geopolitical domain distinct from both state sovereignty and the nation as a whole, and thus a plausible target of intervention by a national government. The "crime corridor" provided a way of imagining the nation as something beyond the capacities of states to effectively address and yet small enough to be undertaken by a national government not seeking totalitarian dominance of society.

The roving criminals also underscored the connection of Americans in almost every community to the possibility of direct encounters with violent criminals. People in the still-populated and vital rural and small-town America of the 1930s might avoid confronting a Jewish or Italian gangster by staying out of Chicago, Detroit, or Kansas City. But the highway bandits of the era struck in small towns where they would expect less law enforcement preparedness. The linkage meant that almost any town in America could become the scene of unpredictable and savage violence.[9]

If crime served as a powerful metaphor for the evils addressed by the embattled New Deal economic recovery program in 1934, it was also available directly as a way to intervene in the economy. The early stages of the New Deal suggest that Roosevelt was willing to use the weapons of criminal justice against recalcitrant businessmen as well as bandits.

Roosevelt would go down in history as the leader who morphed from Dr. New Deal to Dr. Win the War. His war on crime turned out to be a rather interesting sideline that never became a central focus for his government. A real war on Nazi Germany and Japan soon made a widespread war on crime logistically impossible and politically unnecessary. In retrospect, however, we can also see the New Deal's war on crime as an early reflection of a central tendency toward governing through crime created by the law-centered model of the executive into which the New Deal was somewhat reactively cast by its bruising battle with the conservative majority on the Supreme Court.

Bobby Kennedy: Prosecutor as Politician

The administration of President John Kennedy (1961–1963) returned to crime as no administration had since the first Roosevelt term, and once again it was the Department of Justice and a close alliance between a president and attorney general that lay behind the initiatives. This was partly a result of the unique relationship between the two brothers. Few doubted that the Justice Department was the second command station of the Kennedy administration under the president's loyal brother, who had run John's tough campaign for president in 1960. Though the president showed some interest in crime, it was Robert Kennedy who more than any other executive of the 1960s forged a path toward governing through crime. Both Kennedys had worked on the organized crime problem in the 1950s,

John as a member of the Senate subcommittee on organized crime and Robert as the Democratic counsel to the subcommittee.

Robert Kennedy's Department of Justice developed a crime-focused program that highlighted crime as a model problem for federal solution. While Kennedy's approach had elements that anticipated both the Great Society strategies of Lyndon Johnson and the law-and-order campaigns waged by Richard Nixon and George Wallace in 1968, Kennedy fused this with a prosecutorial sensibility fashioned in highly stylized battles with mafia suspects and their lawyers and a comfort speaking as the people's seeker of justice that was unique in his period. Robert Kennedy's Justice Department is more famous for noncriminal aspects of the attorney generalship, especially civil rights, but crime was central from the start and identified as such by the administration's most acute critics (Navasky 1971).

Perhaps the most recognizable strand of Robert Kennedy's crime vision in today's terms was his highly public, no-holds-barred pursuit of organized crime in general, and Jimmy Hoffa in particular. During his '50s stint on the organized crime subcommittee of the Senate, Kennedy found a path that would take him beyond the anticommunism that defined most politicians of the era.[10] In his role as majority counsel to the organized crime subcommittee, Kennedy operated as a kind of special prosecutor, with the power to cross-examine persons suspected of leadership roles in organized crime and their associates in organized labor and business. Among the latter was James R. Hoffa, leader of the powerful Teamsters Union, and allegedly an accomplice of organized crime in conspiracies involving conversion of the Teamsters' pension fund. Kennedy and others considered the massive pension fund to be the federal reserve of mid-twentieth-century organized crime.[11] In terms that would help define the moral richness of the war on crime, Kennedy characterized organized crime as a secret evil in American society. "The American public may not see him, but that makes the racketeer's power for evil in our society even greater," he said (Lowi 1964, 143). "Lacking direct confrontation with racketeering, the American citizen is all too likely to fail to see the reason for the alarm" (ibid.). Aided by gangland turncoat Joseph Valachi, Kennedy chose a path that brought him into direct conflict with the large urban ethnic (Italian and Jewish) organized crime that President Roosevelt and FBI Director J. Edgar Hoover had chosen to avoid confronting. In doing so, he challenged an important base for his political party and his own family's wealth.[12] For many who revere Robert Kennedy's stand on civil rights and his willingness to use executive power to enforce judicial decrees on desegregation, this prosecutorial side is largely hidden or explained away.[13] Kennedy had a broader vision of social as well as criminal justice, but, like Roosevelt, he recognized in crime a powerful way to build a stronger bond between the executive and the mass public the executive serves.

> I do not object at all to more police, improved court procedures or more effective treatment facilities. Crime has to be repressed and communities must be protected. . . . But we should be pouring as much, or even more, money, manpower and imagination into preventing those early law violations that start criminal careers. (Lowi 1964, 25)

If the pursuit of Hoffa anticipates the prosecutorial zealousness of John Mitchell, Ed Meese, and John Ashcroft, two major initiatives of the Department of Justice under Kennedy—his Mobilization for Youth, aimed at drawing juveniles away from crime and into community action, and his efforts to model bail reform—anticipated the war on poverty that President Johnson would pursue from the White House after the assassination of President Kennedy. Both were aimed most immediately at the poor and at minority groups. Both represented a continuation of the project, first articulated by the Wickersham commission in the Hoover administration, to modernize the administration of justice in America from the federal level. At the same time, each dealt with aspects of crime and its control that were being made into problems in the popular perception in the early 1960s.

Robert Kennedy's focus on bail reform was intended to allow more people to be released from jail pending trial. Kennedy, however, saw bail as a bottleneck of a criminal justice system that often did terrible injustices to the poorest members of the community while failing to prevent many crimes. By allowing defendants' wealth to determine who was held and who was freed, the justice system made it likely that the poorest, rather than the guiltiest, would be convicted. Drawing on the then-recently published sociolegal work of the Vera Institute, Kennedy's department pursued legislation aimed at promoting broad use of the Vera method, which favored community ties over cash bond (Goldkamp et al. 1995, 7). Unlike the attorneys general who would come in the later phases of the war on crime, Kennedy embraced social science–oriented legal expertise, including leading academic stars like Francis Allen at the University of Chicago.

Juvenile Justice Reform ↓ Rehab

All of these themes—modernization, juvenile justice, and bail—would remain central to the war on crime that emerged fully only after Kennedy's assassination in 1968, just as the crucial Omnibus Crime Control and Safe Streets Act of 1968 was being passed by an overwhelming majority in Congress. His top crime policy priority, juvenile justice reform—a position advocated by both the Democratic and Republican platforms in 1960—reflected an optimistic rehabilitative approach quite different from the focus on juvenile criminals today. Since juvenile justice at the time was dominated by optimism about rehabilitation, so was the crime policy that came out of the Robert Kennedy Justice Department. But in the 1980s and 1990s a more pessimistic view of juvenile offenders would come to dominate a renewed effort to make the juvenile a key point of federal intervention in state policies—this time to harden the punitiveness of sanctions rather than emphasize rehabilitation (Feld 1999).

Avoided to some extent, protecting of Con. Rights in South

Robert Kennedy's tenure as attorney general is probably most famous for his confrontation with southern governors over the desegregation of state universities. His method in these confrontations, however, reveals something of how his prosecutorial vision of the attorney general's powers played out in an area quite distinct from the department's normal prosecution roles. Wary of alienating southern states ahead of his brother's re-election campaign in 1964, Kennedy positioned the department as a law enforcer, responding to court decisions to justify each escalation of executive action. In maneuvering to register James Meredith at the University of Mississippi, the department waited until mob violence was apparent before using direct federal police power to move Meredith onto campus. Rather than affirm a federal obligation to enforce constitutional rights in the South, the Justice Department positioned itself as the passive instrument of the law.

Kennedy = America's prosecutor

Robert Kennedy is remembered today through the lens of his 1968 presidential campaign, in which he powerfully represented the aspirations of the Civil Rights movement, the antiwar movement, and many other outsider constituencies in the United States. But in his years as attorney general, he emerged as one of the first American politicians at the national level since Roosevelt to grasp crime as a crucial anchor for activist government. More than any of his predecessors, Kennedy made the attorney general "America's prosecutor." As with Roosevelt and Cummings (only more so), Kennedy combined this crime focus with a powerful political relationship to the president. President Kennedy's speeches in the fall of 1963 suggested he planned to use the Department of Justice's campaign against organized crime in his upcoming 1964 electoral battle. His likely opponent had already signaled his intention to question the toughness of the Democrats on crime.

The Kennedys sought to revitalize the New Deal model of leadership with their New Frontier. Crime policy was to be only a part of a refurbished crisis manager model of the presidency, one that handled the Cold War, the economy, and the deeper problems of communities isolated from affluence. President Kennedy's assassination dealt a complex blow to this model of the New Deal leader. As a catastrophic failure of an executive branch whose central purpose had become to protect us from other (most notably, nuclear) catastrophes, the assassination left the nation doubly deprived of comfort.

Prosecution Complex

With some notable exceptions, every attorney general since Kennedy has maintained or increased the importance of criminal law to the attorney general's mandate and public presentation.[14]

Nixon followed Kennedy's move and appointed an attorney general, John Mitchell, who had been his close confidant and campaign manager. Mitchell was a corporate lawyer, not a crime fighter by background, but upon reading clearly the popularity of Nixon's crime criticisms in the campaign, Mitchell was more than willing to promote an escalated war on crime as a partial compensation for winding down the Vietnam War. The Justice Department under Mitchell quickly reversed Ramsay Clark's positions on wiretaps and other sensitive evidence issues. As a candidate, Nixon had castigated the Supreme Court under Chief Justice Earl Warren for setting the constitutional balance such that it was too favorable toward criminals and burdensome to law enforcement (Nixon 1968). Nixon was able to make a large number of appointments to the Supreme Court in his first term. Readiness to strengthen the constitutional position of law enforcement was a crucial concern to the selection process, as shown by the early decisions of all three of Nixon's first-term appointees: Warren Burger, Harry Blackmun (who for his first 10 years was a reliable conservative vote on crime issues), and William Rehnquist.

Much of Nixon's actual program on crime paralleled Johnson's goal of funding improvements in law enforcement, but he visibly moved closer to a prosecutorial role, advocating (even if not implementing) longer prison sentences, preventive detention for "dangerous" offenders, and criminal code reform to strengthen prosecutorial power. The reach of federal criminal laws available to the administration to directly fight crime in urban America was limited to creative extension of federal statutes written in the 1930s to combat Dust Bowl bank robbers.

Nixon and Mitchell helped turn the Kennedy-Johnson war on crime into a Vietnam-like conflict with federal funding and training of state and local police to fight the war. Ironically, Nixon and Mitchell became, by coincidence, the two most dramatic examples of criminality at the highest levels of government in recent American history. That crime expectations and criminal scandals have haunted the occupants of those offices ever since is part of that legacy. More important, it is a product of their prescience and effectiveness in fashioning crime into a new platform for national executive governance.

The Ford and Carter (1974–1977, 1977–1981) administrations seem like a time-out in the escalation of the war on crime. The unwinding of the Nixon administration took with it a series of attorney generals including Mitchell and his replacement, Elliot Richardson, who resigned rather than fire special counsel Archibald Cox in the infamous "Saturday night massacre" (N. Baker 1992). President Ford was first appointed to replace Spiro Agnew as vice president following Agnew's resignation because of unrelated charges of corruption while governor of Maryland. President Ford replaced Richard Nixon when the latter resigned in the face of a great likelihood of an impeachment trial in the Senate. Ford's subsequent use of executive clemency to pardon Nixon almost certainly contributed to his narrow defeat by little-known Georgia Democrat Jimmy Carter in November 1976. The war on crime and the new prosecutorial model of attorney general and president had been temporarily halted by a scandal that crossed crime and governance in a presumably independent but spectacular way.[15]

Following revelation of crimes committed by agents of the executive branch overseen by the attorney general and perhaps the president himself, both Ford and Carter sought to model an executive of limitations and legality, and both appointed attorney generals with independent reputations associated with academic law and the private bar. For a time, the Justice Department remained a central focus of executive government because of the post-Watergate interest in law. Congress passed a series of laws aimed at curbing public and private intrusions into privacy and limiting the cooperation of law enforcement and intelligence agencies within the federal executive (limits that are only now being dismantled in response to the "war on terrorism"). The Carter administration made human rights a touchstone in foreign policy. Domestically, he confronted mounting inflation and pressures to trim back the size and regulatory role of government. In this regard, he anticipated his Republican successors in the 1980s. Unlike them, however, he did not appear tempted to reshape the appearance of a direct role of the American executive in fostering the well-being of individual Americans (a post-FDR expectation) by invoking crime and the retributive capacity of government. As the first of a series of openly religious presidents, Carter sounded themes of forgiveness and laid America's plight in the malaise of its virtuous citizenry rather than the perfidy of its bad actors.

Neither attorney general Edward Levy under Ford, nor Griffin Bell under Carter, were much inclined to expand their role as champion of the war on crime. Levy was a law professor, dean, and university president appointed to represent scrupulous attention to legality. Bell, a prominent Georgia lawyer and former president of the American Bar Association, was primarily concerned with the politics of school desegregation, which in the mid-1970s remained a very big practical concern for the Justice Department and especially for an attorney general from the South.

During the debates of 1976, the death penalty and crime in general barely came up as issues, despite a high level of reported violent crime. When President Ford was reminded by a reporter of his pledge to do more to fight crime, he acknowledged that is was not easy to make progress while holding down new spending, and he urged reform of the federal criminal code as an inexpensive step. Carter eschewed any opportunity to attack Ford on crime. A decade later, any governor of a state such as Georgia would virtually guarantee that a politician would have major exposure to the crime issue and a strong stand on the death penalty. Carter, interestingly, served his one term as governor from 1971 to 1975, at precisely the moment when the death penalty was off the table for politicization as the Supreme Court considered the basic question of constitutionality. If crime shadowed the executive in the Ford and Carter years, it was in the form of Watergate and in the implicit presence of the prosecutor as adversary.

Perhaps the strongest hint of the priority of the prosecutorial executive that was to come in the 1980s was in the consequences of Ford's pardon of Nixon. As was demonstrated more recently by criticism of President Clinton's use of the pardon power in the last hours of his presidency, the pardon decision is today seen as an executive one rather than a judicial one. The president is expected not to judge whether sufficient repentance has been done but to ask, as a prosecutor does, whether the public interest of the potential victim class is to remove the sanctions of criminal law from a particular individual. Ford saw it as an issue of healing and pardoned Nixon at the same time that he issued a limited pardon to Americans who had resisted the Vietnam War draft. His message of healing and forgiveness met with mixed success, and Nixon's pardon came back to haunt him in his debates with Carter.

Message of pardon / forgiveness / mixed success

Reagan had an early experience with the importance of the crime issue during his years as California governor. Though crime was not his dominant issue in California politics, he made the death penalty for murder one of the signature differences in his 1966 campaign against incumbent governor Pat Brown. Brown had enforced the death penalty but had made public his opposition to it on religious and moral grounds. Against the background of the nation's rising homicide rate, Reagan modeled what would become a familiar circuit in suggesting that Brown's moral calculus represented a choice to identify with the killer rather than his victim.

Reagan's first attorney general, William French Smith, was a California business lawyer with important Republican connections but little public record on crime. By naming Edwin Meese as Smith's successor, Reagan fit more into the Kennedy and Nixon model of appointing a crime warrior and close personal advisor. Meese was a career prosecutor, one of the few attorney generals to actually have practiced as a prosecutor before taking office, and his political career was tied to the rise of crime. He had been an assistant district attorney in Alameda County, California, which includes the politically volatile cities of Oakland and Berkeley, during the heaviest period of radical political activity and conflict with the police during the 1960s. Governor Reagan picked Meese out of relative obscurity in part because of his public war with Berkeley. Meese became a political advisor to Reagan and an intermediary to the growing grass roots of right-wing property owners in California and nationally for whom crime was a major concern.

Once in office, Meese brought his career as a trial prosecutor to the center, pursuing a prolonged attack on the Fourth Amendment exclusionary rule under which courts often refused to admit accurate evidence of a crime gathered in violation of the defendant's Fourth Amendment rights. Using the public posture of the nation's chief prosecutor, Meese openly attacked even the conservative Burger Court as betraying innocent Americans and victims by refusing to completely overrule Warren Court precedents enhancing the rights of the criminally accused. "Neither *Mapp* [*v. Ohio*] or *Miranda* [*v. Arizona*] helps any innocent person. They help guilty people," he said (Baker 1992, 92). Meese went beyond Nixon and Mitchell and openly questioned whether the Supreme Court was the final arbiter of the meaning of the Constitution. The fruits of this attack were substantial. In the mid-1980s, the Court began carving out major exceptions to the Fourth Amendment exclusionary rule. First was a 1983 decision to abandon strict evidentiary requirements for warrants based on the tip of an anonymous informant; a year later, the Court recognized a general "good faith" exception to the warrant requirement when the police rely on a warrant reasonably obtained.

George H. W. Bush, who had served as Reagan's vice president and succeeded him in office, broke with this pattern by making himself a more prominent crime warrior than his attorney general. Even more than the 1968 Nixon campaign, the 1988 presidential campaign of George Bush marked the emergence, for the first time, of the war on crime as a primary basis for choosing a president (Dionne 1991). In the most well-remembered sound bytes of the campaign, Democratic nominee Michael Dukakis was linked to the furlough of a Massachusetts prisoner named Willie Horton, who absconded while on release, kidnapped a couple, and raped the woman. Dukakis was also painted as soft on crime because he opposed the death penalty. Bush did more than take advantage of vulnerabilities in Dukakis's record or his wooden and technocratic persona; in his own speeches, Bush laid out a vision of his presidency in which crime operated as a central problem.

Bush's nomination acceptance speech in 1988 contained hints that crime was not just another social problem, but rather a metaphor around which a whole range of popular needs might be expressed, a metaphor whose crucial entailment was punishment and a punitive state. Taking up one of the great conservative causes of the late twentieth century (and one of the most immediate pillars of Ronald Reagan's electoral victories in 1980 and 1984), Bush characterized inflation as a crimelike phenomenon.

> There are millions of older Americans who were brutalized by inflation. We arrested it—and we're not going to let it out on furlough. We're going to keep the Social Security trust fund sound and out of reach of the big spenders. To America's elderly I say: "Once again you have the security that is your right—and I'm not going to let them take it away from you." (Bush 1988)

Elderly people, an important base of support for the Democratic Party in recent decades, feel especially vulnerable to both inflation and crime. Bush's speech tied these two themes together. Reagan and Bush had triumphed in 1980 over a Democratic administration that was widely blamed for its inability to bring down inflation rates (notwithstanding the fact that the inflation built up during the Nixon and Ford administrations). By speaking of furloughs, the speech artfully linked Dukakis and Horton with Carter and the stagnant economy of the late 1970s. The furlough reference also points to a common form of government power that Bush wanted to claim: confinement and prison. Both crime and inflation needed to be held in check or else they would threaten vulnerable citizens.

Bush also defined his executive power in the posture of a prosecutor more than any other previous chief executive of the United States. Whether addressing drug dealers or the unnamed group interests behind federal spending and inflationary demands, Bush promised in his nomination acceptance speech to confront wrongdoers with severe punishment. His administration delivered on this in rising incarceration rates and in the enduring influence of punishment in general and punishments that confine and exclude people in particular. As president, Bush pushed the war on crime in a new direction, toward long prison sentences for drug dealers and the death penalty for so-called drug kingpins when convicted of murder. This direction was signaled in Bush's filmlike mantra, "you're history."

Clinton defeated Bush because he was able to neutralize the advantage of Bush's identification of president and prosecutor by embracing much of it. As the governor of a southern state, Arkansas, Clinton could also deploy a mechanism that Bush could promote only in theory: the death penalty. In a particularly dramatic instance, Clinton actually flew back from the contested and crucial New Hampshire primary battle to oversee an execution of an Arkansas prisoner with limited mental capacity who had killed a police officer. Clinton had absorbed the political lessons of 1988 and was prepared to match Bush on punitiveness toward crime and drugs. Once in office, he signed every bill extending punishments or contracting rights of prisoners presented to him by Congress, and he promoted many of them. Like Bush, Clinton would be an even more dedicated crime warrior than his Attorney General, Janet Reno, who quietly favored more emphasis on rehabilitation and personally opposed the death penalty.

The election of George W. Bush in 2000, contested as it was, can be seen as marking the stability of the prosecutorial executive model. The campaign was relatively free of controversy about crime mainly because there was so little visible difference between the two candidates on long prison terms or the death penalty. When campaigning for governor of Texas, Bush had made juvenile crime one of his four major themes for attacking popular incumbent Ann Richards. The governorship of Texas comes with administration of the nation's largest prison system and most active death penalty. The latter fact, especially, may well have hurt Bush in swing states Oregon and Wisconsin during the presidential election. During his first year in office, George W. Bush did not embrace crime fighting with the directness his father had in the war on drugs, but he elected to embrace the most punitive policies, resisted the softening of current harsh penal laws, and embraced opportunities to make punishment his preferred response to social problems.

George W. Bush's controversial choice of John Ashcroft to be his attorney general brought to the office a man who had shaped his political career around crime as much as had Bush himself. As a political leader in Missouri, Ashcroft used the politics of crime to rise through the state executive ranks from attorney general and then governor. Though not personally close to President Bush, Ashcroft was closely linked to the president's most important political constituency, right-wing Christian activists. As attorney general, Ashcroft moved strongly to reinforce the prosecutorial orientation of the department and to consolidate his own power over it. One striking feature of Ashcroft's political approach on crime, especially in light of the traditional role of the attorney general as link between the executive and the judicial branch, was his high-profile attack on Ronnie White during White's confirmation process in the U.S. Senate after being nominated to a district court judgeship by President Clinton. White, the first African American to sit on Missouri's

Supreme Court, and some of his colleagues had dissented in a death penalty case involving a man convicted of murdering law enforcement officers and the spouse of a law enforcement officer. (Police, as we shall see in the next chapter, are potent symbolic victims.) Ashcroft rallied Republicans to block White's nomination. Justice White testified at Ashcroft's own confirmation hearings regarding that earlier confirmation process:

> I was very surprised to hear that he had gone to the Senate floor and called me "pro-criminal, with a tremendous bent toward criminal activity," that he told his colleagues that I was against prosecutors and the culture in terms of maintaining order. . . . Ashcroft's rhetoric left the impression that I was calling for [convicted murderer] Johnson's release.[16]

In a little-noticed gesture that testifies to the endurance of Robert Kennedy's crime-centered model of the executive, in 2002, Ashcroft dedicated the Justice Department's new headquarters to Kennedy. Artfully lifting the mantle of the slain liberal hero, one of the most conservative attorney generals in modern times invoked Kennedy's zealous pursuit of organized crime as a precedent for his own controversial tactics in the administration's "war on terror." Ashcroft particularly noted the shared willingness to go to the absolute limits of the law to combat evil in the name of justice. "Robert Kennedy," Ashcroft said in his remarks at the dedication of the new building, "led an extraordinary campaign against organized crime that inspires us still today in the war against terrorism. He was unafraid to call his enemy evil and unapologetic about devoting all his resources, his energy and his passion to that evil's defeat."[17]

Death and the Resurrection of the Governor

In the twenty-first century, a state governor represents the last vestige of the "divine right of kings," because he has absolute power over life and death.
                    —Sister Helen Prejean, "Death in Texas"

The attorney general combines the functions of a post–New Deal administrator in charge of a large and influential agency with the actual powers of a prosecutor. In this latter regard, the attorney general (federal and in many cases, state) is one of the few high-profile political officeholders who can exercise a direct power of prosecuting crime; others have to associate themselves metaphorically with the state's power to punish and the opportunity to represent the victims directly in their pursuit of punitive justice. One of the most powerful opportunities for this kind of role construction was created incidentally by the Supreme Court's decision in *Furman v. Georgia* (1972), which nullified all existing death penalties. The decision gave governors in every state in which the death penalty had been nullified, regardless of whether it had recently been used, an opportunity to become personally and affirmatively involved with restoring a specific political power, one that would come to be associated not with the imperial power of the state but with the righteous demands of the individual victim.

To governors whose leadership role had been subordinated in important ways to the federal government since the New Deal, the rebirth of public interest in executing murderers offered a unique way back to relevance. Federal agencies might clean air, renew downtowns, or build university dormitories. They could even wage a war on crime with federal law enforcement and massive investment in state law enforcement. But the one thing the federal government could not do from 1972 until the late 1990s was seek and carry out the death penalty. The residual liberal opposition to resumption of the death penalty kept the federal government out of the death penalty for all practical purposes until the mid-1990s, when the first broad federal death penalty in a generation was adopted.

The Avengers: Re-creating the Power of Death

Although generally denied the prosecutors' unique ability to seek the death penalty in a particular case,[18] governors have found in the death penalty multiple benefits to their standing as representatives of victims and as fighters of murder, a kind of crime widely seen as expressing the deepest threats hinted at by all crime. Those governors involved in reestablishing the death penalty after *Furman v. Georgia* have been able to participate in a unique act of political creation, the formation of a political will to power, specifically, the power to kill, in a way that dramatically materializes the stakes of being part of the state as political community (Sarat 2001; Zimring 2004; Zimring and Hawkins 1986).

In those states with the greatest popular support for the death penalty, the move was nearly immediate and generally represented a moment of unity between liberals and conservatives as well as Republicans and Democrats. In Florida, a relatively liberal Democrat, Governor Reuben Askew (1971–1982), called the legislature into a special session and enacted by near acclamation a statute that has proven highly productive of death sentences.[19] The popularity gained through that initiative in his first term kept him in office across a decade in which Florida was increasingly voting Republican in national elections.

In those states with substantial opposition to the death penalty, where often the state Supreme Court had struck down the death penalty independently of *Furman*, restoration came later and after bitter battles pitting conservatives against liberals and, usually, Republicans against Democrats. In California, where the state high court had struck down the death penalty shortly before *Furman*, the power was restored by a triumphant constitutional amendment of the sort that was to become a dominant feature of California politics. George Deukmejian's identity as the legislator most identified with restoration of the death penalty was a major factor in his election as governor.[20] These governors became highly identified with the death penalty itself, and left that as a part of the job description potential successors will have to fit. In the case of New York, one of the latest states to have restored the death penalty (only to have it judicially struck down again recently), voters elected a Republican Governor largely on the basis of his promise to restore the death penalty after years of resistance from Democratic predecessors Hugh Carey and Mario Cuomo (Culver 1999, 291).

The Governor as President

The reshaping of the presidency along more prosecutorial lines has gone along with a rise in the relative advantage of governors as candidates for the presidency as opposed to senators and other federal officeholders. No other executive officeholder was better equipped to act in a prosecutorial manner than governors, whose duties often included formal roles in the parole of prisoners and the execution of condemned inmates. This pattern is even more striking when contrasted with what observers only a generation ago thought of the post–New Deal presidency, encapulated in the title of an article analyzing the 1960 presidential election. Pollster Lou Harris published in the *Public Opinion Quarterly* of autumn 1959 the article: "Why the Odds Are against a Governor Becoming President." Harris argued that governors and senators had reversed their longtime pattern of fortunes in presidential politics. Harris observed that since the start of the twentieth century, governors had dominated the presidential nominations of their national parties based on a number of features of the office. As chief executives, governors appeared to be prepared for the administrative tasks of the presidency. Their state role gave them a good excuse for ducking national debates. Their control of state revenues and jobs gave them a natural political base in their state. Senators, in contrast, were recorded as taking up or down positions on virtually every issue of national prominence but having little opportunity to stand out as singular leaders.

Harris saw 1960 as shaping up very differently. Richard Nixon, vice president after being a representative and senator from California, appeared likely to win the Republican nomination. Several senators, John Kennedy of Massachusetts among them, seemed likely to dominate the Democratic nomination fight according to Harris. Harris speculated that the 1960 election might in retrospect be the beginning of a period of senatorial domination of the presidency.

Harris pointed to a number of factors that arguably would explain a shift in relative fortune between governors and senators. The most significant was the rise of foreign affairs as a central feature of the presidency, where governors seemed presumptively out of their areas of expertise. "Somehow in a cosmic, atomic, mass-media age, Governors have shrunk to being thought of all too often as local figures" (Harris 1959). Another advantage enjoyed by senators was greater national recognition, a virtue in a nomination fight more likely to be nationally covered and contested in primary elections than resolved among party leaders at a convention.

In addition, the governors' position had been disadvantaged by the difficult fiscal circumstances of the states in the 1950s as they moved to address the myriad of demands placed on them by the baby boom cohort without the modernized revenue collection system of the federal government. Lots of things that states were responsible for—highways, schools, and universities—were all suddenly in high demand.

It is not clear that Harris's era of senators ever fully materialized. The Kennedy/Johnson ticket (both senators, supporting Harris's prediction) won two terms, followed by two more for the Nixon side of the 1960 face-off. Thus from 1961 to 1976, the presidency was dominated by figures from the Senate (indeed from the 1960 election). But the next 18 years would be dominated by governors—Jimmy Carter of Georgia, Ronald Reagan of California, Bill Clinton of Arkansas, and George W. Bush of Texas—interrupted only by the term of Vice President George H. W. Bush, who enjoyed considerable residual appeal from the Reagan presidency.

Texas governor George W. Bush defeated Senator/Vice President Al Gore (precisely Richard Nixon's position) in 2000 (or did he?). By the time Massachusetts Senator John Kerry squared off against George W. Bush for the 2004 presidential election, media observers were noting the historic pattern against senators, pointing out that only Kennedy and Warren G. Harding had entered the White House directly from the Senate and by-passing altogether Harris's thesis of a shift in favor of senators.

Throughout the nineteenth and much of the first half of the twentieth century, governors were at least as important as presidents in setting the agenda for national political change. Governors controlled the national political parties, and often chose one of their own to receive the party's nomination in presidential election years (Harris 1959). This ascendance was reversed for a time by Franklin Roosevelt's New Deal. Although his own rise to political prominence included a term as governor of New York (1929–1933), Roosevelt's response to the Depression as a national political problem, and the new laws and institutions put in place by the New Deal, transformed American federalism as much or more than had Reconstruction, and in the process, the power of the states was diminished. Until very recently, at least, this recasting of federalism seemed permanent, a constitutional moment even if lacking a formal pedigree as such (Ackerman 1991).

Since 1976, we have experienced a reversion back to the historic primacy of the governorship, notwithstanding the renewed interest in foreign affairs in 1979 and again after 9/11. I argue that we can explain this reversion, at least in part, as an effect of the influence on American political culture of the death penalty, a small but symbolically explosive penal practice, highlighted by the national government's war on crime, whose dynamics have peculiarly benefited governors on the national political stage.

The influence of the New Deal as a model for politics and governance in the United States has been widely recognized by historians and political scientists (Fraser & Gerstle 1989). I focus here briefly on just those aspects of the New Deal governing approach most relevant to the shift from governors to senators as likely future presidents. Politically, Roosevelt's election to an unprecedented four terms was particularly important. The customary pattern of two terms helped preserve the power of state party leaders (governors) over future nominations against the risk that the White House would become a platform for sustaining national prominence for cabinet officers and key legislators. With four terms, Roosevelt assured that a generation of leaders shaped by his administration would have a huge head start in future presidential contests.

Roosevelt also proved to be enormously adept at taking advantage of radio as a national medium that had something close to universal penetration in the 1930s. The national broadcast media, greatly expanded by World War II and the Cold War and transformed by television, created a permanent circuit of knowledge about Washington, D.C., and those political figures who were celebrities there. Though the Twenty-Second Amendment (1951) fixed a two-term presidential limit in the Constitution, the Cold War and post–New Deal social policies helped keep the president at the forefront of the political leadership for at least the next half century. Aside from the president, a variety of federal officials, including generals and cabinet officers, senators and representatives, became familiar players in the national and global drama of political life.

As Table 2.1 shows, the ascendance of candidates prominent primarily for their federal role rather than their role as a state chief executive began with Truman and continued with Eisenhower, whose status as a national star began with his role as the nation's chief military leader during World War II. The eclipse of governors continued in the post–World War II period and reached its peak in the 1960s, when the liberal administrations of Kennedy and Johnson began pumping federal money directly into local government and civil society, largely bypassing the state capitals and their chief executives.

As Harris (1959) argued, these years saw considerable public focus on foreign affairs, especially the Cold War and various hot wars in the 1950s and 1960s. Consistent with his argument is the fact that the 1950s and 1960s also saw continuing agenda setting by Congress and by the New Deal domestic agencies, as well as an emerging role of the Supreme Court. All of these

Table 2-1

Federal Politicians v. Governors as Presidential Nominees and Winners 1948–1976

	Republican	*Democrat*	*Winner*
1948	*Dewey*	**Truman**	**Truman**
1952	**Eisenhower**	*Stevenson*	**Eisenhower**
1956	**Eisenhower**	*Stevenson*	**Eisenhower**
1960	**Nixon**	**Kennedy**	**Kennedy**
1964	**Goldwater**	**Johnson**	**Johnson**
1968	**Nixon**	**Humphrey**	**Nixon**
1972	**Nixon**	**McGovern**	**Nixon**
1976	**Ford**	*Carter*	*Carter*

Bold indicates that the candidate's most important political experience previous to the run for president was in the federal government. Italic indicates that the candidate's most important political experience previous to the run for president was being governor of a state.

changes made the actions of federal officeholders more important to citizens. Senators were particularly well positioned to take advantage. Few enough in number that they could emerge as individual personalities within the drama of congressional action, senators also enjoy the constitutional role of voting on Supreme Court appointments, two aspects of presidential power that became even more visible and important in the Cold War period.

Not until 1976 was the dominance of senators brought to a close in favor of governors. Governor Jimmy Carter of Georgia was elected in a close election after a period of extraordinary losses of federal prestige brought on by the defeat of the United States in the Vietnam War and the scandals of Watergate.

During the previous period of federal ascendancy, there were two distinct paths for politically ambitious state governors to follow. One was to emulate the New Deal by pursuing strategies of public investment in infrastructure and human capital. Governors of both parties in the 1950s through the 1970s sought to establish credentials as reformers with strong connections in Washington, and progressive strategies that could be developed first on the state level. This was true of Republicans like Earl Warren and Nelson Rockefeller as well as Democrats like Adlai Stevenson and Edmund "Pat" Brown—all leaders who were considered serious contenders for the White House but never reached it, although Stevenson was twice the nominee of his party. These governors led their states through successful modernization drives in the crux years for coping with the post–World War II baby boom generation and the demands they placed on the roads, schools, and university systems of the nation (all largely state and local functions of government). They all had claims on combining New Deal activism with a discipline unique to state responsibilities ("responsible liberalism" was Pat Brown's version).

The other was to claim a unique role in protecting the citizens of the state from an overly aggressive central government (freely analogized to the demonized Soviet threat abroad), a role that came to be most dramatically developed by southern governors in the confrontation with federal court desegregation orders in the 1960s under a pre–Civil War constitutional doctrine known as "interposition" (Dallek 2003, 514). On September 4, 1957, Governor Orval Faubus of Arkansas called out the state militia to prevent nine African American students from entering Little Rock's Central High School on the order of a federal court. On June 11, 1963, Governor George Wallace physically blocked the entrance to the University of Alabama to prevent the execution of a federal court's desegregation order. Although they lost their legal battle against desegregation, Faubus and Wallace succeeded in casting themselves as defenders of traditional sovereign prerogatives within the state. Ironically, they were both New Dealers who combined both strategies, working to expand state services in traditionally backward states, while using their public fight with the Supreme Court to demonstrate their loyalty to the populist tradition of white supremacy.

Table 2.2 shows almost a clean reversal of the trend described in Table 2.1. Governors reverted to being the common nominees of the two major parties and were almost always the winner (the exception being 1988, when Michael Dukakis, governor of Massachusetts, lost to federal politician George H. W. Bush). Below, I will explore some reasons why the death penalty might alter the political dynamics of governors versus senators. Here I note the close fit between the pattern of reversion to "governor power" and the death penalty hypothesis.

The pattern of reversion to governors as presidents can be traced in lines that correspond to changes in the status of the death penalty. First, the year in which the shift back to governors arguably begins, 1976, is the first presidential election cycle to unfold fully after *Furman v. Georgia* (1972). Though Jimmy Carter benefited from avoiding close identification with the death penalty (closer identification might well have denied him the nomination, given the abolitionist leanings of the Democrats in 1976

Table 2-2

Federal Politicians v. Governors as Presidential Nominees and Winners 1980–2004

	Republican	*Democrat*	*Winner*
1980	*Reagan*	*Carter*	*Reagan*
1984	*Reagan*	**Mondale**	*Reagan*
1988	**Bush I**	*Dukakis*	**Bush I**
1992	**Bush I**	*Clinton*	*Clinton*
1996	**Dole**	*Clinton*	*Clinton*
2000	*Bush II*	**Gore**	*Bush II**
2004	*Bush II*	**Kerry**	*Bush II*

Bold indicates that the candidate's most important political experience previous to the run for president was in the federal government. Italic indicates that the candidate's most important political experience previous to the run for president was being governor of a state.

* Bush lost the popular vote and won the electoral college only after intervention by the Supreme Court.

(Banner 2002, 277); it is interesting that his state was the one most closely identified with the Supreme Court's attack on the death penalty, in *Gregg v. Georgia* (1976) as well as in *Furman*.

Second, although Carter's election was consistent with Harris's argument that the attention to foreign affairs is a driving factor in the selection of a senator to be president (the post-Vietnam and post-Watergate mid-1970s was clearly a period of domestic concerns), the pattern of the 1980s remained favorable to governors despite the attention given to foreign affairs after the Soviet invasion of Afghanistan and the Iran hostage crisis of 1979, just as it was favorable after September 11, 2001.

Third, the one exception to the governor-wins pattern was the 1988 election, when quintessentially federal politician George H. W. Bush (congressman, CIA director, vice president) defeated a sitting governor whose profile reprised many of the themes Harris had noted as relevant to the traditional dominance of governors. As governor of Massachusetts, Dukakis had gotten enormous national attention as a decision maker who could maintain fiscal discipline at a time of ballooning federal deficits and work successfully with legislatures. Though Harris blamed the tough fiscal circumstances of the 1950s for the eclipse of governors, Dukakis benefited from a relatively strong and revenue-producing economy in Massachusetts during the 1980s. Moreover, with the Soviet Union still intact but undergoing Perestroika, the Cold War drama of the first Reagan term had wound down and not been replaced yet by the astounding revolution of 1989; the election seemed destined to focus on domestic issues on which a fiscally successful governor should have been well positioned to win—and indeed, Dukakis was up 17 points in the polls after his nomination. In short, 1988 should have been a winning year for a governor in the midst of a run of such election cycles.

As has been much noted, the election seemed to turn on Bush's success in making the death penalty, and Dukakis' opposition to it, a defining issue about his leadership (Sarat 2001, 152). Dukakis's unwillingness to support the death penalty even for his own wife's hypothetical murderer, and the existence on his watch of a prison furlough program under which convicted murderer Willie Horton had been temporarily released before committing new violent crimes, undercut his leadership advantages as governor. This is especially so if being governor supposedly qualifies a person for leadership in part because it brings the power to execute on behalf of the people. Despite being a classical post–New Deal federal politician, Bush Sr. seemed a better leader because of his avowed loyalty to the death penalty. His support for the death penalty made him more like a governor than Dukakis (a real, but abolitionist, governor).

This points to a fourth feature of the aggregate pattern: no governor from a state that has outlawed executions was elected president in this period. All the successful governors were associated with their enthusiastic support for the death penalty as governor. As previously noted, Bill Clinton famously flew back to Arkansas to preside over the execution of prisoner Ricky Rector in the days before the New Hampshire primary, making him once again the front-runner (Banner 2002, 276; Sarat 2001, 259). If the resurrection of the governor as the source of national leaders is a sign that states are once again crucial to how Americans imagine themselves as a nation, this pattern suggests that only those states with the death penalty are fully American, and that the abolitionist states stand out as deviant cases.[21]

By wounding and not killing the death penalty, the Supreme Court placed every governor and state legislature in the nation in the position of having to either rescue the power to punish with death or allow it to disappear from among the tools available to the people of a state to protect themselves from violent crime. More than any other hot-button issue of the period, including busing and abortion, capital punishment placed state political leaders between the citizens of the state (and their perceived risk of murder) and an apparently unaccountable part of the federal power. The controversy around capital punishment may have helped crystallize and universalize a common theme in the earlier controversies about busing (1971) and abortion (1973), the sense of the importance of individual lives (those of fetuses and white school-age children in the first two cases and of everybody who is not a murderer in the death penalty context). This suggests that the evocative phrase "culture of life," which has been adopted by many conservatives and right-wing Christians to describe their opposition to abortion, and more recently, to characterize their stands on issues ranging from stem cell research to infant safe haven laws (see Sanger 2006), all of which may have at their core a sensibility of criminal victimization stemming from the war on crime. In terms of executive leadership, the post-*Furman* wave of reenactment legislation was a replay of the interposition fight without the discredited subject of segregation.

Thus, beyond any generic features of capital punishment, the Supreme Court's constitutional intervention on the death penalty created an enormous opportunity for both political authority in general, and an opportunity almost singularly available to governors or state legislators with an eye to being governor. The death penalty came eventually to be important in federal elections and directly in presidential elections, but for the first decade after *Furman*, abolitionist sentiment among liberal Democrats in Congress meant that the opportunity to enact a new federal death penalty would be blocked. The so-called drug-kingpin sections of the 1987 crime bill provided the first occasion for a new federal death penalty affirmation, just in time for Vice President George H. W. Bush to successfully use the death penalty against Massachusetts Governor Michael Dukakis in the 1988 election.

Conclusion: The Dialectic of Prosecutor and Criminal

Prosecutors have long been a distinct American innovation in executive government. Almost everywhere in the world, prosecution is exercised by local representatives of a national, or at least, state/provincial-wide executive. Only in the United States and other countries that have adopted the model do local elected officials exercise these deep but jurisdictionally limited powers and a special claim to represent the local community as a whole. In the last decades of the twentieth century, however, the war on crime reshaped the American prosecutor into an important model for political authority, while also giving real prosecutors enormous jurisdiction over the welfare of communities. For the modern chief executive, especially governors, the expanded war on crime has created numerous opportunities to govern like a prosecutor, including:

- spending crime control dollars from the federal government or state revenues
- supporting legislative increases in punishment
- exercising executive discretion to sustain and maintain punishments by denying clemency or parole, signing a death warrant, or seeking to protect the death penalty

At the same time, the executive's prosecutorial shift has created powerful new vulnerabilities, including:

- political responsibility for criminal acts that could conceivably have been prevented by different executive actions (parole denial or revocation, furlough programs, etc.)
- failure to satisfy the demands for security or vengeance by victims and publics aroused to consider their potential for victimization
- competition with other prosecutorial executives
- accusation of sympathy with criminals or even criminal activity

For a long but now largely forgotten stretch of American history, chief executives were produced by negotiation among networks of local partisan clubs (only an evolutionary step or two away from the street gang) ascending to state and ultimately national political campaigns. Franklin Delano Roosevelt may have been the last president to be nominated that way and elected by an all-out partisan effort only loosely tied to the person and personality of the candidate. Roosevelt and the New Deal changed that by constructing powerful federal agencies that would forge a new and direct circuit of power with mass society. Roosevelt's four-term success marked the emergence of two independent models of executive authority, one emphasizing social welfare and the other global military dominance. In both, the executive's reliance on an army of political volunteers was replaced largely by claims of scientific expertise communicated to the public through mass media and popular culture. Governors and presidents no longer answer first to powerful party bosses but instead through grids of polls, news, and social programs to millions of citizens who can in turn express their sentiments at the ballot box, in polls, and in the interpretation of a 24-hour-a-day news commentary.

Today, the social welfare strategies of the New Deal and Great Society eras have been powerfully discredited and no longer unify a stable electoral majority. The appeal of global military dominance appears slightly more robust, especially after 9/11, but in fact was permanently damaged by the Vietnam debacle, leaving a substantial resistance to military adventure (now reinforced by the problems being encountered in Iraq). As national security crises from the Bay of Pigs to the invasion of Iraq have shown, the executive is as much endangered as empowered by the expanded importance of military power.

The attraction of crime control as a basis for executive power begins with its immunity from the political collapse of support for both the liberal social welfare state and the conservative message of global military dominance. Here, the prosecutor has by far the most politically promising position as the unique advocate of the people's right to seek criminal justice. Though both welfare and militarism seem to many Americans to be perverse and corrupt, prosecutors represent a purer aspect of public interest that seems free of interest-group factionalism.

How does the prosecutorial model change the nature of executive power? How does ascendance of the prosecutor alter the relationship between the executive and the citizen? The triumph of executives over legislatures and parliaments has been one of the most contentious questions of political theory. Many theorists, beginning with Carl Schmitt, maintained that the executive has the advantage in legitimately representing the citizens under conditions of modernity (Schmitt 1923/1985). But this comparison ignores the grave problems contemporary executives have had maintaining their legitimacy in the face of the same political contradictions that confront parliamentary leadership. The prosecutorial model of the executive offers a unique alternative.

In associating their executive authority with the role of the prosecutor, presidents and governors are able to tap into a logic of sovereign representation largely independent of, and unimpaired by, the discrediting of the general welfare state constructed by the New Deal. At the same time, prosecutors operating mainly at the local level have found themselves pulled to act in a wider sphere of governance that was largely abandoned by the retreat of welfarism.

The political attractions of both trends are apparent, but the costs to the feasibility of democratic governance in the long run are disturbing. In establishing a posture of punisher, executives favor program development that requires punitive responses toward individuals and institutions whose reform may require other strategies. Governing behavior through the power to punish raises maximum amounts of resistance. It also underdevelops programs that do not lend themselves to a prosecutorial posture. Allowing prosecutors to take increasing responsibility for assuring the social well-being of the most disadvantaged and impoverished parts of our urban society also exacts costs. Even the most community-minded prosecutor is likely to be heavily anchored in the resources and metaphors of criminal justice. The fact that prosecutors are generally elected in countywide elections makes them less sensitive to minority interests in all but predominantly minority jurisdictions.

The competition between executive and prosecutor can become dangerous to both. Since the Watergate scandal, the executive branch has been shadowed by a kind of evil twin of the attorney general who pursues the crime of the administration with the same kind of force applied by the contemporary attorney general to the national crime problem (Woodward 1999). The presidencies of Nixon, Reagan, Bush, and Clinton were all visibly wounded in varying degrees by the activities of special prosecutors. The pursuit of Clinton by special prosecutor Kenneth Starr in the late 1990s, culminating in Clinton's impeachment in 1998, virtually paralyzed a potentially activist administration for much of its second term. Clinton had made his mark in part by addressing the penchant of Democratic presidential candidates for not seeming serious enough about the public's fear of crime. Ironically, Clinton, who had done so much to associate himself with the prosecutorial position, found himself in a mortal battle with a special prosecutor over who was the real criminal.

Trying to leverage the legitimacy of the prosecution model for a broader task of governance also runs the risk of narrowing any real mandate for reform. In their own ways, both Bush and Clinton faced the limitations of their successful invocation of the prosecutorial model for achieving any major institutional transformations (e.g., national health insurance or privatizing Social Security).

Perhaps no contemporary politician better exemplifies the perils of the prosecutorial executive than Gray Davis. Davis pursued tough-on-crime policies with a vigor that offended fellow liberal Democrats in the California State Assembly. Davis took every opportunity possible to personally place himself between citizens and individual criminals, opposing the parole of even the small group of parole-eligible life-termers that his tough-on-crime Board of Prison Terms had recommended for parole. For a time, this seemed to give him an edge. In 1998, Davis defeated a conservative Republican state attorney general by refusing to cede anything to him on crime while winning liberals on issues such as abortion. But crime turned out to be too thin a basis for building support in an era of declining crime rates. Less than two years later, with state revenues having collapsed and the state mired in recession, a petition drive for recall caught on, and in November of 2003 an overwhelming majority of the voters elected to recall Governor Davis (Seelye 2003).

We the Victims

Fearing Crime and Making Law

Would I move into another gated community? The short,
wimpy answer is yes. I'm getting old, and in this post-9/11
world it's not such a bad thing having someone—even a
rent-a-cop—to watch over you.

—Joe Modzelewski, *Miami Herald*, November 10, 2002

Starting in the late 1960s, state legislatures and Congress produced a remarkable stream of laws concerning the power to punish criminals.
Most of these laws increased that authority to punish and invested, either
directly or indirectly, more public money in criminal justice operations,
especially the vast and expensive prison system that now characterizes the
federal government and virtually every state. This outpouring of legislation (and the related output of courts and administrative agencies) is just
beginning to receive its due from political scientists and historians as a significant swing in the legal construction of the American Republic (Guest
2005; Murakawa 2005). But it is not just the scope of this wave of lawmaking that makes it impressive, it is also the coherence of this body of law as
reflecting a vision of how institutions govern through crime. Crime, to be
sure, is an ancient subject of legislation. This chapter argues that starting
with the federal Omnibus Crime Control and Safe Streets Act of 1968,[1]
crime legislation in the United States has had a distinctive legislative rationality, that is, a way of imagining the needs of the citizenry as framed by the
problem of crime, the purposes and means of intervention, and the means
of achieving a higher level of success against crime.

At the center of this new lawmaking rationality is the crime victim.
Crime victims are in a real sense the representative subjects of our time
(Garland 2001a, 11–12). It is as crime victims that Americans are most readily imagined as united; the threat of crime simultaneously de-emphasizes
their differences and authorizes them to take dramatic political steps. As a
result, a remarkable proportion of lawmaking by contemporary American

representative institutions concerns crime. The vulnerabilities and needs of victims define the appropriate conditions for government intervention.

The nature of this victim identity is deeply racialized. It is not all victims, but primarily white, suburban, middle-class victims, whose exposure has driven waves of crime legislation. As I shall explore further below, crime legislation has an imagined location: safe and respectable residential areas, typically in the suburbs, with a definable margin against which crime, poverty and, typically, minority demographics are pushing. Victims of violent crime have formed the public face of the justifications for the war on crime, even as that war has targeted mainly crimes that are not violent and, indeed, that have no specific victims, such as violations of drug laws and laws against firearms possession by felons (Dubber 2002).

But while victims have been successful at winning attention and intervention from law makers, this strength cannot easily be converted into modern welfare benefits. Instead, in the logic of modern crime legislation, victims can benefit only by the production of overall security through the punishment of the person responsible or, in the case of a loved one's death, by psychological acts such as "closure" (Zimring 2004). Were victims to instead receive something akin to, say, workers' compensation, they would become just one more rent-seeking interest group, rather than the model of the "general will" they currently reflect.

This has produced one of the most anomalous features of modern crime legislation. Though victims are the key subject addressed by crime legislation, they are not always or even often directly referenced. Instead, crime legislation has created elements within the state that have come to symbolically stand for victims; two in particular are police officers and prison cells. As we shall explore further in chapter 5, prison cells have succeeded far more than have police in capturing public funding, but as we shall explore here, police have captured the greatest amount of symbolic investment. Not only are their interests treated in modern crime legislation as a proxy for victim interests, but police are often portrayed in such legislation as victims themselves, not only of criminals, but of defense lawyers, soft-on-crime judges, misguided parole and probation officers, and so on. Prison cells, meanwhile, are the purest expression of the public's embrace of and promise to protect the victims, and potential victims, of crime, especially because they promise to produce a security effect that is generalized to the whole state, while policing is always spatially concentrated (and usually also locally funded).

Whatever else it does, contemporary crime legislation invests these elements with truth and power, causing government agents and subjects to further invest their own attention and capacities in responding. Crime legislation is not *just a symbolic way to signal* to particular constituents or an instrument to accomplish particular policy objectives, but also an influential model of how to make law in a democratic way.[2] Classifying the citizenry into types of actual and potential victims allows for a broad recognition of diversity within the unifying framework of "fearing crime"—while our contemporary catalog of "monsters," including sex offenders, gang members, drug kingpins, and violent crime recidivists, forms a constantly renewed rationale for legislative action. Radiating out from the victim and the offender are metaphoric chains,[3] along which the representational security of legislative bodies found in crime legislation can be extended both by repetition and application to other governmental problems.

The point is not that contemporary crime legislation has covered up an authentic political subject. The crime victim is only the latest in a whole parade of idealized subjects of the law, including the yeoman farmer of the nineteenth century, the freedman of the Reconstruction era, the industrial worker of the early twentieth century, and the consumer who became the central concern of economic policy after World War II. All of these survive in American politics and include real political organizations that continue to lobby on their behalf, but at the same time it is in the experience of victimization and (much more commonly) the imagined possibility of victimization that lawmaking consensus has been redefined in our time. Indeed, to the extent that earlier ideals seek to recuperate their political currency, it is through a narrative representation of themselves in crime victim mode. Thus, in an era when Congress attends little to civil rights, hate crimes have emerged as the dominant focus for those lobbyists and legislators loyal to that cause.[4] When workers want to contest the decisions of managers in the post-unionized, at-will labor market, they must define themselves as potential victims of crimes by customers, co-workers, or others, or as victims of immoral behavior (sexual harassment).

The rest of this chapter explores crime legislation and the rationality of governance it has helped form. The first section provides a quick sketch of the major idealized citizen subjects that have been the focus of legislation since the birth of the Republic. The second section examines the foundational piece of legislation for the war on crime, the Omnibus Crime

Control and Safe Streets Act of 1968. Without erasing the line between ordinary legislation and constitutions, we can productively read the act as a kind of quasi-constitutional law, one that calls into being a number of dynamic processes that will help to shape and define a mode of law-making. That law was not a piece of crime legislation in the traditional sense. It did not specify a crime within the field of federal criminal jurisdiction and seek to protect Americans from it, and it did not change the penalty of an old crime. Rather, it focused on the operation of state and local law enforcement within their far broader field of criminal jurisdiction as a problem for federal intervention. This began an era of federal investment in state and local criminal justice institutions, but it was much more than money that flowed out of the law and into the cellular structures of state and local governments. Rather, along with the money came a cluster of ways of knowing and acting toward crime that have profoundly influenced and deformed American democracy. The final section follows the development of the crime legislation model into the 1990s.

Making Up Legal Subjects: The Idealized Subject of Legislation

In claiming that crime legislation since 1968 reflects a distinctive logic of law making we are not suggesting anything abnormal about the legislative process. One might suppose that laws always have an underlying legislative logic or rationality, a way of imagining subjects who will be responding to the law and the purposes of intervening among them. We can identify other periods of American history, when distinct and recognizable styles of lawmaking emerge around a particular subject over a period of years or even decades. As with crime, earlier waves of lawmaking have anchored themselves in compelling narratives of the representative citizen and their needs. The crime victim is only the latest in a whole parade of idealized subjects of the law, including the small landowning or yeoman farmer of the nineteenth century, the freedmen of the Reconstruction era, the industrial workers of the Depression and post–WWII eras, and the at-risk consumer of the mid-twentieth century.

Whatever else they do, laws define categories of subjects to which consequences, negative and positive, attach. When laws address us in specific statuses—as primary school students, those convicted of one or more felonies, or those looking for work in the past month—they invest power and meaning in those identities while taking such away from others (Simon 1988). None of these need be dominating identities, nor do they deprive individuals of forms of agency derived from their other identities.

It is tempting to think of such legislative subjects as ideological fictions through which the needs of real people were often disguised to suit the advantage of the few over the many. But whatever the strategic value *behind* the promotion of a certain system of classification, its *effects* are undeniably real. The investment of power into certain identities creates incentives for people to invest their own will in the maintenance and re-formation of those identities. Classification produces symbolic effects, investing certain identities with stigma and valorizing others (Edelman 1964; Scheingold 1984, 84). These laws achieve important practical effects as well (although not always those promised) by constituting flows of information between governors and the governed that in turn create new surfaces for action and unleash new flows of information.

The following sections offer brief sketches of what can best be thought of as lawmaking rationalities. They involve not just one or two pieces of legislation, but a template for producing new law on an ongoing basis. As such, they involve identifying broad sectors of the American population through subject positions that help further elaborate the purpose of legislation and the best means to accomplish those ends, including which "enemies" must be confronted by the government to protect citizens. Farmers, freedmen, workers, and consumers have introduced new subjects of the law and come to define, for a time, the dominant meaning of representational integrity. They continue to have ongoing resonance in lawmaking even after competing projects have been introduced.

Landowning Farmers

At the beginning of the Republic, Thomas Jefferson and other believers in the vision of a nation of free small landowners saw that the federal government had one major asset that could lift the estate of the ordinary citizen: unimaginably large land holdings. These advocates sought legislation to use this extraordinary power to intentionally create a population of small landowning farmers who would, by virtue of owning land, have a practical independence unavailable to the serf, slave, or tenant farmer

(Clawson 1968). Their opponents—including the first treasury secretary, Alexander Hamilton—believed the federal government should simply maximize returns by selling large pieces of land as expensively as possible to the highest bidder, which would result in the creation of huge, plantation-like private land holdings and the inflation of land costs beyond what ordinary individuals could afford. This was a conflict not only between speculators and settlers for the economic bounty of the new nation, but also between two quite different visions of whether the national government should promote or discourage a society of families capable of self-government as a result of ownership and economic exploitation of land.

Jefferson's election to the presidency in 1800 helped secure a significant victory for the small landowning settler vision. Federal land sales were kept inexpensive, and the minimum size unit available remained relatively small, dropping to just 80 acres in 1820. Free land to anyone who would agree to farm it in an appropriate way became the dominant ideal. As the nineteenth century progressed, however, political tension over control of the federal government between slave and free states began to invest the land issue with new meaning. The ideal of many small independent farmers was resisted by other leaders, particularly from the slave-holding states, which were dominated by large plantation owners who saw in that ideal both a challenge to their internal hegemony and a further advantage to the free states in their mutual competition for population growth. The most important piece of federal land legislation promoting the small landowning farmer as a privileged subject of the national government prior to the Civil War was the General Pre-Emption Act of 1841. This allowed settlers who had been "illegally" squatting on federal land to purchase the land at low prices. The law unabashedly converted outlaw subjects into functioning members of a property-owner society. Consequently, it sent a major signal to urban families who didn't have enough money to buy land "free and clear" to risk settling new areas in hopes the act's terms would eventually legalize their claims.

Once the coming of the Civil War emptied Congress of its southern representatives, the promoters of governing through land had a free hand to expand. They responded by enacting the Homestead Act of 1862, which provided units of 160 acres to any head of family or person over 21 who was a U.S. citizen (or intended to become one) on condition they farm it for at least five years before any transfer of title, to make it less attractive to hidden speculators. Even as the war unleashed economic and demographic forces that would doom the vision of the small landholding Republic, the act succeeded in creating vast numbers of new subjects with a stake in land and thus a relationship to government mediated through the conditions applying to the holding of former federal lands.

Land legislation in the nineteenth century reflected not just a specific social policy, but a master strategy for fostering democracy and for governing.[5] These laws recognize a certain kind of citizen subject as the dominant interlocutor of government; the white male farmer who, with family or employees, works a relatively small piece of land. It is through the needs of such a small landowner that the proper scope and approach of government is projected. It is through the needs and capacities of this idealized citizen subject that federal lawmaking attempted to achieve other objectives, for example, producing timber for the market or irrigation of the land. Indeed, notwithstanding the rise of new competitive subjects like the freedmen, industrial working class, and new giant corporations, land remained central to how Congress governed.

Nineteenth-century land policy also introduced certain political technologies for fostering a landholding public, including forms of expert knowledge applicable to the individual farmers through institutions like "land grant" universities and a network of "land agents."[6] Decades later, these pathways of knowledge and power would be expanded by the New Deal, which drew much of its intellectual capital from those same universities, and used land grant agents as a capillary system to help small land holders negotiate the increasingly complex system of federal regulations and benefits surrounding the agricultural use of land.

Land legislation also created new consumers and producers of knowledge about the land and its resources. Landowners engaged in active cultivation and development of the land produced new knowledge about the resources and developmental needs of the land. Meanwhile, they formed a powerful consumer base for knowledge about how to exploit the land. States coming into the union were granted large federal land tracts to help finance the creation of public elementary schools.

By the end of the nineteenth century, any serious notion of a nation of farmers was fading into nostalgia, but the circuitry of knowledge and power created around this idealized political subject remained (and continues even to this day) as an appreciable effect on legislation. In the complex battles around western mining and ranching rights, water, and the environmental protections of species and habitat, we can see the continuing centrality of the impact of this idealized legislative subject.

The Freedmen

During the Reconstruction era (1864–1880), Congress passed a series of sweeping measures to address the post–Civil War political and legal ambiguities left by the uncertain status of both former slaves and the property of slave masters and Confederates. Two of the most famous were the Civil Rights Act of 1866 and the Freedmen's Bureau Act of 1866. Andrew Johnson vetoed both, escalating his conflict with the Republican leadership in Congress that would lead to his impeachment and near conviction by the Senate. The Freedmen's Bureau Act failed to receive sufficient votes to override the veto, but the Civil Rights Act became law, and an empowered Congress went on to constitutionalize its vision in the form of the Fourteenth Amendment. Both together offer a good diagram of Reconstruction lawmaking.

These laws established not just specific rights but broad government enterprises designed to sustain new legal subjects whose recent invention was plain. They marked the start of a new way of making federal law. In this regard, they shared a consistent set of features. As with the land settlement program, the Reconstruction acts valorized new kinds of political subjects, implemented new political practices, provoked cascades of knowledge production, and re-imagined the role of a representational body.

Reconstruction legislation highlighted a whole range of *idealized* political subjects—most importantly freed slaves, but also federal officers, federal employees working under hostile conditions in the South, and pro-Union citizens of the former Confederacy. The laws also recognized important new *negative* subjects requiring attention, especially the former rebels and slaveholders and formations like the Ku Klux Klan, which threatened freedmen and other federal subjects. The new forms of power and new modes of knowledge introduced by Reconstruction have been duly noted by historians (especially Foner 1989). Whole new kinds of federal agencies came into being, among them the Freedmen's Bureau, while older ones, such as the U.S. Army, were put to novel assignments.

The Reconstruction laws created new federal rights that would be the model for many subsequent efforts. They established a broad federal police power to collect data about basic social conditions in the states, constituting a new link between federal government and individual subjects unmediated by the states. Most important, they envisioned the national government as governing through rights invested in individuals. The federal government, once the subject of the constraining "bill of rights," now found its jurisdiction and its powers enormously expanded in the name of protecting rights-bearing individuals against other levels of government and private forces.

The Reconstruction Congress projected a new kind of representational relationship between Congress and the people, one based on assuring access to all citizens on an equal basis to the freedoms of a market economy. This was crucial to the legitimacy of a body that could no longer claim to be playing by the model of representational government that prevailed prior to the war. Written to guide the federal government through the unprecedented landscape of the defeated rebellion against the Constitution, Reconstruction legislation openly contemplated the problem of how to govern people during a transition from nonfreedom to freedom. Although written for the South, the Reconstruction vision ultimately reshaped governance nationally, leading to three constitutional amendments; indeed one of the great constitutional transformations in U.S. history.[7]

Political compromises in the 1880s brought about a rapid end to serious efforts at Reconstruction. The new legal forms continued to operate, often in novel fields. For example, the ability of a vulnerable subject to force a hostile institution of state or local government into federal court to answer to charges of violating those federal rights came to be used most voraciously by corporations. The possibilities of a civil rights governance, one governing through the protection of rights, would remain dormant until the rise of the Civil Rights movement in the 1950s brought about what some have described as a "second Reconstruction."[8]

The Civil Rights movement of the 1950s and its legislative triumph in the mid-1960s represented a genuine renewal of the Reconstruction project and the style of legislation associated with it. Like the laws of the first Reconstruction, the Civil Rights Act of 1964 and the Voting Rights Act of 1965 created new federal agencies, empowered federal courts to hear civil suits by citizens against their state and local government agencies, and produced over time a host of internal responses by state and private organizations to enhance compliance. The new laws also expanded the relevance of the civil rights citizen-subject from the laws' original focus, African Americans (especially in the South), to women, gays and lesbians, Latinos, and whites who perceived themselves as the victims of affirmative action programs. In its broadest form, the civil rights subject merges into the subject of human rights and the burgeoning bodies of transnational and international as well as national laws being produced around it.

The Industrial Worker

The New Deal legislation of the 1930s, including the National Industrial Recovery Act of 1933, the Social Security Act, and the Wagner Act of 1935, brought about one of the great constitutional transformations in American history. Like legislation during Reconstruction, this legislation has been seen in the context of constitutional politics (Fraser & Gerstle 1989). Here I focus on the New Deal as a new model of lawmaking that recognized a new set of idealized subjects. In its first phase, best known for the National Recovery Act and the Agricultural Adjustment Act, the main subjects were producers in industrial capitalism and its agricultural equivalents. Because of the strong alliance that developed between the Democratic Party and the large industrial unions of the Congress of Industrial Organizations, it is easy to think of the New Deal now as focusing on industrial workers, just as we think of Reconstruction as focusing on freedmen. But right from the start, New Deal legislation saw the worker, even the unionized worker, as just part of a productivity alliance that included capitalists.

The National Recovery Act called for industry-based coordination of firms that would have paralleled the industrial logic of an emerging trade unionism where the Congress of Industrial Organizations was the leading agent of industrial workers.[9] The statute laid out an elaborate administrative code for the regulatory power of industrial associations that would enjoy legal power over firms. Firms that chose to disregard new associational standards for an important ingredient of production (e.g., labor) found themselves defined as outlaws, and their executives could face criminal penalties. The Supreme Court struck the National Recovery Act down in a closely divided vote that marked the beginning of overt tensions between the conservative majority on the Court and the Roosevelt administration.

The president ultimately prevailed in his battle with the Supreme Court, but by then his strategic vision for economic recovery had shifted away from the broad regulation of production decisions of the National Recovery Act. In the second phase, exemplified by the Social Security Act, New Deal lawmakers focused instead on the citizen as consumer, a subject whose flow of income, and thus purchasing power, was critical to sustaining demand for the producers. Federal governance over production was not over. The Wagner Act, for example, legalized collective bargaining and established federal authority to resolve disputes over the recognition of unions, strengthening the position of workers but otherwise leaving the market largely competitive rather than overtly corporatist. Ultimately, it was the worker as wage earner that became the greatest interest of unions. A nation of organized workers was in fact a nation of reliable consumers. If the worker served the economy as a consumer in producing demand just as much as when working to fill the demands of others, whole new possibilities for government existed in maintaining and fostering that consuming demand (Cohen 2003).

Historians have debated just what model of governing the New Deal represented (Brinkley 1989). The political technologies of the New Deal were manifold and rapidly changing. They ranged from direct federal oversight of all aspects of private management, to the use of federal subsidies as tools to shift the equilibrium results in certain markets. More consistent, perhaps, was the understanding expressed in a wide variety of New Deal legislation, including the measures discussed here, of what features of the American citizenry needed governing and what made them governable.

One feature, expressed in many of these specific laws, was a vision of the economy as driven by collective agents, such as workers in a particular industry or investors. These mass participants might be composed of individual choices, but it was at the aggregate level that their real effects operated. The role of government was to foster the recognition and well-being of these mass agents or collective agents who were in a sense the new subjects of government. To govern through this organization of mass interests meant the enactment of laws that helped mass agents like unions gain recognition and become self-organizing; laws that protected mass publics by enforcing collective savings, as in the payroll taxes that have paid for Social Security since the 1935 Act; and laws that protected the collective interests of whole industries by punishing deviation from cooperatively defined standards, those aspects being mostly struck down.

The Vulnerable Consumer

The Second World War (1939–1945) marked both a culmination and the beginning of the end of the era of the industrial worker as an idealized citizen subject. Whether as part of the huge mechanized American military or the great industrial system supplying the war, more Americans than ever before or after found themselves directly embodied in the ideal of an industrial worker. The absorption of millions of American women and African Americans into the industrial economy undermined the assumptions of the previous boundaries of the model of industrial citizenship that even the New Deal had accepted. The great American industrial cities—Detroit, Chicago, Los Angeles, Seattle, and many others—stood at a kind of peak. Their infrastructures, last expanded in the boom of the 1920s and supplemented here and there by New Deal public works, strained under the maximum utilization of the industrial base that had concentrated in these cities over the previous half century (Sugrue 1996, 17–32). Their boulevards teemed with a population invigorated by their economic importance and liberated, if temporarily, by the global emergency of total war.[10]

By the beginning of the 1960s, a mere 15 years later, this industrial tableaux and the idealized industrial subject at its core were in disarray, not so much defeated as outgrown and outcast. For the sectors of America best positioned to benefit from the high tide of postwar affluence, the triumph of the industrial order in World War II paid immediate dividends: new homes in the suburbs, college educations, and white-collar jobs in the vast corporate and government sectors of the new economy (Cohen 2003). Peacetime brought on a rapid transfer of industrial employment to rural areas, the South, and the West. Unable to access most of the benefits of the postwar government largesse because of discrimination and lack of opportunity, minorities and female-headed households found themselves occupying the dying centers of the old industrial economy. Increasingly perceived as dangerous and unproductive, the new urban poor would soon be blamed for the failure of cities like Detroit.

The historian Lizabeth Cohen (2003, 7) has characterized this era as a "consumer republic," "an economy, culture, and politics built around the promises of mass consumption." The vulnerabilities as well as capacities of this consumer-subject in this era opened up new possibilities for governance, reflected in new waves of "consumer" legislation and a range of idealized, or demonized, consumer subjects.

In the 1950s, an important line of development concerned the different vulnerabilities of consumers as economic, sociological, and biological entities who are threatened by toxins and carcinogens in their food and larger environment or exposed to malnutrition, poor education, and inadequate health care. The consumer subject of the New Deal was largely subordinate to the logic of national emergency government, whether the government was fighting the Depression or the Axis powers. Starting almost immediately after the war and growing with the new affluence of the United States, the consumer subject of legislation thickened and deepened, especially around these three centers of vulnerability.

Perhaps the most widely recognized new locus of governance was the consumer as aggregate economic force whose capacity to spend came to be viewed as the key to postwar economic prosperity. Historians have argued that this formed the crucial direction by which the New Deal yielded a much more conservative form of regulated capitalism than might have emerged from the Great Depression. The key role for at least the federal government was to maintain consumer demand through fiscal and monetary policy, a strategy known generally as Keynesianism after British economic theorist and government planner John Maynard Keynes. A great deal of post–World War II legislation sought to sustain this Keynsian mechanism, not least the great highway building laws that constructed the interstate and invested directly in opening up new economic consumption opportunities in the suburbs.

Beyond the Keynesian consensus, however, the post–New Deal consumer republic gave rise to a range of other, more deviant consumer subjects (both in the sense that they deal with more marginalized parts of the American population and take up vulnerabilities associated with greater stigma. Around each, new centers of lawmaking and governing formed. One center was the problem of the consumer as a victim of machine-age risk, exemplified by the car accident. From the early 1950s on, the U.S. Congress legislated around a whole series of issues defined as "consumer" issues, ranging from debt collection practices to the suffocation of children in refrigerators. New scientific expertise in the study of human safety engineering, spurred by World War II, helped to give the familiar "economic man" a physiological dimension as the subject of catastrophic forces un-leashed by car accidents and dives into aboveground swimming pools.

Another center was forming around the biological subject of envi-ronmental contamination, especially through the food supply. As with economic and physiological subjects, the biological subject needed gov-ernment protection against machine-age forces beyond ready inspection and precaution by the consumer. But unlike the others, the biological sub-ject exposed a kind of intolerable vulnerability that demanded more than improved safety and risk spreading. This new threat had a distinct and al-ready well-known and dreaded face, that of cancer. The need to protect consumers from exposure to carcinogens in the food supply motivated the famous Delaney Amendment of 1958 that forbade food with measurable quantities of carcinogens from entering the stream of commerce, establish-ing the first "zero-tolerance" standard in American governance.

Starting in the Kennedy administration, the problem of poverty be-came a third center for formation of a new kind of idealized political sub-ject. Poverty was negative consumption, those whose chronic inability to draw enough income to support their own families constituted a problem for governing consumption. The wave of legislation during the Kennedy and Johnson administration known as the "Great Society" constituted a new model of lawmaking attuned to this idealized consumer subject, and its targets included juvenile delinquency, urban redevelopment, and mental health delivery systems.

The war on poverty launched by Lyndon Baines Johnson after his election in 1964 constituted an effort to cast this order, creating a post–New Deal relationship between the federal government and its privileged sub-jects. By focusing on poverty, Johnson, presiding over the most buoyant economy in U.S. history, was taking a step away from the almost corpo-ratist logic of the New Deal. The private capitalist economy was to domi-nate resource allocation, but the federal government would have a role in transforming the conditions of Americans isolated from the wellsprings of economic success: the poor, the elderly, and those disabled by disadvan-tage and disease.

> Each program singled out the "inner city" as its main target;
> each provided a basketful of services; each channeled some por-
> tion of its funds more or less directly to new organizations in the

"inner city," circumventing the existing municipal agencies which traditionally controlled services; and, most important, each made the service agencies of local government, whether in health, housing, education, or public welfare, the "mark"—the target of reform. (Rabin 1986, 1273)

This complex consumer subject with its economic, physiological, and biological sides remains an omnipresent force in contemporary politics. In the 1970s, social scientists pondering the "new social movements" (such as environmentalism and gay rights) and the emergence of postindustrial trends across the wealthy west believed that a new political balance of power was in the process of forming around "postmaterialist" values (Inglehart 1980), including environmentalism (Douglas and Wildavsky 1982) and civil rights. But the expected political strength of this complex consumer subject has never fully been realized in the United States. Whether as a cause of this failure, or simply a beneficiary of the resulting space for a political solution, the victim of violent crime came in the 1980s and 1990s to squeeze out both the civil rights subject and the vulnerable consumer subject.

Crime Victim: Contemporary Crime Legislation and Rise of the Crime Victim as the Idealized Subject of the Law

I draw most of my strength from victims for they represent
America to me: people who will not be put down, people who
will not be defeated, people who will rise again and again for
what is right . . . you are my heroes and heroines. You are but
little lower than the angels.

—Janet Reno

From War on Poverty to War on Crime

One can argue over which piece of Reconstruction or New Deal legislation was the most definitive, but there is little doubt that the Omnibus Crime Control and Safe Streets Act of 1968 (hereafter Safe Streets Act) is the legislative enactment marking the birth of "governing through crime" in

America. As with the great pieces of Reconstruction and New Deal legislation, the Safe Streets Act bears examination on three levels: as a solidifying political victory for a new governing coalition; as a set of strategies for knowing and acting on subjects of crime, including criminals, victims, and also the state and local institutions that address them; and as a framework generating a new set of privileged subjects for government, including victims and state law enforcement, courts, and correctional systems. After briefly outlining the major elements of the act, we will take up each of these dimensions in turn.

The Omnibus Crime Control and Safe Streets Act and Lawmaking Since 1968

The legislation was enacted June 6, 1968 with only four senators and seventeen representatives voting against it. As befitting its "omnibus" designation, the law was actually a conglomerate of numerous measures addressing a wide variety of crime and law enforcement–related topics. There were four major themes, each accorded a distinct title, in the statute. Title I authorized more than $400 million in federal funds for planning and innovation in law enforcement, corrections, and courts. The act created a new federal agency to distribute funds through a system of competitive grants to those state and local agencies ready to improve criminal justice along federal lines. Title II established a new rule of evidence for federal courts regarding the admissions of confessions in criminal cases.[11] Such statements should be admitted, according to the statute, if the judge deemed them "voluntary." The new standard, if read literally, had the effect of mandating that federal courts ignore several new criteria that the U.S. Supreme Court had established on top of the traditional voluntariness test.[12] Title III authorized both federal and local police to engage in wiretapping and other forms of electronic eavesdropping with and without a court order under certain circumstances. The law also set internal regulatory criteria for the use of these devices. Title IV set up a federal licensing structure for gun dealers, requiring them to keep information on the purchases of weapons and banning pistol sales by mail order, and banning sales altogether to a range of such presumptively dangerous subjects as dishonorably discharged veterans, felons, and the insane.

Though the Safe Streets Act was enacted during the heat of the 1968 presidential campaign, its origins lie in the aftermath of Johnson's 1964 landslide victory. Johnson understood intuitively how dangerous violent crime was to the post–New Deal coalition he was seeking to reestablish. Barry Goldwater had invoked "crime in the streets" in his campaign, and although LBJ succeeded in turning the campaign on Goldwater's own extremism, not Democratic permissiveness, he recognized presciently that crime was driving a stake through the heart of the Democrats' urban coalition even while leading liberal criminologists of the day continued to doubt the seriousness of the surge in armed robberies in the very largest cities.

From almost the start of Johnson's own term, public anxiety about riots and crime was constantly in the news. Even the *New York Times,* a paper not easily swayed by short-term popular interests, documented the political rumbling of this issue in the headlines of the mid-1960s: "Hasidic Jews Use Patrols to Balk Attack," "Philadelphia Police Using Dogs to Curb Violence in Subways," "[Mayor] Wagner Orders a Night Patrol on All Subways," "Fear of Muggers Looms Large in Public Concern over Crime."[13] The apparent rise in violent street crime, primarily armed and unarmed robberies, was concentrated in the big cities that were the traditional anchors of the New Deal style of government. This kind of one-on-one crime linked the term "violence" to the riots and antiwar protests that had become common for the first time in a century during the mid-1960s. Both riots and protests were associated with urban blacks and college students, two subjects highly associated with federal aspirations in the New Deal and Great Society eras.

Johnson's speeches and legislative proposals from the start of his term suggest a consistent strategy to address violent crime as a political problem of growing proportions to his liberal coalition. Three elements of this strategy that were to become an enduring part of governing through crime in America were President Johnson's expressive solidarity with crime victims, his promise of technical solutions to crime risk, and a federally led and funded rebuilding to modern standards of local police departments and criminal courts, as well as jails and prisons.

First, conscious as he was of the need to position the Democratic Party on the side of crime victims, he spoke frequently and forcefully of his concern about the harm crime was causing, and the absolute necessity of combating it.

Second, the president's Commission on Law Enforcement and the Administration of Criminal Justice, put into action his faith in social science expertise as a tool of value to the criminal justice system; this was a continuation of the New Deal emphasis on the need to address social problems with new forms of expertise. The commission, headed by Attorney General Nicholas Katzenbach, began work in 1965 and issued reports in 1966 and 1967. Although overshadowed by the conservative-dominated law that followed, the commission proved highly influential to the direction of criminal justice reform at the state and local level. Some of the most significant features of contemporary criminal justice, the modern emergency telephone system (911), and the rationalization of dispatching, were promoted by the commission as was the regular use of victimization surveys to determine the levels of crime independent of reports made to the police.

Third, the president pumped federal money into planning and innovation at the local level. The heart of the original crime legislation Johnson had introduced in Congress in 1967, and one largely retained by the 1968 act, was the start of a massive federal investment in the material and intellectual technologies of criminal justice. Few aspects of state and local government were more derelict and backward than criminal justice in the 1960s. Today no part of state and local government has been more extensively reconstructed. What our schools, public health systems, or environmental management systems might look like today with similar investment is an open question.

From its inception in 1968, the law's gestation was controlled by an emerging congressional coalition of southern Democrats and western Republicans who shared a social conservatism and a growing anxiety about crime.[14] Despite growing criticism of the legislation by the Democratic left in Congress—led by Senator Robert Kennedy, who harshly criticized the provisions on wiretapping and interrogations—by the end of May 1968, a large majority of both parties was poised to adopt it in a season of growing concern about disorder following the assassination of Martin Luther King, Jr. The law finally came to a vote on June 7, the day following the assassination of Senator Robert Kennedy.[15] In a gesture toward the manner of his death by gunshot, Congress reconsidered the recently defeated gun control measures and made them Title IV of the law.

To its liberal critics, the Safe Streets Act represented a moment of reactionary regression on the part of government. British journalist Richard Harris (1969, 41), writing in the *New Yorker* and later in a book on the law, described it bluntly as "a piece of demagoguery devised out of malevolence and enacted in hysteria." Johnson's strategy to fight poverty and reform local governance was still in its infancy, both administratively and as a political successor to the New Deal consensus of the previous generation. Along with the administration's implementation of the landmark civil rights decisions of the previous decade, these new programs engendered strong resistance from both traditional Republican opponents of expanding the New Deal and southern Democrats defending segregation. The Safe Streets Act represented the first fruit of the union between those forces that have dominated American politics ever since.

The Safe Streets Act reflected for the first time the power of law making about crime to bring together representatives from across the ideological spectrum. Many of the southern democrats and western republicans were drawn by what became Title II of the law, with its repudiation of the Warren Court's major decisions on police interrogations.[16] Conservatives and moderates were also drawn to Title III, which for the first time authorized wiretaps and other forms of electronic surveillance. Liberals, like Senator Edward Kennedy of Massachusetts and ultimately President Johnson himself, primarily cited two elements of the law: huge federal outlays for improving local criminal justice, and the nation's first federal gun control laws (Harris 1968, 104). The act was enacted June 7, 1968, with only four senators and 17 representatives voting against it.

Title I was the heart of the administration's own proposal first presented to Congress in 1967. There it functioned as a pure Great Society program. It set up a new federal agency, filled it with experts, and authorized it to pump money into local projects all over the country to reform local law enforcement and corrections. As originally envisioned, the new Law Enforcement Assistance Agency would have been a vehicle for implementing the crime control strategy outlined in the report of the President's Commission on Crime published in 1967, which combined a focus on raising the technological level of policing with a focus on advancing therapeutic rehabilitation strategies in state correctional systems.

The form Title I took in the Safe Streets Act was in the end quite different. Most important, the law rejected the Great Society funding structure and adopted instead a structure known as "block grants," which would soon become well known as the core of the Nixon administration's "New Federalism." While Johnson' Great Society approach used funding to create direct circuits between the federal government and the community, the block grant approach channeled the federal government funding back to the traditional state governments, and indeed within their executive branch (see the discussion of how the war on crime helped restore the power of governors in chapter 2).

Johnson was keenly aware of all this when he signed the Safe Streets Act despite the various ways it had been written to attack his administration's other domestic initiatives. Having already withdrawn from seeking a second term, and deep into last-ditch efforts to negotiate a cease-fire in the Vietnam War, Johnson vacillated on whether or not to sign the bill, waiting until the last possible day before it would become law without his signature. He asked for the comments of each cabinet agency; none advised him to veto it.

Johnson's official statement on signing the bill provides ready evidence of his ambivalence. He described the law on balance as "more good than bad." He rejected the wiretapping and police interrogation portions of the law, and, following the advice of his liberal attorney general, Ramsey Clark, made clear those parts would not be federal policy for the remainder of his administration. He touted the enormous commitment of federal money to reforming local law enforcement, avoiding mention of the law's new block grant structure, although it represented the first major step away from the New Deal/Great Society–style legislation he had pushed through Congress earlier.

Crime victims themselves remain just beneath the surface of the 1968 Act, the subject intended by law rather than those directly targeted by it. No doubt, their direct presence might have generated more resistance from the still influential body of jurists, academics, and lawyers whose conception of modern criminal jurisprudence was inclined toward society rather than the victim as the main concern. Instead, the victim is represented indirectly in three related foci of the 1968 act: the streets, law enforcement, and the diminished role of judges.

Metaphors We Govern By

The idea of titling the administration's proposal the "Safe Streets Act" came from Housing and Urban Development Secretary Joseph Califano.[17] One of the administration's leading liberals, Califano wanted to emphasize that anticrime measures were not goods in themselves but ways to "restore public and private safety" (Dallek 1998, 407). In the name of the Act and the language of Johnson's signing statement, "streets" operates as a metonymy for American society generally, and especially the great cities. Following the lead of cognitive scientists like George Lakoff and Mark Johnson (1980), we can read his "streets" metaphor not simply as a reflection of an ideology or a set of beliefs, but as a strategic vision for retooling liberalism to govern the changing demographic and economic conditions of the great American cities on which Johnson's Democratic majority remained dependent.[18]

> I sign the bill because it responds to one of the most urgent problems in America today—the problem of fighting crime in the local neighborhood and on the city street. (Johnson 1968, 725)

Johnson defines crime as one of America's "most urgent problems," but his strategic message is embedded in the images that follow: "fighting crime," "local neighborhood," and "city street." The idea that the law is a way of "fighting" crime is an extension of the war-on-crime metaphor. "[T]he local neighborhood" and "the city street" point to subtly different terrains. Local neighborhoods, to be sure, contain city streets (and in many older cities, they are mostly streets), but the referents of "local" and "neighborhood" suggest something more culturally specific. By multiplying "local" against the semantically close "neighborhood," the Johnson statement invokes the intimacy of private homes and the immediate surrounding area, including a person's "block" and perhaps a neighborhood school or park.

The term "city," modifying streets in the next image, "city street," gives us one final clue. The "local neighborhood," while apparently a generic location in the spatial order set up by play of metaphor in Johnson's signing statement, has a defined spatial relationship, i.e., away from the "city" or at least the "inner city." The "local neighborhood" is in the suburbs, and in 1968, it included the traditionally prestigious outlying neighborhoods of the great cities and the tidy industrial neighborhoods where many working-class Americans were made property-owning members of the middle class by New Deal governance. While "local neighborhood" suggests the familiar and intimate, the emotionally private (even if technically public) streets just around the home, the residential, the local, and often the parochial, Johnson contrasts this with "city street" implying something far more specific than municipal roadways. These are downtown, public, business, and shopping streets. City streets are the places where any one can go, and they were, in the public imagination of 1968, becoming a place where anything violent and terrible can happen to anybody, even a president.

The menace of crime in the city streets was undermining the political coalition and methods of the New Deal at two of its most crucial sectors: the urban working and middle classes that had been made into a new kind of rights-based middle class by New Deal policies and postwar affluence; and the organized interests represented by those downtown streets, such as municipal unions, banks, insurance companies with large real estate holdings, large public institutions including museums and universities and the large corporations that sustain them, and, by 1968, the civil rights community as a representative of black America. Delivering more effective security to citizens as potential crime victims was imperative to prevent fear of crime from undermining both the new property and the social sector of capital.

Law Enforcement

The crime victim is perhaps most present in the 1968 Act as a substitute subject that is simultaneously a kind of representative victim itself and a form of security that government can provide victims. Just as "street" becomes metonymic for society, "police" becomes metonymic for the state as a whole. This is a metaphor that remains potent today, as presidents and candidates for high executive office seek to pose as often as possible with uniformed police. It is also a remarkable reversal in political currency. As late as the 1950s, sociologist William Westley, in his pioneering 1953 article on police violence, noted that one of the problems facing the police officer as a member of a service profession was that "he is regarded as corrupt and inefficient by, and meets with hostility of, the public" (Westley 1953, 35). Movies of the first half of the twentieth century almost uniformly portray police as corrupt and inept. It is the job of private investigators like Sam Spade (most memorably played by Humphrey Bogart in movies like *The Maltese Falcon*, 1941) to get the truth and the bad guys. Today, police are treated in both public discourse and popular culture in mostly heroic terms.[19] Movies sometimes portray corruption and failure, but those are treated as aberrational. It is left largely to minorities and some white liberals to have a deep suspicion of the police.

Johnson in 1968 could not presuppose that kind of consensus, but the law he was signing was in fact helping to call it into being. Throughout the text, Johnson uses law enforcement to mean at least the entire criminal justice process. In a complex movement, Johnson simultaneously offers law enforcement as an answer to the community beset by crime and fear of crime—stain and shadow—and as a special victim class of its own needing special federal attention. The end result is to mark both citizens fearful of crime and state and local law enforcement as requiring a privileged status as federal subjects.

Though later presidents would conflate themselves with local law enforcement—and Congress has followed suit by federalizing much local crime—Johnson saw the federal government largely as an agent for the improvement and reform of law enforcement. True to his New Deal heritage, Johnson emphasized the expert knowledge behind his program. The job of the executive was to bring together on a national level the kind of expertise that was unavailable at the local and state levels.

> My program was based on the most exhaustive study of crime
> ever undertaken in America—the work of the president's na-
> tional crime commission. That commission—composed of the
> Nation's leading criminologists, police chiefs, educators, and
> urban experts—spotlighted the weaknesses in our present sys-
> tem of law enforcement. (Johnson 1968)

In touting the part of the Safe Streets Act that he liked the most, the Great Society–like action grant program designed to motivate innovation and reform, Johnson promised to "strengthen the sinews of local law enforcement—from police to prisons to parole." Here the statement deploys one of the oldest of governmental metaphors, one so old that it is inscribed as a dictionary meaning of sinew. Literally, "sinew" is the term for tendon, the connective tissue that lies between bands of muscle and key bone structure. Metaphorically, sinew has long stood for the "source of strength, power, or vigor."[20]

The metaphor offers a subtle response to loud criticism from the right, that crime in the streets was a response to the liberal administration's failed policy of rewarding morally and socially bad behavior in the name of fighting poverty. By locating the problem of crime in the weakness of

state and local law enforcement, Johnson denied both that there is an essential weakness in American society and that the federal government is the source of it. He was saying that, on the contrary, the federal government alone can lead the kind of reconstruction of local power that will be necessary to make American streets safe in the last part of the twentieth century. The ambition is nothing less than reconstructing the power of law enforcement at a molecular level. The federal role would be to collect a national base of expertise through the new National Institute of Law Enforcement and Criminal Justice, later the National Institute of Justice, which the president referred to as "a modern research and development venture which will put science and the laboratory to work in the detection of criminals and the prevention of crime" (Johnson 1968, 726). Federal money would flow to pay off college loans and attract a new college-educated workforce into law enforcement, and open up new training and salary enhancements. In short, the war on crime for Johnson looked a lot like a war on poverty with police in the role of community development agencies.

Law enforcement agencies also emerge as a subject in the Safe Streets Act, perhaps even more strongly than victims. The largest portion of the federal revenues directed to the states under the Act was intended to directly benefit law enforcement agencies. The goal in the original Johnson administration proposal was aimed at "reforming" local law enforcement (taking the status quo as in bad need of modernization), but the tone of the 1968 law and its implementation instead created a federal income stream for the benefit of and under the authority of existing law enforcement agencies and their leadership. Research also prioritized policing. Police emerged in the law not simply as a tool to repress crime, but as a prime example of the victims of crime, injured both by criminals and by the lax handling of criminals by courts and corrections. The most controversial parts of the Safe Streets Act—the evidentiary rules regarding confessions and the authorization for electronic surveillance—were directed to both enhancing the police as a crime control agency and redressing the injuries presumably caused by "liberal" judges who were lax in enforcing the law.

One of the most consequential features of the Safe Streets Act, revealed in Johnson's statement is the intertwining of police and citizens as victims. Police are believed to be the party that can most effectively prevent victimization: "But at a time when crime is on the tip of every American's tongue, we must remember that our protection rests essentially with local and State police officers" (Johnson 1968, 727). At the same time, law enforcement would become the privileged subject of governance itself, parallel to the citizen in the local community in relation to the nation and its executive.

In the concluding paragraph of the statement, President Johnson brings the whole constellation into view: the war on crime, its territorialization into streets, and the centrality of law enforcement. He does this in a paragraph that addresses itself to other governing officials.

> Today, I ask every Governor, every mayor, and every county and
> city commissioner and councilman to examine the adequacy
> of their state and local law enforcement systems and to move
> promptly to support the policemen, the law enforcement officers,
> and the men who wage the war on crime day after day in all the
> streets and roads and alleys in America. (Johnson 1968, 728)

The Safe Streets Act is a call to reform governance, "state and local law enforcement systems," a mandate from the federal government to state and local leaders. The war on crime is situated between parallel structures of repeated invocations of law enforcement and streets. First comes the human element of law enforcement, "policemen," "law enforcement officers," "men who wage the war on crime day after day." Second comes the naming of "America" through its "streets and roads and alleys."

In retrospect, the Safe Streets Act was the signal event marking the end of the Great Society era and of the liberal pro–Civil Rights dominance of federal policy.[21] It would rapidly produce its own theorists, political scientists Richard Scammon and Ben J. Wattenberg, who published *The Real Majority* in 1969, only a year after the Act and the Republican takeover of the White House. The book used crime as the central example of how the Democratic Party was in real danger of losing its two-generation-old majority status by ignoring a profound shift of its traditional supporters on a host of "social" issues, including the race problem, abortion, family values, and so on. Democrats, in their view, had to move fast to stop talking about the root causes of crime, and instead support tougher law enforcement measures to repress existing criminals, even if that trampled on civil rights concerns.

With remarkable speed, Democrats in Congress followed suit. Although Richard Nixon introduced numerous crime proposals during his first year in office, he had no control over the legislative agenda because Democrats held large majorities in both houses of Congress and had no intentions of allowing Nixon to brand the crime issue as his own. As the 1970 election approached, however, the Democrats rapidly took up and enacted with little debate virtually everything on the administration's list, including "no-knock entry" and "preventive detention" proposals for the District of Columbia, measures that would have been considered far too extreme for the Safe Streets Act. On the campaign trail, liberal Democrats sought to explicitly define their moral commitment to rejecting crime. Edward Kennedy, running for reelection in 1970, told an audience at Boston University:

> Those who seek change by the threat of use of force must be identified and isolated and subjected to the sanctions of the criminal law. They are the hijackers of the university . . . and like hijackers, they must be deterred and repudiated. . . . Any person who lends them aid and comfort, any person who grants them sympathy and support, must share the burden of guilt. (Herbers 1970)

History would show that this rapid turn would not restore liberals to their influence. Some would argue that they never moved far or fast enough to the Right. Once the game of who could be tougher came to dominate, there was little chance of outrunning the issue because each election cycle brought a new crime bill with a new array of opportunities to test one's commitment to punishment.

The primary political legacy of the Safe Streets Act is to have shaped, in defining ways, the logic of representation that exists today across the political spectrum, at both the federal and state levels. Simply put, to be for the people, legislators must be for victims and law enforcement, and thus they must never be for (or capable of being portrayed as being for) criminals or prisoners as individuals or as a class. To do so is damning in two distinct ways. First, it portrays a disqualifying personal softness or tolerance toward crime. Second, it means siding against victims and law enforcement in a zero-sum game in which any gain for prisoners or criminals is experienced as a loss for law enforcement and victims.[22]

Although the Safe Streets Act did little directly to increase criminal penalties or expand the prison system, the representational system it modeled has led to both. Any vote to expand punishment is defined as a vote for law enforcement and victims that has become the paradigmatic act of lawmaking in our time, akin to dispensing federal lands in new size bits with new conditions in another time. Likewise, representatives seeking to recognize constituents have developed considerable creativity in using the penal code as a source of social capital. They have, for example, sought to accumulate such capital with a measure that would lengthen a sentence for killing a person over 65. In another act, the same ambition has taken the form of enacting a hate-crime bill that targets people who would attack others because of their sexual orientation. Crime legislation has been open into a broad grammar for recognizing and rewarding.

Fear This: Crime Legislation and Its Public

Congress may have taken the lead in placing crime legislation at the heart of the governance process in enacting the 1968 crime act and frequent measures since, but state legislatures have followed suit, and many of them have gone further in making crime legislation the paradigmatic form of legislation. Though Congress is burdened by an ongoing process of demand for lawmaking growing out of its own earlier activism in many areas outside of crime, state legislatures have more leeway to devote their time to the subjects they want. Criminal law has always formed a much larger share of state governance than federal governance. Even so, legislatures have devoted an increasing share of their time since the 1970s to enacting laws creating new criminal offenses, increasing the punishment of existing ones, and producing innumerable procedural laws designed to promote the other processes.

These laws reflect, in important respects, the twin principles underlying the federal crime legislation model: (1) the system is the problem; (2) the victim is the key. Nothing has moved legislatures more than the idea that public safety has been sacrificed to the convenience or indifference of the judiciary and the correctional bureaucracy. Since the 1970s, a steady flow of laws has attacked virtually every step of the criminal justice system for decisions perceived as favorable to criminals, ranging from bail law, to the insanity defense, to sentencing law, to corrections law. Discretion at any of these steps is viewed as something being used to favor criminals. Reform has taken the form of "zero-tolerance rules" that make favorable discretion impossible, transferring effective discretion to law enforcement and prosecutors to decide when to invoke the decision-making process. For the most part, lawmaking has also spoken in the voice of punishment, both in the prison and in the application of the death penalty.

In the 1970s, many of the perceived problems of the system were blamed on discretion, then held by judges and parole authorities. A number of states abolished parole and introduced legislatively determined sentencing ranges that limited the discretion of judges. The federal system followed in 1987. Studies of the reformed systems have generally noted that discretion was shifted to prosecutors rather than being eliminated. This may mark a failure of legal reform but a success for the principle that law should reflect loyalty to the victim of crime. Police and prosecutors have been popularly perceived as those actors in the criminal justice system most aligned to the interests of victims (despite the fact that a great deal of scholarship documents how much the interests of victims diverge from those of police and prosecutors).

The Violent Crime Control and Law Enforcement Act of 1994

The image of safe streets never appears in the title of the 1994 Violent Crime Control and Law Enforcement Act. In an era in which the modal picture of a good family life is driving back to a gated community subdivision in a military-grade SUV, "safe streets" has a nostalgic ring to it, evocative but not fully relevant. In a deeper sense, there is no optimism in this law that crime can be eliminated. Instead it reflects what David Garland (2001a) has called the "culture of control," a presumption that management of crime risk must be built into the fabric of everyday life.

Like the 1968 law, the 1994 law was enacted by a Congress fully in the control of the Democratic Party, with a Democrat in the White House and in the face of a competitive election campaign. In 1968, that campaign culminated six months later with a Republican capture of the White House and clear signs of potential for Republicans in a Congress that remained solidly Democratic. The 1994 law was adopted with only days to spare before that year's congressional elections, which resulted in an historic shift in power in the House of Representatives—the first such major shift in four decades—and a swing in the Senate to the Republicans for the first time since 1986.

Indeed, the size and scope of the 1994 crime bill suggests how many governable interests have been recast as problems of crime and victimization. This behemoth of a law—many times bigger and more expensive than the Safe Streets Act—reflected the stunning variety of groups now seeking to be represented in crime legislation: women's groups, minority citizens living in urban poverty, the elderly, and law enforcement agencies. Size also reflects the fact that competition between the parties in Congress and many state legislatures has created a proliferation of different approaches to fighting crime and securing victims.

The law provides a window into the breadth of ideological variation possible within the crime legislation model. In 1994, the administration of tough-on-crime Democrat Bill Clinton and his congressional allies like Charles Schumer of New York pushed primarily the theme of community policing and, secondarily, in an appeal to their liberal wing, the idea of crime prevention in the form of programs for at-risk youth and their communities, exemplified by the jazzy title of one funded program that received media attention, "midnight basketball." The Republicans were primarily pushing mandatory incarceration for violent crime. The death penalty, once a dividing line, became a consensus issue in 1994, with most of the liberal Democrats supporting an expansion from a narrow federal death penalty concerned with hijacking and drug kingpins to a whole host of crimes and special victims.

The very intensity of this blizzard of information gives rise to all kinds of new subjects and objects of governance. The federal war on drugs since the 1970s has produced a huge knowledge enterprise about drugs that has changed the way we know crime. In 1968, the idea of drugs as the driving force of crime was a purely speculative argument. In 1988, when the war on drugs reached national crisis proportions, government-collected data presented a measurable picture of the drug involvement of the criminal population.[23]

The Violent Crime Control Act might be seen as inaugurating the era when crime information in a broad sense becomes so dense that it becomes possible to present other interests and concerns in this medium. With crime the most visible and measurable phenomenon around, it becomes possible to legislate on ever more detailed aspects of it, even in the absence of a convincing strategy of control. For example, Section 210402 of the act requires the Department of Justice to produce an annual report to Congress. In filling this mandate, the Justice Department has in fact instituted a new series of public surveys regarding contact with the police that produced a pretest cycle in 1996 and a full national survey in 1999. The data from the survey provide the first national data on police-citizen contacts and collect information on citizen views of the police contact as well as the race and gender of both police and citizen. For an even longer time, the department has conducted surveys of police officers, and these surveys provide a picture of policing in America independent of that presented by police agencies themselves.

Observers such as Feeley and Sarat (1980, 41) were struck by the sense that for all its talk of planning and innovation, the Safe Streets Act provided little content for changing strategies or practice. The Violent Crime Control Act of 1994, in contrast, bristles with branded approaches such as "cops on the beat," prevention programs for "at-risk youth," and "truth in sentencing." The 1968 structure envisioned research shaping practice through the planning and grant-seeking procedures grafted onto state government. In fact, many of the approaches promoted in the 1994 act owe their origins to innovative programs started with federal funding in one site and publicized to others. Many of these programs have been developed through the federal research process and are promoted through various publications of the Department of Justice. There is no claim to a silver bullet here, but rather a collection of partial strategies aimed at specific targets.

The 1968 act left states quite free to develop strategies so long as they were willing to engage with some version of a research and planning process. The 1994 act, in contrast, has a much more specific agenda. Though the 1968 act privileged experimentation over paying for fixed assets like buildings and long-term employees—and in fact was used to buy far more equipment than may have been originally intended—the 1994 act devotes substantial funds to paying for community service police officers, new prisons, and a variety of prevention programs. In a 2001 law reauthorizing portions of the Violence Against Women Act that was part of the 1994 law, Congress aimed to punish those states that declined to adopt such measures as "truth in sentencing," which is designed to lengthen the years in prison actually served by convicted criminals. The law established a cost-shifting scheme whereby a state obtaining a conviction for murder, rape, or a dangerous sexual offense against someone who had been previously convicted of one of these crimes in another state can seek compensation for the cost of incarcerating the criminal from the state that previously obtained a conviction if that state failed to adopt truth-in-sentencing laws or other measures assuring long prison terms for such offenders.[24]

Like its 1968 predecessor, the Violent Crime Control Act of 1994 is a system of revenue sharing with state and local government, but with a twist. The block grants structure for most of the money in the 1968 bill was considered a big step toward the New Federalism that candidate Nixon and other conservatives were calling for: let states develop their own strategies closer to the facts. The 1994 act is as imperially federal as any Great Society program, indeed more so. Money yes, but for community policing, federal style, and long prison sentences for violent felons with no individualizing parole release mechanisms.

The Evolution of the Victim

It took a while for the victim to emerge from the complex of legislation on crime that began in 1968. At first, the victim was primarily there in the motivation for the law rather than in its enactments. The liberal Democrats who anguished over a law laden with so many overtly reactionary elements recognized the force with which crime had risen to the top of the governable concerns of the public. The law itself aimed to fight crime by improving the capacity of law enforcement and the quality of corrections; there was little there to salve the wounds of victims or recognize them as having a special status. But the pathways of knowledge carved by the law did bring the victim into a new kind of relationship to Congress, one increasingly independent of public opinion. Indeed, careful analysis of public opinion data beginning in the 1960s shows tremendous variability in the salience of crime, even after 1968, and the degree of salience is closely tied to the efforts of politicians to mobilize public opinion (Beckett 1997).

What is most noteworthy about the construction of the victim in the 1994 act is the way that the victim category has grown and fragmented to address many of the fault lines of difference around which American social conflict is frequently found. This leads to complicated variations in the harshness of the law. Thus two years later when a harsh law on aliens cut back equitable remedies to deportation orders and required incarceration of those challenging a deportation order, exceptions for domestic violence victims were woven through the law. The claim was that without these exceptions, such victims, generally women, might not alert the police and thus endanger themselves and their children. The domestic violence victim subject had become real enough to Congress to create new rights for a population (aliens) otherwise being criminalized and punished. The 1994 law also instructed the Sentencing Commission to promulgate guidelines to assure that violent assaults on elderly victims receive enhanced punishment to reflect the vulnerability of the victim and the degree of harm actually suffered.

The 1994 law sought to expand the role of the victim as a "voice" within the legal process. The 1994 law specifically speaks of the "victim's right of allocution in sentencing." The 1994 act amends the Federal Rules of Criminal Procedure to allow victims to speak at federal hearings on sentences. The act also includes a sense of the Senate vote that states should adopt the same right of allocution, one "equivalent to the opportunity accorded to the offender to address the sentencing court or parole board."[25]

These laws are also important for the real impetus they provide for more people to partake of the powerful public confirmation that awaits their taking up and affirming the identity as crime victim. These mechanisms are state-sponsored ways to reproduce a certain kind of victim voice that has been promoted by the victim's rights movement, one of extremity, anger, and vengeance. This has important representational consequences within the larger logic of the victim as idealized political subject. To the extent that activist victims define the victim subject position more generally, lawmaking will systematically favor vengeance and ritualized rage over crime prevention and fear reduction. Little wonder that prisons rather than policing have been the primary beneficiaries of the public investment side of governing through crime (Stuntz 2005).

Conclusion: Who Are We Now?

It is a mistake to assume that a political society as diverse and complex as the United States falls into line behind monolithic views of the governable interests of the people. There has almost always been public conflict about the basic terms on which needs and risks should be assessed. Moments of legislative innovation create pathways of knowledge and power that exert enduring influence in the habituated practices of government agencies, including their funding streams, knowledge-gathering patterns, and regulatory activity. Some live with us in such diminished capacity that we acknowledge them as a kind of public myth. The "yeoman" farmer is one such subject. Nobody thinks the needs of such farmers define the dominant needs of the political community, but the enormous sentiment that continues to surround that figure keeps it a potent, if minor, icon in lawmaking.[26]

Increasingly, few think that the fate of the nation hinges on the wellbeing of industrial workers, a position that seemed plausible as recently as the 1980s. It is true that public opinion often targets the economy or even job security as primary concerns—indeed, recently it has once again moved ahead of crime, as it often has in the years since 1968 (Beckett 1997). This helps explain why strong public concern for certain policy objectives does not result in lawmaking. It may be that a whole host of concerns about the economy and even job security weigh on large portions of American voters who would like to see government address issues like health care, pension security, and job creation, but whatever those concerns are, the industrial worker as a model has not effectively organized those concerns into a coherent narrative, has not linked them to effective channels of political organization, and has not produced major new legislation in decades.[27]

The freed slave and the consumer have a somewhat different fate today. Although those actually freed from slavery (and, for that matter, their grandchildren) have passed on, the model of subjects collectively wounded by the effects of racism and other forms of state sponsored discrimination remains a potent lens for viewing the governable interests of the people. Recent history is replete with witness to the fecundity of this model for producing effective narratives, organizations, and laws on behalf of women, Latinos, Asians, as well as religious and sexual minorities. Though what we might call the "civil rights subject" has been the target of some political counterattack, it can in no way be dismissed in the way the industrial worker as subject has been by its political opponents. Rather, the battle here has been for opponents of the traditional objectives of civil rights movements to claim their language and precedents for themselves (e.g., the anti–affirmative action movement that constantly invokes the value of equality).

Yet even the relatively robust civil rights subject is most successfully reproduced in legislation today when it coalesces with the crime victim subject. There is irony here. The crime victim as subject of national protection was once framed by the civil rights subject. Jim Crow segregation came to be seen as a kind of crime against African Americans by the 1960s, a resemblance deepened by acts of overt criminal violence against civil rights workers of both races. The appeal to northern opinion makers was even more compelling in the mirror of the Nazi Holocaust and its victims. The Nazis were unquestionably criminals, and their victims, especially the "survivors" as they came to be called in the 1960s, were admired as well as pitied subjects as witnesses to a kind of redemptive sacrifice or "holocaust."

Feminists made the link between crime victims and the civil rights subject even stronger when they presented the raped woman as the idealized political subject of second-wave feminism (Gruber 2006). Rape victims were betrayed by a criminal justice system that overidentified with the criminals and subjected the victim to her own trial by ordeal in the form of an intrusive and judgmental inquiry into her sexual history. Victims of domestic battery were a closely related subject, abandoned by the police and the courts to rule by violence of their husbands and boyfriends.

Both the black victims of racist violence and female victims of rape and assault tied the personal witness of crime victims to the historical and sociological narrative of racial and gender domination. The fact that criminal behavior in the form of lynchings, rapes, and beatings (the latter two primarily of women by husbands and other male intimates) largely went unsanctioned constituted searing proof of the extreme asymmetries of race and gender relations, forms of violence that belied the claims of a moral foundation to existing hierarchies.

In the 1980s, the crime victim emerged from the shadows of the civil rights subject as its own idealized political subject. In a kind of "everyman" extension, the claims of crime victims adopted the complicity critique that civil rights and feminist activists had articulated concerning the involvement of the state in criminal violence. It was the failure of the liberal state in the form of the adversary process, bail, and parole that allowed people known (or believed) by the police to be criminals to leave prison early (or evade it altogether) and engage in further criminal assaults against property and person. In the crime victim story, however, the state's complicity with criminality is no longer proof of social domination, but rather of its own perfidy. Crime as a critique of big government is about big government itself, emblematic only of its elitism, poor morals, and perhaps corruption.

Once separated from the civil rights subject, the crime victim subject is easily linked to another key center of political mobilization (especially for Republicans): the taxpayer, victimized by government, threatened with the loss of wealth and even the ability to own a home by an avaricious political establishment.[28] The successful Republican rhetoric on taxes in the 1970s and 1980s linked this to the high costs of welfare for poor, minority, urban residents—the same communities blamed for crime. As a result much legislation produced by the federal and state governments over the last two decades appears to have followed the implicit rule that lawmakers should never appear to be adverse to the interests of a political subject that is both taxpayer and (potential) crime victim.

Political scientists have noted that government programs not only serve citizen interests, they help constitute them (Pierson 1993). The New Deal represented not only a coalition of farmers, industrial workers, descendants of slaves, and consumers, the citizen of mass society, and especially the industrial worker, but it created a great wave of law making that called more people than ever before to these identities and the associated opportunities. Crime legislation since the 1960s represents as big an innovation in lawmaking as any since the New Deal. Today it is in the experience of victimization, and, much more commonly, the imagined possibility of victimization, that the political community and its governable interests are being redefined. It is the outlines of this victim subject, projected by advocacy groups, the media, and ultimately in the language of law itself, which is arguably the most important effect of crime laws: namely, how they succeed. Indeed, to the extent that earlier ideals seek to recuperate their political currency, it is through a narrative re-presentation of themselves in crime victim mode. Thus in an era in which civil rights is little attended to by Congress, hate crimes have emerged as the dominant focus for those lobbyists and legislators loyal to that cause (Jenness and Broad, 1997; Jacobs and Potter 1998). At a time when regulation of consumer industries is increasingly voluntary, laws creating new kinds of safety crimes (e.g., driving while speaking on a hand-held cellular phone) are growing.

For more than three decades, the making of crime laws has offered itself rather explicitly as the most important subject for expressing the common interest of the American people. We are crime victims. We are the loved ones of crime victims. Above all, we are those who live in fear that we or those we care for will be victimized by crime. Although few of us

recognize this as a primary identity, our social practices and the way our lawmakers make laws for us testify to that. By writing laws that implicitly and increasingly explicitly say that we are victims and potential victims, lawmakers have defined the crime victim as an idealized political subject, the model subject, whose circumstances and experiences have come to stand for the general good.

The Jurisprudence of Crime and the
Decline of Judicial Governance

The great political theorists of the first half of the twentieth century argued about whether legislative or executive power could best express
the will of democratic mass publics (Schmitt 1996). Those of the last part
of the century could not help but see courts, and the judicial actors within
them, as a serious competitor for dominance—at least in the style of mass
democracy for which the United States became the distinctive global model
(Ely 1980; Habermas 1996).

The American judge, a transplant from English common law, had *Are judge*
always been something of a hybrid, combining the freedom to decide associated with the executive in modern states and the legitimacy of deliberation and expertise associated with the modern parliamentary government
(Schmitt 1923/1996, Wilson 1900/2002), along with its own distinctive
professional expertise and neutrality. In the twentieth century, this active
and robust institution became even more important. American courts
had long involved themselves in the governance of society at the micro
level of interpersonal relations. Progressive reforms, such as juvenile court
and probation, expanded traditional judicial powers over individuals and *self-confi-*
interpersonal relations (Willrich 2003). The formation of professional- *dence of*
ized corporate and public interest lawyers also stimulated the intellectual *courts*
production and self-confidence of courts (Epp 1998).

This growing potential of courts in the early twentieth century was reflected in different popular faces of American courts in this period. At the
beginning of the century, the idea of courts producing a distinctively modern form of governance appropriate to the ills of industrialized societies
found its most charismatic and expansive vision in the figure of the juvenile

111

court judge, a local figure working among the cities' poor and immigrant classes who had nearly dictatorial power over adolescents and their families and discretion to pursue the public interest in the child's being saved from a life of crime.

A more critical view of courts as policy makers played out in the federal courts, fanned by the conflict between Progressive regulations at the state and later federal levels and the very conservative justices who dominated the federal courts and the Supreme Court until the mid-1930s. This is reflected in the title of Louis Boudin's 1932 critique, *Government by Judiciary*, which anticipated the New Deal's court battles and the framing of the judiciary as reactionary that would follow from it. After World War II, these two images would merge, with the federal courts taking up the mantle of Progressive reform in such fields as voting rights, school desegregation, and the confinement of the mentally ill. It would be left to right-wing activists to attack "government by judiciary" (Berger 1969; Neely 1981).

Since the 1980s, however, the idea of courts as appropriate movers of social policy has been in decline. The federal courts have reduced their intervention into public institutions and embraced a very different model of authority, one based on adherence to popular sentiment and deference to private ordering. Juvenile courts have found themselves under attack as too weak a deterrent against violent youth crime, and have been stripped of much of their control over minors accused of serious crimes. Changes in the sentencing of adults convicted of crime in the federal courts and many state courts have also seen a decline in the authority of judges.

There are too many levels and types of courts in America to allow us to assume that courts as such are rising or falling. This chapter argues that American courts have been hobbled by the unique challenges posed by the framing of street crime as a fundamental political problem to be solved by government, including courts, and the resulting "war on crime" from the 1960s through the end of the twentieth century. The war on crime, and changing mentalities and logics of government it has encouraged, has been harder on judges, including those of rightist political or legal persuasion, then on any other category of governmental actors. It is not their neutrality and judgment that have come to be mistrusted, but neutrality and judgment themselves. The very virtues that made courts an attractive solution to many twentieth-century governance problems—their relative autonomy from normal political and market pressures; the roles of argumentation, deliberation, and interpretation in shaping judicial decisions; and the ability to consider different voices and many kinds of information—have come to be seen as flaws that bespeak a lack of alignment between judicial judgment and the common good. These same decisions now seem to be precisely the kind that judges cannot be trusted to make.

The resulting jurisprudence is neither liberal nor conservative, but increasingly convoluted, result-oriented, and defensive. This is manifest in the way American courts have come to respond to issues of criminal justice, including punishment, capital punishment, and juvenile justice. Courts from the mid-1970s on have turned out a broad body of law favoring the government's power to punish (Bilionis 2005). Much of this work has been accomplished through valorization of police, victims, and prosecutors.

The way courts dealt with the crime problem has also influenced their performance in legal fields as diverse as employment discrimination and the interpretation of insurance contracts. What might be called a "jurisprudence of crime" has emerged that operates to limit judicial interventions. This jurisprudence is reflected across different doctrinal fields in defensive moves aiming to protect courts from the kind of exposure they felt when crime emerged as a defining problem after the 1960s. The central lesson of this crime jurisprudence for contemporary judges is to protect those who fear crime to the maximum extent possible by deferring to more politically accountable branches, and setting firm if arbitrary limits on the ability of courts to engage in institutional reform remedies.

Judges in the "War on Crime"

Having exemplified the most optimistic hopes of twentieth-century modernism in government, by the last years of the century judges found themselves regularly portrayed by members of the executive and legislative branches as betrayers of the common good. Judicial "policy making" in police procedures, school and housing desegregation, reform of mental hospitals, and so on came to be widely criticized even, in some cases, by those who remain sympathetic to the substantive goals. This view of judges as dangerous power holders, prone to acting against the interest of ordinary citizens, is nowhere more rooted than in the public's perception of the judicial role in crime and criminal justice. Since the 1960s, and with remarkably little change over the next forty years, judges have been widely blamed by politicians for being "soft on crime." Public opinion surveys of Americans from the 1970s through the 1990s showed that this charge was believed to be true, although it was often deeply misleading because many states in that period placed basic control over prison sentences in the hands of administrative parole boards and, more recently, prosecutors.

The war on crime as it emerged from the late 1960s on brought critical scrutiny to bear on courts in all kinds of ways. Here we will focus on three episodes that exemplify the larger problem of courts in the war on crime: the criminal procedure decisions of the Warren Court, which placed a variety of new requirements on police regarding arrests, interrogations, and searches; the Supreme Court's near-abolition of the death penalty in *Furman v. Georgia* (1972), followed by its acceptance of a new generation of reenergized death penalties; and the role of judges in criminal sentencing.

The Warren Court and the War on Crime

The criminal procedure revolution was part of the Warren Court's overriding concern for the the Fourteenth Amendment's promise of equal protection of the law, which had also led to major precedents in school desegregation and free expression. It was not intended to respond to a rising tide of violent crimes that was not visible when the Court decided *Mapp v. Ohio* (1961). *Mapp* required courts to exclude evidence gathered in violation of search-and-seizure rights of suspects, while *Gideon v. Wainright* (1963) required states to provide counsel for indigent felony defendants. Later, when the headlines made the seriousness of violent crime trends and political alarm about them undeniable, the Warren Court clearly recognized and sought to address this concern in cases very helpful to law enforcement, such as *Terry v. Ohio* (1968, 30), which allowed police to "stop and frisk" suspects without a warrant or probable cause of crime if they were "reasonably suspicious."

In 1968, when fear of crime became a highly visible issue in the national political arena, the "due process" revolution carried out by the Warren Court was one of the central targets of political criticism.[1] Richard Nixon, who won that year's presidential election, openly accused the Court of ignoring the safety of law-abiding citizens. The rapid rise of violent crime during the mid- to late 1960s, and the parallel rise in media attention to crime, lent credence to the claim that such decisions, by making it harder to arrest and convict criminal suspects, undermined deterrence. The general effects of this revolution on law enforcement and the criminal process have been much debated but need not concern us here. The effect we care about is the way these decisions, and political criticism of them, helped frame the debate about how courts govern.

The empirical case that these decisions significantly undermined crime control and thus fed the crime wave is not particularly strong. At the same time, it is likely that the attention these decisions focused on the judicial role in governing law enforcement, at a time of rising public alarm about violent crime, helped to turn a crime wave into an axis for critical scrutiny of government. Seen retrospectively through the war on crime, these decisions would have a lasting effect on the stance of the courts toward crime and other social issues. First, cases created a repetitive competition in which police and criminal suspects were locked in a zero-sum game over whose rights would receive greater protection. As the war on crime raised the salience of the crime victim as citizen, it became clear whose interests were the proxy for the rights and liberties of the ordinary citizen—and it was not those of criminal suspects. In a disturbing way, the cases, which rarely mentioned race explicitly, may have suggested a parallel zero-sum game between white and minority citizens—notwithstanding the fact that on average blacks and other minorities had far more actual exposure to crime victimization than whites.

Second, the criminal procedure cases also established that judicial intervention was inevitably a trade-off with crime control effectiveness, a framework captured by Herbert Packer's (1968) famous reading of these decisions as a battle between due process and crime control perspectives. This framework suggested that court-enforced rights inevitably produced more victims; the only question was how many. This effect was quickly and effectively linked to the higher violent crime levels of the late 1960s and 1970s by critics of the Court. Thus, although these decisions might have been seen as helping modernize American criminal justice in time for its great expansion—placing courts along with the executive and legislative branches as organs of the war on crime—the criminal procedure revolution marked the court as a deviant actor in need of restraint by the other branches.

Third, the controversy about the criminal procedure cases would allow a series of arguments made against court interventions in other fields—e.g., the defense of state institutions of racial segregation—to be recast in terms of the threat of violent crime to ordinary citizens (Beckett 1997). Although delegitimated by the association with segregation, these arguments against federal judicial intervention in state institutions, and against judicial intervention more generally, would survive to expand again during the conservative ascendancy of the 1980s.

All three of these patterns would emerge in even starker outline after Chief Justice Earl Warren resigned in 1969, to be replaced by the far more conservative Warren Burger (and subsequently the even more conservative William Rehnquist). Although Warren Court decisions like *Mapp* and *Miranda* had been prominently criticized by conservative politicians— including those who appointed most of the justices between 1969 and 2000 (Richard Nixon, Ronald Reagan, and George H. W. Bush)—the more right-leaning Supreme Court refrained from overturning any major precedent. Instead, these leading precedents were defined down to a reaffirmation of core rights, while new questions about the seemingly peripheral application of those rights were, for the most part, resolved in favor of police and prosecutors (Bilionis 2005). This approach to criminal justice has had the paradoxical effect of removing much of the significance for the defense of constitutional rights, while leaving courts themselves frozen in a tableau of apparent antagonism toward police, prosecutors, and ordinary people perceived as potential crime victims.

The result is that while courts have retreated from any serious effort to reform law enforcement practices through the application of exclusionary rules, they appear responsible for what are perceived as continuing crime problems. Lacking the ability to openly signal their favoritism toward potential victims (although judicial elections have strained even the limits of decorum on that), courts appear unreliable. In the meantime, law enforcement benefits doubly. Police enjoy a presumption of being under strong legal restraint; this has helped increase their legitimacy. At the same time, courts take the blame for failures to prevent and punish crime.

Backlash: The Supreme Court and the Resurrection of the Death Penalty

Three years after Chief Justice Warren resigned, and over the dissents of the more right-wing justices appointed under Richard Nixon, the Court struck down all the capital sentencing procedures at use in every death penalty jurisdiction in *Furman v. Georgia* (1972). This nullified the death sentences of hundreds of prisoners on death rows around the country temporarily leaving the United States a "death penalty" abolitionist country. Though no opinion garnered a majority of justices, it seemed possible the decision was the first of several steps that would lead to the complete abolition of the death penalty in the United States (Banner 2002).

Instead, the opposite happened. The response to *Furman* was fast and furious. Five state legislatures announced their intention to draft new statutes the day after the opinion was published. In November 1972, California voters, responding to a ban on executions passed by that state's supreme court a few months before *Furman*, approved by a ratio of 2 to 1 an amendment to the state constitution restoring the death penalty. Historian Stuart Banner notes:

> If *Furman* did not influence the *direction* of change, it almost certainly influenced the *speed* of change. *Furman* suddenly made capital punishment a more salient issue than it had been in decades, perhaps ever. People who previously had little occasion to think about the death penalty now saw it on the front page of the newspaper. *Furman*, like other landmark cases, had the effect of calling its opponents to action. (2002, 268–69)

The opinions finding the death penalty unconstitutional helped frame the death penalty issue in ways that ultimately played into this backlash (Gottschalk 2006). Unable to rely on the language or original intent of the Constitution, some in the majority relied on a notion of evolving standards of decency to support their argument that capital punishment had become cruel and unusual in American society. Justice Brennan, for example, pointed to the declining number of death sentences handed down in the 1960s as indicative that Americans had rejected the death penalty as too severe for even the categories of violent crime it had been narrowed to in the twentieth century. Justice Marshall famously predicted that if the public "were fully informed as to the purposes of the penalty and its liabilities, [it] would find the penalty shocking, unjust, and unacceptable" (*Furman*, 361). Although these arguments built on earlier precedent, they made public opinion itself a central part of the debate about capital punishment and the state's power to punish more generally (Gottschalk 2006). In the center, opinions by Justices White and Stewart emphasized the apparent arbitrariness of the distribution of death sentences, a stance that shifted the question from the death penalty as a punishment to the capital sentencing system as a process.

The populist focus on victims and public opinion was even more prominent in the dissenting opinions. Justice Blackmun, although expressing personal opposition to the death penalty, noted ominously that the majority position might create a populist backlash because of their apparent empathy with the victims of capital punishment rather than the victims of capital crimes.

> It is not without interest, also, to note that, although the several concurring opinions acknowledge the heinous and atrocious character of the offenses committed by the petitioners, none of these opinions makes reference to the misery the petitioners' crimes occasioned to the victims, to the families of the victims, and to the communities where the offenses took place. The arguments for the respective petitioners, particularly the oral arguments, were similarly and curiously devoid of reference to the victims. There is risk, of course, in a comment such as this, for it opens one to the charge of emphasizing the retributive. . . . Nevertheless, these cases are here because offenses to innocent victims were perpetrated. This fact, and the terror that occasioned it, and the fear that stalks the streets of many of our cities today perhaps deserve not to be entirely overlooked. Let us hope that, with the Court's decision, the terror imposed will be forgotten by those upon whom it was visited, and that our society will reap the hoped for benefits of magnanimity.[2]

Justice Lewis Powell, a Virginian who made no comment on his personal beliefs but probably supported the death penalty at this point, interjected a similar note, pointedly calling into question the assumptions about public repugnance against the death penalty and highlighting the role that murder and violent crime were playing in mobilizing the public.

> If, as petitioners urge, we are to engage in speculation, it is not at all certain that the public would experience deeply felt revulsion if the States were to execute as many sentenced capital offenders this year as they executed in the mid-1930s. It seems more likely that public reaction, rather than being characterized by undifferentiated rejection, would depend upon the facts and circumstances surrounding each particular case. Members of this Court know, from petitions and appeals that come before us regularly,

that brutish and revolting murders continue to occur with disquieting frequency. Indeed, murders are so commonplace in our society that only the most sensational receive significant and sustained publicity. It could hardly be suggested that in any of these highly publicized murder cases—the several senseless assassinations or the too numerous shocking multiple murders that have stained this country's recent history—the public has exhibited any signs of "revulsion" at the thought of executing the convicted murderers. The public outcry, as we all know, has been quite to the contrary. Furthermore there is little reason to suspect that the public's reaction would differ significantly in response to other less publicized murders.[3]

These dissenting comments, although technically irrelevant to the grounds of their dissents, reflected a very different idea about the role of government that was coming into focus in relation to violent crime and capital punishment. First and foremost is the prominence given to the victims of violence and the truth they proclaim about their losses, feelings, and fears.

Modern penology, with its emphasis on deterrence, incapacitation, and rehabilitation, had little to say about the victim (Garland 2001a). As against a New Deal consensus shared by many of the justices themselves that punishment should serve the ends of social control, Blackmun and Powell emphasized the centrality of the victim, the importance of personal experiences of terror and pain, and popular satisfaction as independent and sufficient purposes for capital punishment. The death penalty, as it began to renew itself after *Furman,* was coming to represent a kind of populism in governance, that is, a willingness to define key aspects of law to accommodate popular feelings and fears, with implications far beyond criminal justice, and for the role of courts themselves. Neither Blackmun nor Powell precisely embraced this vision[4] (that would await Justice Scalia a decade later), but in their warnings about the danger of mobilizing public retributive rage, they suggested a jurisprudence of avoidance that has come to pass.

When the new death penalty statutes drafted in the months after *Furman* reached the Supreme Court in 1976, they found a Court seemingly anxious to retreat from its earlier intervention, something very much like the "switch in time" that came about in 1937.[5] Justices Stewart and White, joined by a fourth Republican appointee, John Paul Stevens, found that the new statutes addressed the concerns about arbitrariness and overly broad discretion raised by the Stewart and White concurrences to *Furman*.[6] Together with Chief Justice Burger, and Justices Rehnquist and Blackmun who had dissented in *Furman*, there was now a solid 6–3 majority in favor of allowing the states to reform their death penalty systems.

Moreover, the new death penalty would not be the sluggish institution that seemed to be slowly dying in the 1960s. The new statutes produced in response to *Furman* were put into use with an intensity unseen even during the 1930s (Banner 2002, 270). More important, the reaction to *Furman* soon made the death penalty an issue in virtually every American election, especially for executive offices.

For a period from the mid-1970s until the early 1980s, the Supreme Court signaled to both death row prisoners and the states the availability of the federal courts to "regulate, and even sometimes categorically prohibit, executions when constitutional values or norms were at stake." The death penalty would be permitted, but under a regime of federal judicial scrutiny similar to that applied to segregated public school systems and prison systems. But by taking this stand, the Court won no friends. Opponents of the death penalty, who still made up one quarter to one third of the public, considered the promise of *Furman* betrayed. Supporters of the death penalty, from two thirds to three quarters of the public, credited their politicians, not the Court, with its resumption. As detailed in chapter 2, politicians who led successful legislative or referendum fights to bring back the death penalty were often rewarded by being elected governor, while courts got little credit for upholding the new statutes. In contrast, the cost of the new system, its growing pattern of long delays between rounds of appeals that was beginning to take shape in the late 1970s, was tied to the courts and their review.

The relationship between courts and the death penalty was paradoxical. On the one hand, no other branch of government held as dramatic a role in deciding who would die and when. Because of the burgeoning number of capital cases by the early 1980s and the relative paucity of lawyers, judges in some states found themselves compelled to rule on petitions filed only hours prior to an execution (Banner 2002). Judges had the final say on whether an execution would go forward or not. But unlike all the other political actors involved in the death penalty process, judges were denied the opportunity to openly embrace the objectives of the community in punishment. Again and again, they were compelled to make dramatic last-minute decisions to halt executions, and to frustrate victims, based on inevitably summary legal analysis.[7]

Since the early 1980s, the Supreme Court has overtly signaled an end to any presumption created by *Furman* and *Gregg* that the Court intended to police the rationality of state normative choices over the death penalty, or even whether prosecutors and juries were adhering to those choices, effectively "deregulating death" (Weisberg 1983). In the 1987 case of *McCleskey v. Kemp*, the Court declined to place new burdens on the death penalty in the face of powerful statistical evidence that those who killed white victims were more likely to be sentenced to death, especially if the killers were African American. In the view of the Court, the historic choice of local prosecutors and juries was too integral to criminal justice to be set aside based on statistics. Only proof of discriminatory intent against a particular defendant would violate the constitutional guarantee of equal protection.

In the 1991 case of *Payne v. Tennessee*, the Court overruled a four-year-old precedent and upheld a death sentence in a case in which jurors had been allowed to hear a statement from the victim's surviving family members about their suffering. In his concurring opinion, Justice Scalia explicitly acknowledged the victims' rights movement and its influence on the Court.

Notwithstanding the Supreme Court's efforts since the early 1980s to back off from taking a close look at the operation of state death penalties, a formidable body of case law devoted to the remaining protections implied by *Gregg v. Georgia* (1976) has meant that the time gap between sentencing and execution can be years or decades. Some states have kept it to as little as five years, based on harsh state procedural rules and regional consensus among state and federal judges not to interfere much with the death penalty. In states with more generous procedural rules and/or more protective courts, executions can take as long as 20 years. This often arduous procedural path, attacked frequently by victim advocates and politicians, has itself become a major vector for criticism of courts, access-limiting legislation, and judicial decisions. On the federal level, the most striking of these is the 1994 law that reduced access to a successive claim to those prisoners who can show one of two things by clear and convincing evidence: either (1) that a new rule of constitutional law held by the Supreme Court to be retroactive applies to the case, or (2) that newly discovered evidence which could not have been discovered before constitutes clear and convincing reason for altering a legal judgment. The law deepened restrictions that the Supreme Court itself had placed on successive habeas petitions. Even the law's title emphasized Congress's mistrust of courts as protectors of public safety. Invoking the horrors of the terrorist attack on the federal building in Oklahoma City the year before, Congress titled the law the "Antiterrorism and Effective Death Penalty Act."[8] As a result, the development of a legally correct argument that could well persuade a court that a death penalty was inappropriate in a particular case will not be heard at all if it could have been raised by a better lawyer on the first petition.

Thus, although courts began the resumption of capital sentencing in the 1970s in a position of power over executions, as time went by, the forces in the states driving toward an overproduction of death penalties (Liebman 2000) were able to thrive in the climate of emergency, which the courts inevitably contributed to, and in which they were made to appear as a kind of criminal again and again frustrating the exercise of state justice.

The examples above are mainly of federal courts and especially the Supreme Court. The structural association created by the death penalty that places courts as obstacles to the safety of citizens and the recovery of victims has generated powerful political incentives in the states as well. California's Supreme Court was a national innovator, especially in areas of civil justice, from the 1950s through the 1980s. But its decisions in the area of the death penalty became a flash point of political criticism that ultimately led to popular backlash and an electoral realignment of the court. The cycle of abolition and restoration cemented the California court's reputation as being too concerned about murderers and indifferent to victims. In 1982, another state constitutional amendment passed by voter referendum limited the ability of California state courts to exclude evidence based on violations of the state, but not federal, constitution. Finally, after a bloc of liberal justices continued to vote to reverse many death sentences in the 1980s, a campaign was mobilized against Chief Justice Rose Bird and three of her colleagues, all of whom were removed from the bench. The resulting appointments produced a court that has been docile on criminal justice and pro-business on civil justice and environmental matters.

Florida provides a striking recent example where the death penalty has been at the center of a cycle of extraordinary lawmaking that emphasized the problem of representation and cast courts as enemies of the people. With its diverse population and highly competitive elections, Florida gives politicians few safe grounds to compete without the risk of alienating one voter group or another.[9] Fear of crime is one of the strongest consensus concerns in Florida, and unremitting toughness on crime, reflected in a strong commitment to the death penalty, has been the dominant strategy for politicians of both parties. These conditions lend themselves perfectly to the "overproduction of death" (Liebman 2000). This means that the governor and legislature have a compulsion to create new death penalty laws in order to sustain the legitimacy that has come from reclaiming the death penalty. This practice, whose features I examined above, expands the reach of the death penalty, even though the post-*Furman* system was supposed to narrow it. But at the constitutional level, new death penalty laws promote something even more distorting, an increasingly compulsive and fatal battle between the branches of government over loyalty to a public that is represented by victims of crime. At the operational level of police and prosecution, sustaining the legitimacy of the death penalty means strong incentives to push marginal cases into the competitive process of producing capital sentences, with the result of a high rate of judicial error. Five Florida counties rank among the top fifteen in the nation for seeking the death penalty and for the rate of error in capital cases (Gelman et al. 2004). This rate of systematic error suggests a judicial culture fundamentally shaped by the value of capital sentences to investigators and prosecutors building careers. Once committed to capital charges, both police and prosecutors have powerful incentives to rely on forms of evidence that are at high risk for contaminating the process with falsehood (e.g., the testimony of other prisoners claiming to have heard the defendant confess) and to seek advantages over the defense that can lead to technical reversals.

Ironically, the most immediate effect of attempts to sustain legitimacy of the death penalty at both the political and operational levels is the creation of numerous cases with so many questionable elements that their legal complexity ultimately leads to delayed executions. Constant changes introduced by the legislature and governor produce substantial delays while courts review new features of laws. Aggressive conduct by police and prosecutors leads to frequent reversals and subsequent retrials. Not surprisingly, in states such as Florida executions typically come a cruel twenty years or more after conviction.

One might assume that a delay in execution would undermine the authority of the state. Indeed, politicians in states such as Florida have made delayed executions a boogey man during elections since the 1980s. But while support for quicker executions is reliably good politics, it is not clear that political leaders pay any price for delay, at least as long as responsibility can be laid at the foot of courts and defense attorneys. It is this thinking that pervades the two successful ballot initiatives around the death penalty in a remarkable episode of antijudicial politics that would be noteworthy even if it had not formed part of the backdrop for the contested presidential election of 2000.

Twice in four years the Florida legislature, as permitted under the state's constitution, presented a constitutional amendment on the ballot for approval of the voters. The proposed amendment declared the death penalty to be a constitutional mode of punishment and amended the text of Article VII, changing the phrase "cruel or unusual" to "cruel and unusual" and explicitly requiring that the new phrase be interpreted consistently with the decisions of the U.S. Supreme Court.[10]

Placed before the voters in 1998 and in 2002, the amendment was approved by large majorities both times. During the intervening years the Florida Supreme Court decided *Armstrong v. Harris* (2000), invalidating the amendment adopted in 1998 on the grounds that the ballot language misrepresented the effect of the amendment to the voters.[11] The decision in *Armstrong* turned on a well-developed body of referendum law in Florida. Florida ballot initiatives must be limited to a "single issue" (although they may make numerous technical changes of law necessary to accomplish this issue resolution). They must also present the issue clearly before the voters. The latter is particularly tricky because the actual wording of the laws being enacted (or the amendments being enacted to existing statutory law) is not printed in the voter guide that comes with the ballot. Instead, the initiative author, in this case the Florida legislature, writes a statement limited to 73 words. The actual text being inserted into the constitution is not typically presented to the voters on the ballot.

In proposing an amendment to place the death penalty into the constitution and to hog tie the jurisprudence of the state supreme court, the legislature was laying down a dramatic challenge to the power of courts as a coequal branch of government framed in terms of loyalty to the death penalty and to the machinery of the death penalty itself. The Florida legislature not only claimed to be institutionally superior at representing the wishes of the people of Florida (something most lawyers would concede) but claimed, in effect, that the court could not be trusted to consider that representational superiority in reviewing death penalty cases. In holding that the legislature's 1998 death penalty amendment misled the voters, the Florida Supreme Court seemed to join the issue of institutional capacity and representation, but here to invert the legislature's equation and suggest that the death penalty is deforming the representational process.

Great battles between branches of government are not new, but few have been determined to a greater degree by conflicting ambition than the one over amendment 2. The controversy began when legislators became concerned that a number of death penalty cases were likely to place the constitutionality of the electric chair before the Florida Supreme Court. Concerned that the court was "soft" on the death penalty, the legislators decided to preempt the court by taking the issue over its heads to the voters as a constitutional amendment.

The *Armstrong* majority held that the ballot title and summary were defective in a number of ways. First, the summary made it seem as if the amendment was creating a right for Floridians when, in the view of the court, it was narrowing one. Citing crucial doctrinal language in earlier cases, Justice Shaw described this as "flying under false colors." The title and summary misstated the actual legal effect of the amendment—namely, to nullify the "Cruel or Unusual Punishment" clause.

Second, the text implied that the main purpose of the amendment was to "preserve the death penalty," but the ballot language dramatically misstated the effect of the amendment in two respects. It implied that the death penalty was in danger of being abolished if not "preserved," and that a yes vote was necessary to save it. While having nothing to do with preserving the death penalty, it would, in fact, alter the rights of Floridians with respect to all other possible penalties as well. This amounted to concealing intent from voters, and it robbed the authors (in this case the Florida legislature) of their claim to represent a majority of the voters in amending the constitution.

The dissenters angrily criticized the majority for placing themselves in the position of the voters (precisely what the legislature was trying to accomplish). This position was taken up and carried further by individual legislative leaders who discussed the need to dramatically alter the composition of the court either through adding new positions or creating a new "death court" to review capital punishment exclusively. Either solution would permit the incumbent governor (Jeb Bush) to appoint an effective majority on the death penalty. Thus in the aftermath of *Armstrong* and in the period leading up to the November 2000 presidential election controversy in Florida, the legislature and the state's supreme court had openly accused each other of engaging in a fundamental betrayal of the representational process over the subject of the death penalty.[12]

A year later, acting with an urgency and a sweep indicative of a compulsive motivation, the Florida legislature reintroduced precisely the same amendment. To remove *Armstrong v. Harris* problems, the statement prepared for the November 2002 ballot provided the entire text of the constitutional amendment, word for word. This required the legislature to exempt itself from strict rules that require citizen initiatives to be represented by brief summaries, which the legislature did with virtually no dissent.[13]

The 2002 initiative is also remarkable because of the disappearance of the issue that was the specific motivation for the 1998 version. The goal of preserving the electric chair was always a puzzling focus. Death penalty states like Texas and Virginia had decided long ago that lethal injection was easier to administer and less prone to legal challenges. For the most driven supporters of the death penalty in the Florida legislature, it seemed possible that the electric chair was attractive precisely because it was harder to administer. The pictures of Allen Davis's corpse still in the electric chair suggest that Florida's execution procedure was an ordeal for state employees charged with strapping a recalcitrant individual into what amounted to a kind of barbeque and then removing the "cooked" body.

While the Florida Supreme Court was considering the appeal in *Armstrong v. Harris*, it examined directly whether the Florida execution procedure violated the U.S. or Florida constitution (using the older, presumptively more protective language of "cruel or unusual") and in a split decision upheld the constitutionality of the chair. After this decision, which contradicted the very reasons for the amendment at issue in *Armstrong*, the Florida legislature, with the support of Governor Bush, preemptively adopted a new capital sentencing procedure with an option for lethal injection. The law was enacted over the objections of many die-hard supporters of electrocution because proponents feared that there was a very real chance that the U.S. Supreme Court would soon find electrocution unconstitutional. This gutted another reason for a constitutional amendment. To tie the Florida Supreme Court more tightly to the conservative majority on the U.S. Supreme Court, the Florida Supreme Court had preserved the electric chair while the majority on the U.S. Supreme Court seemed to some observers poised to strike it down (they have not thus far).

Thus the new constitutional amendment proposal placed before the voters in 2002 no longer had any instrumental goal other than to complete the process of demonizing the Florida Supreme Court as a clear and present danger to the death penalty. This might have made some sense in a state like California where a liberal supreme court majority during 1980 was willing to resist pressure to speed up executions and held a hostility toward the death penalty, and might have been tempted by a novel attack on the constitutionality of the death penalty (and where a voter initiative placed the death penalty in the constitution in 1978). Florida's Supreme Court, in contrast, had never shown any interest in systematically challenging the viability of the Florida death penalty. While some years in the 1990s saw a 50 percent or higher reversal rate in death cases before the Florida Supreme Court, most of these were traditional statutory and evidentiary issues that reflect more the sloppiness of prosecutors than an activist attack on the death penalty. The same reluctance to challenge the political branches on capital punishment was reflected in the Florida Supreme Court's decision upholding the electric chair.

The behavior of Florida's elected officials, especially the legislature, in this process of death penalty higher lawmaking reflects the grip that crime, raised to the capital dimension, has on modern government. Florida is a twenty-first-century state whose citizenry uses the constitutional amendment process to call for things such as bullet trains and smaller class sizes in public schools. In the meantime, the state and its major counties have suffered public scandals in their management of basic functions such as protecting dependent children, providing reliable election equipment and procedures, managing pension funds, and graduating minority high school seniors who fail the state's standardized tests. But in the midst of these crises the legislature and governor act in many respects in and through the death penalty.

Fear of Judging

As the war on crime began in the 1970s, judges came under attack as too prone to individualize justice to suit the particular circumstances of defendants in ways that limited punishment and diminished deterrence. In fact, the indeterminate sentences that were then in use in many states, and the federal system, gave broad authority to administrative bodies to set precise prison terms, although they often allowed judges wide latitude in deciding who got probation rather than prison.

The actual path of sentencing reform has been complex and often contradictory, but one of the clearest trends is the diminishing role of the judge. This has taken place primarily through two mechanisms at work in many states: mandatory minimum sentences and mandatory guidelines for calculating prison sentences.

The U.S. Sentencing Guidelines, adopted by Congress in 1987, are the best-known version of the mandatory guideline approach (Stith & Cabranes 1998).[14] Restructuring the federal criminal code had been a fixture on the crime agenda of administrations since, at least, the Roosevelt administration (Marion 1993, 45). In the 1980s, however, the mandate had changed from rationalizing the way federal crimes are defined and graded, i.e., ranked in terms of penal severity, to revising the way federal defendants are sentenced. Most of the complaints against the federal sentencing process of the time concerned the broad discretion held by federal judges over whether to send convicted criminals to prison and for how long. Critics charged that widely varying use of this discretion had been detrimental to both the fairness and effectiveness of the criminal sanction. When a coalition of liberal and conservative representatives in Congress came together to support the creation of the Sentencing Commission, reform was clearly directed to curb the power of judges and the role of case-by-case judgment itself.

Prior to adoption of the guidelines, federal judges could sentence convicted defendants to probation, or to prison terms within wide minimum and maximum sentences established when the crimes were committed. A federal parole authority could release prisoners prior to their maximum sentence, but not before the minimum sentence, which judges could set as high as they chose. Judges thus had real power over who went to prison and over the sentence's length. In making their sentencing decision, judges could draw on the help of probation officers trained in the style of social-work case analysis. Their reports would typically provide a detailed biography of the defendant that discussed family, school, work life, and criminal record.

The history of the adoption of the guidelines suggests a quite deliberate intent to reject judicial governance as such. The legislative record is loaded with discussion of the evils of arbitrariness and deep suspicion of federal judges as individuals. Thus, even though the Sentencing Commission was made part of the judicial branch by Congress, the number of sitting federal judges permitted on the original commission that drew up the guidelines was limited to two (Stith & Cabranes 1998, 44). The guidelines have altered the power of judges at both the systemwide and individual levels. On the system-wide level, judges have ceased to be a major determinant of federal prison sentences. On the individual case level, the guidelines have put the judge in a position, which many of them find personally humiliating, of having to hand out sentences shaped more by lawyers and probation officers than by the court. Probation officers were key figures under the old system as investigators who would provide the sentencing judge with a comprehensive social report on the criminal and the crime. Under the guidelines, they have become, in effect, agents of the Sentencing Commission, charged with making sure that the guidelines are accurately applied and aiding the judge with much of the complicated analysis required to calculate the appropriate sentencing range.

The role of the judge in the guidelines system is, by any definition, circumscribed. Probation has been taken off the table for most federal felonies and is limited to only those with no prior offenses. The length of a prison sentence is established in its basic parameters either by a complex and prescribed calculus of sentencing factors or by a crude mandatory minimum. Judges are permitted to then set a prison sentence within a range (limited to 25 percent) determined by a calculus of these factors. In some instances, if a judge decides that facts in the case are different from the ordinary run of cases on factors that the Sentencing Commission did not consider in establishing the guidelines, the judge may make a further upward or downward departure. S/he must explain the reasoning behind the adjustment, which is subject to appeal. Even though some recent cases have suggested that trial judges may have more leeway to grant such departures than was previously thought, departures remain limited to extraordinary facts, leaving the great majority of cases limited to the 25-percent range of discretion to express any individualized judgment regarding the facts.

Though the guidelines transfer much authority to the Sentencing Commission to shape the overall structure of sentences, Congress has retained and used the right to set mandatory minimum sentences that override the guidelines if the latter would recommend a more lenient sentence. Mandatory minimums, mostly in drug trafficking cases, have generated some of the most publicized criticisms of federal sentencing practice from judges.

Though creative federal judges can find ways to do individual justice in many criminal cases, the judge remains a figure of suspicion, a person with a propensity to violate public safety, little different in public confidence from the figure of the criminal before them. In both cases, the prosecution has gained power as the agency capable of holding both criminals and judges in check. In many states, existing laws give judges far more discretion to individualize sentences, discretion they sometimes use, but fierce political backlashes regarding crime and the fact that many judges are elected works as powerfully as mandatory guidelines might.[15] In California, for example, judges were initially thought to have little discretion over whether to impose the state's infamously harsh three-strikes law—but later were found to have discretion to withhold the effects of the law "in the interests of justice." However, research on judicial practice and examination of the numbers of persons who received harsh sentences for nonserious and nonviolent crimes suggests that judges rarely utilize their "safety valve" role under the law (Ricciardulli 2002). Likewise, the Federal Sentencing Guidelines were declared to be merely voluntary guidelines in the *U.S. v. Booker* case in 2004, but there appears to be little willingness by judges to depart from the guidelines.

Crime Jurisprudence: How the War on Crime Disciplined Courts

Led by the Supreme Court, American courts have produced a reactive judicial posture toward the war on crime reflected in a broad array of legal doctrines. This jurisprudence of crime has generally altered how courts govern, and specifically limited the expansive role that federal courts had begun to play in modernizing state institutions. In its compromised attempt to modernize the death penalty in *Furman* and *Gregg*, the Court's framing emphasized the importance of public opinion, played up the conflict between victim and defendant rights, and preserved credibility in the theory that capital punishment deterred murders (Gottschalk 2005). In terms of criminal justice, this posture and new doctrinal developments greatly favored the government's powers to police and punish and helped promote the growth of mass incarceration (Gottschalk 2005).

Legal scholar Louis Bilionis has recently argued that the Rehnquist Court's strategies for rolling back the liberal criminal procedure decisions of the 1960s provided a template for the reversal of liberal jurisprudence, and the growth of a new conservative jurisprudence, in such areas as antidiscrimination law, environmental law, and federalism. For Bilionis, the key elements of this jurisprudence include an antipathy toward the liberal regime in crime, a ready set of conservative policy ideas on crime, mainly emphasizing the deterrent and incapacitating potential of harsh punishment, and a strategy of distinguishing a narrow core of liberal defendants' rights, while cutting back those same rights at their supposed peripheries (Bilionis 2005, 998).

The Even Less Dangerous Branch: Elements of a Crime Jurisprudence

The influence of crime and judicial thinking has been more than one of proximity. In shaping the doctrines that have altered how courts govern in American society, the Supreme Court seems to have been influenced by the substance of the war on crime, as well as by the formal methods of distinguishing liberal precedents. This crime jurisprudence includes several elements that have already emerged in our discussion of executive and legislative government.

One is the centrality of victims to the meaning of crime and to the force of law. Starting in the 1970s, Supreme Court justices began to worry out loud about the effects their decisions and even discourse were having on crime victims. By the 1990s, this concern had become a driving force in decisions.[16] This has often showed up as a kind of populism. It has also emerged in an embrace of police officers as distinct synecdoche for the public in its victim status.

A second element of the Court's crime jurisprudence is trust that the executive will make the right trade-offs between individual liberty and collective security. In criminal justice cases, courts have, with some important exceptions (e.g., the issue of preemptive strikes against members of the jury pool), treated prosecutorial discretion as resolving all questions of the fairness of charge selection—and at the same time made it very difficult for litigants even to discover the pattern of prosecutorial decision making. For example, in *McCleskey v. Georgia* (1986), the Supreme Court held that the existence of a statistical pattern correlating the race of victim and the imposition of capital punishment in homicide cases did not suffice to show a violation of equal protection, relying heavily on the necessity of leaving space for individualized decision making by prosecutors (and juries).

A third element of the jurisprudence of crime is a skepticism about the role of courts in intervening in institutional decisions and a preference for formal barriers, such as procedural defaults and other bright-line rules, that limit the scope of judicial review and remedies. This is exemplified in the Supreme Court's rules governing successive habeas corpus petitions by criminal defendants, capital prisoners in particular. The result is often a visibly destabilized law that often fails to distinguish between the law and what might reasonably have been taken to be the law.

These three elements, as articulated in criminal and noncriminal cases after the 1960s, spell out a kind of memo to the lower courts. From now on, conflicts about institutional reform should be resolved with the goal of making people who feel threatened by crime (especially white suburbanites) safer to the maximum degree possible, by deferring to those political authorities—governors, prosecutors, school boards—most accountable to these voters, and by limiting the courts' role in implementing large-scale reform.

Desegregation Meets the War on Crime: A Case Study

All three of these elements defining a jurisprudence of crime are visible in the Supreme Court's reshaping of constitutional antidiscrimination law in the mid-1970s. This period saw a dramatic turnaround in the willingness of the Supreme Court, under the imprimatur of the Constitution's "equal protection of the laws" provision, to support lower courts in carrying out major institutional reforms. Notwithstanding the appointment of conservative Warren Burger as Chief Justice in 1969, the early 1970s saw rapid advancement of the Court's involvement. In the 1971 decision of *Swann v. Charlotte-Mecklenburg Board of Education*, a unanimous Supreme Court for the first time upheld a massive school desegregation plan for the city of Charlotte, North Carolina, one involving substantial use of student busing and other methods to eliminate as much as possible racially identifiable schools in a segregated urban setting.[17] The Court said that judges, having discovered a violation of the equal protection guarantee, should "make every effort to achieve the greatest possible degree of actual desegregation" (*Swann*, 26). Just three years later, in *Milliken v. Bradley* (1974), a divided Supreme Court rejected a similarly broad plan aimed at eliminating racially identifiable schools, this time in Detroit, Michigan, on the grounds that the desegregation plan anticipated busing of children from suburban school districts not shown to have been involved in the practice of segregation.

To its contemporary critics, *Milliken* appeared to end the quest for substantial school desegregation in the United States some 20 years after

Brown v. Board of Education (1954) had begun the project, and to signal that the Supreme Court would henceforth restrict the efforts of courts to reform state and local institutions more generally.[18] These prophesies have proven correct. In a series of decisions coming after *Milliken,* the Supreme Court rapidly ended any prospect that the equal protection guarantee of the Constitution would be used to persuade courts to dismantle the substantial social and economic barriers that the country's history of state-supported racism had all too visibly left. These decisions were about not only racial justice but also the scope and nature of how courts governed.

Although limiting the reach of school desegregation in particular, and courts in general, were goals associated with the political Right in the United States during the 1970s, several key features of crime jurisprudence are visible in the course of the Court's antidiscrimination decisions from *Milliken.* A close look at *Milliken* and its context illuminates these.

The Detroit desegregation battle unfolded at a stark moment in the city's history, less than three years after the July 1967 riots—five days of violence in the heart of the city's African American community that resulted in 43 deaths, looting, and arson damage to thousands of properties. Criminal violence had long been associated with Detroit's system of residential race segregation. Detroit lacked southern-style laws enforcing the geographic boundaries of its black residents, whose numbers increased rapidly during World Wars I and II. Instead, it relied on the legal tactic of exclusionary racial covenants in property deeds and more direct vigilante acts of criminal violence against black families who sought better housing in white neighborhoods (Sugrue 1996, 259). Racial subordination—as opposed to segregation—was also imposed by the symbolic and real violence used by the virtually all-white Detroit police force.

White Detroit was also riven by its own class, ethnic, and religious conflicts, but the battle to maintain racial segregation against African Americans was a point of unity. This battle was carried out into the 1960s through homeowners associations, the police, and the Detroit's elected city government (Sugrue 1996). This white alliance found its primary ideological justification in crime, especially as legal decisions in the 1940s and 1950s made overt racism less acceptable in public discourse. The riot of July 1967 reflected the rage in the black community about the continued power of this alliance over daily life, especially through the police, and the failure of reform to keep pace with rapidly growing expectations as a more liberal political alliance.[19] For all but the most liberal white Detroiters, the riot's images of arson, looting, and battles with police confirmed the historic linkage of African American residential presence and crime.

By the spring of 1970—when the liberal dominated Detroit school board—began to develop a voluntary desegregation plan, none of these tensions had improved. The war of neighborhoods that had dominated Detroit's urban racial politics in the mid-twentieth century continued, as homeowner associations fought to maintain solidarity among remaining white residents. School segregation was a critical feature of this strategy. At the same time, this long war was giving way to a new territorialization based on the city limits, around which an almost exclusively white ring of incorporated municipalities stood as a wall.[20]

After a modest voluntary plan was overturned by a remarkably rapid white backlash—the legislature acted to suspend the plan two days after it was adopted, and liberal members of the school board were recalled within months—the legal battle that became *Milliken v. Bradley* (1974) began. The plan that was proposed by District Judge Stephen Roth after finding the Detroit Board of Education and the state of Michigan guilty of segregating schools in Detroit was far broader. Convinced by demographic evidence that no substantial integration could be achieved within the boundaries of Detroit, Roth made suburban districts part of his plan and ultimately involved more than 56 separate school districts in southeastern Michigan.[21] The political response to Judge Roth's order received national attention, especially when Alabama segregationist George Wallace narrowly won the Michigan Democratic primary in 1971. Huge numbers of white, blue-collar Democrats who had moved to segregated suburbs and the whites who lived in the remaining segregated neighborhoods of Detroit itself felt exposed to the core on the issue of schools and were outraged that the national Democratic Party would not act on their behalf. The populist response to Judge Roth seethed with threats of criminal violence and allusions to the threat of black crime endangering children. One popular bumper sticker stated, "Roth is a child molester" (Dimond 1985, 76).

As the case went to the Supreme Court in 1974, a right-leaning political and legal alliance—representatives of the white suburbs; the Detroit Board of Education, by then controlled by the members elected to replace the recalled liberals; and the Nixon administration via Solicitor General and legal scholar Robert Bork—focused on what they considered the major vulnerability of the multidistrict plan: the relatively undeveloped record of the role of segregation in suburban school districts. The remedy was unlawful because the "innocent" suburbs were being compelled to solve the problems of the "guilty" city of Detroit. The plaintiffs—who had not come into the litigation committed to a multidistrict remedy, but now found themselves defending it—argued that *Swann*'s principle of maximum feasible desegregation required crossing the district lines. They argued that the specific kind of segregation practiced in Detroit, in which African American students had been contained in all-black schools, had produced a citywide identification of Detroit schools with a black threat in need of containment, a violation that a Detroit-only desegregation plan would not remedy but complete. The two sides also squared off on correlative issues. Just how important are district lines as opposed to the state of Michigan?[22]

In *Milliken*, the majority in the 5–4 ruling accepted almost all of the arguments supported by the parties seeking to overrule Judge Roth's multidistrict plan. The Court held that suburban districts should be brought in only if a showing could be made that they had practiced segregation or collaborated in the maintenance of segregation in Detroit. The notion articulated in *Swann* of maximum feasible desegregation was to be limited to the guilty school district. The Court also embraced local school districts as important vessels of democratic will independent of the state, and foreclosed any shortcut to showing the role of the state of Michigan in promoting a segregated system.

The opinion makes no overt mention of crime, nor are its doctrinal moves in any sense derived from those of its criminal procedure decisions. But neither is the link to crime limited to the strategies of judicial craft. Instead, we see central elements of the crime jurisprudence operating in a distinct doctrinal context.

One is in the Court's consciousness of the victims. Critics of *Milliken* and of the Court's subsequent equal protection jurisprudence have often characterized the Court as abandoning the victims of segregation by assuring that no meaningful remedy could be applied. Constitutional theorist Lawrence Tribe, for example, describes these cases as reflecting a "perpetrator" perspective rather than a "victim" perspective (Tribe, 1509). Indeed, the majority's main reference to the term "victim" is ambivalent, seeming to promise remedy, and at the same time severely limiting that remedy to the effects directly traceable to the perpetrators' wrongdoing. "But the remedy is necessarily designed, as all remedies are, to restore the victims of discriminatory conduct to the position they would have occupied in the absence of such conduct."[23]

In his dissenting opinion, Justice White questioned the sensibility of the majority's focus on limiting the remedy to the direct effects of the wrongdoing. "It is unrealistic to suppose that the children who were victims of the State's unconstitutional conduct could now be provided the benefits of which they were wrongfully deprived," he wrote. Rather than focus on direct effects of wrongdoing on the victim, the focus should be the remedy that "will achieve the greatest possible degree of actual desegregation."[24]

This unrealistic quality, its reassuring promise of restoration while staying efforts at desegregation, reflects precisely the hold of the crime victim idea on the Court's remedial thinking. In *Milliken*, the victim of discrimination is recognized, but only in the frame of the wrongful conduct. *Swann* and other desegregation cases had clearly indicated that the remedy was not to be limited in scope to the direct acts of wrongdoing, but should seek maximum feasible desegregation. In *Milliken*, the legal personality of the wrongdoer emerges as a decisive limiting factor. The crime victim can be celebrated in American governance as an ideal citizen subject in part because his or her demands are limited to what the state already knows how to produce relatively effectively, i.e., punishment.

The ambivalent reference of the *Milliken* majority to the victims of discrimination may also reflect the fact that they compete for the status of victims with another class unnamed but clearly recognized in the opinion: the "innocent" white children, referenced in the briefs for the suburban districts, who might be bused to black Detroit schools under a multidistrict remedy. If crime victims, and potential crime victims, have become a privileged subject, then it is not surprising that the *Milliken* majority feels more empathy with the plight of suburban white students than with African American students in Detroit. In the whole context of northern desegregation generally, and specifically in post-riot Detroit, the idea that white students were being exposed to violent crime by busing them to Detroit was too palpable to require stating. This element of Court deference to populist fear of crime—and rage at government policies blamed for it—makes an explicit appearance only at the very close of Justice Marshall's anguished dissent:

> Public opposition, no matter how strident, cannot be permitted
> to divert this court from the enforcement of the constitutional

principles at issue in this case. Today's holding, is more a reflection of the public mood that we have gone far enough in enforcing the Constitution's guarantee of equal justice than it is the product of neutral principles of law.[25]

The second element of crime jurisprudence is deference to the executive as a more reliable and legitimate representative of the people in the context of crime. In *Milliken*, the executive is present in multiple forms: the school boards both in Detroit and the numerous suburban districts; the state of Michigan, which was represented by its attorney general before the Supreme Court; and the Nixon administration, represented before the Court by Solicitor General Robert Bork. The *Milliken* majority takes a deferential stance toward all these executives, refusing to allow suburban districts to be brought into the plan, declining to hold the state of Michigan responsible in any substantive sense for Detroit's segregation, and following the Nixon administration's policy preference to limit busing. But the suburban boards of education come in for an especially strong proclamation of deference, one laden with exactly the sort of emotional obeisance that the Court had begun to take toward prosecutors and police officers. Rejecting the idea, associated with the dissenters, that district lines were "mere administrative convenience," Chief Justice Burger wrote:

> No single tradition in public education is more deeply rooted than local control over the operation of schools; local autonomy has long been thought essential to both the maintenance of community concern and support for the public schools and to the quality of the educational process. . . . [L]ocal control over the educational process affords citizens an opportunity to participate in decision-making, permits the structuring of school programs to fit local needs, and encourages "experimentation, innovation, and a healthy competition for educational excellence."[26]

A third element of crime jurisprudence is a contrast with the second. If executives such as prosecutors and school boards have a relationship with the people rooted in tradition and political accountability, courts are the most suspect of governing agents. Indeed, the crime-related populist politics that came to the fore in the late 1960s and early 1970s revealed an often explicit analogy between judge and criminal, as evidenced in the

"Roth Is a Child Molester" bumper stickers in suburban Detroit in the early 1970s: both menaced the citizen, taxpayer, and homeowner through the imposition of arbitrary acts of power. Chief Justice Burger's majority opinion never makes such an explicit link, but by specifically focusing on the district judge as a kind of lawless actor pursuing his subjective desires over the interests and rights of suburban white students, Burger draws on this culturally laden analogy. The chief justice criticizes both the district court and the Sixth Circuit Court of Appeals for having "shifted the primary focus from a Detroit remedy to the metropolitan area" arbitrarily in order to pursue "a racial balance which they perceived as desirable."[27]

Paradoxically, Judge Roth is also portrayed as overreaching and punitive toward innocent white students and districts, whose inclusion in a multidistrict busing plan was labeled judicially imposed punishment (Dimond 1985, 100). The majority opinion in *Milliken* never directly says this, but Justice White's dissent names it directly in the opinion in which he wrote, "The task is not to devise a system of pains and penalties to punish constitutional violations brought to light."[28]

The result in *Milliken* was highly significant for the course of judicial-led reform under the banner of equal protection. The number of large cities where single-district desegregation plans could make a meaningful difference were dwindling. Approving a multidistrict remedy in *Milliken* would have opened the door for many more district courts in the Midwest and Northeast to begin restructuring metropolitan school systems. Such a major new vein of cases might have kept the federal judiciary busy for another decade or two, and further inculcated the mentalities and skills necessary for judges to comfortably assert a governing role in running institutions.

The Court's retreat from broad judicial governance of metropolitan school systems in *Milliken* would prove to be more than a temporary halt. Confronted by the populist anger directed at school desegregation orders, the Court turned to its crime jurisprudence as a model for addressing that rage. Several years later in *Washington v. Davis* (1976), the Court directly limited the definition of discrimination to harmful actions taken with an invidious intent, a malicious purpose to harm because of the characteristic at which discrimination was directed. (This has been a shameful and very powerful legacy.)

In framing discrimination in this way, the Court drew again from the metaphoric link to crime as it had in *Milliken*. Discrimination as a target for judicial action was to be narrowed to those acts that followed the model of crimelike behavior. Tribe criticized *Davis* and its progeny for adopting a perpetrator perspective from which discrimination is seen "not as a social phenomenon—the historical legacy of centuries of slavery and subjugation—but as the misguided, retrograde, almost atavistic behavior of individual actors" (Tribe, 1509). Tribe argues that this "pseudo-scienter" requirement (borrowing the criminal law term) was adopted precisely to address "the Supreme Court's trepidation about embracing the highly intrusive structural remedies that may be required to root out the entrenched results of racial subjugation" (1510).

Conclusion: Crime, Risk, and the Crisis of Judgment

For many, the 1960s and 1970s was the apotheosis of judicial government. Findings of constitutional violations by school boards, welfare agencies, mental hospitals, and prisons, and the consent decrees that followed, placed judges and their appointed agents at the center of most important public institutions. The "rights revolution," as some described it, increasingly made courts the addressee for demands on government, although it did not secure them a popular mandate. Even spaces of rational despotism, such as the prison, came under judicial control. Since the 1990s, courts have increasingly withdrawn from, or been pushed out of, these institutions. Sometimes this has been through legislation limiting the ability of courts to hear cases, such as the Prison Litigation Reform Act, or through legislation prohibiting public interest lawyers that work for legal services offices receiving federal funding from engaging in class actions. In other regards, the courts themselves, especially the Supreme Court, have done the retreating. Both developments have diminished the power of courts to help govern America.

Some would attribute this to the rise of a jurisprudential shift to the right. No doubt it has been a major goal of the legal and political right to limit the institutional reform role of federal and even state courts. But the war on crime, and the critical gaze on government that the war on crime brought, played a critical role in breaking down the status of judges in American political culture. At the highest level, the Warren Court decisions expanding the rights of criminal suspects and defendants in the 1960s displaced the ongoing legal effort to desegregate American institutions as the most controversial judicial interventions, and in important ways they projected a new meaning back on the Court's broader civil rights agenda. Trial courts in the federal and state systems were widely criticized for a collapse in the deterrent power of the criminal law and for enforcing remedies for racial discrimination that both white and African American parents perceived as exposing children of all races to more crime and violence. The claim that courts were indifferent or even hostile to the fate of "ordinary" Americans stuck and became an influence on the way courts govern today.

Perhaps even more disabling for judges as decision makers has been the rise of the crime victim as the central figure to which the government must respond. In ways the preceding two chapters have attempted to elucidate, governing agents in the executive and legislative modes have forged pathways by which to route their own power and knowledge to and through the victim. Governors in many states can use their power to slow or stop parole of violent criminals. Legislatures can enact reams of new laws, lengthen prison sentences, and strip convicted criminals of more aspects of their dignity or well-being. Whether making decisions perceived as "soft" on criminals, ordering remedies for racial discrimination, or closing asylums for the mentally ill, judges have become symbols of a mode governance that is not sensitive to the crime victim as idealized political subject. Ethical features of the judicial role have prevented judges from engaging in open embrace of the crime victim. In criminal trials, the victim has no specific role other than as witness. Judges are required to remain neutral in form and substance during trials.

Though judges have meant a great deal more to twentieth-century governance than is captured by their role in criminal courts, these distinctively criminal law narratives of judgment have come to haunt the judiciary. Whether yoked to a panoply of calculative rules such as the sentencing guidelines, or to their own imagined jury of vengeful victims, many contemporary judges now experience themselves as what we might call "judgment machines": people who are no more responsible for the consequences of their judgment than a pregnancy test is for the condition it declares. It is not simply judges, both federal and state, who have suffered a decline in autonomy, power, and prestige. In a real way, all roles calling for any independent judgment—including, but not limited to, parents, school administrators, and business executives, among others—have become vulnerable to a seemingly limitless panoply of ill-defined yet emotionally powerful suspicions.

Project Exile | **5**

Race, the War on Crime, and Mass Imprisonment

America since the 1980s has created a historically unique penal form
that some sociologists and criminologists have called "mass imprisonment" (Garland 2001b). The term is meant to point to three distinctive
features of imprisonment in the United States: its scale, its categorical application, and its increasingly warehouse-like or even waste management–like
qualities (Feeley & Simon 1992). All three are inevitably relative features.
Prison was once an aberrational experience for all segments of the community, even those with the highest levels of imprisonment. If present
trends continue, nearly one in 15 Americans born in 2001 will serve time
in prison during their lifetimes (6.6 percent of that birth cohort). Broken
down by race and gender, the odds are even more daunting: one in three
black men, one in seven Hispanic men, and one in 17 white men will go to
prison in their lifetime, given current trends (Bonczar 2003). The odds of
an African American man going to prison today are higher than the odds
he will go to college, get married, or go into the military.

As these figures suggest, "mass" does not mean racially uniform. This is
because of the second feature of "mass imprisonment": it applies to whole
categories. Not only was prison aberrational in a demographic sense, it was
individualized. Whether someone went to prison for many crimes and for
how long turned on their individual circumstances and the particular
judge who sentenced them. In varying degrees, virtually all the states in
the United States have reoriented their penal systems toward more uniform
application of prison sentences. The federal government embraced these
trends strongly in its sentencing guidelines system adopted in 1987. This
categorical aspect of mass imprisonment is double-edged in its interaction

141

with American racial formations. Because many of the categorical factors that send people to prison are targeted at circumstances highly correlated with race, they help produce the dramatic skewing in the odds of imprisonment faced by Americans with different racial backgrounds. For example, the notorious crack/powder cocaine distinction in federal guidelines makes possession of crack, which is commonly associated with African Americans, far more consequential for prison sentences. Likewise, federal laws prohibiting felons from possessing guns (Dubber 2002) are far more consequential in African American communities, where young men are more likely to arm themselves for self-defense. At the same time, because imprisonment is often triggered by categories of behavior or circumstances rather than individualized assessments, a white person from a very affluent background who might have benefited from individualized assessment in the past is more likely than before to go to prison in America.

In the nineteenth and twentieth centuries, prisons operated in accordance with a number of competing and succeeding principles. Among them were coercive monasteries—where penitence was produced through solitary confinement; locked factories, mills, and mines, and where criminals were subjected to the discipline of silence and group labor under the ever-present threat of the whip—and correctional institutions, where prisoners were forced into group therapy and received college educations. Each of these "penal regimes" had ways of imagining the nature of the criminal and forms of knowledge that would allow the prison to act on that "criminal nature." Often as not, criminals disappointed, and knowledge of all sorts remained shallow. But the prison project itself succeeded because in distinct ways it served as a crucial relay within the broader political order (Bright 1996). Building prisons served to remove troubled and troublesome individuals from the community while supporting investment in construction contracts, in the production of a docile labor force, and in new forms of psychiatric and psychological expertise.

The distinctive new form and function of the prison today is a space of pure custody, a human warehouse or even a kind of social waste management facility, where adults and some juveniles distinctive only for their dangerousness by society are concentrated for purposes of protecting the wider community. The waste management prison promises no transformation of the prisoner through penitence, discipline, intimidation, or therapy. Instead, it promises to promote security in the community simply by creating a space physically separated from the community in which to hold people whose propensity for crime makes them appear an intolerable risk for society. In the political order linked to waste management prisons, political leaders compete to protect the public in their willingness to stretch the concept of "unchanging propensity" to fit ever larger potential offender populations.

All of these features are summarized in the federally promoted program from which this chapter takes its title, "Project Exile." Developed in Richmond, Virginia, in response to a spike in homicides in the mid-1990s, Project Exile has won support from across the political spectrum. It was originally developed during the Clinton administrations and got its first national model status then. Shortly after taking office, the Bush administration and Attorney General Ashcroft warmly embraced Project Exile as the paradigm they would follow in crime control (Richman 2001). The key to the program is the categorical application of tougher federal gun laws (which criminalize a felon's possession of a firearm for any reason or anyone's possession of a gun in the commission of a drug crime) to all persons arrested in applicable situations (Raphael & Ludwig 2002). By focusing on the link between guns and violence, but only in contexts that are otherwise criminal, the strategy has won support from both sides in the polarized gun debate in America.

This chapter argues that it is not the prison per se (or any complex of interests associated with it) that endangers American democracy but rather mass imprisonment in all three senses of scale, categorical application, and the shift toward a waste management vision of corrections. Were contemporary prisons modeled, even in predictably flawed ways, on schools, mental hospitals, or even plantations, they would be less destructive than is their current configuration as human toxic waste dumps. Further, the prison population boom, and its descent into waste management, is a cumulative product of the way American government has become enthralled by the logic of crime, as I traced in earlier chapters. Project Exile can be our name for this larger constellation of commitments that presents Americans with the option of obtaining more security for its beleaguered urban cores only by sending the young men of those communities into "exile."

The first part of this chapter provides a context for the toxic-waste-dump prison by briefly describing some of the earlier forms of the prison and how they functioned within distinctive American political orders or states. The second part analyzes the waste management prison as a distinct penal strategy in American history, one linked to the emergence of governing through crime as a political rationality in America since the 1960s.

The third part analyzes how the self-understanding of government promoted by the war on crime has locked in mass imprisonment.

The Prison and American Political Culture

The United States was not the first society to develop prisons or use them for persons convicted of crimes, but from the beginning of the eighteenth century it has embraced the prison more fully and imagined it in more ways than has any other society.

The Penitentiary and the Early Republican Political Order

The Eastern State Penitentiary, built in Philadelphia, became perhaps the most famous example in the world of the solitary confinement penitentiary. Along with its archrival, the congregate system of New York, Eastern generated great excitement among penal reformers globally. Philadelphia's "separate" or "solitary confinement" approach used the elaborate seclusion of individual cells to cut off both visual and sound contact and produce a space of internal penitence. Inmates were kept in self-enclosed living and working units that required no interaction with other inmates day or night and that totally controlled interaction with staff. In theory, a prisoner would enter, live for years, and leave the penitentiary without meeting anyone but the religious counselors and staff that tended to their needs. No criminal underclass would form in such a prison to feed back into the community when prisoners returned. In the eyes of early observers, it appeared to work, if sometimes too well, leaving some of its inmates mentally scarred.

More than any other North American prison of the early nineteenth century, Philadelphia's Eastern State Prison staked the good order of the prison on its architecture (Meranze 1996).[1] Its individual cells, designed for the prisoners to live and work in full time, day and night, aimed at achieving total isolation of prisoners from other prisoners and allowing for total administrative control over what came in and out of the cells. Enclosed monad-like in a cellular space for living and working, the prisoners had no ability to disrupt the order of the prison or even shape its operation.[2]

This order proved vulnerable in a number of respects. Even isolated in cells, inmates were quite capable of resisting in ways that took their toll on staff and possibly on other inmates. Staff responded with a variety of strategies aimed at coercing cooperation including pressure on the body (although seeking to avoid the visible and intense contact of whipping). There is also compelling contemporary evidence that solitary confinement went too far in breaking down inmates' subjectivity, leaving them incapable of constructing a new reliable self. Its persistence, even in the face of these problems, owed to the fact that whatever its penological faults, the Pennsylvania solitary system fit well with the political order that was taking shape in the early Republic.

The Philadelphia model helped to constitute a political order outside the wall in two quite distinct, even contradictory ways. First, the prison would become the center of a vast, informal web of stories about the horrors of life for those locked up. In a way, this would make the solitary confinement system more akin to the public scaffold because it was capable of producing a powerful emotional experience for the public, although one no longer connected directly to visual experience but rather tied precisely to the imagination. Visitors to the famous prison, including Charles Dickens (1842), did precisely this. His notes on his American tour included vivid descriptions of the horrific condition of solitary confinement. The prison in this sense functioned as the source of a kind of republican mythology or lore, one that could compete with tales of monarchical excess in providing a popular face to the law's threat.

For Benjamin Rush, this symbolic production could exist independently of an internal practice focused on the quiet accumulation of positive knowledge regarding moral pathology. The disciplinary practice at Eastern State Prison included one of the earliest systematic efforts to make individual case files a critical tool of prison decision making. Pennsylvania law required court officials to produce case files on inmates detailing their past history, both criminal and social, their crimes, and their conduct since arrest and to forward these files to prison officials. These files were designed to shape prison treatment but also to reach out into the community and produce a workable knowledge of what later sociologists would call "social disorganization." The solitary confinement prison was intended to decode the individual sources of delinquency and thus map the process by which criminals were produced.

The second way that the Philadelphia model of prison order linked to the larger political order being established by the political class of Philadelphia in those years operated in a kind of medical-spatial strategy in which the confinement of the morally corrupt in prison, like that of the physically ill in the hospital, cut off infection, enabled objective observation, and concentrated efficient therapeutic procedures (Foucault 1977). In the post-Revolutionary generation, governing elites viewed the "sovereign" individuals of the new Republic as vulnerable to the unregulated circulation of demoralizing images, what historian Michael Meranze calls "mimetic corruption." This concern extended itself to the tradition of public punishments (which some feared would degrade the solemnity and justness of the law through identity with the malefactors), as well as to the theater, street conduct, and even the behavior of law enforcement. Though sovereignty belonged to the people, the government had to assure that the circulation of unhealthy images did not corrupt the people. This paternalistic underside to freedom required authority that was based on "character and specialized knowledge," virtues expressed in the prison (Meranze 1996, 318).

In time, the prison came to endanger the legitimacy of the political order that promoted it. In the eyes of many Philadelphians, prison, its internal regime of isolation and penitence having failed, had become a great channel pouring the dangerous classes of Pennsylvania's countryside into the city (Meranze 1996, 243). The news of uprisings within the prison escaped the walls and merged with such public outrages as the riot at Vauxhall that followed an aborted balloon launch in 1820 (Meranze 1996, 250). In both respects, the output of the Eastern State Prison helped to support but also to delegitimate its operation, a pattern that would be repeated again and again in the history of the prison. Scandal would prove to be an important dynamic in the game of party politics that was still establishing itself in Philadelphia in the 1830s. The population of ex-offenders would provide a pool of highly volatile individuals available for all kinds of political agendas and for justification of the need for an intensification of penal measures. In any event, the dialectic of horror and medical optimism would remain a fundamental feature of the prison's contribution to the larger political order.

The Big House and the Patronage Political Order

New states entering the union, including California in 1851, set about almost immediately to construct penitentiaries. Like a constitution and a state flag, the penitentiary had become a hallmark of statehood. By the middle of the nineteenth century, in most prisons, solitary confinement remained limited to disciplinary cases. The congregate system of group labor became the general rule for keeping inmates in control during the day with a return to a single cell (room permitting) at night. Notwithstanding the use of whipping and other punishments, inmate culture grew in the inevitable gaps of surveillance and discipline.

As resistance to prison industrial labor by organized labor and business grew, the dream of profitable and abundant labor as a source of reform inside the prison died. In its place, a kind of shadow version of the industrial economy and its culture arose in prisons. A modicum of work existed for most prisoners, whether focused on providing "state use" items such as filing cabinets and license plates—marginal products for the civilian economy—or simply the production of goods and services needed inside the prison. When sociologists began to observe prisons in the 1920s and 1930s, they found that this limited economy anchored an extensive inmate social system based on rackets in illicit pleasures in a tacit alliance with the official custodians. It was this prison order that was captured vividly in both the "big house" sociology and the movies of the 1930s and 1940s. The big-house prison operated as a major source of capital spending by the state, which was in turn a major excuse to distribute jobs and contracts (Bright 1996). This made the prison a significant political asset. The main "currency" of this system, the links that tied governors through myriad arrays down to individual voters in the counties, was patronage. Controlling the office of governor guaranteed the candidate and his partisans access to a large number of state jobs distributed across the state and, with the cooperation of the legislature, public works investments that could enormously expand the capital available for patronage.

The big-house prison was well situated to produce numerous effects capable of being distributed at the local level, where the "patronage state" received its votes. Like highways (the other great form of state building in the 1920s), prisons provided a subject for spending well beyond the needs or capacities of local areas. Jackson Prison, one of the largest ever built, provided a particularly rich treasure, divided over many years of construction, and would produce jobs and demand supplies for decades. The prison assured an even larger flow of capital. From this, capital rewards were drawn for political supporters, and a greater opportunity extended the forms of corruption that kept these complicated political machines lubricated.

The big-house prison also provided symbolic goods appropriate to the small-town values that dominated the patronage state. At a time when Detroit and other cities were experiencing high levels of immigration and

Prohibition-fueled violence (associated with immigrants), the construction of a new generation of big-house prisons in the 1920s signaled an intent to get serious about punishing and containing these "dangerous classes." The huge size of Jackson may have been particularly telling in that respect. It signaled an effort akin to the leap into solitary confinement at Eastern State Prison in Philadelphia a century earlier to capture the imagination of the public with an indirect promise to discipline the unruly new inhabitants of the cities.

When things worked well, both prison and state provided functional inputs to each other. They also produced by-products that were destabilizing to each other. The big-house prison, for example, inevitably produced a steady stream of scandals as the accommodations behind the prison order came to light in newspapers, grand juries, and state legislative committees. Since prison managers were linked to the governor, scandals among even low-level prison employees could produce problems for the very top of the structure. The sudden changes and crackdowns in discipline that such scandals generally produced could be expected to rattle the internal order of the "big house" as the forms of official laxness and accommodation that created the surplus pleasures needed to support inmate society were withdrawn. The social peace of the prison could collapse, leading to violence among inmates and between inmates and guards. Violence in the prison in turn produced more scandal.

The Correctional Institution and the New Deal Political Order

The crucial difference in the New Deal political order was the projection of a direct relationship between the executive political authority (president or governor) and the population through the news media—newspapers and radio and, later, television. These allowed the voter to receive a steady stream of information about social problems, the state's solutions, and the political background to the doings of government. Another crucial link was the construction of statewide services, such as universities and agricultural research stations, that provided direct state benefits to individuals. Such institutions had existed since the nineteenth century, but after World War II, expanded state investment in education and expertise made such assistance far more available to individuals at the grass roots. In the New Deal style of rule, political leadership could produce popular loyalty through these new institutions as an alternative to and way of reinvigorating old patronage networks. The local political machines survived into the 1960s in part by helping their clients access benefits of the New Deal, but their appeal was limited. They might help you get a job on a state highway project, but they could not promise your child a chance to advance to the middle classes.

These new institutions made meritocratic competition and abstract evaluation methods increasingly important in determining the distribution of government benefits, but these did not so much replace as parallel traditional mechanisms of loyalty and local knowledge. Science and professional expertise also played a prominent role in the New Deal style of governing along both dimensions. The institutional capacity to access and make use of the best scientific advice in managing social problems was an important form of government prowess. Scientific discourse was critical to running the regulatory and benefit systems that the New Deal increasingly developed to service its direct relationship to the people. In particular, the language of the social sciences became essential to the dialogue between the state and the new array of quasi-corporatist collective subjects that formed their most important constituents: unions, trade associations, and interest groups.

As New Deal–style governors began to take power after World War II, they made the reorganization of the prison administration a chief concern. In Michigan, riots in 1952 at Jackson provided the basis for reworking the narratives and strategies of the prison (Bright 1994). In California, prisons began to be reshaped even earlier, in 1944, when Governor Earl Warren reorganized the Department of Corrections and hired Richard McGee, a progressive administrator who had worked on federal prison policy for the New Deal. In both states, the new approach emphasized rehabilitation and the claim that the prison could be controlled through individualized, scientifically oriented treatment of offenders.

The residual stock of big-house prisons meant that physical structure would remain dominant, but the new model of classification reshaped routines and individualized treatment carried out by a staff of treatment professionals. Though rehabilitation talk had continuities with the reform talk of the big-house prison and the penitence talk of the solitary confinement prison, it promoted a very different interpretive grid upon inmates and their conduct and implemented a very different set of interventions. Labor had been central to earlier reform hopes, but even after the end of the Great Depression and the return of full employment, labor never regained its place in the prison. In its place, education and therapy were the major forms of treatment and the building blocks of the new control regime that was taking shape in prisons dubbed "correctional institutions." Education was already a dominant theme in the New Deal style of rule, with its great universities and high-quality public schools. Therapy, predominantly on a group basis, had roots in scientific psychology and became a significant private option for middle-class citizens in affluent America encouraged by generous social insurance policies.[3] Inside the prison, these themes came to be wrapped around each other as reading, defined as "bibliotherapy," which was seriously viewed as an important part of making a record of progress for release (Cummins 1994).

In those states in which the New Deal mentality of rule was most successfully articulated, the state's claim to reform criminals through punishment was greatly expanded. The penitentiary and the big-house prison promised to reform prisoners by giving them the opportunity to repent spiritually or by submitting them to discipline and a life bereft of comforts. But neither the early republic nor the patronage state staked its legitimacy on reform. In both cases, the individual prisoner was thought to have the major responsibility for reforming. The correctional institution, in contrast, very much staked its legitimacy (and through it the state's) on an ambitious aspiration to transform recalcitrant subjects who had typically "failed" in the softer sectors of the New Deal, including the school system and social welfare agencies. The routines of the prison would not simply expose sinners to their consciences or scrub rogues clean of their bad habits, but reach inside with scientific techniques to address deep individual pathologies. Moreover, the correctional institution promised to accomplish this in conditions of relative transparence, using social science not only as a technology of rehabilitation but as a way of evaluating its own success. In contrast, Philadelphia prison reformer Benjamin Rush at the turn of the nineteenth century envisioned bifurcating the clinical benefits of living in the penitentiary from the horror stories of solitary confinement that would circulate in and help constitute a public law-abiding community.

California is a good example of the New Deal style of rule between 1945 and 1980 (Schrag 1998). Its economy, driven by industrial manufacturing from automobiles through aerospace, supported as developed a set of New Deal institutions as any state in the United States. In universities, public schools, and highways, California led a national pattern of heavy investment. Prodded by a series of progressive state Supreme Court justices, California also went further than most states in developing welfare, health, and educational entitlements for the poor. The California Department of Corrections was clearly the national leader in forging a scientific model of correctional treatment and prison management.

Administering resources such as universities and colleges bathed state government in the glow of technical competence, economic growth, and scientific progress. The gleaming California system was perhaps the best example in the country. With eight major research universities, a number of four-year colleges with master's programs, and an array of free community colleges, California envisioned that virtually all of its high school graduates would receive higher education. This established something akin to an entitlement touching nearly all state residents, something as valuable as the old patronage links, but now tying the citizen directly into the governor and the professional state administration.

By the 1960s, however, prisoners and college students were demonstrating to many observers not the triumph but the failure of the New Deal state. Model subjects of a form of government staked on the ability to reap major social gains from extensive investment in the subjectivity of ordinary people had become increasingly agitated and seemed to be turning on the New Deal state that privileged them.[4] Not surprisingly, both became symbols of a perceived threat to "law and order" around which the first new political coalition since the New Deal would take shape.

Crimes, especially violent crimes such as robbery, rape, and homicide by people with established criminal records, pose a deep problem for the legitimacy of any political authority, but especially those depending on the New Deal style of rule. The personal relationship between government and citizen is directly endangered by the failure of the former. Victims of violent crime are particularly vulnerable to feelings of dramatic alienation from others, including those closest to them. Their experience opens up a divide from the common ground of collective progress promoted by New Deal institutions.[5] To the extent that people imagine themselves in the light of this victim experience, they partake of much of the same alienation and rage. Indeed, as I will discuss shortly, the mentalities of rule that have replaced the New Deal state have come to depend often on just such rage.

The Waste Management Prison and the Post–New Deal Order

California since 1980 presents the most striking case of the transformation in the style of rule in America since the rise of the social activist state during the New Deal. In less than 20 years, California went from being the most ambitious and generous version of the New Deal state to one organized along lines familiar in the American South, where the New Deal type of rule was truncated by the politics of white supremacy and the New Deal state was largely stillborn. Much of this was accomplished through a series of popular ballot initiatives beginning with the famous Proposition 13, which rolled back property taxes, embedded a whole set of mechanical controls on fiscal policy, and generally deprived the New Deal style of rule of the maneuverability and accountability it requires (Schrag 1998). These initiatives have also bolstered a new circuit of power linking political consultants, pollsters, the media, and an increasingly disaggregated voting public, one that both resembles and rivals that of the New Deal mentality of rule.

The Waste Management Prison

The waste management prison no longer works through broad efforts at shaping the personalities and personal relations of inmates but relies instead on specific behavioral objectives to be enforced over any degree of resistance. In place of the rackets of the big-house prison and the compulsory self-narration of the correctional institution, the order constructed by the toxic-waste-dump prison increasingly relies on total segregation of the prisoners considered most threatening. Ironically, this harkens back to the solitary confinement regime of the Philadelphia silent system penitentiary. There, however, isolation was part of a process aimed at compelling a transformational and spiritual crisis of the prisoner upon which prison experts could work their influence. Solitary confinement also became an important disciplinary tool in the correctional institution, where it served to separate out those deemed unreformable and an immediate threat to the security of the prison population. It is only with the contemporary waste management prison that solitary confinement is deployed as a general status and aimed at achieving internal security only. This prison lacks an internal regime, whether based on penitence, labor, or therapy (or something else), and increasingly relies on technological controls on movement and violent repression of resistance.

As with earlier shifts in the order of the prison, the physical plant changes much more slowly than the strategies of power deployed with them. The big-house regime made use of the old penitentiary prisons and built new ones such as Jackson. The era of the correctional institution saw relatively few new structures built, but those that were resembled college campuses or hospitals. The waste management prison has come in at a time of massive prison expansion and thus has found its logic realized in physical structure. This has meant a rigorous focus on risk and custody. The primary mandate of the prison has been to sort inmates by the danger they pose to the order of the prison and then sort them into prisons designed primarily to deal with risk of a certain level (Feeley & Simon 1992; 1994). Throughout this hierarchy, the goal of building the prisons as quickly and inexpensively as possible has been the other principle of the toxic-waste-dump prison.

Despite its superficial resemblance to the penitentiary, the super-max prison uses its architectural and technological capacities not to transform the individual but to contain his toxic behavioral properties at reasonable fiscal, political, and legal costs. The forms of knowledge at work in the super-max are not the disciplinary sciences of normalizing inspection advocated by Benjamin Rush and other promoters of the penitentiary, but the sciences of managing risk through rigorous external controls.

Unlike either the big-house or the correctional institution, the waste management prison needs to make few promises about its ability to penetrate and influence the mentality or will of criminal offenders. Indeed, the state can produce more security on this theory simply by building more prisons and filling them, no matter what happens inside those walls. The strength of this claim is that it minimizes the exposure of the state to failure by concentrating on the simple task of containment.

This logic helps explain why prison construction has been such a major initiative even in states with strong antitax sentiment. These include Texas, which built 120 prisons between 1980 and 2000, and California, which built 59 during the period. Prison in California has become a major tool for government to take action against the risks that the public fears the most.

The Emerging Post–New Deal Political Order

Where the New Deal political order has declined most precipitously (or never caught on), especially California in the first category and other Western and Sun Belt states in the other, political mobilization has concentrated on two related subjects, taxes and crime. The first is about reducing the size and power of government accumulated since the emergence of the New Deal. This includes reducing taxes most clearly, but by implication reducing regulations and social programs. The other axis has been crime and the perceived failure of government to bring punishment to bear on lawbreakers. This has manifested itself primarily in increases in the severity and scope of criminal law.

Both reflect what political journalist Calvin Schrag (1998) describes as "neo-populist" politics. Like the populist movements that influenced state government at the end of the nineteenth century, the new populism is strongly distrustful of expertise and of elite normative judgments about society (Garland 2001; Zimring, Hawkins, & Kamin 2001). Unlike the earlier populists, however, the new populism is not aimed at empowering ordinary citizens to have a more direct role in government. Instead, the ideal promoted is a kind of abolition of politics, one in which some mythically simple system of rules allows individuals to abandon politics altogether in favor of self-interest without any sustained agreement on collective goals. Thus the popularity in California of ballot initiatives and a wide body of law (produced by both initiative and conventional lawmaking) that produce "mechanical" decision methods, such as the property tax caps imposed by Proposition 13 and a whole panoply of mandatory sentence rules, including propositions and statutes.[6]

In this new configuration, it is not surprising that prison has become even more central to the political order than it was to earlier styles of rule. Like property taxes, which can become so burdensome to a fixed-income retiree as to force sale of his home, fear of crime affects people in their very sense of belonging to a specific community through their home and their use of neighborhood parks and streets. This is especially true for homeowners, for whom crime threatens in a special way only distantly suggested by the term "property values." Since World War II, stoked by government lending policies and tax credits, home ownership has become critical to the financial viability and social status of the middle classes in the United States. During much of this time and for most places, this has meant a steady increase in home values. But for parts of every large city and large parts of some cities, the worth of homes collapsed in the late 1960s and 1970s as a fear of crime marked whole neighborhoods as unattractive to families with suburban options.

The home is often, at least in American mythology, viewed as a bulwark against a wide variety of individual and collective threats, but taxes and fear of crime attack subjects precisely in their homeowner status, and individuals can do very little to protect themselves without cutting their ties to community and relocating. Certain kinds of crime did rise rapidly in California (and nationally) during the 1980s and stay high during the early 1990s, especially violence associated with young males in the inner city communities devastated by many of the economic changes that have undermined the resources and legitimacy of the New Deal style of rule. Most of this crime did not directly threaten suburban white voters who dominate competition among factions in the electoral battles of the populist state, but incidents throughout the 1980s and especially after the Los Angeles riot of 1991 suggested the potential for violence to break into the lives of the middle class.

A noteworthy incident in the early 1990s was the kidnapping and murder of 12-year-old Polly Klaas from her northern California suburban home in October 1993 (Zimring, Hawkins, and Kamen 2001). The murder galvanized the electorate in time for the 1994 election and led to the reelection of a conservative Republican incumbent widely seen as vulnerable because of the state's worst recession in decades. The public outrage was mobilized by the emergence of two fathers of murdered girls as media spokespeople for harsh punishment. Marc Klaas, Polly's father, met with politicians and set up a foundation addressing criminal justice policy, from which he initially castigated soft-on-crime judges and laws. Mike Reynolds, a Fresno-based businessman whose daughter had been murdered several years earlier, was the original proponent of the three-strikes law (Proposition 184) and helped turn public outrage over the Klaas kidnapping and murder into support for his voter initiative.

The Klaas murder and the three-strikes law reflect the ethos of fear of crime and mistrust of governing institutions that has fueled the logic of mass imprisonment. Richard Allen Davis, convicted of murder in Polly

Klaas's death, was a parolee who had been in prison several times for serious crimes. Critics seized upon Davis as an example of the apparent unwillingness of the judicial system to protect the people from known criminals. The three-strikes law, with its expressly populist tone and scarcely disguised contempt for the judicial process, embodies the categorical logic of mass imprisonment, which promises to substitute rigorous rules for the soft and untrustworthy judgment of judges and other government officials insulated by bureaucracy and expertise from direct engagement with the public.

As an episode of crime lawmaking (see chapter 3), the three-strikes initiative also illuminated the competitive logic of representation that lawmakers often find themselves in. The Klaas kidnapping and murder invigorated what had been a relatively weak signature campaign to place the three-strikes initiative on the ballot. The initiative qualified faster than any other voter initiative in California history (*Ewing v. California*, 15). By March of 1994, against the advice of all the criminologists in the state and much of the state's own prison bureaucracy, the California legislature had approved a bill conforming in all crucial respects to Proposition 184, and it was immediately signed into law by Governor Pete Wilson. Despite the fact that the legislature quickly enacted the harshest version of the law more than six months before the November 1994 election, the voters by 72 percent to 28 percent voted to place the three-strikes law in the California constitution so that no ordinary legislative majority could remove it.

In contrast to the New Deal order in which government promoted its own role in fostering the economic and social well-being of subjects, the post–New Deal order presupposes pervasive public fear of downward mobility associated with strong mistrust of government. In the face of this complex pattern of political mobilization in which public fear and rage sparked by property taxes and crime lead to rigid and mechanical decision rules for government, the prison represents a winning solution for politicians.

In cities like Los Angeles, Miami, and Seattle, social disorders (e.g., gang violence and riots) blend with natural disasters (e.g., earthquakes, hurricanes, floods, and fires) to form what Mike Davis (1998) calls an "ecology of fear." The prison plays a paradoxical but central role in this new spatial and political order. On the one hand, prisons provide a plausible promise of security against the risk of crime by concentrating "high-risk" subjects in a series of depots or dumps. On the other hand, prisons appear as little more than an incubator for criminal risk. In this sense, they are the ultimate bad neighborhoods, a space that, notwithstanding its walls and bars, routinely releases hundreds of thousands of prisoners into the larger space of society.

Prisons provide a public good that is directly aimed at insecurity, the form of public need that crime legislation has made both visible and compelling. More important, it does so in a way that does not raise the problems that have delegitimated the social programs of the New Deal that channeled benefits to preferred constituencies or special interests. The prison, conceived as a means of isolating and incapacitating the dangerous (and as perhaps deterring would-be criminals), provides a public good and benefit that works (if it works at all) for everyone equally, or at least in proportion to how they are actually exposed to crime risks. Each prison cell built by the state adds to the capacity of the state to provide this public good in a way that is beyond any "program failure" of the sort that haunted the projects of the New Deal, such as public housing, school desegregation, and so on. Not surprisingly, California governors in the 1980s and 1990s embraced prison construction with an enthusiasm matched by few other states (Schrag 1998, 94). The California legislature made sure it would stay in need of more by enacting more than 400 pieces of legislation increasing criminal penalties.

The logic of imprisonment in the post–New Deal order was aptly captured by California governor George Deukmejian. A conservative legislator from the central valley town of Fresno, Deukmejian first came to statewide fame when he led the fight in the legislature to draft a new death penalty law. That statute was struck down by the California Supreme Court in 1976.[7] Deukmejian ran for governor in the same 1982 election cycle in which a popular initiative to restore the death penalty by amending the state constitution was adopted. In Deukmejian's two terms, he initiated the huge increase in prison construction that has made mass imprisonment possible in California (notwithstanding the fact that epic overcrowding remains a problem).

In his State of the State speech in January 1990, at the start of his final year after two terms in office (the constitutional maximum permitted), Governor Deukmejian indicated the place that imprisonment would have in the new political order of California. In his very first comments on his government's priorities, before he addressed anything about the environment, AIDS, or homelessness, all of which had been major California issues in his terms, Deukmejian spoke of what he saw as the pride of his governorship:

> In 1983, California had just 12 state prisons to house dangerous criminals. Since then, we have built 14 new prison facilities. That has enabled us to remove an additional 52,000 convicted felons from neighborhoods to send them to state prison.[8]

This logic has helped make growing the prison population a positive project of state legitimacy in its own right, quite apart for any positive effect on crime rates. The absolute size of the prison population was not particularly important in earlier periods. The value of the prison to the production of political authority and order was tied to its symbolic message, the prestige of the techniques it demonstrated, or the opportunities for patronage that building and maintaining prisons created. Sometimes growth advanced these interests, but as we have seen, in each regime, important institutional checks and limits to prison growth also existed. In contrast, for each of the past regimes, the form and substance of imprisonment played an important part in the contribution that prisons made to governability.

Locked In: Why Mass Imprisonment Escapes the Policy Dilemma

The first wave of scholars to study the Safe Streets Act of 1968 in operation were skeptical about the effectiveness or innovativeness of the law. Sociolegal scholars Malcolm Feeley and Austin Sarat (1980) interviewed frontline bureaucrats at all levels of government and the criminal justice system to see how deeply the act had penetrated the tissue of American criminal justice a decade after its passage. They concluded that the act had largely failed to generate substantial change in practices because its vague mandates of planning and innovation were never tied to substantive proposals on how to repress crime more effectively than did current practice. Instead, they found the triumph of process, a world where expertise was devoted not to solving the problems but complying with procedures. In this regard, Feeley and Sarat saw the Safe Streets Act of 1968 as ultimately a product of the same larger paradigm of the New Deal welfare state and subject to its primary pathology, which they dubbed "the policy dilemma." Law has a tendency to define its task as solving social problems that, because they are deeply embedded in variable social circumstances, are largely unsolvable with the tools of government. Thus, such laws as the Safe Streets Act only place government in a position to fail repeatedly (Feeley and Sarat 1980).

It makes perfect sense that Feeley and Sarat would view the Safe Streets Act as another variation on New Deal governance, with security from crime as the public good to be distributed by yet another welfare program. But if the argument of the last several chapters is followed, the Safe Streets Act was not just another New Deal variation, but in fact was the first legislative fruit of a reordering of government around the problem of crime. If Feeley and Sarat were correct that the policy dilemma they describe is a structural failure of the New Deal order, it would not be surprising if a hallmark of the new crime-centered model of governing would be precisely its freedom from this dilemma.

In this light, we can see mass imprisonment not as a social strategy to reconfigure the domination of African Americans or discipline the margins of the labor force to support the increasing demands for exploitation of the neoliberal economic order, although it may well have these effects, but as a policy solution to the political dilemmas of governing through crime. Mass imprisonment allows the political order to address its most vulnerable problem, crime, with a solution that is solvable precisely at the process level where Feeley and Sarat (1980) and many political scientists before and since have thought government was pretty successful.

Mass imprisonment is a stable solution to the highly competitive political logic established by governing through crime. As the following examples will suggest, executives (especially governors and presidents), lawmakers, and courts attempting to play to their strengths in the era of governing through crime must embrace mass imprisonment.

Executive Decisions: Life Means Life

Here is a sobering thought for those who believe that restoring more indeterminacy to American sentencing law might reduce mass imprisonment—the only real limitation on how much governors will do to keep prisons

Governors have the power + (handwritten margin note)

full is how much they *can* do. In California, the governor exercises the power (installed there by citizen initiative) to review specific decisions of the parole authority in the case of prisoners serving an indeterminate life sentence (which today includes persons convicted of second-degree murder and third-strike offenses). Governors in such states can wield a unique power to hold a person in prison indefinitely even when the Board of Prison Terms, filled with the governor's appointees, recommends parole.

During the period of mass imprisonment in California, parole rates dwindled to 5 percent of eligible prisoners under Governor Deukmejian (1983–1991), to 1 percent under Governor Wilson (1991–1999), and to an effective parole rate of 0 percent under Governor Gray Davis, who served until he was recalled in 2003, shortly after winning election to a second term (Moran 2000).

A lifelong Democrat with liberal positions on major social issues (gay rights, abortion, and so on), Davis had a long-established tough-on-crime posture on the death penalty and prisons. He became, with his election in 1998, the first Democrat to capture the statehouse in some twenty years. His victory over Republican Attorney General Dan Lungren was largely credited to being closer to California's center on social issues such as abortion, but Lungren might have won anyway had he succeeded in making crime policy the issue that it was for Deukmejian or Wilson. The difference was that Davis made clear from the start of the campaign that he would not be outflanked when it came to being tough on crime. During a debate he framed his perspective on crime policy by stating: "Singapore is a good starting point, in terms of law and order" (quoted in Downey 1998, A3). Singapore has been discussed in the United States most recently in terms of its harsh punishments, including the frequent use of caning for public order offenses and the death penalty for crimes such as drug trafficking. Davis explained his reference in similar terms.

Idea of Parole decreasing ↓ Increase on power on death penalty (handwritten margin note)

> I'm trying to let people know that I'm not going to tolerate violent crime. I believe strongly in the death penalty. I put it in all my ads. . . .
>
> I think Singapore has very clear rules. . . . They don't fool around and they have very little violent crime. And if you don't like it, you can get on a plane and go somewhere else. (quoted in Downey 1998, A3)

In his public statements on parole for people serving life terms for second-degree murder, Davis came closer than his conservative predecessors dared in acknowledging that he will not parole any killers, even those whom the law explicitly anticipates parole for. His appointees to the Board of Prison Terms found no prisoner sufficient to warrant parole with one exception that was produced by a court order threatening them with contempt if they failed to recommend parole. Even in that case, the governor used his power to reject parole.[9] As one of Davis's aides described his vision of the parole power: "He's deadly serious about stopping crime, and he also takes into account the impact that the crime has had on the victims and the victims' families" (Sams 2000, A1).

The terms seem to self-consciously invoke the death penalty (you'll die here, life for a life). Victims and their families are identified as crucial stakeholders along with the general public as the intended beneficiaries of Davis's "deadly serious" attitude. Against these interests, the rehabilitative progress made by the prisoner, made difficult by warehouse-oriented prisons, is readily outweighed by the interests of victims in not having their special fears intensified by the release of the person who killed their loved one (fears that are unlikely to be salved by the mitigating circumstances that led to a conviction for a lesser homicide offense or the progress the prisoner has made in prison). To the side of continued imprisonment is also weighed the risk that others might be injured in the future by the same person, whose capacity for lethal violence has already been demonstrated. However small that risk may be, it becomes almost infinitely large when compared not simply against the victim family but against the generalized California population.

The policy of denying any real consideration of parole to prisoners serving life terms for noncapital murder and potentially other crimes places the governor on the side of victims and potential victims and against courts, which have given life with parole sentences; legislatures, which have permitted them; and even prosecutors, who may have chosen not to lobby for parole denial. This kind of conflict is politically beneficial to governors.

The logic of this new kind of gubernatorial sentencing is well illustrated by a case in which Davis' zero-parole policy was tested and ultimately upheld by the California courts.[10] On the night of his high school graduation party, Robert Rosenkrantz was outed as gay by his younger brother and one of the brother's friends, Steven Redman. The circumstances of the outing were severe. The brother and friend burst into a beach house where Rosenkrantz and his friends were staying and screamed the word "faggot." In a fight that followed, Rosenkrantz had his nose broken. The brother then reported his discovery to Rosenkrantz's parents, who responded by throwing Rosenkrantz out of the family's house. Rosenkrantz asked his brother and Redman to retract their story and tell his parents that it had all been a joke. The brother agreed, but Redman refused. Enraged, Rosenkrantz acquired an Uzi, practiced at a range, and later confronted Redman with the weapon, demanding that he retract the story. Redman laughed in Rosenkrantz's face and again called him a "faggot." Rosenkrantz then shot Redman 10 times and drove off.

Rosenkrantz Case.   Rosenkrantz was charged with first-degree murder because of the premeditated quality of the act. The jury rejected that theory, convicting him instead of second-degree murder with a sentence of 15 years to life plus two years on a separate charge of using a weapon. Rosenkrantz came close to receiving a recommendation to the governor for parole on his first hearing after achieving his minimum eligibility. A panel of three commissioners of the Board of Prison Terms recommended Rosenkrantz be paroled, finding expressly that he "would not pose an unreasonable risk or danger to society." The panel noted a number of features of Rosenkrantz himself, his crime, and his prison life. Rosenkrantz had no juvenile record and had been accepted into a college at the time of the crime. In prison, he had used self-help and therapy programs and had reached an understanding of why he reacted so violently in the instant offense. The panel noted that he "committed the crime as a result of significant stress in his life and because of his homosexual tendencies which he had attempted to conceal from his family, friends and community."[11] A Decision Review Unit of the board reviewed the parole recommendation and reversed it, apparently disturbed by Rosenkrantz's seeming minimalization of his crime in referring to the incident the night of his graduation as an "attack" on him.[12]

In subsequent hearings before panels of the Board of Prison Terms, Rosenkrantz's case was bolstered by support from the sheriff who had arrested him, the district attorney who had prosecuted him, and correctional officers in the prisons where he had served time. But notwithstanding the improved posture of his parole file, subsequent panels of the Board of Prison terms has with increasing intensity rejected Rosenkrantz as unsuitable for parole. The rationale for this judgment came to be narrowed to a single factor. Because of its premeditated quality—buying the gun, training, confronting the victim—the crime was one that suggested "a callous disregard for the life and suffering of another."[13] In short, the board rejected the jury's decision that the murder was second- rather than first-degree murder.

In 1999, a California trial court granted Rosenkrantz's habeas corpus petition and ordered the Board of Prison Terms to set a parole date "commensurate with Rosenkrantz's conviction of second degree murder." After a protracted legal battle, the board held a hearing in which it found that Rosenkrantz was unsuitable for parole, repeating its previous rationale, but setting a parole date nonetheless. Governor Davis invoked his authority to reverse the board's decision granting parole.[14] The governor's statement of reasons noted that the board's decision was based solely on the court order. A further trip to court followed, and in April of 2000 the Court of Appeals sent the case back to the board one more time for a new suitability hearing "and to render a new determination in strict accordance with both the letter and spirit of the views expressed in this opinion."[15] The court noted that unless new information not previously present in the record should be presented, it would be incumbent on the board to set a parole date commensurate with a second-degree murder conviction. The court refused to actually order a date for Rosenkrantz's release. Instead it left that to the board's discretion, but with the following remarkable caution from the judiciary to the executive branch:

> At some point, a failure to follow the law, or the continued application of an arbitrary and irrational standard, will rise to the level of a substantive due process violation. . . . It is at that point (if at all) that the enforcement issue will be decided. In the meantime, however, we flatly reject the Board's contention that (a) Rosenkrantz's only remedy is the continuing charade of meaningless hearings, and (b) that the superior court lacks the power to compel the Board to follow the law.[16]

This extraordinary battle over the scope of the governor's constitutional power expresses a number of themes central to the governor as prosecutor. First, in their focus on Rosenkrantz's crime, the actions of the board and of the governor reflect a will to achieve a prosecutorial goal, the conviction of

Rosenkrantz for first-degree murder, which a jury denied to the original prosecution and which is therefore legally beyond the reach of any future action of ordinary prosecution. Second, in rejecting even the residual elements of correctionalism left in the California system after the shift to determinate sentencing in 1977, the board and the governor are removing precisely those parts that authorize a state interest in the reintegration of prisoners into society. Moreover, they are doing so in a constitutionally extraordinary way that in effect replaces the legislature's claim to represent the people of California with a special executive mandate. Thus the governor as prosecutor introduces himself as a new model of law, one focused on command and control without appeal. Third, in embracing the prison as a permanent exclusion for those convicted of homicides, the governor's policy embraces exile or death as the only satisfactory response of the state to lethal violence.

Gray Davis may represent an extreme interpretation of executive power on crime, but it is one that resonates with the approach of many other contemporary executives who have also sought to identify themselves with prosecutorial fervor and loyalty to victims by rejecting any power role of neutral judgment or individualized assessment with respect to violent crime (and perhaps all crime). Mass imprisonment is the only sure policy for such governors to adhere to.

Zero Tolerance: Lawmaking Without Pity

One might pick any number of laws to reflect on the legislative investment in mass imprisonment. As political scientist Naomi Murakawa (2005) has found, the biannual cycle of congressional elections produced a regular escalation of punitive federal statutes throughout the 1980s and 1990s. From the original Safe Streets Act of 1968, Congress shaped a crime legislation model that emphasized loyalty to victims (symbolically expressed in support for the police) and increased monitoring of criminal justice activity itself. These twin imperatives that have been reproduced repeatedly by federal and state legislation both tend toward mass imprisonment. In a competition for demonstrating loyalty to victims as an abstract and generalizable public, prison will always prevail (unless capital punishment is a possibility) because only prison provides the illusion of total security for the victim and complete deprivation for the offender. Any kind of supervised release is a compromise on both and is seen as such by victims and their political advocates (Kahan 1996).

The parallel demand to make visible the activity of criminal justice agencies and the implied distrust of discretion within the criminal justice system (other than in the hands of prosecutors) also leads to mass imprisonment. There is an old law school game that pits "rules" against "standards." You can always show that establishing a rigid rule will leave lots of individuals with an outcome that seems normatively unjust, whereas leaving a broad standard will place great power with decision makers (police officers, inspectors, judges). The heightened political cost of discretion means that decision makers themselves will opt for rules over standards, if only to protect themselves against charges of making the wrong judgment. In the business of criminal sentencing, these imperatives will lead to rules that favor incarceration and readily determinable criteria for the application of incarceration.

These are the incentives that lawmakers have themselves set up for administrators and courts who must implement crime legislation (Stuntz 2006). Mostly they can then allow those incentives to produce and sustain the mass imprisonment we have seen take shape across the 1980s and 1990s, until the next election cycle calls for a ratcheting up of some dimension. But something of the tightness of this logic and its powerful resistance to change was showcased in 2003 when Congress enacted legislation calling for tighter restraint by federal judges in the use of downward departures from the sentences determined by the federal sentencing guidelines.

The background of the Feeney Amendment and the controversy that followed goes back to the U.S. Sentencing Guidelines, which established a new regime of federal sentencing for all cases commenced after January 1, 1987 (see the discussion in chapter 4). Until that date, federal prisoners were sentenced within the very broad statutory maximum and minimum sentences established by Congress for specific crimes at the discretion of a federal district judge acting with a detailed case history prepared by a federal probation officer. If sent to prison, a federal prisoner would have an actual release date set by the Federal Parole Commission. After that date, federal prisoners faced sentencing under a narrow range of months in prison or probation based on the seriousness of the current offense and the prisoner's past criminal record. The new sentencing guidelines did not replace the statutory maximum and minimum sentences that Congress had established over the years when establishing various crimes, but they purported to establish a range from which trial judges were to depart only under specific and extraordinary circumstances.

Until 2004, when the Supreme Court held that the guidelines were not at all binding on federal judges, the general perception of the guidelines (including that of federal judges themselves) was that they had removed virtually all of the judges' discretion in sentencing; some judges found this situation especially galling in drug cases in which defendants with relatively small roles faced very long prison sentences if the quantities of drugs were high enough. In 1996, however, in the case of *United States v. Koons*, the Supreme Court held that district courts retained discretion in sentencing to consider factors not explicitly disapproved by the Sentencing Commission (originally established by the Sentencing Reform Act of 1984 and charged with setting up and maintaining the guidelines). This limited affirmation of discretion did little to affect federal judges' view that they were highly restricted by the guidelines; downward departures were possible only in extraordinary cases and even then under the threat of appellate review.

It was in this context that in 2003, the Feeney Amendment set off a rare riff between the federal courts and Congress. Representative Tom Feeney of Florida offered his amendment primarily out of concern for one of Congress's favorite governing-through-crime topics, child pornography. To a package of measures creating new crimes and enhancing penalties for others, Feeney proposed a set of measures expressly aimed at reducing the number of downward departures in federal criminal sentences. Feeney claimed this was particularly a problem in child pornography cases, but the amendment applied to all criminal cases. The proposal drew a broad response from judges, including Chief Justice Rehnquist, who criticized Congress for seeking to pressure a coequal branch. But Congress ultimately passed a strongly confrontational measure anyway with a title intended to highlight Congress's fidelity to victims: the Prosecutorial Remedies and Other Tools to End the Exploitation of Children Today (PROTECT) Act.[17]

The PROTECT Act included a strong narrative denunciation of judges who were hostile to the guidelines and depicted them as looking for opportunities to depart from it. The law sought to limit such departures both by direct action on the sentencing practices of judges and by indirect action through the Sentencing Commission. The law required federal judges to provide written reasons for any downward departure, and it required district courts to set up systems for gathering and relaying specific documentation about such departures to the Sentencing Commission within 30 days of a final judgment. The law reset the standard of review in cases of departure to allow appellate courts to consider the case with virtually no deference to the sentencing court, a standard known as "de novo." It required the commission to make reports on departures available at Congress's request and to develop guidelines to diminish the frequency of downward departures; it also forbade the commission from recognizing any new grounds for permissible downward departures for three years. The law even reduced the number of federal judges on the Sentencing Commission itself for the first time to a minority.

As Professor Marc Miller has commented, the Feeney Amendment was noteworthy as much for what it revealed about Congress's feelings about the performance of the sentencing guidelines as anything else:

> The Feeney Amendment showed true anger towards the system as a whole, and especially the departure function, and revealed frustration with every major actor in the federal sentencing system, including the Department of Justice, or at least with line prosecutors. It might be extraordinary for many observers to believe that Congress could find the tough federal sentences under the guidelines to be too moderate, but that appears to be one of themes of the provisions as well. (Miller 2004, 1248)

There was virtually no debate about why departures might be sought and when they might be appropriately granted. The fact that nearly a third of all criminal sentences decided in 2001 departed from the guidelines, almost all of them downward, might mean that these guideline sentences are too harsh for the federal judiciary (many of them appointed by Republican presidents) or that law enforcement itself requires the assistance of accomplices to convict other criminals (and indeed this is a primary purpose of harsh sentences in their view). As Miller points out, both parties in Congress were angry at the very idea of departure and distrustful of all the agencies involved (including the Department of Justice, but only insofar as it was not prosecutorial enough). But the point for us is not to note the major failures in Congress's logic as a matter of crime reduction policy but to note in this extraordinary moment of interbranch public discourse how intense and how bipartisan was Congress's embrace of the twin imperatives of crime legislation (do not do anything to improve the fate of criminals, for this hurts victims; and make the process of criminal justice more visible and accountable to public reaction).

The Supreme Court's 2004 decision in *United States v. Booker* throws into doubt any practical implications of the Feeney Amendment. In the short run, the Supreme Court appears to have freed district courts to depart from the guidelines even more, but the long-run possibility exists that Congress will act again to establish a harsher regime of sentences that meet the constitutional objection (and the issue in *Booker* was not the severity of punishment). What the PROTECT Act and its Feeney Amendment suggest is that for the foreseeable future, Congress in the hands of either major political party is unlikely to permit any backing down from mass imprisonment and views its own primary (and imminently achievable) goal as policing the performance of other government agencies (that, again, is part of the legacy of the Safe Streets Act of 1968). In a revealing picture of interbranch relations with the executive branch, PROTECT even castigated the prosecution for failure to vigorously enough contest the downward departures.

Judgment of Intolerable Risk

Perhaps a look at the judiciary is not necessary to complete our case that mass imprisonment, whatever its social effects, remains a robust solution to the political problem of governing through crime, which can be dislodged only by dislodging governing through crime itself. The judiciary in an era of crime is on the defensive and anxious to demonstrate that it is not a source of criminal risk to victims. Few could expect an important blow to mass imprisonment to come from the Supreme Court of the United States. But if for no reason other than constitutional habit, Americans have litigated mass imprisonment before the Supreme Court, and the most recent decision provides in its own terms a reiteration of the themes of governing through crime that provides a helpful summary and another measure of the grip of crime on our political imagination. This is all the more true when we read this seemingly split 5-to-4 decision as hiding a deep underlying consensus that the Constitution sets only the most marginal limits on the power of democratic state governments to exact imprisonment.

Ewing v. California (2003) upheld a 25-years-to-life sentence (with no parole consideration for 25 years) for a man with two previous convictions who was convicted of grand theft for stealthily leaving a golf club pro shop with three golf clubs worth about $400 each. In California, grand theft is a property crime that can be either a felony or a misdemeanor, but the judge chose to treat it as a felony in Ewing's case. Combined with two earlier burglaries (classified as strikes under the California three-strikes law, which counts "serious or violent" felonies as strikes), the grand theft conviction made Ewing eligible for sentencing under the third-strike provision, which provides for a sentence of at least 25 years before possible consideration of parole.

Ewing claimed that this sentence violated the "cruel and unusual punishment" clause of the Constitution's Eighth Amendment, which past Supreme Court precedent describes as having a proportionality principal. Five justices agreed that Ewing's sentence was constitutional. Two of them, Justices Scalia and Thomas, would have held that the Eighth Amendment contains no proportionality principal at all. The three others, O'Connor, Kennedy, and Rehnquist, held that although a proportionality principal may exist and might apply to some theoretical prison sentence, Ewing's sentence of 25 years to life did not amount to a constitutionally disproportionate one.

Justice O'Connor's opinion places the political context of the three-strikes law front and center.

> Polly Klaas' murder galvanized support for the three strikes initiative. Within days, Proposition 184 was on its way to becoming the fastest qualifying initiative in California history. On January 3, 1994, the sponsors of Assembly Bill 971 resubmitted an amended version of the bill that conformed to Proposition 184. On January 31, 1994, Assembly Bill 971 passed the Assembly by a 63 to 9 margin. The Senate passed it by a 29 to 7 margin on March 3, 1994. Governor Pete Wilson signed the bill into law on March 7, 1994. California voters approved Proposition 184 by a margin of 72 to 28 percent on November 8, 1994. (*Ewing v. California*, 14)

From this political framework, the plurality opinion goes on to identify a set of frameworks that establish the constitutionality of mass imprisonment. The first element of this analysis is the Court's recognition of the waste management prison, one focused primarily on incapacitation and secondarily on deterrence, but aimed at reducing crime in the community outside the prison. There is, according to the Court, no constitutionally required penology; instead, each state is free to determine what it expects the prison to achieve (*Ewing v. California*, 25). Reading the history of the three-strikes law, the plurality found a major shift in penology toward something very much like our waste management model. Yet having marked its distinctive qualities, the justices suggested that it belongs in the long history of state penological choices to which the Court has traditionally deferred:

> Throughout the States, legislatures enacting three strikes laws made a deliberate policy choice that individuals who have repeatedly engaged in serious or violent criminal behavior, and whose conduct has not been deterred by more conventional approaches to punishment, must be isolated from society in order to protect the public safety. Though three strikes laws may be relatively new, our tradition of deferring to state legislatures in making and implementing such important policy decisions is longstanding. (*Ewing v. California*, 25)

Precisely because three-strikes laws evidence a new penal mentality not rooted in traditions of democratic penal government (as both retribution and rehabilitation in their own ways may claim to be), it might be appropriate to question whether the same deference is due. Indeed, our analysis of executive and legislative styles of governing through crime would suggest that many of the traditional checks and balances have been eliminated by governing through crime (a conclusion shared by scholars using more conventional public choice analysis; see Stuntz 2001, 2006).

Having promised that it would defer to the state's own definition of what is a rational approach to punishment, the Court nonetheless comes back in to assure us that "California's justification is no pretext":

> Recidivism is a serious public safety concern in California and throughout the Nation. According to a recent report, approximately 67 percent of former inmates released from state prisons were charged with at least one "serious" new crime within three years of their release. (*Ewing v. California*, 26)

The Court, again over its own insistence that it is deferring to the state's judgment, summarized a study conducted by a newspaper of three-strikes offenders, which appeared to show that most such offenders had long records of serious crime.

If the incapacitation argument were not enough, although the plurality seems to believe it is, the opinion also recognizes the possibility that the law makes sense as a deterrent. The Court cites California Department of Justice data showing a drop in recidivism after the three-strikes law was passed. And even "more dramatically":

> An unintended but positive consequence of "Three Strikes" has been the impact on parolees leaving the state. More California parolees are now leaving the state than parolees from other jurisdictions entering California. This striking turnaround started in 1994. It was the first time more parolees left the state than entered since 1976. This trend has continued and in 1997 more than 1,000 net parolees left California. (27, quoting a report of the California attorney general)

The Court did note that other empirical evidence contradicted those findings (citing among other things, Zimring, Hawkins, & Kamin 2001), but politely demurred from deciding such controversies.

Before rushing on to the unsurprising conclusion that Ewing's sentence was not disproportionate, we would do well to step back to see the state of governing through crime reflected in the *Ewing* picture of the three-strikes law. Fueled by populist anger over the kidnapping and murder of a little girl by a man who could not have been free to commit the crime had he received an enhanced sentence sometime earlier in his criminal history, California amended its constitution to allow prosecutors to send anyone guilty of two serious felonies to prison for the rest of their life if they commit another felony of any kind (even one that in other cases is classified a misdemeanor). The legislature and the governor abandoned their own reform plans and adopted the harsh approach of the ballot initiative. This law constituted a fundamental shift in the theory of punishment at work in California prisons to a major emphasis on incapacitating repeat offenders to produce a possible return in security to California's law-abiding populace. It is also noteworthy that on the way to finding this new penology constitutionally adequate, the Court turned repeatedly to evidence for the effectiveness of this strategy that came directly from the existing system of mass imprisonment and had virtually no direct relevance to Ewing himself, who was never treated as an individual case by the Court.

Perhaps I am making too much of the holding in *Ewing*, which was, after all, 5–4 (and O'Connor's opinion was only for three justices). But our main interest here is not with the holding of whether Ewing's case presents

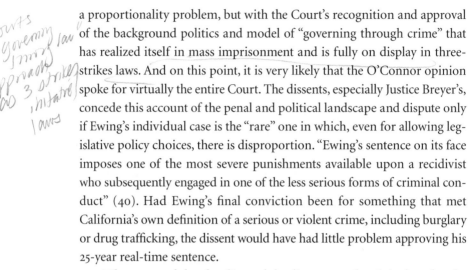

a proportionality problem, but with the Court's recognition and approval of the background politics and model of "governing through crime" that has realized itself in mass imprisonment and is fully on display in three-strikes laws. And on this point, it is very likely that the O'Connor opinion spoke for virtually the entire Court. The dissents, especially Justice Breyer's, concede this account of the penal and political landscape and dispute only if Ewing's individual case is the "rare" one in which, even for allowing legislative policy choices, there is disproportion. "Ewing's sentence on its face imposes one of the most severe punishments available upon a recidivist who subsequently engaged in one of the less serious forms of criminal conduct" (40). Had Ewing's final conviction been for something that met California's own definition of a serious or violent crime, including burglary or drug trafficking, the dissent would have had little problem approving his 25-year real-time sentence.

When we read the plurality and the dissent together, it is clear that the system of mass imprisonment does not pose a constitutional problem, at least not an Eighth Amendment problem (it's hard to see right now what alternatives there might be). The vast majority of prisoners would find no relief in court even had the dissent picked up an additional vote to become a 5-to-4 majority.

Technologies of Exile: Detention, Expulsion, and Dismissal

It is worth considering whether the prison and its close analogues, such as immigration detention, should be seen as the hard end of a continuum of technologies for addressing threatening persons and behaviors by removing them from the community more or less permanently. There is in fact evidence that in a variety of analogues, we can discern a parallel rise in what we might call "technologies of exile." Not all these practices involve confinement; some shut out, and others shut in. Three in particular are almost certainly on the rise: school detentions, suspensions, and expulsions; employee dismissals; and gated communities.

We can observe the power of the waste management prison as a model for governing in the parallel rise in recent decades of sanctions aimed at removing from schools or workplaces individuals who have violated the rules of the institutions. Families themselves engage in a kind of inverse function in the pursuit of controlled residential and recreation settings in which family members are protected against encounters with strangers who might pose some risk. The gated community is in its own way a kind of reverse waste management prison. Whereas the latter is designed to keep dangerous people in, the former is designed to keep them out. Something similar has happened with the abandonment of streets, parks, and public libraries as the after-school venue for older school-age children. Instead, for middle-class or upper-class families with the resources to address these concerns, managed recreation has come to be perceived as essential to responsible parenting.

Schools were once seen as institutions of normalization—"normal" schools were where teachers went to learn how to be teachers—and thus shared an orientation toward rehabilitation of which the correctional institution was hoped to be at least a faint echo. When students act in ways that violate the rights and raise the risks of others, schools have long responded with sanctions aimed both at protecting school order *and* at reintegrating the wrongdoer through corrective punishment. More serious misconduct, especially that taking place away from school, might warrant juvenile justice intervention, but schools took responsibility for enforcing their own normative order through rules of discipline. Expulsion and its more limited cousin, suspension, have long been the hard end of school disciplinary sanctions.

After a period during the 1960s when both the substantive reach and use of hard-end sanctions seemed to decline, recent decades have seen a swing back in the other direction, with more attention to school behavior, harsher sanctions, and greater readiness to bring juvenile justice system intervention for school-based misconduct. Because expulsion and suspension raise immediate problems of supervision of a minor, schools have increasingly relied on in-school detentions as a sanction that removes the student from the social and educational life of the school while maintaining the school's custody. Like expulsion, suspension, and the waste management prison, school detention is designed not to correct or normalize, but to remove the subject from the normal school population (Ferguson 2000). This is true not only of schools in communities already afflicted by high rates of crime and criminal justice system penetration. In a recent study of metropolitan schools, political scientists William Lyons and Julie Drew (2006) compared a central city and suburban school in the same part of Ohio. They were surprised by the density of security practices at both schools, including technologies of exile, notwithstanding the fact that the suburban students were overwhelmingly from white, middle-class families and that little crime or disorder existed in or around the school. In interviews with students, staff, and parents, the investigators found that many held a racialized view of the threat as associated with the inner-city school and saw harsh discipline as a way to reinforce the distance between the two.

There is no precise equivalent to the waste management prison in the workplace. Adults cannot readily be detained for violation of institutional rules. But something similar is going on in American workplaces. In the absence of strong unions or expectations of responsibility to the community, firings have become a favored response to conduct that violates rules or signals a heightened level of risk. In the 1960s—after decades of growing union strength, then just beginning its long slow decline, and the perception of an economy capable of reaching near full employment of existing workers—some labor experts referred to job termination as an outdated workplace sanction. Tellingly analogizing it to capital punishment, these observers expected firings to virtually disappear in favor of corrective and even therapeutic responses. Today, dismissals are rising.

The decline of unions, and a generally soft market for unskilled labor, has no doubt made it easier to exercise the power to dismiss. But it is hard to show that profit in some generic sense drives the inclination to dismiss, which can generate costs as well as savings. Instead, as with the family and the school, managers of workplaces increasingly understand their responsibilities to include early identification and removal of subjects who violate rules and/or pose risks to other members of the organization. We can say that in each of these settings, part of the concept of "governing well" for those charged with institutional leadership is to practice crime prevention through the prophylactic exclusion of rule breakers and other risk makers.

Conclusion: The Limits of Project Exile

Though governments have found considerable political advantage through investing in waste management prisons, and analogous techniques of exclusion and exile are spreading, there is a danger that their security-conscious publics will question this arrangement. There is increasing public discussion of the criminogenic effects of prisons that send back into society inmates who not only are not rehabilitated but who have been made more dangerous or rendered dysfunctional by imprisonment. This is especially salient in the case of the celebrated super-max prisons that are sometimes touted as if their technology presented some major new protection to the public. However, the technological achievements of the super-max prisons are all aimed at protecting the staff and other inmates. There is no warrantee that this regime is well calculated to produce more docile ex-prisoners; quite the contrary, there is a growing body of evidence that suggests inmates held for prolonged periods in the near-total solitary confinement conditions of many super-max prisons are at risk for escalating behavioral abnormalities (Haney 2003).

The massive prison buildup conducted by states enamored of the populist style of rule poses a risk of delegitimizing the current political order. Just as the correctional institutions, welfare systems, and universities ultimately weakened the New Deal political order that invested so heavily in them, the post–New Deal order finds itself mass-producing subjects, namely prisoners and other internal exiles, that it can neither govern adequately nor eliminate permanently. This vulnerability is likely to emerge in the coming decade as the fiscal costs of an aging prison population and the economic losses of a heavily criminalized underclass both grow.

In families, schools, and workplaces all over America, costs incurred due to a lockdown, life-trashing, exclusionary, exile strategy are becoming apparent. The imperatives for isolation plus supervision of children creates an increasingly untenable set of demands on parents who must arrange for the constant transportation of children to and from various sites of security or must earn incomes high enough to pay for someone else to take on that responsibility. The demand to rid schoolrooms and playgrounds of disruptive students is causing the growth of a security dimension to every aspect of schooling, a dimension ill suited if not downright antagonistic to educational goals. Likewise, the growth of a professionalized security apparatus within schools and the routines and practices of using them are diminishing the pedagogic role of the classroom teachers to little more than test preparation instructors. In the workplace, the strategy of firing people with little provocation, where it is practiced, erodes the role of solidarity and trust, and incentives increase for employees and other constituents to look at ways of gaining opportunistic advantage over others.

Crime Families | **6**

Governing Domestic Relations Through Crime

The dominant modern metaphors of the family usually cast it against the marketplace as a "haven in a heartless world" (Lasch 1977), although more recently sociologists have questioned the wisdom that the family is a less competitive space than the workplace (Hochschild 1997). Indeed, the family and the workplace have both become concentrated zones of concern about crime, and the responsibility for governing it. Families as we idealize them are crime free, bound by lawful and natural bonds of mutual protection. If the family is crime free by definition, it is not secure; in fact, it is the ideal space for crime to invade. Here are consumer goods galore. Here are women and young people vulnerable to abuse and sexual aggression. Here are family secrets stored on computer hard drives and in filing cabinets.

The role of crime in the governance of the family has virtually flipped in the last two generations. At one time, truly violent conduct by parents over children, or adult men over women and girls in the family, was largely immune from the force of the criminal law out of deference for what legal decision makers—legislators, judges, prosecutors, and police officers—articulated as the special needs of family governance (Seigel 1996). Today, the problem of crime, starting with violence but including many other kinds of acts, has extended the institutional and metaphoric force of the criminal law into families with a scope and intensity at least as great, if not greater, than that of the marketplace. The haven, with its implication of privacy and refuge, is now a zone in which potential responsibility for criminal action is even greater than in other social contexts.

177

Divorce law represents another striking reversal on the axis of crime. Before the era of "no-fault" divorce, divorce law mimicked criminal law with its claims of wrongdoing, adultery, abandonment, and cruelty. These rules had the clear intent to mobilize some of the stigmatizing and humiliating features of criminal prosecution to bear upon those violating marital norms, but with few real-world links between the drama of the divorce court and the force of police or prisons. Today, in contrast, the claims of abuse that emerge in divorce, especially disputes concerning the custody of children, amount to real crimes—e.g., drug use, sexual abuse, and domestic violence—that are taken quite seriously by the state (Kay 1987).

Even the intact family is treated as a locus of suspicions about crime that require other institutions interacting with the family to maintain surveillance and intervention. A whole panoply of helping professionals developed around the family in the nineteenth century, including doctors, social workers, and teachers, in the name of assuring eugenic, physical, and mental health in a process one leading history refers to as the "policing of families" (Donzelot 1979). Today, professionals involved in the servicing of families find themselves acting as extensions of the actual police and the criminal justice system for which police operate as the gatekeepers.

When we carefully examine how crime becomes a problem for us in the roles we occupy in the domestic household, as parents, spouses/partners, and children/other dependents, we see not simply a growing role for traditional criminal justice agencies over the family, but an intertwining of crime control and family governance responsibilities as well.

As a parent, I am mobilized by crime in a number of different but overlapping ways. Sometimes I am encouraged to fulfill my role as the front-line protector of my children and partner against criminal assault by being attentive to the whereabouts of sex offenders who live in my "community." Sometimes I am viewed as a potential criminal; as a man, a husband, and a father, I stand at some calculable risk of assaulting my wife and children. I may also function as an enabler to crime, allowing my kids to join gangs, tolerating their drug abuse, or permitting them to ignore school attendance laws.

In this regard, contemporary American adults, especially parents, find themselves under a moral and sometimes legal mandate to manage crime risks in their domestic domain. Not surprisingly, Americans have become major consumers of security technologies, expertise, and services. Institutions and organizations that address the family (e.g., schools, churches, medical providers, and insurers) also find these crime pathways becoming a larger part of their mandate; some of which will be discussed in other chapters. Increasingly, crime provides the framework by which oversight of the family is integrated into these other, noncrime-oriented institutions.

Crime Begins at Home

Story 1

Consider the real-life situation of Al and Pammy (not their real names), an upper-class couple with two young children. Pammy, who had moved to the United States to marry Al, was depressed and missed her family in South Africa a great deal. Sometimes she would drink too much, and at those times she and Al would fight. On one occasion, Pammy slapped Al and threw several dishes at him while the children were sitting some distance away, safe but in visual range. Al, uncertain of what to do and afraid that he might frighten the children if he tried to physically restrain Pammy, called 911. Although Pammy had calmed down by the time the police arrived, both Al and Pammy found themselves in a complex legal nightmare that they could do little to control.

First, the policy of the police in their urban county was to make an arrest whenever they have probable cause to believe that an assault has been committed in the home, even if the victim does not want the arrest to take place. The policy is gender neutral, and it did not matter that it was Pammy, not Al, who was acting out. Nor did it matter that no actual harm had been done. Violence is broadly defined to include reckless acts that could cause harm. Al and Pammy knew a lawyer who quickly arranged for Pammy to be released on bail, but under a policy designed to deter domestic violence, she had to spend a night in jail while the "victim," Al, was given a window of time to seek a legal restraining order, which he chose not to pursue.

The district attorney's office in this urban county has a no-drop policy for domestic violence, a policy designed to deal with the historic pattern of domestic violence victims dropping charges as part of the cycle of abuse. Using the police report, the prosecutor can win a conviction for domestic violence even when the victim spouse exercises his or her statutory privilege not to give testimony against the offending spouse. Under an evidentiary rule known as the "excited utterance doctrine," many courts allow police to testify to what they were initially told by the victim when they called 911 or when the police first showed up.

Due to careful work by Al and Pammy's lawyer, however, the district attorney agreed to drop charges in exchange for Pammy's completion of a program of treatment for batterers. If the program is completed, the charge of domestic violence is expunged from the record. The couple also agreed to a period of probation, during which a probation officer, specially trained in domestic violence work, would make frequent unannounced visits to their house at stressful times, such as before dinner and during breakfast.

With their private lawyer and considerable resources, Al and Pammy might have prevailed at trial, but there was substantial risk that she might have been convicted even without Al testifying against her. Had she been convicted in some states, she would face a mandatory jail term of at least five days even for a first offense, followed by probation and treatment. She would also have faced a growing number of civil disabilities, including loss of the right to own a firearm. More important for Pammy, who has lived in the United States for five years as a legal resident alien without naturalizing, harsh changes in immigration law in the 1990s define domestic violence as an "aggravated felony" that requires mandatory deportation, even for those with significant ties in this country, like a husband and young children, and detention until deportation can be affected.

The above scenario is not meant to suggest the typical case of domestic violence in America. One might just as well describe a case that ends in the murder of a woman who had sought police help on previous occasions (as did Nicole Brown Simpson) or even obtained a restraining order that was ignored by her obsessed attacker. In both kinds of cases, however, a growing set of criminal justice responses now dominate public response to the threat of violence between adults in families. Domestic violence has emerged over the last three decades as one of the clearest cases where a civil rights movement has turned to criminalization as a primary tool of social justice.

Today, feminist legal scholars who fought to get criminal justice agencies to take domestic violence seriously are now in the forefront of those questioning the process of criminalization. Elizabeth M. Schneider, a pioneering legal advocate for victims and scholar of legal doctrines and practices concerning domestic violence, recently noted with concern the growing role that criminal justice agencies play in defining the public agenda for domestic violence. In her view, this development puts "a greater emphasis on criminalization" than on objectives that feminists would rather emphasize in aiding domestic violence victims to recover and move on including "women's employment, childcare or welfare" (Schneider 2001, 244). Wife beatings and killings have become a political problem for the state at a number of times in our history. Each time, they served as a privileged location for the law to articulate a general model of family governance and to problematize the conduct of specific groups of people—from the late nineteenth century on, mainly working-class and African American men; Siegel 1996). But although crime was the occasion for legal transformation, the scholarship of legal historian Reva Siegel shows that the new ways of talking and acting on families produced by these controversies tended to renormalize family violence within an updated framework of family governance. To the extent the state offered any strategies to actually repress family violence, it was through the general aspiration to stabilize the conditions of the lower classes of industrial society, presumed to be the locus of any real problem. It was not crime, but degraded social practices and conditions, that needed addressing.

The leading authorities on the common law, especially the influential Blackstone, maintained that husbands had privilege and duty to "rule and chastise" wives in which moderate corporal punishment was no breach of law or civil duty. Violence for other purposes, or excessive violence constituting a danger of serious bodily harm or death, was not privileged and thus, strictly speaking, could not be a defense to charges of assault or manslaughter. By the last third of the nineteenth century, courts all over the United States took pains to emphasize that, whatever its former scope, the doctrine of chastisement was no longer operative. Henceforth, any assault that would constitute a crime if committed against a woman by a stranger would also constitute a crime if committed by her husband.[1]

Yet long after a formal legal immunity was abolished, a de facto regime of inattention through police and prosecutorial discretion remained a dominant fact of American domestic life through the 1980s. Siegel shows that spousal violence continued to be sheltered by courts under a new theory stressing the importance of privacy. In an oft-repeated formula, courts reasoned that the publicity and shame produced by a criminal trial would be more damaging to the prospects of the marriage's survival than the crime itself. The core idea here was that "family privacy" was an essential condition for the family's well-being and that legal intervention was inevitably destructive of it.

Today, in contrast, crime provides both the occasion for and logic of state intervention in the family. As in past periods of reform described by Siegel, the contemporary reconceptualization of the governmental interests at stake in domestic violence is oriented toward leaving the structural tensions within the gendered order of both the market and the family out of the picture. As a bus campaign in Ann Arbor, Michigan, during the late 1990s put it: "domestic violence is crime." What is needed, we are told today, is to recognize family crime as crime and treat it as such. The broader features of society that make women less able to use effective self-help against abusive partners, including the special responsibility women generally have for children, are cut off from these discussions altogether. Most forms of status inequality seem in danger of being reproduced in this new era of heavy criminalization (Mills 2003). Poor and minority people—the historically discriminated against—find themselves on the worst end of all the changes driven by governing through crime.[2]

The denial of equality to women in law enforcement practice and prosecution became unsustainable in an era in which victimization by crime was being defined as the most important feature of government's relationship to its subjects. By the 1970s and 1980s, the second-wave feminist strategy of using government's failed response to the victimization of women as a prime focus of mobilization fell exactly in line with attacks on the liberal welfare state coming from rights-oriented property owners. This cross-ideological alignment contributed to the conversion of crime control into a general schema of governance of the family (Burt & Estep 1981). During this period, second-wave feminists who criticized state policies of nonintervention in domestic violence cases as a central pillar of patriarchy in otherwise modern societies began to see a response in state-level changes in criminal law policies (Dobash & Dobash 1992; Daley 1994). The then-dominant approach of police departments and individual officers to treat domestic violence as crime only to the extent that it became a "public" disorder revealed a gendered government not captured by "unequal benefits" battles that had dominated first-wave feminism in the 1960s and 1970s. Here, government was not blindly adopting a male norm that disadvantaged women trying to be different by competing with men; here, government was consciously playing a part in maintaining the violent imposition of male dominance within the household in a way that endangered the lives of women attempting to maintain the "ordinary" functions of the family.

The legislative pathway to success for the feminist movement regarding battered women charts its independence from, but increasing integration with, the larger agenda of governing America through crime. The first public face of the movement in the 1970s emerged with the issue of shelters where battered women could seek refuge (Dobash & Dobash 1992, 36). The first federal legislative efforts to nationalize domestic violence was constructed as a welfare and health problem, and supposed to be lodged in the Department of Health, Education, and Welfare (later changed to Health and Human Services) (137). At a time the Republican Party was devoted to defeating the Equal Rights Amendment, these early efforts fizzled in the face of growing GOP resistance to anything that might seem to empower feminism.

Although hidden as an amendment to a bill on child abuse, the federal government in the 1980s began to promote and finance the spread of domestic violence issues and expertise. Signed by President Reagan as part of the Victims of Crime Act of 1984, the law provided about $8 million a year to be divided between victim service programs and police training programs (Dobash & Dobash 1992, 140).

Domestic Violence Policies

More than a quarter century after the first efforts to win funding for shelters and obtain recognition for domestic violence victims, the criminal justice system in most states now reflects a new consensus that domestic violence of any kind is a crime, and one best deterred by quick sanctions against the violator. Let us briefly review the complex of legal policies at work here.

Mandatory Arrest

More than a dozen states and many more municipalities have adopted policies mandating that police make an arrest when they have probable cause to believe that an act of domestic violence has occurred (Mills 1999). This new vision quickly led to successful lawsuits on behalf of women injured by their spouses after police had exercised their discretion *not* to make an arrest (Dobash & Dobash 1992, 198). Mandatory arrest policies have become popular with governors and state legislatures that would reject feminism in other respects. They permit legislators to vote with organized women's rights and feminist groups supporting a tough law enforcement approach that reflects a concern for victims as a group, even if it requires overriding the wishes of individual victims. Despite growing disputes among feminists themselves as to the costs and benefits of mandatory arrests, legislative support is almost universal. Laws recognizing the interests of same-sex couples would generally spark resistance from conservative legislators, but the crime focus allows even those legislators to support mandatory arrest laws.

Statutory Pressure on Prosecutors

These have followed from mandatory arrest policies in a way familiar in the spread of crime legislation generally (Ford & Regoli 1993). Once discretion in some government function is associated with leniency toward criminals and increased risks for victims, it becomes illegitimate at every level of that system. Prosecution policies are fewer and generally leave more discretion in the hands of prosecutors than do police policies. Indeed, a policy that stripped prosecutors of all discretion to charge might run afoul of the separation-of-powers doctrine (Hanna 1996). States have taken steps to encourage prosecution without directly requiring it, as, for example, in the following Florida statute:

> Each state attorney shall develop special units or assign prosecutors to specialize in the prosecution of domestic violence cases, but such specialization need not be an exclusive area of duty assignment. These prosecutors, specializing in domestic violence cases, and their support staff shall receive training in domestic violence issues.
>
> It is the intent of the Legislature that domestic violence be treated as a criminal act rather than a private matter. For that reason, criminal prosecution shall be the favored method of enforcing compliance with injunctions for protection against domestic violence as both length and severity of sentence for those found to have accountability of perpetrators. . . . The state attorney in each circuit shall adopt a pro-prosecution policy for acts of domestic violence, as defined in s. 741.28 and an intake policy and procedures coordinated with the clerk of court for violations of injunctions for protection against domestic violence. The filing, nonfiling, or diversion of criminal charges, and the prosecution of violations of injunctions for protection against domestic violence by the state attorney, shall be determined by these specialized prosecutors over the objection of the victim, if necessary.[3]

The Florida policy is both less and more than a mandatory prosecution policy. It clearly leaves prosecutors with discretion to file or not file charges, or to seek some diversion arrangement. The mention of the victim here is noteworthy. At face value, the provision clarifies the authority of the prosecutor to make a decision even if it goes against the wishes of the victim. This may seem to diminish the victim, and indeed it is controversial precisely on that ground. On the other hand, the prosecutor generally has a well-understood power (quite apart from this statute) to file whatever charges he or she deems appropriate and sustainable regardless of the victim's wishes. Thus, what makes this passage striking is that the law acknowledges the victim and apologetically frames the prosecutor's normal power as an extreme one of last resort.[4]

The law takes the hitherto unusual step of declaring as a matter of legislative "intent" that domestic violence be treated as a "criminal act." In fact this brings Florida into compliance with the grant requirements under the federal Violence Against Women Act. It also provides a striking example of the process described in chapter 3 of the legislature identifying itself directly with the aggrieved victim's demand for criminal justice. Crime legislation since the 1960s has systematically conflated victims as a class with the political community itself and the legislative body. Like the victims, the Florida legislature itself is limited in its ability to compel prosecutors to file charges, but its right to enter into the process rhetorically is now unchallenged.

One way to further this hardening of the crime approach the law adopts is to create a special interest group, within the prosecution function, oriented toward domestic violence and its victims. It is these "specialist" prosecutors, not any representative of the people, who are empowered to exercise discretion. A further unquoted section of the law requires the prosecutor to undertake a "thorough investigation of the defendant's history," and that information is to be made available to the court at the time of the defendant's first appearance. These steps assure that the inevitable discretion remaining with prosecutors and judges to not pursue criminal charges, or seek maximum custody over the defendant, will be made against a record that can be reviewed ex post, meaning that prosecutors and judges may later have to account for why they did not act.

Mandatory Incarceration

The latest wave of legislation regarding punishment of people convicted in domestic violence cases requires short but mandatory jail terms for first-time convictions. The idea of short but mandatory jail terms for offenses that have a long history of being taken less than seriously by the police and the public was popularized by the campaign throughout the 1970s to make drunk driving a serious crime. Some states now require first-time DUI offenders to spend a short time in jail. These programs also borrow from the popularity of boot camps and "shock probation" programs, with their promise of using a short but sharp penal shock to the system to provoke major individual transformation. All of these reflect the status of incarceration as a government solution for problems.

Domestic Violence Courts

Domestic violence charges are increasingly being heard in specialized courts created to deal with domestic violence exclusively. Advocates have promoted the idea that such courts allow considerable expertise to be built up among the judges and prosecutors assigned to them (Winnick 2000; Lederman & Brown 2000). Critics, generally in the defense bar, fear that such expertise and advocacy will compromise traditional values of fairness and neutrality in adjudication. The new courts tend to combine criminal and civil powers permitting them to issue protection orders and initiate criminal process. Based simply on a complaint from a self-defined victim, with no hearing or preliminary investigation, the domestic violence court can, and does, issue civil orders barring an alleged violator from returning to his or her home.

Children as Domestic Violence Victims

Children have also emerged as an important political subject of domestic violence (Coker 2001, 835). Since the mid-1990s, the federal government has sponsored both research into the implications of domestic violence for children and grants for programs aimed at addressing these effects. As a recent publication of the Department of Justice framed the issue:

> Throughout the United States, millions of children are exposed to violence—current estimates indicate that as many as 10 million children have witnessed or been victims of violence in their homes or communities. Children's exposure to violence has been significantly linked with increased depression, anxiety, anger, and alcohol and drug abuse and with decreased academic achievement. In addition, approximately 2 million adolescents ages 12–17 appear to have suffered from post traumatic stress disorder. (Kracke 2001a)

In a subsequent publication of the same agency, the question was framed as to how often domestic violence and "child maltreatment" go on concurrently. The research cited suggested that "these behaviors co-occur" in 30 percent to 60 percent of the families presenting with domestic violence (Kracke 2001b).

The focus on the link between domestic violence and child abuse exemplifies the way the problem of domestic violence is generalized into a broader schema relevant to the whole family.

First, the status of domestic violence as a serious crime of violence has been hardened by the way it is talked about, counted, and acted upon. Second, having established the unambiguous quality of domestic violence as crime requiring crime control solutions, that crime is shown to be a driving force behind a host of the most serious and intractable social problems afflicting our youth. Third, the victim base for that crime constellation is extended beyond the family to the community itself, marking the entire governable space of the social scheme as a grid of crime effects. This is marked by the active "collaboration" between the U.S. Department of Justice (and four of *its* numerous crime or victim-centered subagencies) with the U.S. Department of Health and Human Services (and four of *its* subagencies focused on children, families, and injury prevention). Fourth, federal responses to this "problem" take the form of research and programming integrated with political advocacy into a strategy that self-consciously blurs the line between program evaluation and program promotion, between responding to local demands for crime control and mobilizing them.

The battle over domestic violence began at the state level but became a national issue in 1994 when Congress adopted the Violence Against Women Act as part of its gargantuan 1994 Violent Crime Control and Law Enforcement Act (see discussion in chapter 3). The Violence Against Women Act was first introduced in 1990 by Senator Joseph Biden. Although it did not become law in its first year, it continued to build support through the explosive response to Anita Hill's accusations of sexual harassment against Clarence Thomas and by charges that O. J. Simpson had murdered his wife in a classic act of domestic violence. Though the Supreme Court struck down a small portion of the act in *United States v. Morrison*,[5] most of it has gone unchallenged, including portions enhancing penalties for repeat offenders and instructing the U.S. Sentencing Commission to remove disparities that provide lighter sentences for perpetrators intimate with the victim than for perpetrators who are strangers.

The law also introduced into federal law the term "survivor" to describe domestic violence victims, and created new grants for state and local programs aimed at combating domestic violence in the style of the funding provisions of the 1968 Omnibus Safe Streets and Crime Control Act (see chapter 3). Some grants specifically rewarded adoption of tough new policies such as mandatory arrest and no-drop prosecutions (Gleason 2001).

Feminist Critiques of Domestic Violence Policy

The emergence of domestic violence as a contemporary crime issue is in large part a result of the work of second-wave feminist activists and their allies in law and the social sciences, and may in fact represent one of the signal triumphs of that generation of feminism.

Since mandatory policies went into operation in the 1990s, a new wave of feminist criticism of this trend has developed that focuses on three issues. First, how effectively does a hardening of the criminal justice response to domestic violence protect women from repeat violence? Second, how does the investment of the domestic violence victim as a crime victim advance the equality of women as political subjects more generally? Third, does the construction of masculine domination as criminal violence alter the larger ecology of cultural support for that domination? I want to provide brief examples of these questions—not to suggest an answer (they are, after all, vastly complicated empirical and theoretical questions) but to place them in a dialogue with governing through crime more generally.

The question of whether more criminalization is actually reducing violence against women remains a prime one for advocates for victims of domestic violence (Mills 2003). The mistrust of the criminal justice system as a major part of the domestic violence problem remains strong even in the era of reform. Advocates have expected that strong laws will be ignored or even enforced against the women that they were intended to help (Pence & Shepard 1999, 7). Recent empirical research has also called into question the specific deterrent effects of arrest on batterers. This evidence suggests that arrest may even be counterproductive precisely in those communities of poverty and high unemployment where many of the most vulnerable victims are also situated (7). There is also a haunting fear that the women coerced into participating in the criminal justice process will find themselves with even less power over their lives than when the system ignored their batterer. This is particularly true for minority communities in which rates for arrests and incarceration of men and older boys are already high (Coker 2001).

Sociolegal scholars studying the domestic violence movement have long predicted that the movement's success at mobilizing state action through tougher criminal justice enforcement comes with a reciprocal involvement in dispersing and embedding criminal justice system values and tactics.

> Once encapsulated within the criminal justice system, reform movements must inevitably serve the needs of that system and potentially assist its expansion into more areas of civil society. The CJS [criminal justice system] may embrace the movement and yet subvert its demands, particularly within the law and or- der agenda, as a means of gaining greater resources and of widening the net of its response. (Dobash & Dobash 1992, 209)

The domestic violence victim has been embraced by the state and the political establishment, but on terms quite different from those that apply to crime victims more generally. The crime victims' rights movement has often been without much theory or even folklore to guide it in shaping a political agenda beyond the next execution or tough-on-crime ballot initia- tive (Scheingold, Olson, & Pershing 1994, 729). As a result, the movement has easily been dominated by prosecutors, correctional unions, politicians, and political consultants.

In contrast, the domestic violence victim has been shaped from the start by feminist ideas and feminist struggles. If crime victims have come to embody the governable interests of the people, domestic violence vic- tims embody those interests in ways that are capable of making visible the power and constraints of the victim logic itself.

One might expect the domestic violence victim to have become a prime focus of crime legislation, as an exemplary crime victim. In fact, the domestic violence victim remains very much in the shadow of more pop- ular competitors, particularly the victims of child abuse and child sexual assault. Both typically involve female children (adult women often face cultural presumptions of having consented). Unlike the child victim of abuse, the adult domestic violence victim is suspected of complicity. Un- like the adult or child victim of sexual assault, the degree of the domestic violence victim's harm remains more easily doubted. Unlike child abusers or rapists, the perpetrators of domestic violence are too broad a class of or- dinary males to easily mark off as moral monsters (Daly 1994a, 779).

Those categories of crime victims that have become the most politically successful are those who can most easily represent the outrage of neighbors against predatory strangers. Those who represent the ease with which good neighbors can become criminals are not politically attractive at all. Unlike the typical victims idealized in the media, the domestic violence victim has interests in incapacitation and deterrence, but she may also have interests in redeeming the criminal, with whom she may well have ongoing contact. Unlike that media victim, the domestic violence victim has a risk profile that does not fit into the zero-sum game in which harsh treatment of the offender can only help and in no way hurt or put at risk the victim.

The uncertain status of the domestic violence victim in the pantheon of crime victims is not the only problem for feminists. Many have raised the danger of the victim role itself for the work of effectively forcing change in the inequality of women within families (Brown 1995; Lamb 1996; Gavey 1999). Stressing the position of women as crime victims may endanger the sense of agency necessary for effective political mobilization.[6] By establishing the bar of women's victimization at the high level of assault, domestic violence policy and discourse may normalize forms of patriarchal oppression that fail to match the popularized image of criminal violence. Those who persist in raising these concerns are easier to marginalize as whiners and moralists. "Normal" abuse gets codified as legitimate by the criminalization of its aberrant cousin.

For present purposes, it is important to observe that domestic violence has become a potent grid of social meaning running through the heart of intact families, a grid that can be activated intentionally and unintentionally by different people in a family and that brings the power of criminal justice agencies into the household. Domestic violence is also a searing example of why governing through crime is not reducible to a set of political interests or ideologies. The feminists who drove the domestic violence movement had no ready, shared interest with more traditional advocates of law-and-order crackdowns, and yet their interaction has created a more potent and productive field of criminalization than existed before. Moreover, second-wave feminists who saw in domestic violence a deep truth of patriarchy that illuminated the role of the state and law in enforcing masculine oppression of women were not deceived. The efficacy that comes from making that truth public and demanding redress is an example of how governing through crime works as a spiral of knowledge and power that enables, empowers, and produces as much as it represses, incarcerates, and stigmatizes.

Child Custody Disputes

Story 2

John and Ariela are in a second marriage. John's first ended with no children. Ariela's first produced three daughters. When Ariela's first husband, Dan, left her, their three daughters were ages 5, 3, and 6 months. Dan agreed that full legal and physical custody of the girls would be with Ariela. After a recent remarriage, Dan got more interested in developing relationships with his daughters. He lived about 45 minutes from John and Ariela and began to have more frequent visits with the girls, with Ariela's support. The oldest daughter, then 10, went on a monthlong vacation with Dan and his family. Shortly after their return, Dan petitioned the court for full custody of all three girls. Dan claims that during their vacation, the oldest daughter accused John and Ariela of using drugs in the house and made other accusations indicative of emotional abuse. In response, Ariela accused Dan of having beaten her several times during their marriage. During an investigation by a state police agency known as Child Protective Services, all three children were removed from John and Ariela's home and placed in foster care. Following an investigation, the case was retained by the family court, which entered a new custody arrangement giving Dan joint legal custody and full physical custody for six months, during which John and Ariela agreed to enter drug treatment and submit drug tests to the court. During this period, they would have supervised visits. Child Protective Services officers would also make unannounced visits to Dan's home during this period to interview his wife and the children concerning any domestic violence.

Narrowing the Context

The story of John and Ariela is not necessarily typical of child custody disputes, but it illustrates a theme that comes up in a great many of them: the role of crime in child custody contests. Interestingly, the increasing role of crime claims in child custody disputes today echo the largely ritualistic narrative of moral wrongness embodied in the old system of fault-based divorce that began to disappear in the 1970s. Under the old fault system of divorce, five different issues were contestable in a typical middle-class divorce: (1) the basis of the divorce, (2) alimony, (3) child support, (4) property distribution, and (5) custody of the children, all of them in large part issues of matrimonial fault; in other words, determining which party to blame for the breakdown of the marriage (Kay 2002/2003, 6). The first of these, the grounds for divorce itself, were a primary subject of contestation. Until the spread of no-fault divorce laws beginning with California in the 1970s, this basic issue was fought out in family court but in terms directly modeled on criminal law.

Joan Shafro (2001), who examined New York cases from the 1950s through the 1970s, found that courts took fault grounds quite seriously and expected the party seeking divorce to prove that the accused party had committed a crimelike wrong against the marriage. The "extreme cruelty ground" was an especially critical pathway for "a divorce seeking wife in the 50s and 60s," and courts would not accept "any farce" but presumed that they had a legitimate preference for preserving marriage. Drug abuse by one spouse, for example, was not sufficient per se for divorce unless the spouse seeking the divorce demonstrated "significant detriment to the nonaddicted spouse" (83).

Today, after the no-fault divorce revolution, the motivations for conflict in situations of dissolution remain, but only two of the five issues are widely available for contest. The old battle about grounds for divorce has mostly been abolished. Potential conflict over property distribution and child support are circumvented by clear legal mandates. Alimony as a permanent payment for breach of the marital contract is gone, replaced by a period of spousal support based on equitable considerations and need. Only the last two, child custody and the issue of property distribution, particularly the family home and who will control it, remain highly contestable. In this narrower contest, crime has asserted itself as the primary domain in which feuding parents seek to distinguish themselves as moral beings.

The Perils of Mediation

One piece of data comes from the field of mediation in California. Virtually all divorcing couples with children find themselves in mediation unless some extreme feature of the case, including the criminal conduct of one or the other, precludes it for preventive purposes. It thus offers a fairly accurate picture of such families. In a snapshot study of families in mediation in California in 1996,[7] half (51 percent) of the mediation sessions studied involved accusations leveled at one or both partners concerning such crimes as "physical or sexual child abuse, child neglect or abduction, substance abuse, or domestic violence" (Center for Families, Children, and the Courts 1996, 6). In nearly a third of all such sessions, both parents made cross accusations of criminal behavior. In 1993 and 1996 surveys of mediation in California, the family court investigators reported conducting an investigation, which suggests the presence of a criminal accusation, in fully a quarter of the families in the snapshot sample (9).

If a claim of violence is brought up during mediation, mediators are required by law to notify police. Such agencies themselves take on a police-like role with trained investigators who typically interview the immediate parties, and likely witnesses including friends, relatives, and school employees. If investigators determine there is probable cause to believe abuse had occurred, they will often initiate an action before a special court charged with the care of dependent children. Courts in California and most states have the mandate to protect children, and the power to remove children from the homes of their parents and place them in foster care if necessary to assure that protection.

Claims that a former partner used drugs in the household when the children were present would be investigated by the family courts as part of determining custody or reviewing a mediated agreement on custody. These courts can and frequently do compel parents to undertake drug treatment and provide drug tests to the court as a way of assuring their compliance. If the drug use was mentioned in mediation, the mediator could make similar recommendations to the court, or if in a county where the parties have a right to terminate mediation with no report to the court, the mediator may still recommend that a custody evaluation be ordered. This would be a signal that most family court judges in the state would recognize as indicating that some fact worthy of the court's consideration had emerged in mediation.

Domestic violence structures the process of mediation in important ways. First, the process of mediation may pose a serious risk to the victim in a pattern of domestic violence. If the mother has left the home and is in a shelter or other secure place, the very trip to the mediation can mean serious exposure to violence. In response to lobbying and lawsuits, most states now make the safety of domestic violence victims a primary consideration in the conditions of mediation and whether it occurs at all. Second, many state legislatures have acted to make domestic violence a dominant consideration in the custody setting itself. California, for example, provides that "the Legislature further finds and declares that the perpetration of child abuse or domestic violence in a household where a child resides is detrimental to the child." Many states also establish a rebuttable presumption against physical custody for a parent if there has been a finding that he or she committed an act of domestic violence within the previous five years.[8]

1 Strike and You're Out: Internalizing Crime Risk to Families

Story 3

Pearl Rucker is a grandmother and a resident of public housing. After her daughter was arrested for possessing cocaine three blocks from the public housing project where she lived, Rucker was informed that she was being evicted from her apartment in accordance with a provision of her lease placed there in compliance with Anti-Drug Abuse Act of 1988.[9] The Act provided that "public housing agency shall utilize leases which . . . provide that any criminal activity that threatens the health, safety, or right to peaceful enjoyment of the premises by other tenants or any drug-related criminal activity on or off such premises, engaged in by a public housing tenant, any member of the tenant's household, or any guest or other person under the tenant's control, shall be cause for termination of tenancy."

Rucker had actively sought to keep her mentally ill daughter off drugs, including placing her in drug treatment programs and searching her room in the family's public housing apartment. She and several other tenants challenged the policy, arguing that the law must be read as not requiring the eviction of "innocent" tenants who did not know that their family member possessed drugs, and that if it so required, the statute violated the constitutional rights of such innocent tenants. The Ninth Circuit Court of Appeals, sitting en banc, held that the requirement was an unreasonable interpretation of the statutory scheme. The Supreme Court reversed that ruling and reinstated Ms. Rucker's eviction, holding that

Congress could rationally experiment with the effectiveness of strict liability policies.[10]

First introduced by the administration of President George H. W. Bush in 1988, the policy under which Pearl Rucker was evicted began as a grant of authority to local housing officials to use leases to remove families with serious crime problems that were endangering other residents. It was reborn in 1996 after President Clinton referred to a strengthened version of the regulation as a "one strike and you're out" standard in his State of the Union Address of that year. The new statute for the first time applied as well to applicants for public housing. The new policies authorize and encourage—but do not require—public housing authorities to do more initial screening of potential residents for criminal behavior, and to evict any current tenant deemed threatening to the safety or security of other residents regardless of whether there was an arrest, a conviction, or whether the incident actually took place in public housing (Renzetti 2001, 686).

An investigation by Human Rights Watch in 2004 found that local housing authorities were in fact using this authority. According to federal figures released to the organization, nearly 50,000 applicants for conventional public housing were rejected because of the one-strike policy in 2002. Human Rights Watch estimates that as many as 3.5 million persons, and thus any household they are part of, could be ineligible to receive public housing as a result of the policy (2004, 33). Using the exclusionary power associated with criminal designation to accomplish other organizational goals (like ridding schools of poor test takers or ridding public housing of waiting lists) is a pattern that we will see recur in the way different institutions respond to governing through crime.

The ratcheting up of the crime exclusion policy from public housing illustrates the most visible aspect of governing through crime: the effort of political leaders of both parties and of both the executive and Congress to embrace crime suppression as a strong policy preference in almost any field of social policy, here housing, and compete openly to establish harsher and more exclusionary rules for the administrative state. The Supreme Court, as noted, upheld the policy unanimously, making it an exemplary case of what I have called "crime jurisprudence." But the one-strike policy reflects governing through crime in two of the deeper meanings identified in our introduction.

In proposing these policies, and defending them before the courts, the government has consistently argued two policy rationales: first, that the safety of public housing residents is the overwhelming interest of the government; second, that in a situation of severe scarcity in which a large population of homeless families and families with deficient housing are on long waiting lists for any public housing, the one-strike rule is a useful and appropriate way to eliminate large numbers of people without a case-by-case determination of either their likely threat to public safety or their needs.

The first rationale is consistent with a theme that spans governing through crime: the clear priority given the prevention of specifically criminal victimization over other kinds of risks or social inequities. These policies build on the zero-sum risk logic of contemporary penal sanctions: virtually any increase in security for the public, no matter how small or speculative, suffices to justify virtually any increase in risk for criminal offenders, no matter how substantial and certain. The unanimous support for upholding this policy against a due process challenge in the Supreme Court reflects the broadly shared assumption that families face grave risks of crime and this justifies government choosing between potential victims and those who have been marked, however lightly, by criminal behavior. Declining to find the one-strike policy unreasonable, the opinion of the Supreme Court noted:

> There is an obvious reason why Congress would have permitted local public housing authorities to conduct no-fault evictions: Regardless of knowledge, a tenant who "cannot control drug crime, or other criminal activities by a household member which threaten health or safety of other residents, is a threat to other residents and the project." . . . With drugs leading to "murders, muggings, and other forms of violence against tenants," and to the "deterioration of the physical environment that requires substantial governmental expenditures," . . . it was reasonable for Congress to permit no-fault evictions in order to "provide public and other federally assisted low-income housing that is decent, safe, and free from illegal drugs."[11]

The second rationale provides a nice illustration of a form of governing through crime that one suspects is typical but is in fact hard to find explicitly acknowledged, in which crime becomes an excuse to pursue another goal or goals. Two distinct goals are visible in the government's own articulation of the policy. One is the efficiency of using criminal conduct as a standard to eliminate marginal cases without significant administrative investment. "In deciding whether to admit applicants who are borderline in the PHA [Public Housing Administration] evaluation process, the PHA should recognize that for every marginal applicant it admits, it is not admitting another applicant who clearly meets the PHA's evaluation standards" (Human Rights Watch 2004, 19).

In this way, crime becomes an unacknowledged way of deciding who does or does not deserve a public benefit. "Because of the extraordinary demand for affordable rental housing, public and assisted housing should be awarded to responsible individuals. It is reasonable to allocate scarcer resources to those who play by the rules." There is also the suggestion here that this strategy will produce a more docile and governable public housing population. "There are many eligible, law-abiding families who are waiting to live in public and assisted housing and who would readily replace evicted tenants" (20).

Whether the one-strike policy makes sense on the merits as a means of public safety, distributional justice, or general administerability is, of course, contestable. One has to factor in the significant distortions in how criminal conduct becomes visible and the vast overconcentration of policing certain populations. For our purposes, however, the more salient point is that the one-strike policy exemplifies the multiple dimensions along which crime as a regulatory ideal shapes something presumably distinct from criminal justice, such as public housing, and one with an enormous impact on families, at least the families of the poor.

In practice, the bundle of housing policies associated with the one-strike rule operates to compel the head of household in a public housing unit, typically a woman, to police the criminal conduct of her children, friends, and boyfriends, and anyone else they bring into the apartment. The implications of this for battered women—who are particularly unlikely to be able to suppress the criminality of the males in her life with acceptable risk to herself—has led to growing criticism of this and similar policies by feminists and advocates of minority women. Some states have actually targeted domestic violence as a particularly dangerous crime requiring zero-tolerance evictions. Under these policies, now being challenged in court, a woman who was victimized in her apartment by her nonresident ex-husband or boyfriend would be automatically evicted. Though they acknowledged that the rule may be harsh on battered women, public housing managers defended the policy as necessary to protect others from victimization by exposure to domestic violence (Lewin 2001).

One-Strike Insurance Exclusions

The one-strike rule in federal public housing finds an echo in the middle-class world of homeownership through a little-recognized, but increasingly common, provision in insurance contracts known as the criminal act exclusion. Originally intended to address the expensive but presumably rare situation in which the victims of an intentional killer are able to recover from the murderer's homeowner policy—notwithstanding standard exclusions for "expected or intended losses"—the broad provisions have been generously interpreted by courts to exclude virtually any loss linked to an arguably criminal action, no matter how accidental the loss.

Insurers justified these exclusion clauses as necessary checks on the courts' expansion of liability to include more deviant and deliberately harmful behavior.[12] More recent decisions, however, show courts inclined to enforce criminal act exclusions, and in situations even more distant from intentional harm than the kind of extreme behavior canvassed in some of the above decisions. For example, in *Horace Mann Insurance Co. v. Drury* (1994), a Georgia appellate court upheld the application of a "criminal act" exclusion to a severe injury occasioned by mishandling of firecrackers. A number of people were riding in a car along with a case of more than 500 firecrackers. With one insured person driving, another insured person tossed a lit firecracker out the passenger front window. The wind blew it back through the rear window, igniting the firecrackers and causing severe injuries to passenger Drury. The homeowner's policy excluded acts "committed by or at the direction of any insured which constitutes a violation of any criminal law or statute."[13] Although neither insured person was charged, the insurer denied the claim. Under Georgia law, it is a misdemeanor to be in possession of or to transport fireworks. After consulting the dictionary definition of crime, the Georgia appeals court held that the exclusion applied.

> Here, the exclusion in this homeowner's policy of coverage of
> acts of an insured which constitute a violation "of any criminal

law or statute" can only reasonably be read to exclude injuries caused by illegal possession of firecrackers.[14]

Such an approach turns the crime into an all-powerful presumption in favor of exclusion, without room for the analysis of risk that courts insisted on under the "expected or intended act" exclusion. Those courts that have limited its reading have emphasized the need to consider the risk, rather than allowing its fit with the elements of a penal statute to define its nature as a risk.

Courts have upheld the applicability of criminal act exclusions even in the absence of criminal prosecution. In this regard, the clauses have become the basis for a distinct kind of criminal law enforcement, one founded on insurance and at the discretion of private interests. Insurance companies have placed themselves in the position of the prosecutor's discretion to charge or not—even if they view themselves as not having discretion—even when the statutory authority prosecutors rely on is absent.

Liability insurance for homeowners, professionals, and businesses has been the major focus of criminal act exclusions, but they have begun to appear as well in "first-party" forms of insurance, so called because they provide benefits to the insured, rather than to parties allegedly injured by the insured. One of the most dramatic examples of this practice, because of its implications, involves employer-provided health insurance. Randy Slovacek was injured in a single-car accident in West Tawakoni, Texas. A blood test at the hospital measured his blood alcohol content at more than three times the legal limit, but no criminal charges were ever filed against him. The company hired to manage claims for Slovacek's employer plan approved his medical bills, but when the plan sought reimbursement from its "stop-loss" carrier,[15] that carrier refused to pay, arguing that its obligation to assume payment for medical bills exceeding $55,000 existed only for "covered expenses," which excluded Slovacek's losses. The stop-loss carrier's argument was founded in an exclusion clause nested within the plan's official description,[16] which purports to exclude coverage for:

> Treatment or service resulting from or occurring (a) during the commission of a crime by the participant; or (b) while engaged in an illegal act (including DWI) illegal occupation or aggravated assault.[17]

The plan administrators claimed in their own defense that they approved coverage on the theory that the exclusion applied only in cases in which "a beneficiary was convicted of an illegal act." The federal district court, however, favored the stop-loss carrier's reading of the clause.

> The Court finds that Exclusion 14 is unambiguous. It is unreasonable to read the term "illegal act" as requiring judicial action and conviction. Driving while "intoxicated," as that term is defined by Texas law, is illegal whether a person is convicted of the crime or not. The drafters of this exclusion could have required a conviction for Exclusion 14 to apply by including such language in the Plan. The natural meaning of the term does not include such a requirement.[18]

The broadening of criminal act exclusions to reach all manner of losses unintended by the insured threatens the safety net that access to homeowner's and commercial insurance is supposed to provide to the American middle class. Homeownership is a key element of middle-class status in America and homeowner's insurance is an absolute requirement for obtaining a mortgage. Other first-party benefits, including health care, could potentially follow the same logic, making crime a basic dividing line between those we enable the modicum of middle-class security associated with insurance and those we abandon to the world of risk and uncertainty to which we regularly relegate the working poor. Imagine, for example, that critical surgery were to be denied your child because he tested positive for marijuana following a severe automobile accident in which he was involved.[19]

Consuming Security

For families, both poor and middle class, these social and legal policies operate to channel responsibility for managing crime risks of household members, especially children, into the family itself. As other institutions, from preschools through colleges, ratchet up the significance of behavior they deem criminal or crimelike, governing the crime risk of one's children has become a major concern for parents in all social classes. For those with sufficient economic means, the new initiatives to police the family are simply the other side of the new social contract they have consented to by living in gated communities, sending their children to high-security schools, and shopping in high-security malls. For these parents, the policing of the family is likely to be delegated to the same kind of professional security-oriented services that already manage so much of the lived environment. A growing industry of private family disciplinary institutions are cropping up to replace the old treatment-oriented social sector that juvenile courts created. The most costly and coercive are expensive private boot camps that combine physical discipline with militaristic drilling and motivational messages about obedience, aimed at parents coping with immediate consequences of school expulsions and threats of worse.[20] A search on the Web locates dozens of companies operating boot camps and treatment facilities aimed at specific problems with children ranging from drug use to disobedience and dating issues. Here we are at a great remove from the state prisons to which a largely minority population is relegated by state actors; we deal with a range of middle- and upper-class consumers exercising their market power to bring a crimelike model of governance to bear on themselves and their children.

Boot camps and other commodified forms of criminal justice governance (e.g., home drug testing kits, home surveillance technology) aim at internalizing the costs of crimes committed by dependent minors within the family but in a way that bears little necessary relationship to actual risks. Criminal acts of children become the occasion for what amounts to a partial disenfranchisement of the family from the common institutions of risk sharing in America, such as public schools and private insurance. Because the effects of exclusion can be potentially devastating to a family—loss of public housing, eligibility for college loans, etc.—and far out of proportion to the risks created by the criminal conduct of the children, parents are compelled to invest heavily in disciplinary technologies and knowledge.

The softer side of this is coextensive with the arrangements many middle-class families already make to secure their family from crime. Living in a security subdivision, going to a security-conscious suburban middle school, being driven between these places in SUVs marketed as crime resistant, children are surrounded by technologies and services aimed at making them secure from criminal attack. Many of the same approaches are key to helping parents prevent their children from committing crimes, especially the public-order and drug crimes that suburban parents most fear. When parents are encouraged to make sure their children are in some

*preventing
children to
be victims
+ offenders
to costly*

kind of organized after-school program until the parents themselves come home and resume control, and are encouraged to provide their own private motorized transportation between the school and any such program, all in the name of lowering their odds of becoming a crime victim—they are also preventing their child from opportunities to sell drugs, commit acts of vandalism, and assault other children. Yet this circuit of parental attention driven by the risk of their children's behavior being defined as criminal or crime like is costly.

For parents with few resources to access the market, or little cultural understanding of the priority that Americans place on security from crime, the encounters are likely to be more state centered and coercive. The message to parents is that the repression of criminal conduct must take priority over any other objectives of child rearing and that parents will be expected to accomplish this largely on their own or with what they can purchase. Anthropology graduate student Thomas J. Douglas writes in a recent academic newsletter of a parenting workshop for Cambodian immigrants he observed in West Seattle:

> I knew from my previous volunteer work, that social workers
> view Cambodian children as "high risk" for not completing their
> education. So, I was not at all surprised to see a West Seattle
> school offering "education" for Cambodian parents. I went ex-
> pecting to hear presentations from teachers, counselors, and
> school administrators on what parents can do to help their chil-
> dren be successful students. I was taken aback when I learned
> that the only two speakers for the event were a lieutenant from
> the police department and a former law professor who currently
> sits as a municipal judge for the juvenile courts. Rather than fo-
> cusing on education, they spent the evening on domestic vio-
> lence, truancy, and especially, issues of parental liability. (Dou-
> glas 2001, 1)

*support publics
that lead
to imprisonment*

It is also primarily as parents that Americans from a whole range of economic and social positions have found themselves supporting the legal policies that lead to mass imprisonment. The highly privatized security system they have invested their families in produce collective insecurities that can be addressed only by incapacitating incarceration. But the same publics whose party independence and high voter participation give them extraordinary political influence in the election system are unwilling to agree to virtually any development that increases the risk of crime or disorder, no matter how valuable those might be to the community as a whole. The centrality of fear of crime as a motivation and the centrality of security as a promise create a strong sense of entitlement. One indication of this is the fearsome degree to which the phenomenon once known as NIMBY (Not In My Back Yard) has proliferated from local struggles against drug treatment centers or halfway houses to even sports fields and schools because these are perceived as linked to disorder and, ultimately, crime (Herszenhorn 2000).

Because contemporary suburban spaces are organized to address the fears of parents about their young children, they provide almost nothing but provocations to teenagers. The same landscape that enabled the control of small children makes it very hard to keep teenagers under control once they leave the house. In such a context, it is likely both that teenagers will inevitably generate lots of the public-order crimes that contribute to fear, and that measures to collectively police such problems will be ineffective. One result may be continued pressure to make parents accountable as governors of their children through homeowners' associations (if they do not exclude children altogether) or criminal liability (a topic we take up below).

It is most difficult to imagine what the boundaries of "personal security" are. There is always a moment when a person must get out of an SUV or walk out of an airport or hotel or shopping mall. The more secure the design, the fewer such situations will be, and the more the design will attempt to address such problems with additional surveillance, private security, and screening that make parking lots or urban mall entrances an extension of the security space. Personal security extends and supplements these extensions, but always at the cost of adding new possibilities of failure and loss.

In several ways, this suggests that the gated community and its analogues, built to address the problem crime posed for the family, are likely to guarantee that crime dominates the governance of the family for a long time to come. First, these landscapes are not only conducive to the kinds of public-order crimes that generate fear of cities in the first place, but also produce, because of the hypercontrolled nature of their internal spaces, a standard of security comfort that virtually no external environment can sustain, unless that external environment itself becomes a larger internal space. As the family is placed in ever more nested security, the goal is redundancy. Locked inside SUVs, parked in a secured garage, locked inside a "gated" and privately policed subdivision, the contemporary suburban family is arriving at an "equilibrium" as circumscribed as the much-feared career criminal, locked inside a high-technology armored cell within a super-max prison.[21]

Conclusion: Crime-Centered Families

The "child-centered family" was the description often used to describe the post–World War II families being grown in America's new "bedroom communities." This interpretation captured a good deal of the energetic innovation in governance concentrated around issues like the food supply, public morality in schools, prayer, integration, and so on. As our examination of the governance of the family suggests, the child, now reconfigured as a nexus of crime, remains very much at the center. This is true both for the family and for the penumbra of helping professions that operate around it.

The fact that the state now prioritizes the family as a site of crime (domestic violence) and criminals (juvenile delinquents) is one of several key factors. Parents, and the institutions like the market and the state, that they turn to for help in fulfilling their governance roles, have also become saturated with crime. It also means, at its most perverse, that individuals for whom the meanings and metaphors of crime become truly compelling may act out their own conflicts within the potent terms of this scenario.

This is not to say that a single monolithic trend is altering the family. The picture of the family as a governable space regarding domestic violence is much different than the one that emerges from the gated community. In one context, the family appears as a nest of potential conflicts and abuses with the possibility that surveillance, deterrence, and punishment must be carried down to the micro level. In another, the family appears as a "crime-free zone."[22] In one frame, parents (father and mother) are potential offenders; in another, they are potential victims and, most important, the parents of potential victims. In one context, the state operates as a coercive agency ready to involve itself in intimate family decisions should violence and crime emerge either from or near their midst. But at the same time, in a different context, the state, so powerful for some, devolves into a distant and largely ineffectual force that cannot be relied upon to provide even minimal family security.

What is remarkable is how much the three themes we have explored in this chapter—domestic violence, the growing priority for parents of crime suppression in their childrearing, and the ceaseless quest to keep the spatial site of the family crime free—coalesce. It is not that they are all subject to the same grand theory, but rather they can exist in a common space of knowledge and power, a space in which the family as both analytic and political unit is splayed along surfaces of crime.

There is also a normative case for worrying about governing the family through crime, that is local to the family, (rather than simply derived from my global claims about democracy and governing through crime), that takes a weak and a strong form. The weak concern is that governing the family through crime ties families to a set of strategies and technologies that are increasingly burdensome, especially at a time when either one or both parents provide income essential to the family.

The stronger concern is that governing the family through crime, at least as it has developed in the United States, is making a functional post-patriarchal domestic order harder to imagine or negotiate, leaving men and women to seek to shape order through their capacity to articulate fear of crime. The culture of crime fear around the family is in part a displacement of social unease with the new roles of women in the workplace and family (Glassner 1999, 31; Garland 2001a). The endless stories of pedophiles and Halloween sadists trying to hurt children that anyone coming of age in America after 1960 can remember personally, operate both to produce guilt on those parents who cannot dedicate personal time to the policing of their children and to valorize those parents who represent "the antithesis of those trends—full time housewives and employed moms who returned early from work to throw safe trick-or-treat parties for their children and their children's friends in their homes or churches, or simply to escort their kids on their rounds and inspect the treats" (Glassner 1999, 31).

Once a space deemed too private for the intrusion of criminal justice, the family has become crisscrossed by tension resulting from crime, domestic violence, child abuse, school misconduct, and housing and insurance exclusions. The family is also where we most directly experience the arts of governance, both as subjects and, for those of us who become parents,

rulers of a most uncertain and frail sort. Perhaps no other set of relationships more powerfully anchors the constellation of meanings and practices
we call governing through crime. In a very real sense, our ability to roll back
the penal state and its mass imprisonment may depend most on our ability
to talk ourselves down from the way we prioritize the avoidance of crime
risk in shaping our family life.

Reforming Education Through Crime

A generation ago, racial inequality served as the pivot around which a vast reworking of governance of public schools took place.[1] As David Kirp observed of this period:

> Support for schooling increased dramatically at every level of government. . . . The ideas of racial equality and educational re-form were closely intertwined. The demand for racial justice formed part of the call for modernization, and the availability of new resources made attentiveness to race specific issues politi-cally more palatable. (1982, 297)

Today, crime in and around schools is playing a similar role as the problem that must be confronted and documented by a reinforcing spiral of political will and the production of new knowledge about school crime. Ironically, the genealogy of crime as a political problem in schools may have had its most salient recent origins in the desegregation era and the of-ten violent conflicts that arose around efforts to dismantle racially bifur-cated public school systems. Although the stamp of desegregation remains on many public school systems today, by the late 1970s, it had largely run its course, defeated by private action and judicial retreat. In the same pe-riod, crime became an increasing influence on school governance.

In the succeeding decades, the criminalization of schools (Giroux 2003) has been accelerated by several other factors arguably external to them. First, there are fresh historical memories of the high tides of youth-ful violence during the 1960s and again in the 1980s. Second, the associa-tion of youth culture with drugs and drug trafficking, a linkage that began in the 1960s, and during the 1980s was framed as a major source of threat to the safety and educational mission of schools. Third, a growing right-wing movement against public schools—at least those that also involve unions and elected school board supervision—has found it extremely useful to frame the public schools as being rife with crime.

The media have picked up on all these themes. Few issues are as likely to keep parents awake for the 11 P.M. local news broadcast as the latest breaking story on crime in schools.[2] For many middle-class Americans whose children will virtually never encounter guns or even knife fights at school, the real and imagined pictures of violence-plagued public schools in inner-city communities have created a neural pathway to the concept of public school. The result has been policies in suburban schools that parallel, in sometimes softer forms, the fortress tactics employed at front-line inner-city schools. As of the 1996–97 school year, 96 percent of public schools required a visitor to sign in before entering a school building, and 80 percent had "closed-campus" policies barring most students from leaving during school hours (Riley & Reno 1998, 14). More than three-quarters of all public schools in a national sample study completed in 2000 included "prevention curriculum, instruction, or training" and had "architectural features of the school" that were devoted to prevention of crime and "problem behavior" (DeVoe et al. 2004, 3).

But even the harder edge of fortress tactics themselves—including mandatory drug testing, metal detectors, and searches—are hardly confined to a handful of the most crime ridden schools in America. More than half of all schools in the same 2000 sample had security and surveillance systems in place at the school (DeVoe et al. 2004, 3). In the 1996–97 survey, 22 percent of the schools had a police officer or other law enforcement representative stationed on the premises at some time during the school day (6 percent for at least 30 hours in a typical week), 19 percent conducted drug sweeps, 4 percent conducted random metal detector checks, and 1 percent routinely screened students with a metal detector (Riley & Reno 1998).

Consider the signs that now surround the entrances to public schools in cities all over the United States, including Ponce De Leon Middle School, located in high-income Coral Gables, Florida: "DRUG FREE SCHOOL ZONE, minimum 3 years in prison," and "YOUTH CRIME WATCH, to report: 757-0514 or Your Local Police Department." The school is not considered among the worst or among the best in the system. It has a highly diverse student population including whites, Hispanics, and blacks. In front of the school, parents wait to pick up their children driving everything from a Mercedes SUV to a Ford Escort.

Schools have long been considered the most important gateway to citizenship in the modern state. Symbolically, few places are more laden with sovereign significance than the entryway to a public school, which for millions of citizens is their first, most enabling, and most enduring experience of governance in action. In the real and iconic experience in which a parent conducts a child to the entrance of a school and then bids him or her farewell are the beginnings of the transformations that conduct a subject from the pure monarchy of the family to the status of a free and responsible adult. In France, a nation rarely shy about enforcing nationalism with law, schools are mandated to inscribe the words "liberté, éqalité, fraternité" over their entrance. Today, in the United States, it is crime that dominates the symbolic passageway to school and citizenship. And behind this surface, the pathways of knowledge and power within the school are increasingly being shaped by crime as the model problem,[3] and tools of criminal justice as the dominant technologies. Through the introduction of police, probation officers, prosecutors, and a host of private security professionals into the schools, new forms of expertise now openly compete with pedagogic knowledge and authority for shaping routines and rituals of schools.

My primary interest in this chapter is the way crime has become an axis around which to recast much of the form and substance of schools, and the effects of this enormous channeling of attention to schools through the lens of crime. One result is a reframing of students as a population of potential victims and perpetrators. At its core, the implicit fallacy dominating many school policy debates today consists of a gross conflation of virtually all the vulnerabilities of children and youth into variations on the theme of crime. This may work to raise the salience of education on the public agenda, but at the cost to students of an education embedded with themes of "accountability," "zero tolerance," and "norm shaping."

Another result is a legal "leveling" of the space between education and juvenile delinquency. In an earlier era, progressives dreamed of expanding the juvenile delinquency model into an overall expert regulation of youth. We seem to be approaching this horizon in a wholly different way. Today, the merging of school and penal system has resulted in speeding the collapse of the progressive project of education and tilting the administration of schools toward a highly authoritarian and mechanistic model.

Serious crime is a substantial problem in a relatively small but hardly random portion of American schools and a small but understandably frightening problem in many others. In the first part of this chapter, we will take a look through the lens of recent ethnographies at some of those schools where the threat of violent crime—of males shooting other males or sexually assaulting females—is real enough to influence almost everybody's actions. Crime in such schools is truly a mode of governance at the individual level in the sense that it is a strategy for conduct on the conduct of others. Punishment and policing have come to at least compete with, if not replace, teaching as the dominant modes of socialization. But the very real violence of a few schools concentrated in zones of hardened poverty and social disadvantage has provided a "truth" of school crime that circulates across whole school systems.[4]

Governing Crime in Schools

Crimes, including crimes of violence, are a real part of the American school experience at the turn of the twenty-first century, and not only in the poorest communities. Since the mid-1990s, crime in schools has become the subject of almost frantic data collection. Numbers, like the 3 million school crimes per year cited by President Bush, bounce from Web page to magazine article to speech. In response to federal mandates, states have begun their own process of data collection. According to recent federal statistics, 56 percent of public high schools in the nation reported at least one criminal incident to police in the 1996–1997 academic year, and 21 percent reported at least one serious violent crime in that period. In more than 10 percent of all public high schools, there was at least one physical attack or fight involving a weapon, and in 8 percent there was at least one rape or sexual assault (Sheley 2000, 37).

Schools with serious incidents of violence have increasingly become high-security environments. Anthropologist John Devine describes a decade of ethnography at one such high school in New York in his book, *Maximum Security* (1996). Devine's ethnographic "cover" was running a tutorial program in which graduate students at New York University did both research and tutoring in academically needy public schools. Consistent with our genealogy, the older teachers interviewed by Devine could not remember any regular security guards in the school before 1968 or

1969, when some schools began to post a guard near the main entrance in response to volatile demonstrations over teacher strikes and decentralization.[5]

By the late 1980s, the security response had become a dominant presence for both staff and design, "as space is rearranged to accommodate metal detectors and the auxiliary technologies they spawn" (Devine 1996, 76). New York employed 3,200 uniformed school safety officers at the time of Devine's observations, constituting the ninth-largest police department in the United States until it was integrated into the New York City Police Department by Mayor Giuliani. When various assistant principals and "deans" are factored in, the security apparatus that Devine observed amounted to 110 people in one school that had a teaching staff of 150 (78). Entrance to school required passing by a guard-supervised computer that read the student's ID and kept a time log of entrances and exits (80).

Devine consciously resisted being drawn into the debate about objective crime trends, the various metrics of violence in schools and how much it differs from years past, metrics that are themselves the products of governing through crime. He situated his account against both liberal critics of school policy, who saw school crime as a complete charade to justify oppressive administration of a failed educational program, and the conservative view that school violence demonstrated either the ultimately corrupting process of liberal secular education or that public schools were too chaotic to be saved. More relevant to the experience of students and staff was the very real possibility of guns being introduced into conflicts at school. Of the 41 schools with the greatest violence problems in the system, several of which fell into his tutorial program, Devine reports a total of 129 "gun incidents" in a year (23).[6] With an average of three gun incidents a year happening in each of these schools, it would be reasonable for every student, teacher, and staff person in the school to consider gun violence a real possibility to be taken into account in the management of everyday life.

One result of the prevalence of violence and the importance of responding to it is that teachers have increasingly been withdrawn from the field of norm enforcement in favor of the professional security staff.[7] The corridors, the site of most significant social behavior in high school, are wholly the space of security personnel. The classrooms remain the sanctum of the teachers, but the security personnel are even called into classrooms when behavior becomes disruptive. Indeed, Devine (1996, 27) finds that security guards have become critical sources of normative guidance for students. Despite the vastness of the technosecurity apparatus—surveillance, metal detectors, drug tests, and locker searches—the remarkable fact is how much that apparatus overlooks, and how often it fails to function. This is not a system bent on discovering every violation, but rather one that ignores violations that do not reach a sufficiently dangerous level. "Meticulous observation of detail has given way to a willful determination *not* to see misbehavior and even outright crime."[8]

A central node in today's inner city schools—competing with the classroom and the playground as spaces of education and self-fashioning—are the spaces given over to in-school detentions that informants in Ann Ferguson's (2000) study of Chicago schools called "the punishing room."

> In the Punishing Room, school identities and reputations are constituted, negotiated, challenged, confirmed for African American youth in a process of categorization, reward and punishment, humiliation, and banishment. Children passing through the system are marked and categorized as they encounter state laws, school rules, tests and exams, psychological remedies, screening committees, penalties and punishments, rewards and praise. Identities that are worthy, hardworking, devious, or dangerous are proffered, assumed, or rejected. (40–41)

These in-school detentions are considered necessary to maintain an educational atmosphere in the classroom and a better alternative than suspension, but they are producing something similar to what criminologists once called "prisonization" (Clemmer 1940), a powerful normative pull of peer culture that undermines the institution's goals.

At the level of whole school systems, many of these inner-city schools themselves have become larger instantiations of punishing rooms, identified by students and parents as places of disorder and risk. New York's highly hierarchical and largely merit-based system of high schools means that, for students living in the poorest sections, the only way to avoid the neighborhood high school is through competitive admission to one of the city's well-known magnet programs (Devine 1996). Crime plays a crucial motivating role in this dynamic. Students are exhorted to compete for the elite special-admission high schools and even the broad middle tier of educationally oriented magnet schools not simply for what admission would do for their college admissions prospects and future earnings, but quite specifically to avoid the chaos and violence of the large neighborhood high schools that are the catchall for those left behind.

Crime, and especially gun violence, has touched an astoundingly wide variety of American high schools. In the 1996–97 school year, for example, 10 percent of public schools nationwide reported at least one serious violent crime (Riley & Reno 1998, 11). A recent study found that "nearly all U.S. public schools are using a variety of delinquency prevention programs and disciplinary practices" (NIJ 2004, ii). When a problem for 10 percent becomes a paradigm for all, it is the mark of the hold of crime over our contemporary political imagination. Most violent crime is concentrated in sociologically identifiable communities, especially urban minority neighborhoods with high rates of unemployment and poverty. Thus out of every 1,000 teachers, nearly 40 in urban schools in 1996–97 were (nonfatal) crime victims, in contrast with 20 in suburban schools and 22 in rural schools. The framing of the danger as a national problem facing schools everywhere is an essentially political act that has consequences for schools environmentally, physically, pedagogically, and in terms of governance.

As in the earlier era of reforming schools for racial equality, the federal government has played a crucial role in making crime a national problem for schools, and crime prevention a national agenda for school reform, using incentives and sanctions to spread it across state and local systems. David Kirp (1982) described the implementation of desegregation as creating a standard operational meaning of equality:

> Policy aspires to uniformity. Policy is proposed for the country
> as if equality had an unvarying meaning from place to place,
> and in terms of fixed goals, as if there existed an ideal end state.
> Such remedies as extensive busing, vouchers, special "magnet"
> schools, or metropolitan-wide districts are proffered with little
> attention to context; each is advanced as if it were a panacea for
> all the ills of racism. (xx)

In both desegregation and the war on crime, court cases and legislation have played a significant role in constructing a national problem and national solutions to making schools work. For racial equality, the signal year was 1965, when the Elementary and Secondary Education Act invested billions of federal dollars in poor schools provided they complied with desegregation orders.[9] For safe schools, the pivotal legislation was the Safe Schools Act of 1994.

Nationalizing the Problem: The Safe Schools Act of 1994

Though the battles over schools and racial inequality in the 1960s helped forge an initial link between schools and violence, by the end of the 1970s this had largely faded, along with the conflict over desegregation plans that had sparked it. By the time schools came back on the national agenda with the 1983 Carnegie Foundation Report *A Nation at Risk*, it was not racial inequality or crime but educational failure that was the dominant concern, especially declining test scores of American students at all levels. Even as late as 1990, when the first President Bush convened a national conference of all 50 governors to frame a national education agenda (with then-Governor of Arkansas, Bill Clinton playing a leading role), concerns about crime formed only one of six goals to be achieved by the year 2000:

1. All children in America will start school ready to learn.
2. The high school graduation rate will increase to at least 90 percent.
3. American students will leave grades four, eight, and twelve having demonstrated competence in challenging subject matter, including English, mathematics, science, history, and geography; and every school in America will ensure that all students learn to use their minds well, so they may be prepared for responsible citizenship, further learning, and productive employment in our modern economy.
4. U.S. students will be first in the world in science and mathematics achievement.
5. Every adult American will be literate and will possess the knowledge and skills necessary to compete in a global economy and exercise the rights and responsibilities of citizenship.
6. Every school in America will be free of drugs and violence and will offer a disciplined environment conducive to learning (Gronlund 1993).

This last short statement sets up a complex equation among three elements—drugs, violence, and lack of discipline—which helps explain why more than any of the other goals, number 6 has become central to the reshaping of schools. This formula has been productive for several reasons.

First, by emphasizing violence, goal 6 was the only one that gestured in the direction of the largely poor and minority school populations in neighborhoods where armed violence among youths was a real risk to spill over into schools. Meanwhile, racial justice—once the dominant model of educational modernization—had disappeared altogether in the 1990 statement. Second, by linking drugs to violence, it brings a far broader swath of American schools into the problem. Violence truly plagues only a small number of schools concentrated in areas of hardened poverty. But drugs are as likely to be sold among, and used by, students in suburban high schools as inner-city ones. Third, by linking both to lack of discipline among students, the equation makes crime control a vehicle for improving the educational function of schools. Schools dominated by a culture friendly to drugs and marked by violence were presumed to be a causal explanation of the declining educational achievement of American students. Still, as late as 1990, the violence-drugs-discipline triangle constituted only one of six points highlighted by the chief executives. In this context, it's not hard to understand how the escalation of the youth homicide rate beginning in the late 1980s became a major political issue in the 1990s. Though most of the attention focused on whether the juvenile justice system could respond adequately to such lethal violence, the age of the perpetrators and victims put schools in the picture. At the political level, the mid-1990s saw the locking into place of a broad consensus that school violence was a primary problem for American education and that the problem could be addressed only by more security and technology. There has been little confusion about what this means in terms of where the ideas and methods will come from in reshaping American schools. Police had been around schools for a generation as a service function. Now they were to become a moralizing force. John Devine (1996) quotes the then-current report "rethinking" school safety in New York as advocating a wholesale adoption of the approach of enlightened police departments:

> We recommend that in many respects, large and small, the Division [of school safety of the Board of Education] should look for guidance to the practices of other law enforcement and public safety organizations, and then tailor those practices and policies to the unique environment of the school. (204)

The creation of a national model of crime governance for schools moved rapidly after Congress enacted the Safe Schools Act in 1994 as part of a larger bill on crime that followed the collapse of the Clinton health reform plan and culminated in the 1994 elections.[10] Following the pattern set down in the landmark 1968 Omnibus Crime Control and Safe Streets Act—notice the parallel of qualifying streets and schools as safe by legislation, the actual logic of which is to define both as dangerous—Congress appropriated significant new funds, conditioning eligibility for this funding on the adoption by states and local school districts of techniques of knowledge and power calculated to focus more governance attention and resources on crime in schools, while assuring a more rapid and punitive response toward it.

This move to nationalize the security response has had impressive results. According to one survey, more than 90 percent of schools have zero-tolerance policies in place for weapons possession. More than 80 percent have recently revised their disciplinary codes to make them more punitive. Nearly 75 percent have been declared "drug-free" zones, 66 percent, "gun-free" zones. More than half have introduced locker searches (Sheley 2000, 39). A national market in expertise and program ideas has come into existence in the last two decades. It provides school administrators with a ready-made set of strategies for raising funds, establishing interventions successful in at least their own carefully defined terms, and creating a flow of information from schools to government and then government to the public about school crime and the response to it.

A closer look at parts of the Safe Schools Act and the federal and state policies that have followed it identifies several main mechanisms through which crime is made a central problem of school governance.

Making Crime Visible

The Safe Schools Act operates far beyond the simple application of money to a local problem; rather, it requires changes in the way knowledge flows and decisions are made within schools. Although many of these provisions reflect the very best social science–informed policy thinking about crime and youth populations, they also represent the triumph of crime over other agendas for reimagining schools. The creation of new pathways for knowledge to circulate within the school, and new rationalities of decision-making, are likely to keep schools locked into the dynamic of crime and security for a long time to come.

To qualify for federal money under the Safe Schools Act, schools must first demonstrate that they have a "serious problem with school crime, violence, and student discipline" (Eckland 1999, 312). This requires schools to develop their own data collection systems for crime, and to assess what kinds of incidents to count, an exercise that school administrators have every incentive to make as expansive as possible.

The law calls into existence a whole series of information streams about crime in schools that assures that whatever else happens, knowledge about crime is going to be brought to the attention of school officials, teachers, and parents. This helps assure that one thing almost everyone interested in schools will know about particular schools, along with the ubiquitous test scores, is information, potentially a lot of information, about the crime scene there. Parents looking for ways to assure themselves they are doing their duty to their children will have this information available. Higher public education officials looking for metrics to evaluate principals will have this information available. While seemingly innocuous, the establishment of such information flows assures a priority for crime in contexts where people are looking for ways to differentiate between competing alternatives (employees, schools, housing complexes, etc.).

Building a Crime Constituency in the Community

The Safe Schools Act also makes clear that schools must build community support for a security program. For example, selection criteria governing funding explicitly favors repeat awards for schools that can turn out the highest levels of participation by parents and community residents for funded projects and activities focused on school crime and safety. At the other end of the process, schools that receive funding must mount a significant campaign to make the public aware of both the crime problem and the progress being made to solve it. Both these features may be laudatory efforts to assure that federal funds flow to programs that receive at least tacit public approval through participation. The result is to build— within the heart of local school districts, one of the oldest institutions of American democracy—enduring structures of intervention, knowledge production, and consent formation, all designed in response to crime.

Hardening School Discipline

A prime target of the 1994 law was the existing disciplinary apparatus within schools. An earlier generation had insisted that, schools, without normalizing deviance, protect young people from criminalization and exclusion. In the early 1990s most schools remained highly protective of students, avoiding sanctions like suspension or expulsion that would genuinely disadvantage their educational prospects, generally distinguishing school discipline from that meted out by the police and court system. At this time, however, such policies became the target of a critique that has since been the cutting edge of governing through crime reform in many institutions. Informal and highly discretionary disciplinary systems are perceived as having denigrated victims, failed to correct offenders, and betrayed the public interest in stamping out crime before it becomes dangerous to the general community.

This critique is built into the qualifying provisions of the Safe Schools Act. To qualify for federal funds under the Act, the school district must already have written policies detailing a) its internal procedures, b) clear conditions under which exclusion will be imposed, and c) close cooperation with police and juvenile justice agencies. The requirement that schools formalize their disciplinary policies is a crucial step in intensifying the flow of information from schools about the disciplinary violations now being constituted as quasi-crimes. At the harder end, violations that would constitute acts of juvenile delinquency under the prevailing legal code must be reported. At the softer end, the accumulation of statistics on incidents will become the raw material for the evaluation studies that the Act mandates as the follow-up to any successful application for funding.

Nationalizing School Crime Expertise

The school must also have put together a crime-fighting strategy. In practice, this means turning to one of a growing number of technologies and forms of expertise that have been nationally "accredited." The school must present a plan for drawing on a range of these resources, and a specific set of goals that the school hopes to achieve with them. These goals become critical in the audit side of the federal grant process. Future funding is contingent on measurable progress in implementing a plan (not necessarily in achieving true declines in crime). Schools that receive federal money must put in place comprehensive school safety plans that address long-term reductions in violence and discipline problems. Encouraged, but not required, is the formation of elaborate emergency plans to respond to school crises, such as the shooting incidents that sparked the law. The law also channels the expenditure of funds into certain preapproved activities that include a host of branded programs whose mission in fact is to reinforce the link between crime and schools by defining routine school activities such as going to school or being at school as occurring in "safe zones" or in "drug- and weapon-free school zones." For example, section 5965 of the Act provides a list of appropriate uses for funds.

> A local educational agency shall use grant funds for one or more of the following activities. . . .
> (11) Supporting "safe zones of passage" . . . through such measures as "Drug and Weapon Free School Zones"
> (12) Counseling programs for victims and witnesses of school violence
> (13) Acquiring and installing metal detectors and hiring security personnel.[11]

State responses have varied widely. Many states have enacted their own versions of the Safe Schools Act to create any authority in the school districts that is necessary to be eligible for federal funds.[12] Like the federal version, these state-level Safe Schools Acts commit the state to the proposition that school violence is the most important problem facing American education and that a security response is the only one possible. The laws typically require school districts to commence the forms of data collection and administrative reform necessary to meet the federal requirements. Some have adopted statewide zero-tolerance policies; others allow districts to do so or to define the incidents serious enough to trigger expulsion. Using fear of crime as an overarching rationale, all of them tighten the net of control around students' movement in and out of schools.

The changes mandated by the Safe Schools Act involve the creation of fundamentally new pathways of knowledge and power within the school community. These pathways are likely to change the educational experience and the status of students, teachers, and administrators in ways that will endure even when the specific conditions that called them into being have disappeared.

Placing a powerful premium on defining an act as one involving school crime or safety alters almost everyone's incentives. School administrators who hope to attract substantial federal and state money will find the crime banner the most productive one available. To be sure, for many schools this incentive will be counterbalanced by their becoming further associated with crime. Administrators are mandated to collect statistics on criminal incidents, and these statistics will ultimately be used to hold them accountable. To survive, administrators must map the sources of these numbers at the capillary level within the spaces they control, using their existing power to shape teaching and learning to better fit desirable states of data. Teachers and others with front-line responsibility for managing students will find themselves facing many of these new mandates and with less ability to reshape the work of others. They will also find that one of the few "buttons" that they can push that will both generate administrative attention and garner resources is the one labeled "crime." Parents or students who want something done will also find it most advantageous to define their children or themselves as victims and others as perpetrators of crimes or discipline violations. It is little wonder that a recent national survey of public schools reported that public school faculty assessment of a principal's leadership ability is "associated with a high level of prevention activity" (read as crime-focused curriculum, security measures, crime data collection efforts, and so on) (NIJ 2004, 5).

One important dimension of this is the eradication of barriers between the juvenile justice and school systems. During the last decade, as youth crime in general has come in for more legislative attention, states have enacted laws giving criminal justice officials greater access to school-based information and administrative systems. Until the Safe Schools Act, however, schools had few incentives to cooperate. Now cooperation will be part and parcel of reconfiguring schools around crime. Juvenile probation officers and police will find themselves valued partners in forming strategic alliances that are viewed favorably by federal funding guidelines.[13] The diminished expectations of privacy accorded to students in primary and secondary education by the U.S. Supreme Court means that these law enforcement personnel will have every incentive to make the school their preferred hunting ground for suspects.[14]

Penal Pedagogy

Against the background of the Safe Schools Act and the broader political pressures that the Act crystallizes, schools have responded by adopting a range of innovations that borrow directly from criminal justice. We have already touched on the presence of professional security agents, advanced security detection equipment (like metal detectors and X-ray machines), and the routine practice of searching, seizing, and interrogating students. These techniques remain concentrated in schools in high-crime areas, but elements of them have spread to schools serving demographic sectors with much less real exposure to violence.

Increasing efforts to police students are perhaps the most natural response to increased pressure to govern crime in schools. More striking and more suggestive of the passage from governing crime to governing through crime are the adoption of practices suggestive of the penal aspects of criminal justice. Three of the most common are uniforms, zero tolerance, and in-school detention.

Uniforms

One technique heavily promoted by the federal government since the 1990s is the adoption of school uniforms. Four percent of all public schools had a uniform policy in the late 1990s (Riley & Reno 1998). Although touted as building school community and saving parents from demands for high-priced designer clothes, uniforms have been implemented overwhelmingly as a response to crime. A Department of Education manual on uniforms, for example, offers the following as potential benefits:

- decreasing violence and theft—even life-threatening situations— among students over designer clothing or expensive sneakers
- helping prevent gang members from wearing gang colors and insignia at school
- instilling students with discipline
- helping parents and students resist peer pressure
- helping students concentrate on their school work
- helping school officials recognize intruders who come to the school.[15]

Unlike policing, which, no matter how intense, still draws a line between security and the ordinary activities of subjects which may suffer some inefficiencies because of security, uniforms invest the subject, here students and parents, with a distinct identity as a governed subject. They are intended not just to act on those subjects (uniforms, for example, make it easier to separate students from nonstudents), but also to encourage subjects to govern themselves and others along certain preferred pathways.

Zero Tolerance

No part of the current crime and safety regime for schools has garnered more attention and more controversy than the requirement that for certain behaviors—most commonly bringing a weapon to school, but also drug-, violence-, or discipline-related misbehaviors—the school response must be certain and specific, qualities often summarized as zero tolerance. The Safe Schools Act explicitly promotes the use of zero tolerance by local school districts in their disciplinary procedures, with at least two implications. First, teachers and administrators will never again be able to overlook acts that are criminal or even capable of being described in those terms. Second, school officials must respond to these visible behaviors punitively. The paradigm example of this is expulsion as punishment for bringing a weapon to school.

Because these policies by their nature are prone to affect the traditionally insulated misbehaviors of middle-class youth, they have produced the only significant resistance met by the whole constellation of crime issues around schools. Whole Web pages are now devoted to criticizing the zero-tolerance aspect of the new regime in terms of its fundamental unfairness and unjust outcomes. Zero tolerance is deemed unfair because it results in a substantial deprivation of rights—that of the student to continue attending the school of his or her choice—even when the substantive goal of the rules—to eliminate real threats of violence—are clearly not served, as when students bring relatively nonthreatening weapons to school with no intent to do violence and little objective chance that violence would ensue. Critics also charge that the outcomes are racially marked. Minorities, especially African American male students, are disproportionately expelled as a result of these policies.[16]

The right to go to school in a safe environment has been transformed from a set of expectations for administrators to a zero-sum game between aggressors who are criminals or criminals in the making, and their victims—a shifting group consisting of everyone not stigmatized already as criminal. Administrators can only improve the lives of victims by subjecting the criminals among them to either the higher risks of expulsion into the streets or special schools full of expelled students that are the super-max prisons of the education system. As a school administrator acknowledged in an interview with William Finnegan, this takes a lot of the anxiety out of the exercise of power:

> "We've quit the 'poor kids' syndrome," he told me. "We now tell
> them what we expect from them, and we remove those kids who

give us trouble. It's an anxiety shift, from administrators to kids." (1999, 223)

In-School Detention

The new emphasis on disciplinary rules and their enforcement has inevitably created pressure for new sanctions. Between merely chastising and suspending or expelling students, an increasingly important recourse is sending misbehaving students to special custodial rooms within the school or on its grounds where they are held in varying degrees of rigor with other such malefactors and apart from the general population of the schools. Ann Ferguson describes a continuum of different penal spaces at the Chicago elementary school she observed. The first, which she calls the "punishing room," was apparently for first offenders and minor infractions:

> The Punishing Room is made up of a small rectangular antechamber with a door opening into a tiny office. The outer room is furnished with a low table flanked by child-sized chairs. The opposite wall is lined with shelves filled with the brightly colored uniforms and regalia of the children who act as the traffic guards before and after school. . . . The Punishing Room is the first tier of the disciplinary apparatus of the school. Like the courtroom, it is the place where stories are told, truth is determined, and judgment is passed. The children who get off lightly in the sentencing process are detained in the outer room, writing lines or copying school rules as their penalty. Sometimes they lose their recreation time as well and have to sit on the bench at recess. (2000, 34)

Punishing Room

Children who committed violations deemed more serious were sent to a room far more isolated from the traffic of the school, a room that the children in Ferguson's study called "the jailhouse." It was hidden away in an outside wall of the school building. Hot and cramped, it looked out on the recreational yard where students at recess would play. Unlike the punishing room, which permitted a fair amount of student conversation, the jailhouse regime enforced silence and the appearance of work on assignments that are part of the punishment (37).

Jailhouse

In-school detention spaces are not, however, limited to schools in traditionally high-crime areas like the one studied by Ferguson. Under current disciplinary regimes, they have become common at schools serving communities across the class spectrum and even in private and religious schools. As disciplinary codes identify more misbehavior as requiring recognition and official response but not warranting suspension or expulsion—which are largely counterproductive because they allow the student to escape oversight—in-house detention is becoming a sanction of choice for various offenses. A friend's son was recently sent to the detention room at a large high school drawing on some of the wealthier sections of Miami, in addition to less privileged areas. His offense involved disobedience of and disrespect for a teacher. Detention, in short, now occupies the space once filled by a trip to the principal's office.

Defining Deviance Up

Another feature of the new regime, overdetermined by many of its other features, is increased attention to behaviors by students that were previously not seen as problems requiring school responses, including schoolyard fights and bullying behavior. An example of one such program is touted in the pages of the federal government's annual report on school safety: McNair Elementary School, a 90-percent white suburban elementary school near St. Louis, Missouri:

> The mission statement of the Fight Free School Program is "To teach the youth of today, the future leaders of our nation, appropriate interpersonal behavior skills. The focus is to provide an improved school environment which will enhance the learning process and allow our children the optimum advantage to excel in their academic careers." (Riley and Reno 1998, 33)

Another exemplar in the report is McCormick Middle School, a rural middle school with an 80-percent African American population, profiled for its antibullying program. The program consisted of an "intense" training of staff, "and administrative policies to support changed student behaviors." The school also instituted "character education, conflict education and mediation programs" in its curriculum and promoted the formation of the students into "Students Against Bullying" (Riley and Reno 1998, 47).

Penal Swarming

Each of the penal features discussed above have melded their own logic and continuity with school traditions, hence constituting the new "normal." In the reform environment shaped by the Safe Schools Act and the other executive / legislative / and judicial changes associated with governing through crime, schools can find themselves host to many of these technologies at once, each promoting some more or less distinctive variant of a common concern to manage the risk of crime. Consider a model school uniform program featured in the Department of Education's on-line "Manual on School Uniforms."

Model School Uniform Policies, Norfolk, Virginia

Type: Mandatory uniform policy at Ruffner Middle School

Opt-out: None. Students who come to school without a uniform are subject to In-school detention

. . .

Support for disadvantaged students: The school provides uniforms for students who cannot afford them

Results: Using U.S. Department of Education software to track discipline data, Ruffner has noted improvements in students' behavior. Leaving class without permission is down 47 percent, throwing objects is down 68 percent and fighting has decreased by 38 percent. Staff attribute these changes in part to the uniform code.[17]

Ruffner, located in Norfolk, Virginia, provides a capsule summary of how many of the technologies and knowledge production strategies already discussed have become intertwined. A school uniform program is enforced by a zero-tolerance policy, with violations punished with in-school detention. The field of visible deviance created by the intensification of discipline is already put to use in evaluating the success of particular reforms. Although the normative ends of this program are called in question by the fact that crucial causal connection relies on the judgment of staff with a clear stake in the success of the strategies, the ability of the new procedures, bolstered by Department of Education software, to make crimelike behavior one of the most readily available handles on schools is evident. These numbers assure that disciplinary violations will play a crucial role in measuring success and failure in schools even if the current moral panics are someday forgotten.

Punishing Educational Failure

In order for an accountability system to work, there has to be *consequences*, and I believe one of the most important *consequences* will be, after a period of time, giving the schools time to adjust and districts time to try different things, if they're failing, that parents ought to be given different options. If children are trapped in schools that *will* not teach and *will* not change, there has to be a different *consequence*.
—George W. Bush, speech on education, January 23, 2001

The No Child Left Behind Act[18] represents another kind of extension of the crime model in education, but one that makes a leap in the generality of crime as a model for governing schools. The Bush proposals and the ultimate measures adopted by Congress trace their origins to theories of education reform espoused in the late 1980s and early 1990s that shared a model of a) linking financial investment in public schools with b) frequent testing to measure success and c) accountability for failure. Grounding itself more in theories of public choice than pedagogy and embracing market mechanisms, this reform strategy sought self-consciously to break out of the pattern in which innovations from the federal government would become simply a stream of resources that remained in place once created because of the heavy constituency in favor of spending on education. Testing and accountability would mean that schools and their stakeholders would have to achieve success and keep trying new approaches or lose the revenue stream.

Critics of the law have pointed to the failure of the administration to fully fund the investment side of the program, and the expensive and unfunded mandates that it places on states. But testing is, after all, relatively inexpensive and brings the imprimatur of scientific rationality. In this section, I suggest that behind this displacement of substantive assistance by testing is something more than budgetary considerations. The framing of the Bush proposals at their launch in the early days of the administration suggests the influence of the crime model. To put this displacement in its most simplistic terms, we might say that the original reform structure of investment/testing/consequences has been shifted in its Bush restatement from an emphasis on the investment-testing leg to the testing-consequences leg.

President Bush, who as governor of Texas made punishment—imposing the death penalty, building prisons, and toughening juvenile justice—his major mode of governing, restates the case for education reform in terms that suggest the way the crime/punishment model of governing can subtly restructure policy directed toward ostensibly different social problems. In his first major policy speech as president, George W. Bush highlighted his education reform plans. Education had been a centerpiece of the Bush campaign, one that had generally won high marks as strategically savvy for a governor best known for carrying out more executions than any other political leader in the Western world. Crime, central to his father's successful campaign for president in 1988, was rarely mentioned by George W. Bush during the 2000 election. Yet in his speech on education in early 2001, Bush inflected his concern with poor reading achievement among American school children with a distinctly different challenge: "We must face up to the plague of school violence, with an average of three million crimes committed against students and teachers inside public schools every year. That's unacceptable in our country. We need real reform" (Rothstein 2001). In short, school reform may signal not the end of crime as an obsession for government, but the progress of governing through crime.

The shocking figure evoked by Bush is, if not a gross exaggeration, a statistical artifact of an expansionist methodology and a mandate to "know" school crime whose origins and meaning are as interesting as its subject. The 3 million figure cited by Bush and others comes from the application of the traditional crime governance strategy of victim surveys to the school environment. Often criticized for being overinclusive of minor violations in the general population version, such crime surveys in schools are even more prone to collect the visible if trivial. Property crime, the dominant form of school crime, includes a vast number of stolen notebooks, and a good deal of assault behavior includes the batteries of schoolyard bullying. Fewer than 10 percent of the incidents reported in the survey that Bush drew on represented serious crimes. Subjects were explicitly encouraged by the survey instructions to report an incident "even if you are not certain it was a crime" (Rothstein 2001). At least in the aggregate, most experts agree that schools are among the safest places for school-age children to be. They are much more likely to be raped, murdered, assaulted, or endure a serious property crime at home or on the street.

The *New York Times* education columnist Edward Rothstein, who called Bush's figures a "gross exaggeration," claimed to be puzzled "that President Bush used the occasion of introducing his education program, focused mainly on testing and accountability, to revive the specter of school violence" (2001). But the central thesis of this chapter is that there is nothing puzzling in this at all. Crime's relevance to the discussion of school reform is dependent not on its actual prevalence but on its success as a rationale for recasting governance.

The original reform proposals, with their emphasis on measuring performance and providing more choices for education consumers, reflect neoliberal (i.e., market-oriented) logics that have dominated policy development in recent years. On this theory, by creating choices for education's subjects, hence making them more like consumers, and allowing their choices to mark the success of individual schools, with their own internal agents and subjects, educational improvement can be obtained without heavy-handed regulations from the center. Educational consumer choice creates incentives for the managers of individual schools, much as monetary rewards and costs stimulate market behavior. The Bush plan, in contrast, emphasizes testing and the promise of serious consequences for school failure. Here the model of prices is displaced by one of sanctions (Cooter 1984). Rather than transform educational subjects like students and their parents into consumers, the Bush vision portrays them as "victims." Rather than transform school agents such as principals and teachers into entrepreneurs, the Bush proposal subtly suggests that at least those in persistently failing schools must be seen and treated as criminals, willful violators of vulnerable subjects, who should be punished and incapacitated.

Consider the president's statement introducing his education proposals back in 2001. In his speech, Bush offered educational failure and crime at school as parallel problems. Although the speech never provides an analysis of what joins them together, it does showcase two powerful governmental metaphors, which it juxtaposes and links: "the scandal of illiteracy" and

Illiteracy as Scandal

"the plague of school violence." By pulling these two out and associating them with the terms "scandal" and "plague," Bush equates illiteracy and school violence but casts them in rather distinctive metaphors. Illiteracy as a "scandal" in the sense of a morally stigmatizing disclosure about a person is a governmental metaphor with deep roots in progressive politics (St. Clair 2004).

Along with Bush's persistent emphasis on improving the reading skills of minority children, his use of this metaphor signals to moderates and even liberals that he shares their outrage at the failure of public education to deliver on the promise of equal opportunity. This metaphor paints the illiterate subject as the bearer of a stigma but also as a victim of the immoral behavior of others or society at large. The metaphor of crime as plague has a long lineage, and its entailments are generally well understood. Criminals, carriers of the crime plague, must be isolated from general populations. Strict procedures must be put in place to define such criminals and make it easier for the system to eliminate them.

Crime as plague

In offering his program as both a way of ending the scandal and controlling the plague, Bush emphasized four elements that he described as "commitments": testing, local responsibility, assistance and additional funding for failing schools, followed by "ultimate" consequences for those that do not improve.

Bush's (4) elements / commitments

Each element is shaded by the crime metaphor. Testing is a classic disciplinary technology that combines normalizing judgment, expert surveillance, and the looming possibility of punishment (Foucault 1977, 184). Long a penal element in the space of education, testing in the Bush plan becomes a central ritual organizing school life superimposed on whatever structure of examination is part of the classroom-based instruction. As the quotation that begins this section suggests, testing here is not linked to a mandate to know the interior truth of the individual. Indeed, it is as an aggregate, measuring the performance of the school as a whole, that testing is deployed.[19] Moreover, the emphasis here is not on a circuit of knowledge and power that runs through testing to diagnosis to treatment but instead a penal circuit of judgment followed after a fair interval by "consequences."

Local responsibility and federal assistance is, of course, the very model of crime policy crafted by the Safe Streets Act of 1968 (see chapter 3). Finally, "ultimate consequences" suggests punishment and was the most frequently emphasized theme of Bush's personal statements on the law.

Conclusion

I began by contrasting the influence of crime on schools today to the influence of the civil rights project and the objective of overcoming a history of racial discrimination through education. In both cases, a subject not directly related to education has become an external framework for reforming schools. In both cases, the federal government has tied its considerable resources and command over public attention to the issue. In both cases, state and local school authorities have changed the way they plan and operate schools to fit the new urgency.

But the analogy is ultimately inapt in ways that suggest why crime is such a powerful metaphor for governing schools.

Educational disadvantage had once been a tool of racial discrimination and oppression and the construction of intraracial solidarity. For a time in the 1960s and 1970s, the federal government sought to reverse the effects of those past actions, and actively use schools as a tool for promoting racial equality and interracial solidarities. But relatively few Americans saw racial justice as integral to the experience of schooling. In contrast, the threat of criminal victimization of their children is at the heart of the schooling experience for many parents.[20] Compulsory education ultimately means surrender of parental control over the safety of their children for the length of the school day. While that fact is in many ways independent of the educational objectives of schooling, it is by no means secondary to it.

Parental resistance ultimately broke the back of federal support for using schools to actively promote racial equality. Yet more than a quarter century later, most metropolitan school districts are still heavily marked by institutions and approaches designed to promote racial equality. Even if parental support for governing schools through crime were to fade, it might take decades to witness the disappearance of internal patterns of governance embedded in technologies of knowing and acting on students, parents, teachers, and administrators.

Ironically, much of the resistance to racial equality in schools was based on a perception that desegregation was forcing parents to send their children to more dangerous schools. Despite some resistance to the excesses of zero tolerance, one should not expect widespread resentment towards the criminalization of schools, because it links the governance of schools to the problem of parental insecurity about their children at school.

The 3 million school crimes that President Bush invoked belong to a parade of numbers that will be continually replenished by existing statutory mandates. But unlike the statistical battles that desegregation cases turned into over the years, the numbers produced by crime governance feed directly back into the sources of parental fears about the fate of their children at school.

Nineteenth-century public school buildings often resembled prisons and asylums because all three drew on a common technology of power for improving the "performance" of their inmates (Foucault 1977). If schools today are again coming to seem more and more like prisons, it is not because of a renewed faith in the capacity of disciplinary methods. Indeed, prisons and schools increasingly deny their capacity to do much more than sort and warehouse people. What they share instead is the institutional imperative that crime is simultaneously the most important problem they have to deal with and a reality whose "existence"—as defined by the federally imposed edict of ever-expanding data collection—is precisely what allows these institutions to maintain and expand themselves in perpetuity.

[handwritten margin note: Schools as prisons]

Crime, Victimization, and Punishment in the

Deregulated Workplace

> If you have rules that allow a lot more freedom, then you need
> much more vigilance and enforcement.
>
> —George Akerlof, *New York Times,* July 28, 2002

> Employers must accept and prepare for the inevitable likelihood
> of experiencing a violent event or behavior at their workplace.
>
> —Jane Philbrick, Marcia Sparks, Marsha Hass,
> and Steven Arsenault, "Workplace Violence,"
> *American Business Review,* 2003

Crime has always been part of the messy struggle for control of the workplace. The modern regime of labor by formally free and equal contract partners arose to dominance in the nineteenth century against a background of labor relations that looked far more like miniature monarchies with a master and his servants including slavery, indentured servitude, and merchants. In such settings, the power to govern work meant the power to define disobedience as crime and respond with sanctions, often physical. Discipline wielded by managers had an undeniably penal element that included flogging, confinement, and loss of pay.

On the other side, employee resistance to these modern labor systems and to the rise of the modern capitalist factory was often defined by law as a form of property crime. Indeed, the rise of capitalism in England during the eighteenth century required a highly rationalized system of property crime to protect the new forms of property essential to capitalist production (Thompson 1975). The creation of a disciplined workforce capable of being profitably employed on the basis of compensation for time worked meant redefining as criminal some aspects of traditional forms of non-wage compensation for employment, such as taking unauthorized time off and taking "surplus" materials home for private use—either as outright theft or at least a breach of the duty of loyalty, its civil equivalent. The work rules of Victorian railways were made by Parliament into criminal laws. A brakeman sleeping or drunk on the job might face jail time or a fine and dismissal. Modern authoritarian regimes have reintroduced penal controls over labor. For example, the Nazis hanged resistant workers and left their bodies dangling on the shop floor of the slave-labor factories where they made the V2 rocket (Yang & Linebaugh 2005).

American history includes numerous examples of how the instruments and metaphors of criminal law play into the cauldron of conflicts of the workplace. Slavery, most famously, was directly governed with the force of the lash and the possibility of death for acts of rebellion against the master. Masters were formally entitled to exercise penal violence in the enforcement of their right to demand the labor of the slave. As the formally free contract became the dominant standard, dismissal replaced physical violence as the ultimate sanction. This paralleled the shift in state punishment from frequent use of corporal and capital punishment for serious crimes to heavy reliance on imprisonment designed to suspend a person's liberty without physically harming them. As in the prison, however, violence reemerged at the margins in the often physical control of supervisors and in the use of criminals to deal violently with those organizing strikes or impeding production in other ways. Unions were often treated as criminal conspiracies by the state courts in the late nineteenth and early twentieth centuries. At the same time, New York businesses turned to the city's organized crime groups to break up union organizing among workers who had the same immigrant backgrounds as the mobsters. Later, the unions would invite similar figures to enforce order on their side, leading to a relationship between unions and organized crime that flourished unchecked until the 1970s.

But if organized crime maintained an influence in some businesses and some unions throughout the twentieth century, the heyday of collective bargaining, from the late 1930s through the beginning of the 1980s in the United States, corresponded to a time when the role of criminal law as instrument and metaphor was minimized in the governance of work. During this period, strikes were mostly considered a legitimate mode of civil conflict,[1] meaning labor could take its grievances with management into open refusal to work without fear of being fired and pauperized as well as criminalized by the state. By the same token, the New Deal labor regime placed restrictions on management's ability to undertake various coercive actions against unions and their organizers, but management was also protected from accusations of crime, and violations of the right to organize became "unfair labor practices" subject to injunctive relief and limited forms of compensation but not criminal sanction. The New Deal also introduced national regulations that treated workplace safety failures as civil failures subject to fines and tended to avoid criminal sanctions even in the case of serious injury or death.

Collective bargaining also ushered in an era of due process in disciplining and dismissing employees. Administrative courts produced a body of arbitration decisions on "just cause" for dismissal that, instead of dismissal, highly favored rehabilitation and reintegration of the "deviant" worker. With 40 percent of the private-sector workforce unionized in the 1950s, the transformation of disciplinary power within the workplace paralleled the efforts of official penology to permanently blend punishment into the New Deal state's expanded education, health, and welfare functions. But by the turn of the twenty-first century, the decline of collective bargaining and the general loss of bargaining power by American workers in the face of global competition for low-cost labor had undermined this regime, and brought a return of crime as a central axis of regulation and resistance in the workplace.

The curve of penal severity from the late 1960s, marked by a nearly five-fold increase in the U.S. imprisonment rate during this period, is strikingly paralleled by the transformation of the governance of work (Weiler 1990). The unionized portion of the workforce entered a period of decline in the 1950s and near free fall since the 1980s; this may only now be ending (if it is). Christian Parenti's (1998) insightful interpretation of America's recent penal severity points out that the intense criminalization of those populations living outside the legal labor market has played a global role in disciplining the legal labor force. In Parenti's view, employers were able to recapture a portion of their declining profit by squeezing a labor force weakened by the decline of unions and the criminalization of alternative survival strategies outside the labor force. From this perspective, the increase in punishment may not have deterred crime, but it deterred strikes, unionization drives, and mobility.

Consistent with the main themes of this book, I see in this the penetration of the metaphors, tactics, and knowledge of crime directly into the workplace. This takes multiple forms. Looking at management first, we can see multiple streams of influence, from concerns about crime itself inside the workplace to the metaphors of punishment. Globally, the general dominance of the "at-will" employment doctrine means that employers enjoy wide discretion to dismiss employees for unsatisfactory performance of almost any kind. From the perspective of the collective bargaining environment, where dismissal was openly seen as a severe punishment appropriate in response only to extreme or repetitive misconduct, the return of dismissal as a ready tool of management reflects a significant escalation in the punitiveness of labor relations.

There is a new emphasis on surveillance and detection of illegal behavior such as drug use, both to prevent the presumptive slacking off that drug use costs the company and to serve as a ready basis for dismissal of employees felt to be uncooperative or assertive. The widespread use of drug testing in American employment is one important component of this (Hoffman 2001).[2] Indeed, the federal government since the 1980s has encouraged drug testing in the workforce.

The combination of the at-will employment environment with the pervasive search for criminal behavior in the workforce creates a similar relationship of support between the penal law of the state and the disciplinary goals of management. Unlike the Victorian railways, the relationship between penal law and private industry is one more of encouragement and modeling than command and control.

In addition, it almost certainly reflects the dark side of the increasingly stark asymmetry of power between management and workers. Crime is returning as a nexus of employee resistance. Once again, return takes multiple forms, none of which is precisely a restoration of the past. The decline of collective bargaining remedies against discipline and dismissal has been balanced in part by the development of a body of civil rights law focused on discriminatory practices, policies, or purposes that may lie behind an employee's dismissal. The aggrieved employee claims that she or he was dismissed because of race, gender, religion, or age, or as a result of the exercise of liberties protected under the First Amendment (e.g., expression, religious freedom). On a formal level, these actions are no more criminal than those claimed in any other civil suit claiming injury, but in the nature of the claim they make, they more closely parallel criminal law, particularly that part of criminal law concerned with truly moral breaches. These claims closely parallel crime in defining victims and offenders, in seeking compensation for harms that violate public policy as well as individual rights, and are intentional wrongdoing, not mere accidents (Minow 1993).

Indeed, in explaining what are, in effect, breaks in the employment-at-will doctrine, courts have defined these kinds of constraints as protecting the public interest. Sexual harassment has constituted another ground of civil liability on which workers are able to contest dismissal, discipline, and work conditions generally.

A different kind of resistance is marked by widely publicized armed assaults by current or former employees directed against co-workers, especially managerial employees. In many cases, discipline or dismissal was the primary incident underlying the employee's lethal resentments. A strikingly high proportion of the attackers are white men, who as a group have relatively poor chances of making a successful employment discrimination claim. It is difficult to determine whether the number of such assaults is actually increasing, and if so, why, but the employee as violent criminal has emerged as a dominant target of workplace governance in recent years.

A terrible realization of many of these themes occurred in a Daimler Chrysler plant in Toledo, Ohio, in early 2005 (Yang & Linebaugh 2005). Myles Meyers, a 54-year-old longtime employee of the plant, came to work with a shotgun and killed one supervisor and wounded two other employees before committing suicide. The incident was explained in the media by a marijuana possession charge that Meyers was facing, but fellow workers blamed the increasingly poisonous climate in the plant, which they said had cut every possible corner to stay profitable and avoid shutdown by the corporation. A once-valuable skilled worker, Meyers had become a source of resistance to corner-cutting, and the company was seeking to dismiss him based on the drug possession charge, which was not easy because this remained a union plant.

As employment lawyers Vicki A. Laden and Gregory Schwartz (2000, 246) note:

> The threat of occupational injury or death, once represented by dangerous machinery or hazardous environments, has now become discursively located in conceptions of the "pathogenic worker," lurking unnoticed in the workplace, poised to explode in lethal violence against his supervisors or co-workers.

The imperative of preventing such assaults has become itself a major managerial theme in business. Violent behavior is not particularly likely at work, and when it occurs, it is rarely committed by workers. Nonetheless, the potentially violent employee, perhaps because she or he represents the most controllable source of workplace violence, has become a major concern. As employers find themselves becoming responsible for the protection of customers and employees from violent behavior of employees, they are necessarily seeking more far-reaching crime-control oriented screening and surveillance in the workplace.

Violence, Drugs, and Fraud: The Specter of Crime and Violence at Work

As we have noted above, violence is no stranger to the American workplace. The history of the last century is marked by innumerable images of defiant workers arrayed outside locked factories as soldiers and private security guards fire rifles at them. The coming of the New Deal saw the decline of collective violence at American workplaces. After World War II, an increasingly secure and well-paid American workforce had little use for violent crime outside of certain notorious industries like the waterfront or trucking. Today, violence has returned to haunt the American workplace, but the specter of collective actions and pitched battles arising out of overt struggles for power has given way to terrifying moments of sudden violence with little political context and often without even narrative elaboration.

Sometimes there are hints this violence is channeling the kinds of tensions that once found an outlet in collective action. Felix Gonzalez, a state worker in California, left a note before he shot his boss and himself stating, "I hope this will alleviate a lot of stress from my co-workers and set them free" (DiLorenzo & Carroll 1995). Many other incidents suggest smoldering resentments that bespeak problems extending far beyond the workplace.

There is considerable debate about how serious the violent crime threat is in the workplace. In 1996, only 4.25 percent of American homicides took place in workplaces. The majority of these were robberies by persons not employed at the workplace: less than 7 percent of these were committed by present or former employees (Laden & Schwartz 2000, 256). From another perspective, however, the success of workplace safety, and the decline of the most dangerous industries like steel and railways has produced an American workplace where death is now relatively rare, compared to the past (although needlessly high in some industries like mining) and violent death by either machines or people rarer still. From this perspective, the fact that homicide is the second most common cause of death in the workplace in the United States, and the highest for women workers, enables management to make it a compelling issue for enforcing discipline (Phillips 1996).

The Bureau of Justice Statistics survey of victimization has produced an estimate of 1.5 million annual workplace assaults, a statistic widely cited even though most of what counts as assault involves neither injury nor even physical contact, as many forms of sexual harassment are counted (Laden & Schwartz 2000, 258). Media images of workplace violence also highlight the seriousness of the threat to most workers. Because a hostage-taking incident in a workplace anywhere in the United States is likely to dominate local news coverage everywhere, the accumulation of such stories can seem enormous and threatening.

Whatever the comparative reality of the threat of workplace violence, there is no doubt it is recasting workplace governance. A host of experts and commercial consultants have emerged with a strong stake in fomenting concern about the threat of violence and fraud at work, simultaneously expanding the range of deviant conduct. An article on the subject in *American Business Review* states alarmingly that "incidents of workplace violence, in public and private organizations, have increased more than 750 percent since 1998" (Philbrick et al. 2003). In addition to the emotional cost to family members and co-workers, such incidents also produce direct costs as high as $250,000 per serious violent incident—a figure that may be compounded many times over by the plethora of liability issues that a business faces when a violent incident occurs on its premises. This is especially so when perpetrated by a current or former employee, on the theory that the business was negligent in hiring, retaining, or supervising the employee. Indeed, companies find themselves in a complex position in which dismissing an apparently dangerous employee may subject them to liability for discrimination against the disabled (under federal and an increasing number of state laws) and not dismissing him may lead to subsequent lawsuits by victims if the employee goes on to injure customers or other workers.

These concerns have led managers to invest in all kinds of technologies and expertise aimed at reducing such risks, from surveillance of the workplace itself to security consultants who profess to screen out potentially

Security

violent employees at the hiring stage. Security is also coming to have a considerable weight in the hiring, promotion, and disciplining of employees.[3] A host of companies now provide packages of business security services. Typical services include preemployment screening; drug testing; fraud prevention and investigation; and violence threat assessment and response. The firms offering these services include Accufacts Pre Employment, ChoicePoint, First American, Isotron, Concentra, Kelly Services, SOURCECORP, kforce, Resources Connection, and Equifax. Since the terrorist attacks of September 11, the scale of expenditures on security in the workplace has received considerable media attention. The sketchy data available on the percentage of revenues spent on security—in many companies, these would be embedded in other categories of expense—are often put forward as suggesting complacency. Thus a 2003 article in *USA Today* (Kessler 2003) noted that "even now most U.S. firms spend 2% or less of revenue on security," far less than the 5 percent spent in more terror-savvy Israel. Yet the other figure offered in comparison by the article—that firms spent, on average, 3 percent on technology—is revealing; given that expenditure for technology is a widespread feature of contemporary business, the 2 percent spent on security would seem to indicate a major trend. Higher numbers, and perhaps our future, can be observed in places like Argentina— where in 2001 more than 40 percent of buildings in the capital of Buenos Aires had private security guards, amounting to more than 38,000 private security guards.[4]

As we shall see below, the "at will" employment environment that dominates private sector workplaces in the United States is especially vulnerable to efforts by management in which preventing violence, drug use, and fraud are consistently offered as the justification for controls that are also aimed at removing discontented workers and keeping others engaged in productivity beyond what their wage incentives alone would explain. Just as health and safety formed the key issues around which employers sought to restore dominance over workers in the period following the New Deal (Klein 2002), today crime has become a structural rationale of the assertion of managerial control over the contemporary workplace.

Key

Beyond violence, drugs have played the most dramatic role in this process of governing the workplace through crime. From the start of the Reagan administration, a major effort was begun to recast illegal narcotics from a recreational drug experience to participation in an organized criminal enterprise, and to blame drug use and the drug business for the high level of violence in American society. The zero-tolerance campaign launched in the United States military in the early 1980s already offered a model for disciplining the workplace generally. Recruits whose tests showed evidence of drug use were to be turned down. Current military personnel were given a chance to clean up and then subjected to drug testing on a regular basis. At the heart of zero tolerance was the sanction of exclusion or expulsion for even trivial use of illegal drugs. Reagan and later President Bush the First and their drug advisors, believed the criminal justice war on drugs in the inner city would not stop the casual recreational drug users in the middle class, at least not without escalating the war into politically problematic directions. Instead, they saw zero tolerance as a way to create a sanction that would be just as feared by the middle class and far easier to police, since the burden of proof would be placed on workers.

In September 1986, President Reagan issued Executive Order 12564, entitled "Drug Free Federal Workplace," that imposed a set of controls on federal workers and requiring federal contractors to impose similar controls on their workers. Reagan asserted that "drug use is having serious effects upon a significant proportion of the national work force and results in billions of dollars of lost productivity each year." The strategy included two elements: "offer drug users a helping hand, and at the same time, demonstrat[e] to drug users and potential drug users that drugs will not be tolerated in the federal workplace."[5]

Reagan's official argument explicitly blended the penal and economic significance of drug use.

> The profits from illegal drugs provide the single greatest source of income for organized crime, fuel violent street crime, and otherwise contribute to the breakdown of our society;
>
> The use of illegal drugs, on or off duty, by Federal employees is inconsistent not only with the law-abiding behavior expected of all citizens, but also with the special trust placed in such employees as servants of the public;
>
> The use of illegal drugs, on or off duty, tends to make employees less productive, less reliable, and prone to greater absenteeism than their fellow employees who do not use illegal drugs.[6]

The issue is one of drug use at any time, not simply such use in the workplace; even off-duty workers are violating the trust placed in them and denying their employer the full productivity of a drug-free employee. The language in the first clause sounds all the major themes of "governing through crime" at the state level: crime in the streets and the breakdown of society.

The language of "special trust" was not just a code word for government to the free-enterprise-minded Reagan. Indeed, the idea that employees are bound by a contractual duty of loyalty to wholeheartedly serve their employers' objectives even outside the work situation has been a crucial part of the criminal law, embodying the same legal asymmetry of the at-will employment situation. In a number of important cases, courts have valorized this duty even over such concerns as consumer protection, worker safety, and free speech. President Reagan was signaling from one CEO to another that the private sector should view drug use as a form of treason against the company because it generated lost productivity through unreliable and absent workers. The goal was a workplace free of not only drugs but those unable to get off drugs. To that end, offers of rehabilitation were combined with drug testing—mandatory for selected employees and new hires, voluntary for others—and ultimately steps to "remove" those who failed to keep a second promise to stay off drugs.

The executive order made clear that its new regime of testing and removals was not to be joined with criminal sanctions. The order explicitly barred supervisors from making drug test information available to law enforcement. Yet at the same time, it placed drugs at the center of a double criminalization of the workplace: first, by making illegal drugs more important than safety, justice, or other workplace concerns; and second, by demanding a hardening of disciplinary sanctions within the workplace. Drug testing today may be less important than the ubiquitous use of background checks and special tests designed to measure what are known in the business as "honesty and integrity," which in this context "are often used interchangeably to describe theft, orientation to safety, counter productivity, workplace withdrawal, time theft, and chemical dependency" (Hollwitz 1998, 20).

In the collective bargaining environment, discipline and dismissal of employees is subject to negotiated procedures. Though the interests of individual workers charged with misconduct are not always and completely in line with those of their unions, unions have generally established due process protection for employees charged with misconduct. More important, unions have established an entitlement to employment, barring economic layoff, if performance is adequate. This entitlement to employment necessarily produces procedural protections because of the high cost of deprivation to the worker. Historically, it also produced a substantive change in the nature of discipline and dismissal. Discipline itself was expected to operate in rehabilitative ways. Dismissal became rarer and more extraordinary, reserved for those whose misconduct was repeated and serious.

Were unions still representing 40 percent of the private labor force, the shape of the current disciplining of the workforce would look different. Drug testing would be permitted only if employees as a collective represented through their union agreed that a common interest required greater vigilance against drug use, as in those cases in which the safety of other workers was compromised. Discipline for drugs and other criminal misconduct would be responded to with a rehabilitative approach at first rather than with dismissal. Indeed, the weight of the unionized sector on market expectations even in nonunion sectors would call into question the whole strategy of recasting workplace governance in terms of violence, drugs, and fraud.

In contemporary America, where unions represent less than 10 percent of private-sector workers, discipline and dismissal are now controlled largely through the employment-at-will doctrine. That doctrine, formed in part as a contrast to slavery in the nineteenth century, provides the worker with a powerful weapon against unjust and cruel discipline: the right to leave at any time with no financial or other sanctions.[7] For the employer, it provides the power to dismiss at any time for any reason that does not independently violate public policy (e.g., racial discrimination).

This power gives employers considerable freedom to reshape the governance of the workplace in terms of crime: screening out employees with criminal backgrounds, firing employees for crimes like drug use or domestic violence (committed off the job), testing employees for drug use, organizing sting operations to uncover employee theft or fraud, and so on. As a result, outside of high-skill industries—where companies have sizable investments in the embodied knowledge of employees, and the few remaining unionized segments of the workforce—the logic of control in workplace discipline has swung dramatically back in the direction of greater punitiveness and arbitrariness. In her participant observation study of low-wage work in the retail, restaurant, and hotel industries, Barbara Ehrenreich (2003) found that crime-focused job interviews, drug tests, and surveillance were the most constant features of the many businesses she worked in. Reflecting on her fieldwork, Ehrenreich reports, "I still flinch to think that I spent all those weeks under the surveillance of men (and later women) whose job it was to monitor my behavior for signs of sloth, theft, drug abuse, or worse" (22). Preemployment interviews were generally introduced with reassurances that there were no right answers. But the questions, many of them dealing with tolerance for misconduct or simply nonconformity, appeared to screen out anyone who did not strongly agree with demands for total conformity. Almost everywhere she applied for work, Ehrenreich was expected to provide urine for a drug test, a practice she estimates is established in some 87 percent of American businesses.

The at-will doctrine means courts are very reluctant to interfere with employer discipline or dismissal decisions unless there is a question of potential violation of a right specifically bargained for in the employment contract. Legal struggle over governance in the workplace comes in the form of civil suits by employees or others complaining of action or inaction justified around the problem of crime. One strategy is for employees damaged by discipline or dismissal to seek, if possible, to bring themselves under the few exceptions to the at-will doctrine that have been recognized in the name of public policy, especially claims of discrimination under state and federal civil rights actions. The other is for employees or customers victimized by employees to sue the employer for negligent hiring, retaining, or failing to supervise. Employers face a dual threat. If they act against an employee whom they suspect to be a criminal threat, they may face liability in a suit for discrimination or defamation. If they fail to act, or warn successor employers who have asked for a reference, they may face liability for damage caused to the employee.

Cody v. Cigna Healthcare of St. Louis, Inc: A Portrait of the Workplace as Crime Scene

Cody v. Cigna Healthcare of St. Louis, Inc., involved the kind of civil rights claims that have become the main channel for employees to contest governance decisions in the workplace, in this case a claim under the Americans with Disabilities Act (ADA).[8] Carol Cody worked as a nurse for the defendant, a health insurer. Her job required her to make "on-site" quality-of-care reviews at physicians' offices in the metropolitan St. Louis area. Cody claimed, then and at the time of her civil suit, that she suffered from depression and an acute anxiety that was worsened by going into areas of St. Louis that she considered "dangerous." Her supervisor refused to help and, according to Cody, intentionally assigned her to such areas. In short, Cody wanted Cigna to protect her from crime and even from exposure to danger of crime. Cody attempted to take her dispute to the executive director of Cigna's St. Louis office, notifying him of her concerns and the fact that she was under treatment. The director set up a meeting for the next day.

According to Cody, when her supervisor learned of the planned meeting, she warned Cody that she "would suffer the consequences" for having complained. Cody also found a Styrofoam cup on her desk with a sign attached reading "alms for the sick"; when she complained about that to the director, she was urged to take the day off, and the meeting with the executive director was delayed. That same day, some of Cody's co-workers began a flow of negative reports about Cody to the director. A call from a co-worker reported that Cody had been behaving strangely and had mentioned carrying a gun. At a meeting the next morning, other employees complained to the director that Cody behaved bizarrely, including sprinkling salt outside her cubicle to "keep away evil spirits," staring into space, and drawing pictures of what appeared to be sperm to observers. There was further mention of a gun. Following the meeting, the director called Cigna's human resources department.

During this call, Cody arrived at the executive director's office, and he advised human resources that she had a bulge in her purse. Human resources then contacted Cigna's security department, which sent to the executive director's office a "local security specialist" who was introduced to Cody as a mediator. He advised the director to deactivate Cody's security access card in advance of the meeting, and he conducted searches of the purses of both Cody and the supervisor. No weapons were found. Human resources advised the director to offer Cody a paid leave of absence, followed by return to work only if she passed a psychiatric screen. The director presented this option to Cody, changing a proposal he had earlier made of switching Cody to another supervisor. Cody apparently accepted the terms after negotiating to be able to see her own therapist at the company's expense.

When Cody left, she was unable to access either the exit from the building or the parking lot because of the decision to deactivate her card.

She was permitted to leave by a security guard who, upon instructions from the director, confiscated the card. Apparently angered by these rituals of mistrust, Cody phoned the director upon her return home and told him that on reconsideration, she would not be returning to work. The director explicitly invited her to reconsider and stated that he regretted her decision.

Cody filed discrimination charges against Cigna, claiming that she was subject to workplace harassment because of her depression, and that Cigna's actions violated both the ADA and the Missouri Human Rights Act. The Equal Employment Opportunity Commission dismissed her complaint, and Cody then filed her case in district court.[9] After conclusion of discovery, the court granted defendant's motion for summary judgment. The court of appeals affirmed the finding that Cody's depression and anxiety did not constitute a disability for purposes of the ADA.

Critics of the decision in *Cody v. Cigna* suggest it is an example of how fear of violence in the workplace undermines the ability of mentally ill workers to achieve the protection that the ADA was intended to provide (Laden & Schwartz 2000). They rightly point to the role played by a body of quite dubious "security" expertise dominating workplace governance today that tends to favor exclusion over accommodation strategies aimed at making the work environment healthier. Because Cody was defined as being a threat rather than as having a disability, the civil rights laws failed her.

Here we can take *Cody v. Cigna* as an extreme but revealing picture of the way crime and its analogues play into the struggle for control over work. I do not claim *Cody* is a "typical" employment discrimination case, let alone a typical example of struggles over governance at work. Yet even if a somewhat freakish case, it serves to suggest how players in the workplace setting are prepared to use crime in a strategic way to deal with issues fundamentally about workplace dominance.

In this context, we can view *Cody v. Cigna* as a window into the way crime operates in the battle for power over labor in the workplace.

First, consider Carol Cody herself. Cody invoked her psychological distress at being in areas of St. Louis that she considered dangerous as an effort to exercise more control over her work, both in relationship to her supervisor and to the executive director of Cigna's St. Louis office. We can assume that "dangerous" areas for Cody meant high-crime areas, rather than places with wild animals, heavy pollution, or prone to flooding. Indeed, it is a feature of our time that "danger" so connotes crime that it does not have to be mentioned independently: "Don't go there, its dangerous."

We do not have enough information in this appellate opinion to begin making full sense of her precise motives. Is Carol Cody white? Were the areas she considered high-crime areas heavily African American? Did her distress at being in these areas overlap in any way with a preference for not dealing with physicians and medical staff who were African American, as medical providers in those areas were more likely to have been? We simply cannot answer those questions with the facts available, although to raise them seriously is to recognize how plausible such motivations remain and to recognize how much crime both channels and effaces the issues of race that not so long ago formed a central focus of workplace governance.

It is also possible that Cody simply existed at the extreme end of the continuum of the fear of violent crime that clearly influences women far more than it influences men of comparable status and power. The power of crime and fear of crime over women's lives has been documented by sociological research (Madriz 1997). This research suggests there is little about the daily routines of contemporary American women that does not reflect some concern for vulnerability to crime. Research from a very different angle on the development of real estate in newer and more distant suburban areas that have been called "edge cities" (Garreau 1991) confirms that making women feel safer is a primary consideration of those who develop large retail, office, and residential projects. If so, the anxiety that Cody felt when making her auditing visits to medical providers, in what she perceived as high-crime areas, was not only a disability but one that disparately affects women as an embodied form of psychic damage.[10] Arguably, Cigna's indifference to her concerns about visiting high-crime areas could be seen as a form of gender discrimination, a ground not raised in Cody's lawsuit.

One also wonders about Cigna's lack of professional interest in her concerns. Cigna's St. Louis office was no stranger to crime risk. One of its security specialists was, after all, readily available on a moment's notice to search Cody's purse; this same person might have been sent with Cody on one of her visits to evaluate the situation, and perhaps make recommendations for technology and strategies that could make Cody feel safer.[11]

We can only speculate about the intersubjective aspects of Cody's claims about her response to being in "high-crime areas." What we can have more confidence about is that Cody felt that her concerns about crime would be taken seriously. In the end, her legal case depended on casting her fear as an individual pathology, but was that how she initially presented it to her supervisor and the director of Cigna's St. Louis office? The frequency with which people lie about being crime victims (or in this case, arguably, being afraid of becoming one)—Susan Smith saying a black man had snatched her two sons away along with her car—tells us that this seems such a plausible phenomenon that almost anyone can get away with faking it.

Even more frequently, people invoke fear of crime as a reason not to do certain things, go certain places, or meet with certain people. Cody's frustration that her supervisor would not accommodate her preferences was undoubtedly real, but her sense that she was entitled to be accommodated on this preference reflects the value of crime as rationale for governance decisions in the workplace and elsewhere. The circulation of claims about crime and fear of crime is both an indicator of the status of crime risk in the workplace, and a source of power that can be used strategically within the struggle over workplace governance.

Cody was far from the only player in the Cigna workplace gaming crime and its intimations for advantage. We cannot tell from the facts in the opinion why Cody's fellow workers sided with her supervisor. Perhaps they felt her demands were unreasonable or would mean they had to spend more time in areas that Cody wished not to visit. At any rate, both the flow of phone calls to the executive director, and the emergency meeting held the next morning in Cody's absence to discuss her "peculiarities" in more detail, speak volumes about the power that the claim of fear of crime can have in the workplace. The fragmentary information they provided the director—real, imagined, or made up—fit into a narrative all of them and us recognize from television: the ordinary person who is about to "blow" or "go postal" and use a firearm to kill her bosses and fellow workers. This widely shared cultural "knowledge" about the threat of crime is one Cody's fellow workers used to brilliant effect in outmaneuvering Cody on behalf of her supervisor, and whatever collective interests she represented.

Why are some crime claims so much more effective than others? Cody's fears about visiting medical providers in supposedly high-crime areas were ignored, but her co-workers' fears that Cody was about to "go postal" received rapid, personal, and effective response from top management. Was it that Cody characterized her problem as one of anxiety rather than fear for her safety? Without looking up the numbers, would anyone want to bet that Cody's fear that something bad might happen to her in the parking lot of one of the inner-city St. Louis medical providers she visited was manifestly unreasonable compared to her co-workers' fear that she would go postal? Was management responsive to the co-workers because they supported their supervisor or simply because Cody was a complainer?

Only interviews with the principals would shed light on these questions. One advantage the co-workers clearly had was that their narrative fit so well with the "worker as violent psychopath" dominant myth. This narrative is one that fits the interests of the new security professionals, who demand an increasing share of the firm's profits to manage all manner of risks under the framework of crime and security (Laden and Schwartz 2000). When co-workers raised concerns about whether Cody was showing signs of going postal, they were appealing to a kind of knowledge and power that these new professionals claim as their own: how to spot dangerous people and manage them. When Cody raised concerns about her anxiety in visiting high-crime areas, she was raising uncomfortable issues about the uneven distribution of security in society, and the corollary question inside the workplace of who is going to have to deal with that.

A final crime frame in the workplace is raised in the *Cody* facts by the ubiquitous and mostly banal presence of security systems and agents. Like most workplaces in late twentieth-century America, the Cigna St. Louis office bristled with security procedures and technologies. The office had a security department that included an on-site specialist offering expertise in managing crime risks as well as direct intervention. The former kind of expertise is often provided by insurance companies as well, and forms a growing part of the expertise they market.

Like many workplaces and public buildings, the entrances to Cigna's offices and parking lot are controlled by electronic key systems that allow entry or exit only to someone bearing an authorized card. As Carol Cody discovered, that authorization can be removed with striking speed. Indeed, no part of her experience seemed to aggravate Cody as much as finding she could not operate the entrances and exits she had used effortlessly dozens of times. One imagines that she got to the first electronic barrier not even thinking about it and may have at first thought that her card was malfunctioning, as often happens with these systems. Perhaps another person came along and opened the door. We are told that at the exit to the parking lot, the attendant, under instructions from the director, took physical custody of the card. At that point, Cody could have had no illusions but that she had been separated from the company as a moral if not legal unit. Her anger and follow-up call to the director were understandable, as was her ultimately failed search for a legal remedy.

The Employee as Victim: Employment Discrimination Law

In the collective bargaining environment, issues like those raised by Carol Cody would almost certainly have been dealt with through negotiation, if the union supported her demands, or by grievance, if not. Employees in the at-will environment cannot generally fall back upon such procedures unless they have sufficient bargaining power to insert such rights into their employment contract from the start. In the absence of clear evidence of negotiated rights, courts in most states strongly presume that a contract is at will.

If an employee is disciplined or dismissed and wants to resist through law, she has to establish an exception to the at-will doctrine, generally by establishing that public policy forbids an employer from disciplining or dismissing the employee for a particular reason. Generally, there are only two ways to determine such an exception. One is to show that the reason you were fired was for refusal to cooperate with something that would be against public policy because it is a crime in itself. These would be actions like fixing a price, dumping environmental toxins, or perjuring yourself on behalf of your employer in a legal matter to which you have been called to present evidence under oath. The second is to show that you were fired because your employer discriminated against you on the basis of some forbidden consideration, such as your race, gender, age, or disability. This area, generally known as employment discrimination law, enables the filing of a lawsuit under one of several broad federal statutes and a host of state statutes that mimic the major provisions of these.[12]

When we look at these employee causes of action in the larger context of the struggle for workplace power, there is a strong parallel with the emergence of crime as a crucial pivot for governance and struggles around governance. When the employee has to show that the employer wanted him to, say, dump pollutants or falsify a legal record, the cause of action requires the worker to prove that a crime was in the offing. Being fired for refusing to be part of a crime constitutes being a victim of crime. Employment discrimination is even more explicit in linking the possibility of a remedy to a showing of personal victimization. Racism, sexism, and many other forms of public and private prejudice are not quite crimes in our society, although they can be criminalized when combined as the motive for some act that is criminal in nature. But like crimes, they are seen as immoral and illegal, and unlike many civil wrongs that are based on negligence or strict liability—which require a defendant to compensate an injured party even though the underlying activity was not wrong or blameworthy—discriminatory treatment is seen as condemned by the law. To accuse someone of discriminating against you is, in that sense, rhetorically much like accusing someone of committing a fairly serious offense.

Strong objections can be raised to my effort to describe employment discrimination claims as kin to claims of criminal victimization. To do so may seem to broaden the concept to the point of irrelevancy and to impugn what are self-consciously civil rather than criminal remedies. As to the first point, we have insisted from the beginning of this book that governing through crime is not only about the imposition of actual criminal sanctions but is also descriptive of situations in which crime provides the metaphors and narratives in which efforts to govern are cast. It is true that as civil actions, discrimination claims are limited in their punitive goals to monetary sanctions and provide a procedural playing field for litigants very different from that of criminal court. Yet as a number of sympathetic scholars of antidiscrimination law have argued, the construction of the civil rights victim shares important features with the victim of crime (Brown 1995; Bumiller 1988). In both cases, the dispute is expressed as an act of harmful wrongdoing that violates public policy. In both cases, the victim is constructed by the law as a passive recipient of the actions of the offender.

Even if civil rights law constructed its notion of victimization in an independent way, the enormous influence of the crime victim as a model for the governable interests of the people has transformed other kinds of victimization claims, especially those, like civil rights claims, that have their roots in struggles for collective rather than individual justice. It is against the background of the decline of legal means for seeking collective justice—including collective bargaining law, institutional reform litigation, and social welfare law—that we can see how much antidiscrimination law has been compelled to reposition itself on a landscape reshaped by crime.

The New Deal state that did so much to build up socially oriented law was notorious for downplaying civil rights. Yet when civil rights politics broke through in the 1950s and 1960s, its primary goals were ones of access and equality in this social welfare state through equal education, housing, business subsidies. In short, the roots of civil rights laws were collective struggles for collective justice. Civil suits for damages or injunctive relief were recognized as one means of pursuing that collective goal. The dominant judicial interpretation of the major civil rights law has tied the core notion of discrimination to a very different model of wrongdoing, one rooted in criminal justice. In this dominant model, discrimination is a purposeful product of the intentional actions of employers or managers. Naturally, problems of intention predominate along the lines of the criminal law with its distinctions of *mens rea* between purposeful, knowing, reckless, and negligent actors.[13] As in criminal law, the invisible space of mind cannot be demonstrated but by the invocation of culturally provocative facts. An employer who discriminates is a deviant aberration, a liar and a bigot, a criminal in fact if not in law.

One can very easily imagine the evolution of employment discrimination law along civil rights lines quite different from the lines of the quasi-criminal model that now dominates. Indeed, the early line of cases associated with the claim of disparate impact self-consciously moved away from the crime model of discrimination and toward a structural view that sees discriminatory outcomes as rooted in habituated social structures and patterns rather than in active malice of individual employment decisions.[14] Lately, however, the Supreme Court has shown increasing hostility to this kind of claim, outside of a few now historically irrelevant litigated examples.

A striking and relevant example of how much the metaphors and models of crime animates the employment discrimination remedy is the law of sexual harassment, the fastest growing and now largest category of employment discrimination suits. Legal scholar Vicki Schultz (1998) argues that the image of sexual violence, and in particular rape, has shaped the legal meaning of sexual harassment. Schultz acknowledges that this body of law reaches some victims of workplace harassment that otherwise had little recourse, especially in an at-will employment context. But she also argues that many forms of gender-based harassment aimed at making it hard for women to succeed in certain workplaces are treated as nonactionable by courts and corporate executives. These are more comfortable with the idea of using law to punish misconduct by individual employees or managers rather than with creating gender justice in workplace governance.

Current sexual harassment law recognizes two legal claims of sexual harassment. One, commonly known to employment discrimination lawyers as a quid pro quo case, typically involves an employee who is promised advancement in exchange for sex, or who faces retaliation for refusing sexual advances. This was the first form of sexual harassment recognized in employment discrimination law, and it had to overcome considerable skepticism that this admittedly bad behavior by men in power was about sex discrimination rather than just sex.

Sexual Harr. (2) legal Claims

Later the courts recognized a second theory of sexual harassment, known as a "hostile working environment case," in which employers participate in or tolerate patterns of behavior that target a woman because of her gender. This was a considerable expansion that opened up a potential sex discrimination claim to a much broader class of workers. Previously only persons who could show an actual decision against them (e.g., a dismissal) for refusing a sexual advance could make a sexual harassment claim for sex discrimination. In the hostile working environment, no specific decision need be shown; it is enough to show there is a pattern of behavior targeting the victim sexually that is tolerated by management. The hostile working environment theory is more removed from the model of intentional criminal assault.

Schultz argues that both forms of contemporary sexual harassment law privilege sexuality as substance of sex discrimination in employment practice and that this overvaluation of the sexual in gender discrimination excludes victims of many other kinds of gender discrimination. Consistent with the theme of this book I want to suggest that the current system leaves too many victims of gender-based harassment at work without a remedy, not just because it privileges sex but because it privileges the metaphors of crime. It is sexual crime and not just sexuality that dominates the model of sexual harassment and deforms it in the direction Schultz indicates.

The sexualization of gender discrimination law was shaped by second-wave feminism in the 1970s and specifically by the turn among feminists to identifying sexual coercion as the core form of discrimination against women in American society. The crime of rape became a symbol for this, a central mobilizing point for feminists, and a metaphor for the dominant tendency of heterosexuality. Feminist theorists like Andrea Dworkin and Catherine MacKinnon openly questioned the possibility of heterosexual sex that was not shaped by the moral economy of rape. The classic *quid pro quo* sexual harassment theory on this model was a diluted form of rape, one in which either the coercion did not rise to the level of overt violence or in which the woman was harmed by being fired for exercising her meaningful consent to say no. In other countries, among them France, this kind of case is handled directly as a matter of criminal law, albeit one with very limited sanctions (Saguy 2003, 24). The hostile workplace theory likewise focused on conduct that sexualized the victim by making her practically or symbolically available for sexual enjoyment.

The importance of the crime or violence component of the sexual violence meaning of sexual harassment was further intensified by the major public scandals that popularized the idea of sexual harassment in the early 1990s: Anita Hill's accusation against Clarence Thomas in 1991 and the Navy's Tailhook "party" scandal in the same year. The behavior Hill accused Thomas of may not have been technically a crime, but it symbolically was presented as one during the hearings by both sides. Most infamously, Republican Senator Orrin Hatch, a major defender of Thomas in the Senate, said that anyone who did what Hill said Thomas had done would be a "psychopathic sex fiend or a pervert" (Schultz 1998, 1693).[15] Tailhook was replete with instances of criminal battery and sexual battery that could clearly have been prosecuted as crimes if specific offenders had been identified.

Schultz's article is a powerful call to expand sexual harassment law beyond the sexual in order to deal with a potentially far greater quantity of workplace harassment aimed at undermining the equality of women. I would join this argument with those of feminist criminologists who call for moving the sexual harassment paradigm away from its crime narrative (Daly 1994b). Much of the harassment Schultz describes is ugly and might also lend itself to being narrated in terms of crime. The question for us is not primarily whether the behavior is equally outrageous, given current cultural standards, but what kind of governance possibilities it sets in motion and what ways of acting and knowing such a move would authorize. One of the problems with criminal law as a governance model is that it encourages decision makers to focus on setting outer limits on behavior, not on addressing the problem of inequality in the workplace. A recent study of sexual harassment law in France, where the charge is explicitly a criminal one, characterizes its effects as remarkably limited in addressing workplace sex discrimination.

> His [the sexual harasser's] action is not condemned as an instance of sex discrimination. Rather, this man has committed a misdemeanor akin to the crime of rape by using his authority as supervisor to try to coerce a woman into having sexual relations with him, much as a rapist uses physical force to compel his victim into having sexual relations. (Saguy 2003, 7)

In contrast, the formally civil status of American sexual harassment law allows for finding the employer's company liable and permits compensatory and punitive damages. This may be far more effective than its French counterpart in producing company efforts to promote gender equity in the workplace environment, but as Schultz's analysis suggests, the effect remains limited by the hold of both sex over gender and crime over inequality as a model of injury. In the current at-will employment context, that consists of judges finding in sexual harassment law the opportunity to rescue a few victims who fit a remarkably narrow vision of workplace power centered on sexual coercion or crime. And since, unlike France, the real financial costs are likely to fall on the company, the response of many managers is to demand a sanitized workplace in which all overt sexual expression is treated as a disciplinary violation and in which such expression can result in rapid dismissal (Saguy 2003, 54–55).

Conclusion: Managing Opportunism

Observing law and society at a very different moment than our own, Karl Marx once described the workplace as split between a visible front, where freedom of contract prevails, and a back side, typified by the factory, where a kind of authoritarian penal law prevails. If one were to try to draw a similar picture today, a kind of legal phenomenology of power struggles in the workplace, it would show contract and crime intertwining in ways far more complicated than Marx's dialectical formalism permits. Claims of victimization, of abuse of power, of danger calls for exclusion and for punishment—all these mix openly with talk of freedom, choice, and contract in the contemporary workplace.

Even political economy, the science that Marx accused of most contributing to the ideology of free labor, has in recent years come to recognize contract and crime as equal partners in the structuring of social relations within and around the firm. Where once crime figured only as the outer bounds that defined an unenforceable contract, in a more subtle form today it is deemed integral to virtually all contracts.

The theory of the rational actor who maximizes well-being by entering into voluntary contracts, dear to both neoclassical economics and penology, has been subtly transformed. Not only is that rationality now limited by the recognition of powerful institutional boundaries to its realization in any particular case, but the rational actor is now characterized as maximizing well-being, not only in seeking the best bargains but also in manipulating every aspect of the implementation of the agreement to achieve asymmetrical advantage.

In place of Karl Marx, today we have the influential transactional cost economics school of Oliver Williamson (1996) to provide the most compelling portrait of the workplace as a field of battle. The task of the company in this model is to govern the opportunism of all its agents. In this perspective, crime is not an aberration at the edges of the employment relationship but an inherent and constitutive struggle. And if the names political economy gives to these features are subtle and scientific—"transaction costs," "agency problems," "bounded rationality," and "opportunism" (6)—the implications are not. This is not bargaining in the shadow of the law (Mnookin and Kornhauser 1979), it is dwelling there.

Thus a recent article on business security spells out precisely the implications of this view of the labor contract for the imperative to secure the workplace.

> In the labor market, employees know more about their skills, work ethic, and performance than do employers. As a result, workers know precisely how much time and effort they devote to their work, whether they use office equipment for personal reasons, whether they write inflammatory e-mail or engage in other wrongful behavior, etc. A problem arises because workers may not exert the appropriate amount of effort or may engage in other behavior that increases firms' costs and decreases their profits.
>
> By monitoring their workers, employers can obtain discrediting information and thus minimize information asymmetry

and accordingly minimize lost profits. For example, employers can monitor to measure job performance or to cut the costs of personal use of equipment. Monitoring also allows employers to determine whether employees have learned their jobs adequately. In addition, since employers are increasingly being held liable for their employees' actions while at work, employers may also need to monitor other wrongful behavior by their employees. These are all examples of ways in which monitoring allows employers to overcome the problem of asymmetric information. (Hartman and Bucci 2001, 14)

This is what Justice Oliver Wendell Holmes (1881) described as law for the "bad man" who must be constantly monitored and penalized, for he cannot be expected to operate on the basis of any loyalties.

The current consensus in political economy, which has enshrined the at-will workplace as an essential element in unchaining economic growth, offers the reassuring assumption that most of this problem can be solved within the contract itself by the ever more technologically sophisticated engineering of transaction costs. But the reality, acknowledged subtly, is that surveillance and punishment remain the inevitable and ever-widening penumbra of the contract, and as the contract comes to govern more and more aspects of the workplace, so too will crime and punishment.

Wars of Governance | 9

From Cancer to Crime to Terror

To the Editor:
My brother was one of thousands of people found last week to
have an aggressive cancer. We, his family, are frantically doing
everything possible to save him.

I read your April 22 Week in Review article about the execution
protocol for Timothy J. McVeigh, the Oklahoma City bomber,
and I am so sorry that we as a society have to spend our time
and energy toward death instead of toward life.

—Sally Stambaugh, Portland, Oregon, April 22, 2001

To a remarkable degree in the post–World War II era, war has been accepted as a metaphor for transformations in how we govern, by both friend and foe alike. We speak easily of the "war on poverty," the "war on crime," and most recently, the "war on terrorism," recognizing as we do that the linkage of the term "war" with the substantive issue transforms it from a question of policy to a model of how to govern. We must once again reverse Carl von Clausewitz's (1832) famous formula, "War is politics carried on by other means." War, in the sense it has been used in phrases like "war on crime" and "war on terror" is a marker that a transformation of the means and rationalities by which elites justify and set the desired dimensions of their own governance.

Cognitive scientists have noted the productivity of the war metaphor in mapping the possibilities for extending power over new domains, mobilizations, attacks, offensives, and so on (Lakoff 1996). Yet there is an historical specificity to the enthusiasm associated with war. For most of the history of governments, it would have been a most inappropriate metaphor. Even victorious wars tend to be remembered by populations through the lens of sacrifice, death, hunger, and deprivation generally. The association of war times with good times, the only reason politicians could invest in such a metaphor, belongs to a specific war and only one of the participants in that war: the United States in World War II.

World War II is the only war in history that several succeeding generations have remembered and re-remembered as a time of unprecedented national unity, high morale, and comparative economic vitality, with full unemployment despite scarcity. By the 1970s, when wars on poverty, cancer, crime, and drugs were all declared, this trope had already been invoked by politicians whose careers began in earnest during World War II. This war offered Americans at home not violence and deprivation, but investment, mobilization, publicity, and new possibilities for advancement, identity re/formation, and innovation, both technological and societal.

But violence and deprivation are never out of the picture. The war metaphor gains purchase from the proximity to danger and the demands for power and knowledge that such proximity brings. The subjects chosen are almost always those that can, in a single semantic leap, strike into the deepest horrors associated with wars, chaos, mass violence, and sudden and irreversible loss. Here the transformative metaphors of governance from the second half of the twentieth century intersect with an older tradition of innovations in governance emerging in response to a fear of power itself as corrupting and monstrous that was highly influential to the generation that framed the American Constitution. Though our best-loved politicians have often invoked American dreams as their guide, it is more accurate to suggest that nightmares have been the driving force in inventing new forms and strategies of government. Ronald Reagan may be our most compelling recent example. Like Franklin Roosevelt, Reagan's popularity was widely associated with his optimism in the face of adversity. He was at his (speech writers') best when he spoke after the Challenger disaster of 1986 of those who break "the surly bonds of earth to touch the face of God," quoting from the poem "High Flight" by John Gillespie Magee (d. 1941). Yet from early on in his post–New Deal Democratic days, Reagan's political appeal was built on a capacity to speak directly to the fears of many middle-class voters concerning national decline generally and rising insecurity particularly. In the 1980 elections, these were framed not so much in terms of crime as in terms that anticipated crime, inflation, mass immigration, and terrorism.

The politics of fear begins earlier, perhaps with Franklin Roosevelt's promise of freedom from insecurity. Fear was separated from its New Deal social action perspective by President Richard Nixon. In choosing two exemplary American nightmares, crime and cancer, Nixon showed his intuitive grasp of what Americans feared as well as the stakes for recasting

American governance. Both share a lengthy and metaphorically linked history in American culture, both would find ready support in the contemporary environment, and were brilliantly placed to cut across many of the existing political divides in American politics. Nixon made little secret of his hope to use the 1972 election to mobilize a decisive majority and mark a new realignment in American politics.[1]

Since September 11, terrorism and a war on terrorism have entered American public discourse with a rapidity that seems remarkable even by the standards of hot-button issues like cancer and crime.

I have shown above how the war on crime fought by federal and state governments since the late 1960s altered the way political authority of all sorts and at all levels has been exercised, including the transformation of American "private" life. The war on terrorism that has unfolded since 9/11 has been profoundly shaped by this field of crime, politics, and governance in ways that may ratify the skew toward security and the "culture of control" (Garland 2001a), even as it covers up the memory of that war on crime. That war on terror has confirmed much of the thesis of this book by highlighting how metaphoric "wars" on social threats can reshape government. We even have a new self-consciousness about fear and risk in our national experience that would seem positive were it not linked to a deep amnesia about how much fear of crime had already reshaped American society during the three decades before 9/11.

This final chapter provides a countermemory to the "forgetting" induced by 9/11, outlining how the response of our major political institutions to the attacks was conditioned by political rationalities previously produced by the war on crime. By comparing the sprawling war on crime with its underdeveloped twin, the war on cancer, this chapter can give us some sense of how the success of the former may have made us more vulnerable to the strategies of those who would use terrorism as an excuse to impose new strategies of governance. The high risks of relying on an essentially penal strategy to achieve global forms of security are already becoming visible in Iraq and elsewhere.

From the War on Cancer to the War on Crime

As social signifiers, crime and cancer are both highly productive. Crime is one of the most ancient metaphors for the moral life of human beings, but cancer is a first-class metaphoric agent of its own (Patterson 1987; Sontag

1977). Even professional discourse about cancer boils with anxiety-provoking terms like "invasive," "mass," and "spread"; other cancer terms, such as "metastases," "remission," and "cancer" itself, have been readily adopted to other contexts (Patterson 1987, 160). Popular discourse about cancer has traditionally been even more vivid, invoking explicitly monstrous themes of aggressive and malevolent flesh- and organ-consuming predators.

While 1971 was the year the Nixon administration formally rolled out its war on drugs, its roots are clear in Nixon's law-and-order message during the campaign of 1968, and in the growing confrontation between the president and the antiwar movement that had helped bring down his predecessor. In that turbulent period marked by high-level assassinations of political leaders and lethal conflict between police and citizens in the center of some of the best-known cities in America, few would have questioned that the U.S. was facing a crisis of governance. Strikes, demonstrations, and violence between citizens were reaching unprecedented highs for the century as the '60s ended (Parenti 1998). In Nixon's first term, his administration looked for opportunities (limited in retrospect) developed through an expansion of federal antidrug efforts and a continuation of his harsh campaign rhetoric against the liberal criminal procedure decisions of the Warren Court (Parenti 1999; Baum 1996). The war on drugs offered great political potential to Nixon because it linked the New Left political base to its broader youth culture penumbra and, through that, to classic themes of organized crime and corruption.

Drugs would also offer a striking metaphoric bridge between the growing political clout of environmentalism and Nixon's center-right majority. Drugs were easily analogized to other "toxic" chemicals placed in water and airways. Building on the Johnson administration's strategy of funding local law enforcement (see chapter 3), Nixon also used the war on drugs to build a new political network, linking the highest levels of national government with local government through law enforcement. By investing federal money in local criminal justice agencies, Nixon was establishing links that bypassed the traditional structures of congressional representation and party machines.[2]

The "war on cancer," a term produced not by Nixon but by the public discussion of Nixon's announcement in his 1971 State of the Union address that he would launch "an intensive campaign against cancer" (Nixon 1971) seems at first glance to be a variation on the welfarist themes most associated with the New Deal and its 1960s spin-off "the war on poverty." The earliest federal government interest in cancer was, in fact, spurred by concern with carcinogenic exposure in war-time industrial work places. This concern fed directly into the expanding federal regulatory concern with carcinogenic chemicals manifest in the Delaney Amendment of 1958,[3] which was perhaps the first piece of modern environmental legislation. A war on cancer along these lines would have meant federal support for workers, consumers, and communities against industrial chemistry.

The war on cancer also has genealogical links with the science-warfare side of the New Deal state, especially the Roosevelt administration's Manhattan Project and, later, the Kennedy administration's race to the moon. Indeed, these were precisely the markers Nixon laid down in his speech to the Ninety-Second Congress. "The time has come in America when the same kind of concentrated effort that split the atom and took man to the moon should be turned toward conquering this dread disease. Let us make a total national commitment to achieve this goal" (Nixon 1971). Rather than dispersing money through a broad political network as did much of the New Deal and the war on poverty (and much as the war on drugs would later do), the Manhattan Project, space program, and war on cancer pumped money into highly centralized research establishments (like the national laboratories in Los Alamos, Berkeley, and Chicago during the 1940s, NASA in the 1960s, and the National Cancer Institute in the 1970s). Though the war on drugs created a new federal local network around law enforcement, the war on cancer presupposed and reinforced one that had already become an important component of government since the New Deal: media, science, and government. Coverage of moon shots, missiles, and presidents was displacing more traditional political circuits that ran vertically through local political machines and news outlets.[4] Rather than threatening industry, this kind of war on cancer would ultimately invest in many of these very same industries as producers of anticancer drugs.

Cancer and crime share a rich metaphoric tradition of trading images. Crime has often been described as a cancer eating away at the integrity of institutions, communities, and whole nations.[5] Cancer is often characterized as a predatory killer that is physically assaulting its victim. Both, in turn, furnish natural metaphors for governance. They provide comprehensive platforms for governance precisely because both are constituted as threats through their lack of control. Crime and cancer are in a sense "antigovernments." Criminal acts are those acts taken in defiance of rules with the greatest social sanction behind them. Cancers are unregulated cells that will neither die nor confine their growth to the functional pathways governed through the body's complex electrochemical guidance systems. As cancers grow, they also act to subvert the functional order of the body's systems in ways that often prove fatal. Although crimes are generally talked about as caused by individual bad actors, especially by conservatives, the same discourse acknowledges a collective climate in which crime may be out of control.

Cancer in the twentieth century has also shared with crime an agonizing proximity to scientific progress. At the end of the nineteenth century, major improvements in medicine—especially bacteriology and the new surgical antiseptic measures it brought with it—generated great optimism that medicine would soon understand and treat cancer with some effectiveness (despite its long being viewed as beyond the reach of medical science).[6] In the same time period, advances in new "social sciences" including criminology, evolutionary biology, and psychology led to a revival of optimism that crime would soon be understood and subjected to therapies or at least preventive measures.[7] In both cases, the confidence in scientific progress was linked with faith that problems were traceable to specific causes in individual human beings that could be prevented and arrested. In both cases, however, scientists and their new audience of politicians and the public were to be disappointed, through a repeated series of supposed "breakthroughs," rapid escalation of hopes, and disturbingly widespread failure. Although cancer was undeniably an objective physiological disorder, its causes and treatment remained so profoundly mysterious that, like crime and other social maladies, it had an essentially indeterminate nature for much of the twentieth century. As with those social maladies, cancer discourse could not easily exclude moralists and "populist countercultures" that saw in the disease primary lessons about the virtues and vices of our culture rather than specific causal events.

From the War on Crime to the War on Terror: Bush, 9/11, and Abu Ghraib

The war on crime as a panoply of political technologies and mentalities has profoundly shaped the strategic context of the war on terror. The Bush administration has made a political theme of claiming that a war on terror is an alternative to a law enforcement approach, a tag it tried, with some success, to hang on Democratic candidate John Kerry during the 2004 election campaign. Yet the administration's approach to that war has been in large part a continuation of the war on crime, as seen in the arrest of suspected militants, both citizens and aliens; the use of harsh methods to extract confessions; and mass incarceration of a class defined by race and religion as "dangerous" in a global archipelago of prisons. Many of the deformations in American institutions produced by the war on crime, developments that have made our society less democratic, are being publicly rejustified as responses to the threat of terror.

This metaphoric transfer between the war on crime and the war on terror has remained beneath the radar for the most part, emerging only obliquely during the 2004 presidential campaign between President George W. Bush and Senator John Kerry in the form of a subdued debate over whether the war on terror could be handled through criminal justice strategies or needed to be handled exclusively at the level of military strategy and foreign relations. President Bush and his supporters argued that Kerry—a former prosecutor and proponent in the 1990s of greater federal attention to global criminal organizations—was locked into a law enforcement model of how to fight terrorism, a strategy they denounced as unrealistic and undesirable for, among other reasons, the fact that it might involve too much deference to international law and cooperation. Senator Kerry likewise attacked the President for being locked into an overreliance on unilateral U.S. military power. Kerry embraced the organized crime model, stating at the height of the campaign that he expected that terrorism would not be eliminated but rather reduced like organized crime to a tolerable problem. Bush supporters leaped to criticize Kerry for accepting something far less than total victory in the war on terror.

These rather tepid exchanges between the candidates revealed more about how porous the boundaries between war and crime control have become than about any difference in principles between the candidates. Having criticized Kerry's law enforcement strategies for fighting terror, Bush moved after his reelection to appoint Michael Chertoff, a veteran federal prosecutor and former deputy attorney general for criminal prosecutions, to lead the Department of Homeland Security. Indeed, other than the short weeks of direct military campaigning in Afghanistan and Iraq, much of both wars and the global pursuit of Al Qaeda has come to look much like a particularly grim war on crime: heavy reliance on a strategy of arrest, incarcerate, or kill, in which the dominant symbols have become not huge tank battles but prisons, including Guantanamo Bay in Cuba and Abu Ghraib in Iraq. For Kerry, the argument that Al Qaeda be pursued as an international cartel of criminals emerged from his earlier focus on international criminal organizations as the growing international threat to U.S. security in a post–Cold War world.

[handwritten margin notes: "President can indefinitely incarcerate", "Enemy Combatant"]

The Executive as Prosecutor-in-Chief

One of the most prominent features of the war on terrorism has been the unprecedented assertion of executive authority that it has sanctioned and justified. Particularly notable has been the president's ability to indefinitely incarcerate someone and subject him to harsh and degrading interrogation techniques as based on a presidential finding that a particular detainee is an "enemy combatant," a classification legal scholar David Cole (2003, 39) has described as the "ultimate move in the government's preventive detention arsenal":

[handwritten margin note: "Lifts all rights of person"]

> Attaching that label takes an individual out of the civilian justice system altogether and places him in military custody, potentially for the duration of the "war on terrorism." The government claims that this power authorizes it to arrest and hold anyone, foreign national or US citizen, for an indefinite period, without charges, without a hearing, without access to a lawyer, and, for all practical purposes, incommunicado, simply on the assertion that he is an "enemy combatant." (39)

In the war on terror, the label "enemy combatant" may exempt the case from the normal rights of the criminal process, but all too familiar from the "war on crime" is the assertion of primacy for the executive in representing the public's interest in security which, as we have noted, has led to a shift in power to the prosecutor over pretrial detention, juvenile court jurisdiction, and the length of prison sentences. The claims of executive autonomy made in the war on terror track closely with the power assumed by prosecutors in the criminal justice system and by chief executives asserting prosecutorial prerogatives.

Though criminal law enforcement is by definition not an emergency power, the expansive role of the prosecutor in it has been justified with reference to the severity of the harm that violence poses to the public. In

claiming to speak for the public's needs for prevention and retribution, the
prosecutor has claimed a direct public trust that requires no review and little
guidance from lawmakers. It is precisely this logic that President Bush and
former Attorney General Ashcroft have invoked to defend the most controversial aspects of the "war on terror," including the harsh interrogation techniques and prolonged detention of prisoners. President Bush has routinely
referred to the persons detained at Guantanamo Bay, Cuba, as "killers"
(quoted in Cole 2003, 42). The term is a highly charged one, and claims more
than would be required to detain them as terrorists if that's what they are. In
implying nothing less than murder, the President draws upon the crime that
tends to condense and intensify the whole complex of public fears that have
supported the war on crime, especially the vulnerability of one's family to the
proximity of violent, racially marked subjects. Vice President Cheney has invoked the same constellation of meanings in describing the detainees held in
the prisons at Guantanamo Bay, Cuba, as "the worst of a very bad lot"
(Higham, Stephens, and Williams, 2004). The death penalty and incarceration
in a super-max lockdown prison, the two harshest punishments in the United
States, are routinely justified as focusing only on the "worst of the worst."

Both Bush and Ashcroft made crime central to their respective political
careers prior to their current positions, so it is not surprising to see them turn
to these narratives, strategies, and rationalities when faced with the challenge
of terrorism. Bush invokes his "solemn obligation to protect the people"
(White House 2004) in rejecting charges of human rights violations in American detention centers. This continues to find acceptance in the opinion of a
public truly sobered after 9/11, that was and is prepared to overlook serious
mistakes made by the administration in its execution of the war on terror.

9/11 and the Citizen Victim

Since 9/11 the nation has had little difficulty applying the logic of trauma
experienced by victims of violent crime to the American people as a whole
and to our national leaders. For example, the Patriot Act,[8] adopted on October 26, 2001, was widely acknowledged, even at the time of its passage, to
have not been read by the vast majority and possibly all of the members of
Congress who voted for it (Priester 2005, 13). This presumably embarrass-
ing fact has been largely explained by noting that the act was passed only
weeks after September 11, 2001, by politicians who had themselves been
witnesses and near victims of the attacks themselves.

The same sense of trauma has been offered to explain the relative lack of interest of the American people or Congress in the scandals at Abu Ghraib and Guantanamo. But whether these explanations make sense empirically or normatively, it is clear that the war on terror as a legislative matter has largely followed the pattern laid down by the role of Congress and state legislatures in the war on crime. In that war, crime victims emerged as idealized citizens whom lawmakers could invoke to expand governmental powers freely without serious political risk, as long as they responded to the twin calls for safety and vengeance that victims are idealized as making.[9]

The core of the Patriot Act, its definition of terrorism, expresses this link between victims and criminal in limiting the crime to "acts dangerous to human life that are violations of the criminal laws . . . [and] appear to be intended to influence the policy of the government."[10] In anchoring a broad expansion of law enforcement powers in the name of human life, Congress was following a pattern well marked in crime legislation: evaluating the reasonableness of policies not by their outcomes but by how well they match the severity of the harm against which they promise to respond. They also follow the path of investing more discretion in the hands of the executive on the premise that due process considerations harm victims in a zero-sum game between victims and offenders. In this respect, the Patriot Act has much in common with the Anti-Terrorism and Effective Death Penalty Act of 1996,[11] adopted after the Oklahoma City bombing, with the express purpose of making it more difficult for death row inmates to raise more legal delays to their executions.

Mistrusted Courts

Three Supreme Court decisions in June of 2004 concerning the detentions of both aliens and citizens under military custody as enemy combatants were widely read as a repudiation of the Bush administration's position in the war on terror. While that may be accurate, such a result reflects the extreme view of the administration regarding executive authority: Federal courts were to have essentially no jurisdiction to question the custody of even a citizen if held under a presidential finding that the detainee is an "enemy combatant." All three rulings, however, were remarkably narrow.

Rasul v. Bush raised the legal status of a large group of detainees who claimed to be innocent of fighting with Al Qaeda or the Taliban, and who had been held at Guantanamo without access to lawyers or an opportunity to challenge their status as enemy combatants. The Supreme Court, in a 6–3 decision, held that the statutory writ of habeas corpus applies outside the political space of the United States, and sent the cases back for further proceedings under the habeas statute in the district court.

In *Hamdi v. Rumsfeld*, the Court was faced with a U.S. citizen held under similar circumstances at a Navy brig in South Carolina. Here the Court divided as to the legal grounds for reversing the denial of the writ. The plurality opinion by Justice O'Connor held that the federal antidetention statute vests citizens with rights against executive confinement that require examination by a federal court. Two other justices, Scalia and Stevens, would have required that the government proceed against a citizen such as Hamdi through a prosecution for treason.

The final case, *Padilla v. Rumsfeld* involved another U.S. citizen, this one detained at the airport in Chicago first as a material witness and then as an enemy combatant in the same Navy brig as Yasser Hamdi. A 5–4 majority sent the case back because it had been filed in the incorrect district court—under the habeas statute, it should be filed in the home district of the defendant, in this case Donald Rumsfeld's district—an outcome that most commentators predicted would have little consequence other than to place Padilla on the same footing as Hamdi once he refiled his complaint in the district court in Virginia.

These decisions may have rejected an extraordinarily broad argument for executive authority, but they did so on statutory grounds that epitomize the judicial craft of parsimony or narrowness. As Michael Reisman (2004) has commented, this kind of parsimony is attractive if a court is seeking to "limit the prescriptive force of its decision," but in these decisions by the Supreme Court, narrowness achieves an extreme in which "the technique closes the aperture of observation to the point where critical facts and law must be ignored" (Reisman 2004, 977).

This self-limiting narrowness is not a new pattern on the late Rehnquist Court, but is instead one that follows a theme most widely developed in that Court's criminal justice decisions from the late 1980s through the late 1990s, particularly in the area of capital punishment. This pattern is characterized by a self-conscious effort to narrow in advance the ability of federal courts to reopen state final convictions by raising the bar of error and prejudice. In these decisions, the Supreme Court essentially barred lawyers for state inmates, mostly on death row, from raising more than one collateral challenge in federal court, and from raising legal claims not adequately preserved in state court, unless they were actually claiming innocence. As a result, the Court has essentially endorsed the execution of prisoners who would not have died had they been tried under correct law.

Mass Imprisonment

Beyond the military campaigns in Afghanistan and Iraq, the most significant component of the U.S. war on terror is the use of long-term detention centers to hold enemy combatants. These prisons' use of torture and sexual-cultural humiliation, as captured in photographs from the Abu Ghraib prison in Iraq, has drawn criticism globally (Weisselberg 2005). Three years or more have elapsed since most of these alleged militants were seized in Afghanistan and Pakistan.

This new emphasis on incarceration based on group association rather than individual guilt represents perhaps the most striking departure from the traditional models of U.S. military action. The military has always run an elaborate and high-quality penal justice system for its own personnel, and has maintained prisoner-of-war facilities for enemy soldiers captured in the Gulf, Vietnam, and Korean wars.

A different and darker precedent is the practice of mass preventive detention against domestic populations who, in the minds of government officials, were associated with foreign enemies of the United States. These include the roundup and detention of several thousand foreign nationals in the Palmer raids in 1919 and the internment of more than 100,000 persons of Japanese ancestry, both citizen and immigrant, during World War II. As David Cole has observed, these past incidents of preventive detention and the current war on terror "all resulted in the mass incarceration of people who turned out not to pose the national security threat that purportedly justified their detention in the first place" (2003, 1753).

What is new today is not only the ambiguous legal status of the detainees held by the United States, but the implication that the incapacitation of available terrorists through long-term, perhaps permanent, incarceration can make a difference for the security of America and her allies. In this respect, the highly publicized difficulty the military has had producing effective and humane penal control in Iraq, and even under far more secure custody in Cuba, is not surprising. And yet it is in this function that the global war on terror most closely tracks the course of the war on crime, which early on committed itself to mass imprisonment of whole cate-gories of people engaged in the underground economies rampant in the United States in the 1980s and 1990s. Then, the race and perceived cultural pathologies of young minority males in the inner cities made them the prime focus of new, harsh laws and surplus police attention. Now, nation-ality and perceived religious pathologies of young Muslim men, mostly of Middle Eastern or Arab descent, are driving a harsh and explicit strategy by the Department of Justice to use criminal and immigration laws to iso-late and confine terror suspects. This use of pre-textual law enforcement as a tool of preventing terrorism is an example of the most literal and instru-mental kind of governing through crime: using crime as an excuse to ac-complish another objective, one that is harder to achieve or perhaps for-bidden (Cole 2003).

[handwritten margin notes: Then: Focus on Race; Now: Religious Affiliation of Muslim men.]

Domestically, the war on crime in the form of a sustained effort to incarcerate certain racialized classes of dangerous lawbreakers has pro-duced only marginal drops in crime rates, in the view of most criminol-ogists, and no real gains in the sense of security in society. Still it remains deeply embedded in the current structure of American politics and pol-icy making, with only incremental signs of reform. The impact of a sim-ilar global military enterprise in security through mass incarceration is not promising.

Another parallel to the war on crime is the considerable attention the Bush administration, especially the Department of Justice, has paid to the death penalty. The administration vigorously sought the death penalty against Zacarias Moussaoui, the only prisoner brought to trial thus far, notwithstanding the fact that security requires denying Moussaoui access to information that would normally be vital to capital cases and very substantial questions about Moussaoaui's mental state at the time of 9/11 and during the course of his federal trial.[12]

Terrorism and the Medium Security Society

Criminologist Thomas Blomberg, has used the phrase "minimum security society" to describe the tendency in late-twentieth-century American society toward raising the security profile of everyday life, and using technology to disperse the mechanisms of surveillance and control associated with the prison throughout social space (Blomberg 1987). The minimum security society has turned out to be part of a trend toward more control over everyone and quite a bit more control for some. By the end of the century, it would have been more accurate to speak of a "medium security" society, as gated communities replaced reliance on good lights and door locks.

The war on terror has thus far encouraged only deeper entrenchment of this lockdown strategy in the home, schools, and workplace. More globally, the major legislative and administrative responses to 9/11 have been to heighten the power of law enforcement and prosecutors to do much of what they were doing before with even fewer avenues for legal challenge. This has been particularly true in the treatment of noncitizens, for whom the already harsh and mandatory reach of criminal alien exclusions has been expanded even further (Cole 2003). It is also true for every American with a criminal conviction or even arrest record. In response to 9/11, new state and federal laws have expanded the already significant pool of jobs for which criminal records checks are now required by law, including, in many states, personal health care attendants, school employees, and truck drivers (Emsellem 2005). New laws have also opened more government data on individuals to security screening firms serving the growing market for prescreening job applicants for crime and drugs, as we discussed in chapter 8.

Disaster: Why the War on Crime Is a Bad Model for Confronting Terrorism

If we look through the window of the losses in New York, Washington, and Pennsylvania on September 11, 2001, we can raise a different kind of question about the way the war on crime has prepared the way for the war on terror: Was it a good security strategy? The answer seems to be no. Indeed, the terrorists highlighted massive vulnerabilities in American security. We were vulnerable not simply because we had no surveillance of a great deal of international and intranational commerce, but because our crime-built culture of control ignores certain kinds of risk while selecting others for investment.

Instead of focusing on aberrational behavior around technical systems with the greatest potential for harm—civilian aeronautics, the chemical industry, trucking, and ports—American domestic security in the 1990s was colored by a traditional criminological bias. The argument there says dangerous acts arise from dangerous people whom you know by their character, to be read in their minor conduct. This has led to a *Broken windows* proliferation of strategies, like the ubiquitous "broken windows" model (Kelling and Wilson 1982), which emphasize attending to even the most minor misbehavior of those we fear, especially minority youth in public places.

The "war on crime" has also created vulnerabilities in the very accumulations it produces on subjects and their institutions. This includes the massive concentration of black and Latino young men and, increasingly, women in the criminal justice system, and the attendant impact on their communities, dependents, families, and neighbors. It also includes a white middle class increasingly taxed by the weight of a private security apparatus that includes gated private police communities, long commutes to safe suburbs in high-polluting, gas-guzzling SUVs, and the high cost of keeping one's children in a state of organized supervision until the parents get home from work.

The Problem With Profiling

Regardless of whether an unambiguous piece of evidence arises proving *Profiling* that our security and law enforcement communities could have discovered and stopped the Al Qaeda plot executed on September 11, 2001, it is clear that the great bulk of our system was not ever remotely interested in these men or their plot. Our institutions, our technologies, and our narratives were all trained elsewhere. After all, the plotters who murdered three thousand people were not born addicted to crack; they did not grow up in single-parent, female-dominated homes; nor did they blow off school, do drugs, or fall into repeated low-level conflicts with the police. In fact, they didn't have any of the risk factors that dominate selection and exclusion practices across our society.[13]

Unfortunately, I do not think the answer lies in developing better risk predictors. Nor should we put huge resources into redirecting the New York Police Department from its endless sorties of street confrontation of single young African American and Latino men towards scrutiny of young men from the Arabian Peninsula—although we should recall that Giuliani was credited in the 1990s with making New York safer by directing police resources at derelicts seeking to wipe car windows at stoplights for donations (known in New York as "squeegee men") and low-level drug, alcohol, and sex consumers.

The focus on minor criminality has kept our police focused on minority youths and their mostly minor criminality. When Mohammed Atta and his colleague stalled their plane on the tarmac at Miami International Airport, they may have panicked, because they left the plane on the field and rented a car. But it took weeks for regulators to respond—and even then, their response was only a letter demanding better behavior from flight school students in the future. In short, we were not afraid of the kind of people who go to flight schools.

Perhaps the greatest contribution that reflection on 9/11 could make to the American governmental imagination is to shatter its faith in the criminological doctrine that violence and disorder are related in some predictable and continuous way to a set of variables, be they sociological, psychological, or even biological. This doctrine, through its manifold different substantive theories, has encouraged a pursuit of minor criminal acts as a logical precursor to more serious crime and profiles of the dangerous that are highly correlated with economic, social, and political disadvantage.

The war on crime has increased dramatically the percentage of minorities in our prisons and jails, many of them through the accumulation of nonviolent offenses. This concentration has done substantial damage to American society. It has replaced discredited racist narratives of exclusion with new and seemingly ethical narratives of crime or terrorism. We must carefully monitor the people arrested, punished, or deported in any war on terrorism to make sure the government is targeting people who act like terrorists and not people who just look, talk, or pray like someone's idea of terrorists. The fact that the Bush administration has thus far fought to maintain maximum secrecy over even whom it holds in custody is a bad sign.

In the war on crime, major initiatives were frequently launched in the name of preventing children from being kidnapped and murdered but they ended up resulting in more frequent imprisonment of drug and property offenders (Ziming, Hawkins, and Kamin 2001). We should be careful that terrorism does not get defined down in ways that make it easier for law enforcement to score points but which may have little impact on the real terrorism problem. We should make clear that September 11 is not a license to stomp out future demonstrations by mostly nonviolent dissidents, such as those who demonstrated against the World Trade Organization in several cities. The prosecutions brought by the federal government against terrorism suspects have thus far (as of 2006) suggested just such a shift from those plotting terrorism to those whose rhetoric or ideologies seem compatible with terrorism.

Locked-Down Government

Even with better screens, the protection of the American public from concerted terrorists is hampered by the limitations of human labor power and administrative resources that government can direct to the effort. Managing 3 percent of the adult population of the United States through the criminal justice system is an extraordinarily costly endeavor. The resource squeeze on all other forms of government spending is widely recognized, as should be the fact that we cannot realistically finance and staff the kind of effort that would be necessary to counter terrorism inside the United States operationally—say, on the scale of Israel during the second *intifada*, or even Italy at the height of the Red Brigades terror of the 1970s—without substantially redirecting resources from criminal justice, medical care, or retirement income, let alone re-funding public education levels back up to those baby boomers enjoyed.

Jose Padilla, best known today for his peculiar legal status as a native-born enemy combatant of the United States, was once a more conventional prisoner of the war on crime, serving a term in prison during the early 1990s, during which time he apparently converted to Islam, like many other prisoners. The conventional wisdom—that whatever advantages Al Qaeda may have, it has no domestic base to which its appeals could possibly be persuasive[14]—should be reexamined, if Padilla turns out to be anywhere near as dangerous as Ashcroft apparently believed him to be when he went on live television from Moscow on June 10, 2002, to announce Padilla's arrest.[15]

People of no reason after prison

The imposition during the last two decades of extraordinarily long prison sentences means that among our 2 million incarcerated Americans are a large and growing body with no reason to ever hope for normal life in the United States, even if they manage to wait out their prison sentences. American prisons once produced revolutionaries like George Jackson and Malcolm X, whose exposure to the deep contradictions of modernist reform-oriented penality led them to envision radical change for American society with the aim of making it live up to its own ideology of freedom and democracy. Jose Padilla reminds us that our increasingly zero-tolerance attitude toward criminals has created a large class of individuals with no reason to work for anything but the destruction of our society.

The Bush administration's strategy in the war on terror has called for deliberate maximum use of the criminal code, as well as penal provisions of immigration law, to obtain control over terror suspects in ways that are likely to exacerbate the isolating effects of the war on crime on young minority men. Even those not targeted on suspicion of terrorism run into the wider net being cast by laws opening up criminal record checks to the private sector in the name of tightening controls.

The criminalization of drugs maintains high profits for supranational drug cartels that Ashcroft said play a role in funding terrorism. When combined with the enormous cost of maintaining a correctional population that is, nationwide, close to 40 percent drug-based, it becomes clear that if our political leadership seriously believed we were faced with a war on terrorism, they would negotiate a peace with honor in the war on drugs.

The war on crime encouraged a lazy reliance by law enforcement on a large pool of usual suspects that could easily be rounded up and detained while a case was made against them, sometimes while the real criminals kept killing. The campaign to do DNA tests on residual biological evidence in already adjudicated murder and rape cases is disclosing scores of cases around the country where the police focused on criminal suspects who fit the preferred portrait of violent criminals, black and young, even while clear signs pointed to other suspects who went on raping and killing.[16] In the name of controlling crime in the 1980s and 1990s, laws were drafted to make it easier for police to operate on their own hunches and harder for defense lawyers to subject the facts of a case to scrutiny. Vehicles like unreviewable deportation of suspected illegal immigrants can easily be used to cover up sloppy investigation and worse.

Raising the Costs of Civil Society

The war on crime has reshaped "private" life in America by placing it in spaces and procedures self-consciously aimed at security from crime and a sense of that security (see chapter 6). Compared with how we lived a generation ago, the lives of virtually all Americans are today more embedded in security technology such as locks of all sorts, alarms, private security, and procedures of stopping, questioning, and searching. But all too often, these technologies, like giant SUVs, increase the security of some only by reducing the security of others.

[handwritten margin note: People now in security frenzy]

In doing so, they constitute a kind of provocation that generates a certain potential threat to security. Both crime and the fortress-like strategies adopted by many Americans who can afford to invest in their personal and family security erode trust and lead to more reliance on both criminal self-help (e.g., vandalism) and on state coercion to work out social accommodation. They also intensify historic patterns of racial segregation in urban areas, especially in the Northeast and Midwest, which lacked a historic ideology of racial separation (unlike the South).

As captured in political cartoons showing Americans "hunkering down" after 9/11, the war on terrorism is imprinting its own logics on this fortress mentality. We can expect it to retroactively ratify much of this security buildup while justifying a further hardening of the segregation of American society. Though crime rates made government at least somewhat accountable, the threat of terror cannot easily be measured or tracked over time. That makes it possible to deploy the possibility of terror as a political tactic in domestic politics. At the same time, it is unclear whether the American public will tolerate the kind of protracted stalemate that marked the war on crime until at least the late 1990s.

Relaunch the War on Cancer

There are, to be sure, different ways that one could imagine governing through crime than the American model as it has developed since the 1960s. At the start of the twentieth century, reformers created in the juvenile court a powerful new form of judicial agency targeted at addressing a broad swath of presumably pathological governance by families and communities, especially immigrant families in the high-population-density working-class precincts of the great cities. Under the auspices of addressing crime, new forms of knowledge and new strategies of governance were explored. By the time the Supreme Court decided that due process required a greater measure of adversary protections for those accused of juvenile delinquency, the ambitions of reinventing community governance had long since given way to the needs of the larger criminal justice establishment (Rothman 1980).

The war on crime invested the federal government in a relationship with a criminal justice establishment that ultimately "blew back" and made criminal justice a kind of reigning metaphor for how to govern, first in Washington, and then in the states and in private institutions. The governing through crime we now experience must be rejected because the narratives it leaves us to do the work of governance in an increasingly complex multicultural democratic society are unsustainable and threaten the alleged principal values of both conservatives and liberals in contemporary American politics.

To mix metaphors, governing through crime produces cancer, or more accurately, cancers: it produces subjects who do not respond to the regulatory signals that allow for effective social coordination and who remain outside any meaningful circuits of democratic will formation.

Consider two examples, the prison population and crime victims. The prison population, now at around 2 million, represents a staggering challenge to the governability of American cities. The war on crime has increased substantially the numbers of people in prison and in legal jeopardy of being sent to prison with minimal effort. Today, large cities throughout the nation—many already stretched to the governmental limits by poverty, AIDS, and the necessity of dealing with children of immigrants—face the prospect of thousands of returning prisoners.

These reentering prisoners, sometimes designated parolees, face extraordinary challenges and pose extraordinary challenges to governability. As a group, they face strong discrimination in the job market; such challenges are only exacerbated by a lack of skills prior to prison and no serious job training in prison. Often, they have burned through local networks of support before committing the crimes that sent them to prison, so that on return they are homeless or soon to be. The experience of prison has only exacerbated many of the very real cognitive and sociability problems suffered by this population. Many have problems with aggression, paranoia, depression, and violence. In a lesser way, the same problem is created by every institution that re-creates the model of exile and exclusion that prison now represents, including zero-tolerance rules removing students from classes, residents from housing, and employees from jobs.

The tendency of governing through crime to produce more victims—and to heighten the potential for victimization to others—produces a different kind of social pathology. Crime victims, especially those of violence, are encouraged to view themselves as facing long-term or permanent damage. In overcoming this damage, they are encouraged to consider the prosecution and punishment of the criminal the primary collective contribution to their healing. They are discouraged from expecting the state to address their medical bills, job losses, or family poverty. At the same time, victims have been empowered by the sense that their experience of this damage is a source of truth unchallengeable by others.

The difficulty posed by this dynamic to institutions was exemplified by the problems faced by governing agencies in dealing with the victims of the 9/11 terrorist attacks. Whether facing off with the mayor of New York over the management of the World Trade Center disaster site or with President Bush over the composition of an independent commission, victims' families have succeeded in insisting on having their own sensibilities accepted as generating the criteria of truth, resulting in otherwise feared politicians backing down from them.

For the vast majority of subjects in contemporary America, the status of victims is experienced mainly as a feared future rather than a present status. It is for them that prisons and the death penalty operate, as much as for the immediate victims. In making the reduction of crime threats such a major objective of family and company governance, governing through crime has exacerbated a whole range of urban problems, including sprawl, the increasing segregation of American residential communities, and traffic gridlock caused by significant commutes between work and home.

Governing through crime produces subjects who are likely to place large demands on governance at all institutional levels. At the same time, it seems to encourage a relatively narrow range of governmental technologies and strategies. As these agents respond to greater demands for governance by a population whose demands on governance are shaped by crime, they find themselves imposing a limited and self-defeating set of strategies. Exclusion strategies—whether putting people in prison, terminating their employment, or suspending them from school—end up raising governance costs somewhere else by placing the threatening subject in an environment with potentially even fewer ways to obtain co-operation.

It is essential that we question the reliance of the war on terror on models from the war on crime. Though Americans may regard the current state of mass incarceration coexisting with violence-producing criminal markets for narcotics as an acceptable price to be paid for a sense of security in the suburbs, we cannot afford this kind of stalemate with terrorism. Here the undeveloped war on cancer may offer important resources for forming alternative questions.

In the war on crime model, the "Why do they hate us?" question is irrelevant. "They" are a pathological or evil force whose motivation is exogenous to the political problem of coping. In the war on cancer model, prevention is always primary. The cancer-causing behavior or exposure must stop, even as we try to search out and destroy every malignant cell.

The war on crime model focuses on willing offenders rather than on conditions that encourage criminal behavior. The emphasis is on tracking known offenders and seeking to reincarcerate them. The war on cancer model is more concerned with identifying risk factors that are correlated with cancer and that can be acted on.

The war on crime model has focused heavily on victims as passive subjects of government. In the war on cancer model, cancer victims are active subjects who must be mobilized to fight their cancer.

Governing through a renewed war on the sources of cancer offers more promising material for restructuring governance than does crime. The current war on cancer, focused on diagnosing and treating individuals with cancer, has been criticized for not achieving up to expectations, but its products do not challenge its operations. It has created institutions, especially large cancer centers and teaching hospitals devoted to treating cancer and training cancer surgeons and specialized care coordinators known as oncologists. The biggest problem associated with this sector has been its rapidly inflating costs. A less inflationary strategy might aim at lifestyle choices that can prevent cancer but might generate resistance from large consumer industries like fast food, alcohol, and automobile producers.

Cancer victims have experienced a significant enhancement as a result of the war on cancer. Once seen as repugnant objects of pity, cancer patients have benefited from the rising prestige of the disease. This is in part a collateral effect of the rising status of their doctors, just as students and teachers may affect each others' prestige. It is also in part a result of a cultural campaign to transform cancer patients from subjects best kept protected from the truth to people encouraged to view themselves as essential partners in the treatment and research process.

The new subject position of the cancer patient is shaped in large part by the creation of extensive knowledge and action networks. One crucial nexus is the National Cancer Institute's patient referral service and its Web page (www.cancer.gov), which provides comprehensive databases for cancer patients and their families to access information on the latest research results, descriptions and protocols for current clinical trials, and a host of self-diagnosis information and links to other resources and cancer organizations. The information helps track patients and their doctors into sponsored cancer research studies. Different aspects of the new subject position of the cancer patient are the target of a growing set of support groups and self-help expertise—disturbingly portrayed in the novel and movie *Fight Club*—all of which grow from the primary recognition of the national status of the cancer population by the National Cancer Act.

By identifying the size of the cancer population and giving patients tangible reasons to seek out such an identity (either by seeking a diagnosis or acting on their diagnoses), the war on cancer has invited the growth of a whole series of markets. There has been tremendous growth in the market for books and articles concerning living with cancer and with people who have cancer. This discourse, much of which valorizes the experience of being a cancer victim, has helped tremendously to promote the vision of the cancer patient as a rights-bearing subject.

Conclusion

Since the beginning of the new millennium, a number of factors have converged to make the shift to a war-on-cancer–style war on crime and terrorism easier than it might appear. Foremost among them is the demographic fact of an aging population, feeling increasingly vulnerable to disease, above all cancer, as they felt to violent crime in the early 1980s. As the baby-boom generation prepares to consider its own mortality, cancer looms large on the horizon indeed, and will only get larger as they and their children age out of the years where exposure to crime is serious. Interestingly, for the first time in many election cycles, promises for major improvements in health care for those already insured, including specific boosts in spending on cancer research, were made in the 2000 campaign by both President Bush and Al Gore, resulting in a rare piece of cancer legislation, the National Cancer Act of 2003.

The experience of mass terrorism itself is a powerful counterbalance to the inertia of governmental ideas. It is doubtful that Americans will settle for the kinds of symbolic solidarity-reinforcing gestures that have marked the war on crime. This is already suggested by the success of the September 11 Commission in pushing for far more access to sensitive intelligence information from the Bush administration than any similar commission has ever enjoyed, much of it because of the panel's alliance with the victim families. The recent disaster in New Orleans after Hurricane Katrina—and the echo disaster in the evacuation of Houston during the approach of Hurricane Rita—underscored the vulnerability of urban America to failures of critical infrastructure, whether or not pressed by human forces bent on destruction.

The new urbanism and the rediscovery of the structural value of urban neighborhoods have also contributed to the formation of a politically engaged public with a far more real stake in the effects of mass incarceration than is true for those already committed to the gated-community approach. The boom in urban real estate means influential people have a much more direct exposure to the results of mass incarceration. This new public is emerging conveniently at a time when the awakening of American journalism and social science to the extraordinary levels of imprisonment in American society is beginning to force a broader public discussion of how well the war on crime has secured America.

These conditions will mean little in the absence of social movements and political leaders ready to break the hold of crime on American governance and animated by the conviction that the American people are being exposed to risks that are largely ignored by institutions laboring under a burdensome set of formal and informal mandates to manage crime and its risks. That conviction will not spread from the major political institutions of the United States, which have been largely made over by the war on crime. If it grows, it will spread from person to person and institution to institution as a discussion breaks out on how crime risks rule our lives. This book was written with the sole aspiration of starting just such discussions. If its interpretation of American institutions, communities, and lives resonates with your experiences, please start a discussion among your friends and colleagues about governing through crime and its consequences.

Notes

Introduction

1. In this novel, first published in 1969 (Vol. 5 of *The Children of Violence*), Lessing imagined a new social order dominated by crime and punishment, arising in the United States from the 1970s on and spreading to Britain in the 1990s. Many thanks to Susan Haack for calling this passage to my attention.

2. Americans did not see Kennedy shot in quite the way that they witnessed the towers being hit and destroyed. News coverage began almost instantly following the assassination, but it was not until some years later that Americans actually saw Abraham Zapruder's hand-shot film of the Kennedy motorcade during the fatal moments. *Life* magazine, however, published numerous stills from the film within months of the assassination, and the Warren Commission published many stills in its appendices.

3. The rate of imprisonment was roughly five times what it was on average before 1980, and 3 percent of the American adult population is in some level of control by correctional agencies (often called parole, probation, or community supervision).

4. As Bernard Harcourt notes (2006), the combined figure of mental patients and prisoners in custody is a better measure of the total confined population and has remained relatively stable and high since the 1950s. Though both settings provide social control, the priority of crime helps determine the possibilities and flexibilities of government.

5. This does not so much involve the formation of new institutions as it does the explosive growth of such familiar twentieth-century institutions as prisons, jails, and parole and probation supervision. Since 1980, the proportion of Americans in the physical custody of the state and federal governments has climbed astronomically, from a remarkably consistent historic base of around 100 prisoners per 100,000 to 470 per 100,000 in 2001. If those under correctional supervision are considered, nearly 3 percent of the entire adult

resident population of the United States is in some form of correctional custody, far more than serve in the military and more than labor in any major industry. The number increases to 686 per 100,000 if jail inmates are considered. See Harrison and Beck (2002).

Chapter 1

1. 536 U.S. 822.
2. *Vernonia School Dist. 47J v. Acton*, 515 U.S. 646 (1995).
3. In contrast, as Justice Ginsburg noted in her dissent to the *Earls* decision, the Vernonia School District claimed that a "large segment of the student body, particularly those involved in interscholastic athletics, was in a state of rebellion . . . fueled by alcohol and drug abuse as well as the student[s'] misperceptions about the drug culture." 536 U.S. 822, 849, Ginsburg, J. dissenting, quoting *Vernonia School Dist. 47J v. Acton*, 515 U.S. 646, 649. Justice Thomas described the full extent of the drug evidence in the *Earls* case as follows: "Teachers testified that they had seen students who appeared to be under the influence of drugs and that they had heard students speaking openly about using drugs. Marijuana cigarettes were found near the school parking lot. Police officers once found drugs or drug paraphernalia in a car driven by a Future Farmers of America member." *Board of Education of Independent School District No. 92 of Pottawatomie County v. Earls*, 536 U.S. 822, 834–5(2002).
4. *Board of Education of Independent School District No. 92 of Pottawatomie County v. Earls*, 536 U.S. 822, 834 (2002).
5. Garland 2001 is a clear exception, arguing strongly that the most profound effects of the experience of high crime has been on the lives of middle-class populations so influential to politicians in liberal societies.
6. This is naturally a gross exaggeration in a country with a quarter of a billion guns in private hands.
7. While growing up in the Hyde Park neighborhood of Chicago, I witnessed my parents and their friends talking about people being robbed at gunpoint on their way home from work or the grocery store or while getting in or out of their cars.
8. 418 U.S. 717 (1974).
9. 347 U.S. 483 (1954).

Chapter 2

1. But executives seize upon such opportunities when they arise. A recent example is President George W. Bush's decision to retain direct control of which terrorist suspects will be tried in the special military tribunals that the administration announced in 2001.
2. John Kerry, the 2004 Democratic nominee for president, had been a prosecutor before being elected to Congress and concentrated his legislative activity on prosecutorial concerns including transnational organized crime. The win-

ner, Republican Nominee George W. Bush, was never a prosecutor (or even a lawyer), but as governor of Texas he presided over one hundred executions, far more than virtually any sovereign outside of Asia or the Middle East.

3. At the federal level, the "weed-and-seed" program begun in the 1990s has given U.S. attorneys, who represent the United States in civil and criminal matters in federal district courts, a role in channeling redevelopment resources in coordination with law enforcement efforts to eliminate gangs and gun violence, often blamed in part for inner-city poverty (L. Miller 2001). Some prosecutors have also experimented with using civil remedies of various sorts to remove gang members from community streets. See Filosa 2003; Alapo 2003; Coen 2001.

4. In theory it continued until the 1950s, but, in practice, from the end of the nineteenth century the police department represented criminal complainants in many cases.

5. This was the position of the American Bar Association (Report with Recommendations No. 107, as Approved by the ABA House of Delegates, February 2, 1997).

6. *Olyer v. Boles*, 386 U.S. 448 (1962); *Inmates of Attica Correctional Facility v. Rockerfeller*, 477 F.2d 375, 2d Cir. (1973); Heller 1997; Davis 1999.

7. Most of the molestation ring cases have collapsed under appeal, and more recently the jogger case did as DNA evidence proved that an individual not among those charged had deposited semen on the jogger. It appears that some of the crimes that led to the most powerful moral panics either never happened at all or were botched by the police and resulted in wrongful conviction.

8. This agency recently moved into the Department of Homeland Security.

9. The highway as channel of criminal violence is one whose resonance would only grow in the middle of the twentieth century. A powerful example from film is the opening of Stanley Kramer's *The Wild One* (1953), starring Marlon Brando. As the credits role, the camera takes the viewer through a pastoral scene and then onto a highway. Starting in the distance, but growing rapidly closer is a seeming horde of motorcycle riding, leather-jacket-clad toughs. We next see them as they take over a small town along the highway.

10. Kennedy, who cut an early posture as an anticommunist in working on Senator Joseph McCarthy's committee, recognized in organized crime a subversion all its own, and one whose influence on American society was far more demonstrable, even if largely ignored by and even cooperated with by government.

11. This was an early and persistent theme of Kennedy's tenure as attorney general. After ordering his staff to pursue Hoffa with every available resource and angle, Kennedy succeeded in indicting Hoffa in May of 1962, about a year and a quarter into his administration. See Lowi 1964, 143–44.

12. Not surprisingly, this has led many to speculate that the assassinations of President Kennedy and Robert Kennedy were products of this "betrayal." See, generally, Kurtz 1982.

13. Although this side of Kennedy is little celebrated by his postassassination image, it lives on in the political career of one of his daughters, Kathleen

Kennedy Townsend. The former lieutenant governor of Maryland (and, until her defeat in the 2002 gubernatorial election, often cited as a rising figure in the national Democratic Party) developed a political profile rooted in a strong response to crime. Ms. Kennedy Townsend has also drawn on her personal experience as a victim of violent crime, through the assassination of her father in 1968. An act that framed the martyrdom of liberalism for many observers in the 1960s has become for her an argument for the death penalty, as when she recently noted the pain she suffers during the periodic and always futile parole hearings for her father's assassin.

14. Ramsey Clark, who served the last couple of years of President Johnson's term, maintained Kennedy's initiatives but spent a great deal of time on the defensive against accusations by Republicans and conservative Democrats that he was soft on crime. Edward Levi, appointed by President Ford, focused on government ethics in the aftermath of the Watergate scandal. See N. Baker 1992.

15. For my ponderings on a similar link between the history of governmental ideas and the far more volatile world of human events, in the case of the Kennedy assassination, see Simon 1998b.

16. "Excerpts from Judge's Testimony at Ashcroft Confirmation Hearing." *New York Times*, National Edition, Jan. 19, 2001, A2.

17. Elisabeth Bumiller, "Putting Name to Bush Justice Department: Kennedy." *New York Times*, National Edition, Nov. 21, 2001, A12.

18. One of the very special features of the attorneys general of the United States is that they combine a broad policy mandate at the federal level (second perhaps only to the president on domestic policy) with the capacity to seek the death penalty in an individual case. Since the renewal of the federal death penalty in the 1990s, the power to seek it has resided with the U.S. attorney in the district where the crime occurred, subject to the review of the attorney general. John Ashcroft, attorney general from 2001 to 2005, was the first to take that decision personally and to actively intervene to reverse decisions not to seek the death penalty.

19. As political scientist John Culver (1999, 292) notes, some states seem to have adopted death penalty laws that legislators could predict would result in relatively few death sentences, and thus serve mainly as a symbolic act.

20. In that case, the association was made even more potent by the fact that Deukmejian's predecessor, Democrat Jerry Brown, had been a strong opponent of the death penalty and had vetoed the legislation. The death penalty was restored in 1982 by popular voter initiative, the same election cycle in which Republican Deukmejian, the major legislative supporter of the death penalty, won handily over Democrat Tom Bradley, the veteran mayor of Los Angeles and the first African American to be nominated by a major party as a candidate for California's governorship (Culver 1999).

21. This deviant status was also implied by Justice Scalia's dissenting argument in *Roper v. Simmons* that abolitionist states should not count for purposes

of gauging national standards of decency on the question of executing people who committed murder when they were 16 or 17 years old.

Chapter 3

1. Public Law 90–351, June 19, 1968, 82 Stat. 197, 42 U.S.C.§ 3711.
2. My analysis of crime legislation since the late 1960s builds on the tradition of studying the role of symbolic politics (Edelman 1964). Rather than focusing on legislative symbols and how they play to win the consent of the governed, however, I follow the path of more recent scholars in treating the language of political narratives as having an operational role in constructing the systems of power and knowledge through which governments act (Rose 1999; Garland 2001a).
3. As cognitive science research has shown, metaphoric links are not purely contingent or completely literary in their logic; rather they build on the embodied roots of reason and work by systematically relating specific guiding action in one domain by application of another. In short, from a cognitive point of view, metaphors are about governance, action on action (Lakoff and Johnson 1980).
4. It is a mystery to me why the unions have failed to launch a national campaign to make violations of organizing rights a federal crime. Their opponents would have a difficult time arguing why premeditated actions intended to disrupt unambiguous federally guaranteed labor rights are not deserving of punishment. If such violations were treated with even the public stigma of insider trading violations (let alone drug dealing) one suspects union organizing would encounter far less illegal resistance from corporate employers who are capable of being imminently rational about their best long term interests.
5. I offer only a sketch of a far more complex legislative history. For present purposes, the elements of my account might be shown to be wrong without basic harm to the thesis that federal land legislation offered a rationality of legislative action.
6. These institutions, the beginnings of the unique investment in higher education undertaken by the United States, were, as the name suggests, targeted very specifically at developing knowledge of immediate practical value to a citizenry of land-owning farmers.
7. The significance of these acts as efforts to recast American governance is described by Bruce Ackerman (1998, 170–73).
8. See Marable 1991; Kousser 1999; Black 1976.
9. The New Deal incorporated the farmer as well, now not quite as independent yeoman but as small business vulnerable to the financial risks of global capitalism.
10. Saul Bellow captured an edgy perspective on these streets in his early novel, *The Dangling Man* set in Chicago, circa 1941.
11. For most of the next three decades, this measure would be of no practical importance. Starting with the Ford administration, it has been the policy of the

Department of Justice to treat the measure as presumptively unconstitutional at least as to the most important of the legal checks on confessions. When that portion of the law was finally tested by the Supreme Court in 2000, it was at the prompting of public interest lawyers and an ultraconservative appeals court.

12. The law also purported to establish by statute that a suspect could be held by the police for at least six hours before being brought to an arraignment before a judge without jeopardizing any confession taken during that time because of failure to bring the suspect to arraignment more promptly.

13. *New York Times*, May 27, 1964; *New York Times*, March 14, 1965; *New York Times*, April 6, 1965; *New York Times*, May 20, 1968.

14. These legislators included John L. McClellan (D-Ark.), James O. Eastland (D-Miss.), Sam J. Ervin (D-N.C.), Strom Thurmond (R-S.C.), Roman L. Hruska (R-Neb.), Burke B. Hickenlooper (R-Iowa), and Paul J. Fannin (R-Ariz.).

15. As attorney general, Kennedy had early spotted the crime issue as a growing threat to the post–New Deal consensus and had tried to push the crime issue on the federal agenda. In the Senate, he became a critic of the Safe Streets Act, rejecting its attack on the Supreme Court and its expansion of electronic surveillance. During his short campaign for president in the winter and spring of 1968, Kennedy argued against what he saw as an effort to criminalize the problem of poverty and civil disorder in America. His murder silenced the law's most influential critic.

16. The Johnson administration had largely allied itself with the liberal wing of the Warren Court, and although the Great Society programs themselves were not at issue in any of the Court decisions sanctioned, they shared with the Great Society a larger set of ambitions to transform the exercise of power at the local level and in everyday life.

17. Interview with Charles Haar, Coral Gables, Florida, 2002.

18. In this regard, he shared the sentiment of many of the more liberal Democrats who had voted for the law because to do nothing courted a "real possibility that the people will lose their faith in the government's ability to protect them" (R. Harris 1968, 99), as Senator Philip Hart, a liberal Democrat from Michigan, and an opponent of the crime bill, said regarding the reasoning of the act's Democrat supporters.

19. The great exception here is *Hip Hop*, but it is an exception that stems generally from a self-consciously oppositional perspective toward the "war on crime" that is a hallmark of that genre and reflects its roots in the experience of the young, inner-city African American males.

20. *The Random House College Dictionary, Revised Edition* (1975), 1226. The entry goes on to give as an example a political metaphor: "the sinews of the nation."

21. From the perspective of the early 1980s, political scientist Stuart Scheingold did see the Safe Streets Act as representing a major shift in the logic of governance. Though acknowledging that its primary goals of repressing crime rates through improving the capacity of criminal justice were difficult to

assess, Scheingold argued that the act remained the "principal piece of federal legislation" defining a new American politics, the "politics of law and order," which now competed with the "politics of rights" created by the New Deal–style welfare state. See Scheingold 1991, 84.22.

22. Of course, the important parallel game between law enforcement and victims is hidden by this dominant picture.

23. Two examples are the Drug Use Forecasting series and the High Intensity Drug Trafficking Areas program. First, since the 1980s, the Department of Justice has contracted with private researchers all over the country to undertake urinalysis of jail inmates on intake (the information is never linked to a particular case and is presented only in aggregate format) to produce a series of city samples of the drug-use pattern in the inmate population. In the 1980s and early 1990s the data showed large majorities testing positive for marijuana, cocaine, and especially alcohol. Second, since 1994 the Department of Justice has identified more than 20 cities in the United States as High Intensity Drug Trafficking Areas based on indicators of the volume of drug trafficking in and out of the area. Becoming one of these "areas" has all kinds of consequences for a community and the people who live there, from access to more federal action grants to more law enforcement agents targeted on users of freeways and airports in the area, to being searched by police elsewhere.

24. The law was appropriately named "Aimee's law" after a victim of violence. See P.L. 107–11, approved May 28, 2001.

25. 108 Stat. 1796, 2078.

26. The increasingly formal nature of this icon is reflected in the fact that President Bush went to a family farm to sign a law repealing the estate tax even though during the debate on the law it was repeatedly acknowledged in the media that nobody in fact could find any family farms that had been sold primarily to meet a federal estate tax liability.

27. Some observers believe that this may be turning around with the growth of unionization among Hispanic service workers in Los Angeles and New York (Erickson et al. 2002.).

28. The home, in particular the privately owned single-family home, has been at the symbolic cross hairs of crime legislation and the anti-tax movement. In the narrative of both anti-crime and anti-tax populism, the home as a locus of family values and wealth is endangered by both rising property taxes (which threaten to make it too expensive to own) and rising crime, which threatens to undercut the market for homes.

Chapter 4

1. As discussed in chapter 3, the Safe Streets Act included provisions attacking two major Warren Court precedents, including *Miranda v. Arizona* (1966).

2. 408 U.S. 238, 413–4, Blackmun, J. dissenting.

3. 408 U.S. 238, 444–5, Powell, J. dissenting.

4. In his later years on the Court, Blackmun increasingly became skeptical of the death penalty. In his last published opinion, an unusual dissent to a denial of certiorari, Justice Blackmun announced that he would vote to find the death penalty unconstitutional. See *Callins v. Collins* (1999) 510 U.S. 1141–1149, Blackmun, J. dissenting.

5. In that year, the conservative coalition on the Supreme Court that had been striking down key pieces of New Deal legislation fragmented in the face of a gathering political storm over Roosevelt's proposal to add several new justices to the Court as a way of breaking the conservative hold. See Carson and Kleinerman 2002.

6. *Gregg v. Georgia*, 428 U.S. 153 (1976).

7. This despite the fact that the overall role of the courts has been, as argued by Carol Steiker, to legitimize and stabilize capital punishment.

> The Supreme Court's project of constitutional regulation of capital punishment since 1976 has played a role in legitimating and thus stabilizing the practice of capital punishment, primarily by generating an appearance of intensive judicial scrutiny and regulation despite its virtual absence. The Court's cases, by continually refining the rules of capital sentencing procedures, have helped to perpetuate (though perhaps unintentionally) a demonstrably false sense that constitutional regulation actually rationalizes the capital sentencing process and thus protects against inaccurate, arbitrary, or discriminatory results. This false sense is conveyed, in different ways, to actors both within and outside of the actual legal process. (2002, 1485)

8. Pub. L. No. 104–132, 110 Stat. 1214 (1996) (codified in scattered sections of 28 U.S.C.).

9. This is a general feature of the post–New Deal political landscape that has supported governing through crime (Caplow and Simon 1998, 71).

10. Since the old text had been cited by the Florida Supreme Court as a reason to provide greater protection to prisoners under that text than provided by the U.S. Supreme Court, the addition of an express requirement to follow the later court might seem superfluous. It is perhaps best seen as an expression of contempt for the Florida Supreme Court placed into the constitution itself.

11. The named defendant, Secretary of State Katherine Harris, would shortly star in a second legal drama that would place the question of representation and the legitimacy of the state supreme court back into contention. Indeed, although the differences between the death penalty amendment controversy and the ballot counting controversy are legion, there is a striking parallelism in the way they pit the branches of government, executive, legislative, and judicial against one another in the context of legal cases generated by alleged flaws in the electoral process of representation. No better confirmation of this parallelism can be found than the fact that Florida's Attorney General, Bob Butterworth, took the highly unusual step in a state law case of petitioning the U.S. Supreme for certiorari (which was, of course, de-

nied). The petition cited *Bush v. Gore* and argued that a similar abuse of judicial role was going on in *Armstrong*. The final twist is that Butterworth was not, like Katherine Harris and Governor Jeb Bush, a supporter of George W. Bush, but instead was the campaign chairperson for Al Gore.

12. The same issues would play themselves out in the posture of the Bush and Gore camps during the final act of the disputed Florida presidential vote and contest of 2000. The Bush camp, allied with the Republican majority of the legislature, attacked the Florida Supreme Court in its briefs as usurping the legislature's unique constitutional role in laying down the ground rules for these crucial moments when democratic will-formation actually happens. The Florida Supreme Court, defended by the Gore camp, could be readily seen as protecting the representational core of democracy by insisting that every vote should be counted if its intent could be reasonably discerned. The continuity between the antagonism of the death penalty amendment fight and the antagonism of the election contest was profound. A remarkable document that provides compelling evidence of how deeply the representational logic of crime and the death penalty has marked political leadership is the brief filed in the Supreme Court seeking review of the Florida Supreme Court's decision in *Armstrong v. Harris*. Attempting to justify a seemingly improbable request for review of an issue of state statutory and constitutional law, the brief overtly references the election fight and accuses the Florida Supreme Court of being little short of a rogue institution in need of extraordinary federal supervision. Interestingly, the brief was filed by Attorney General Robert "Bob" Butterworth, a Democrat, who had been Al Gore's campaign chairperson in Florida and had often faced off with Katherine Harris during the election contest period.

13. Fla. Const. Art. I, § 17. Am. H.J.R. 3505, 1998; adopted 1998; Am. H.J.R. 951, 2001; adopted 2002.

14. Federal courts treated the guidelines as mandatory until the Supreme Court held them to be only advisory in a 2004 decision. My focus here, however, is on how the guidelines were interpreted from the time of their adoption until the end of the twentieth century.

15. Some judges seem eager to read as much guidance as possible into the language of statutes enacted during the war on crime so as to deprive themselves of discretion.

16. Courts have come to identify the victim as independently worthy of judicial deference even in the capital punishment case, where it undermines a remedial scheme painstakingly developed by the Supreme Court. In addition to their direct and indirect weight in cases of criminal punishment, victims have been central to the new crime paradigm in a slightly disguised form: as the police. As argued in chapter 3, police in the war on crime have a dual role of protectors and front-line victims of violence. Judicial deference to police, codified in scores of Supreme Court decisions since the 1970s (Bilionis 2005), evokes both themes.

17. Earlier cases to reach the Supreme Court generally involved communities that were more rural and less geographically segregated, where substantial desegregation could be achieved by ordering new school assignment plans without requiring expensive and intrusive strategies to move large groups of students in multiple directions.
18. See the dissent by Justice Marshall, *Milliken v. Bradley*, at 781 et seq.
19. This was an alliance of organized labor, Catholics, Jews, and African Americans, much like the one that more successfully governed Los Angeles during the same period and into the 1980s.
20. Indeed, one famous stretch of suburban property, hard upon the city limits at Eight Mile Road and across from an early black outpost neighborhood at the edge of the city, was actually fitted with a wall (Dimond 1985; Hayward 2002).
21. This elaborate plan had already been struck down by the Sixth Circuit Court of Appeals, so the issue reviewed by the Supreme Court was only the abstract proposition that an eventual plan would include some number of suburban districts (Dimond 1985).
22. The state had the legal power to create or restructure school districts at any time and had turned toward extreme decentralization in recent years to protect segregation.
23. *Milliken v. Bradley*, 746.
24. Ibid., 780.
25. Ibid., 814–15.
26. Ibid., 741–42.
27. Ibid., 739–40.
28. Ibid., 764.

Chapter 5

1. Foucault offered Jeremy Bentham's unrealized plan for a prison known as the Panopticon as a pure schema of the disciplinary power that many actual prisons of the era relied upon. Eastern lacked the transparency of Bentham's Panopticon, although its spoke-shaped cellblocks and central guard tower invoked that ideal. Meranze (1996) points out that the keepers in the central tower could not observe conduct in the individual cells.
2. In contrast, the congregate system prisons, like that at Auburn, relied heavily on the discipline of physical labor reinforced with whipping to maintain order.
3. This includes direct social insurance programs but also court decisions expanding the value of private insurance, and through the terms of public employment, itself an important feature of the New Deal state in contrast to the contracting pattern of the patronage state. Through setting benefits policies for its own employees, the New Deal state could help influence norms in private sector employment.
4. An extraordinary example of this was convict writer George Jackson whose bestselling volume of letters home from prison made him a celebrity intellectual to thousands of New Left–oriented college students in the late 1960s

and who died in a blaze of revolutionary glory leading an armed seizure of the San Quentin prison's "adjustment center." See Simon 2002, 140–43.

5. This divide is powerfully articulated in the neoconservative jeremiad and memoir of David Gerlertner, a well-known computer scientist when he was mutilated by a letter bomb sent by "Unabomber" Theodore Kacyzinski.

6. Schrag describes this new politics as "a parody of the Newtonian system of checks and balances written by the framers into the United States Constitution, a mechanical device that's supposed to run more or less by itself and spares the individual the bother and complexities of any sort of political engagement" (Schrag 1998, 18). California is Schrag's focus, but the political order he describes can be found in many other states.

7. See *Rockwell v. Superior Court* 556 P.2d 1101 (Cal. 1976).

8. Text of Governor's Last State of the State Message, *Los Angeles Times* (Wednesday, 10 January 1990), Part A. Metro.

9. *In re Rosenkrantz,* 80 Cal. App. 4th 409, 421 (2000).

10. Ibid., 409.

11. Ibid., 414 n. 2.

12. Ibid., 414 n. 3.

13. Ibid., 419.

14. Ibid., 421.

15. Ibid., 428, emphasis in original.

16. Ibid.

17. Public Law 108–21, April 30, 2003, 117 Stat. 650.

Chapter 6

1. Of course, most women in abusive relationships during this period had little real recourse to court, regardless of legal doctrine, because divorce law did not reliably recognize wife beating as a ground for divorce or a basis for ordering financial support in separation.

2. In her article, Siegel addresses the current wave of legislation concerning family violence solely in terms of the provision included in the 1994 Violence Against Women Act that provided a federal civil remedy for victims of violence based on gender. This provision has been the most controversial aspect, and indeed was struck down by the Supreme Court in *United States v. Morrison,* 120 S. Ct. 1740 (2000), by a 5–4 vote, one of a number of recent heated battles on the federalism limits to congressional power. Far more important to the revolution in how families are governed through crime are the provisions encouraging mandatory arrest and tougher prosecution policies.

3. Florida Statutes Annotated, Title XLIII Domestic Relations, § 741.2901 (Supp. 2000).

4. There is in fact a more technical issue of prosecutability that arises when the victim refuses to testify, which she is privileged to do when the defendant is her husband. In practice, even where immunity is not available, prosecutors are loath to place an abused woman victim in custody for contempt of

court. One solution is to allow the prosecution to present police testimony of the statements that the victim made to the police.

5. 529 U.S. 598 (2000).

6. An important literature in feminist jurisprudence has arisen to address this precise question. See Schneider, 1992; Mahoney, 1994; Abrams, 1999.

7. In a snapshot study, as the name suggests, researchers capture information about a system as it existed during a designated time period, with information taken from the stream of clients using the system during that period.

8. These presumptions can create problems for domestic violence victims who have ever engaged in retaliatory "violence." In *Black's Law Dictionary*, "domestic violence" is defined as "violence between members of a household, usually spouses; an assault or other violent act committed by one member of a household against another" (2004, 1564).

9. Anti-Drug Abuse Act of 1988, Public Law 100–690, 102 Stat. 4181 (1988).

10. This story is drawn from the facts of one of the petitioners in *Department of Housing and Urban Development v. Rucker, et al.* 122 S.Ct. 1230 (2002).

11. *Department of Housing and Urban Development v. Rucker, et al.* 122 S.Ct. 1230, 1235 (2002).

12. This is part of the broader critique of tort law mounted by the private insurance industry in support of "tort reform" including punitive damage caps, plaintiff hostile discovery rules, and attacks on liberal judges.

13. As is sometimes the case, the victim had already succeeded in recovering some damages from the automobile policy but probably not enough to cover the full loss. Other than the criminal act exclusion, this case might have been litigated under language in most homeowners policies that excludes losses associated with motor vehicles, a form of risk segmentation exclusion (T. Baker 2000).

14. *Horace Mann Insurance Co. v. Drury*, 445 S.E.2d 272, 274 (Court of Appeals of Georgia, 1994).

15. This describes a form of insurance that becomes effective once certain specified thresholds of loss have been paid by other means (usually other carriers or simply by the plan's own resources).

16. Insurance that is provided as a benefit of employment is generally governed by the Employee Retirement Security Act (ERISA). In ERISA insurance, the "plan" occupies the legal space occupied by the contract in private insurance. Many of the same considerations go into the resolution of disputes about the plan that go into contract disputes in private insurance, but because ERISA preempts the field for federal regulation, many state causes of action and doctrines are unavailable.

17. *SGI/Argis Employee Benefit Trust Plan v. Canada Life*, 151 F.Supp.2d 1044, 1045–46.

18. Ibid. at 1048.

19. So far, this has not been a major feature of health insurance, but as that market becomes more individual–policy-based we can expect criminal behavior

to become a factor in underwriting decisions (i.e., the insurance provider's calculus of whether they want to take on a particular risk).

20. There is actually a trade association, the National Association of Therapeutic Wilderness Camps.

21. This is very much the symmetry Mike Davis has in mind in Davis (1998).

22. Signs denominating spaces as "drug free" have become a regular feature of suburban neighborhoods, some reflecting spatially targeted legislation, and others reflecting the work of private or even voluntary organizations. The term "crime-free zone" never appears, but it seems to be the wish behind the signs.

Chapter 7

1. It is common to emphasize the role of the federal courts, but Congress became deeply involved in creating incentives for school desegregation, incentives that were far more effective in moving school districts along than the often-cumbersome process of courts' administering change with "all deliberate speed." See Rosenberg 1991.

2. The fact that the stories may involve communities far away is unlikely to make most parents feel altogether sanguine. After all, those folks did not expect it to happen to their kids, either.

3. A model problem is not necessarily the average problem, but one that problem solvers, such as principals and teachers, take to be defining for their own success and one that, by consequently occupying much of the thought and imagination of participants, comes to influence others.

4. See, *Vernonia School District 47J v. Acton*, 515 U.S. 646 (1995), in which the Supreme Court upheld suspicionless drug testing of high school athletes in a suburban high school. There had been alarming reports of drug use among student leaders and declining discipline in school.

5. These strikes and decentralization were very much part of the post–civil rights struggle in New York City, around the issues of racial equality and schools. See Podair 2002.

6. It is interesting that this number comes from data collected by the teachers union.

7. Ronald Stephens of the National School Safety Center was quoted in a newspaper story on school police as describing "the modern school officer" as "more akin to an educator than a guard" (quoted in M. Wilson 2004).

8. Malcolm Feeley and I have suggested that this abandonment of individualized normalization in favor of managing high-risk populations en masse is a broad feature of contemporary penality (Feeley & Simon 1992, 1994; Simon & Feeley 1995).

9. For a discussion of the law's impact, see Rosenberg 1991, 47.

10. Public Law 103–227, Mar. 31, 1994, 108 Stat. 200, et seq., 20 U.S.C.A sect. 5960 et seq.

11. 20 U.S.C.A. Sect. 5965.

12. E.g., Missouri's Safe Schools Act, enacted in 1996: Revised Statutes of Missouri Sections 160 et seq.

13. 20 U.S.C.A. S. 5963 (b) (1) "In awarding grants under this subchapter, the Secretary shall give priority to . . . the formation of partnerships among the local educational agency . . . [and] a local law enforcement agency."

14. See, e.g., *New Jersey v. T.L.O.*, 469 U.S. 325 (1985).

15. Available at http://www.ed.gov/updates/uniforms.htm.

16. The civil rights issue received national media attention in the spring of 2000 when Rev. Jesse Jackson led a civil rights protest against the expulsion of a number of black male students for participating in a fight at a high school football game.

17. Available at http://www.ed.gov/updates/uniforms.htm.

18. Public Law No. 107–110, 115, Stat. 1425 (2001).

19. In this regard, it follows another important shift in late modern governance toward treating social problems like crime as aggregate phenomena. See Feeley and Simon 1992.

20. This perspective was captured by Justice Thomas's recent majority opinion for the Court in a decision upholding widespread drug testing of high school students involved in extracurricular activities without any showing of a serious risk or a serious drug problem. Thomas's opinion characterized schools as custodial situations whose overarching purpose is the security of students. Not once did the opinion acknowledge that schools might have functions other than secure custody. *Board of Education of Independent School District No. 92 of Pottawatomie County, v. Earls*, 536 U.S. 822 (2002).

Chapter 8

1. The Taft-Hartley Act of 1947, 29 U.S.C. § 141, introduced restrictions on certain kinds of strikes considered secondary boycotts. Sanctions can be quite punitive although considered formally civil in nature.

2. In 2000, approximately 60 percent of employers tested applicants for the use of illegal substances; almost 90 percent of Fortune 500 companies require submission to a drug test.

3. In some cases this has been encouraged by the state directly. In California, for example, day care centers are required to notify parents of any criminal record of an employee. The law must inevitably discourage day care centers from hiring personnel with even trivial criminal records if equally qualified others are available. California Health and Safety Code § 1596.871 (2003).

4. Economist Intelligence Unit Risk Wire, April 16, 2004.

5. 51 Federal Register 32889, Executive Order 12564.

6. Requirements on federal contractors came in 1988; 41 U.S.C.A Sect. 701, Drug free workplace requirements for Federal contractors. Executive Order 12564. *Federal Register* 51: 32889.

7. Certain exceptions remained, such as seamen, who were held to their work contracts by force if necessary.

8. *Cody v. Cigna Healthcare of St. Louis, Inc.*, 139 F.3d 595 (U.S. Court of Appeals for the 8th Circuit 1998), claim under the Americans with Disabilities Act, Public Law 101–336, 104 Stat. 327 (1990).

9. Plaintiffs may file their case without prejudice in a district court following denial by the Equal Employment Opportunity Commission. If the commission decides in favor of the plaintiff, all further action in court is undertaken by the commission itself on behalf of the plaintiff.

10. It may also reflect the "damage" done by habituation to the new hypersecure spaces that dominate suburban landscapes and tend to make the comparative experience of less ordered environments anxiety-provoking.

11. At their best, security consultants are real wizards in determining fairly low-key and low-cost changes in routine that can make people safer.

12. See 42 U.S.C. § 12101 (1990) (Equal Opportunity for Individuals with Disabilities); 42 U.S.C. § 2000 (Civil Rights Act 1964); 2 U.S.C. § 1201 (1991) (Government Employee Rights); Public Law 95–555 (1978) (Pregnancy Discrimination Act, no currently effective sections).

13. These terms have been popularized by the American Law Institute's influential *Model Penal Code* (1962).

14. *Griggs v. Duke Power*, 401 U.S. 424 (1971), overruled by *United States v. State of North Carolina*, F.Supp. 1257, 1265 (1996), but Congress statutorily authorized the disparate impact approach in the Civil Rights Act of 1991, 2 U.S.C. § 1201. There is, to be sure, a similar way of viewing crime as well, associated with what Stuart Scheingold calls structuralist criminology, but the influence of that form of expertise has been in decline for some time.

15. One need not agree with Senator Hatch's assessment of the gravity of character flaws that Hill's accusations (if true) implied about Thomas to sense that they involve a claim of wrongdoing significantly more invested with the sense of moral wrongdoing associated with violations of the criminal law than with typical contract or even tort wrongs.

Chapter 9

1. Perhaps the most striking evidence of this was Nixon's contemplation in the middle of his first term of abandoning the Republican Party and founding a new political party.

2. In this respect, it closely paralleled what the Kennedy and Johnson administrations attempted to do with the war on poverty, which provided federal legitimacy, expertise, and money to local community development agencies at the expense of traditional political party machines like that of Mayor Richard J. Daley in Chicago.

3. Food Additives Amendment of 1958, Public Law 85–929 72 Stat. 1784 (codified as amended in scattered sections of 21 U.S.C.).

4. Political assassinations became an important aspect of this circuit in 1963 and 1968.

5. One of the most famous instances was John Dean's statement to his client Richard Nixon that Watergate constituted a "cancer on the presidency," March 21, 1973.

6. As late as 1909, general hospitals in the City of New York would not admit cancer patients (or those with tuberculosis and other chronic or incurable diseases). Cancer was so feared that the one hospital in New York in the early twentieth century that was devoted to its care avoided the name altogether, calling itself "Memorial Hospital" (Patterson 1987, 416 n. 52).

7. In the case of crime, this followed a period of pessimism over the perceived long-term failure of the penitentiary as a mechanism of self-improvement by criminals. See Rothman 1980.

8. Public Law 107–56, 115 Stat. 272 (2001).

9. Thus when victims get off script and make demands that do not fit these calls, the response of government is much less automatic. The group of 9/11 widows who became known as the Jersey girls are an example of victims who have extended their calls beyond issues of penal justice in ways that have challenged the political system. They have had remarkable success in getting the 9/11 Commission through its investigation and report against the resistance of the Bush administration (Simon 2005, 1452).

10. Public Law 107–56, 115 Stat. 272, Title VIII, Sec. 802.

11. Public Law 104–132, 110 Stat. 1214 (1996).

12. These extraordinary circumstances might have resulted in a court order not to seek the death penalty were the case being reviewed by any court of appeals other than the ultraconservative U.S. Court of Appeals for the Fourth Circuit.

13. And it is not because they were visitors, since our immigration control laws and practices have tended to exercise the same kinds of screens.

14. The thinking is that Al Qaeda will not be attractive even to immigrants from countries where Bin Laden's views have currency because most will be people who have sacrificed mightily to get to the United States to take advantage of its unorthodox social rules.

15. U.S. Authorities Capture Dirty Bomb Suspect, Associated Press, June 10, 2002, available at http://archives.cnn.com/2002/US/06/10/dirty.bomb.suspect/.

16. The case of serial killer/rapist Eddie Lee Moseley has been thus far most substantially told in the Frontline documentary *Requiem for Frank Lee Smith* (Ophra Bikel producer, 2001). Moseley preyed on literally hundreds of women, mostly in predominantly black neighborhoods of Fort Lauderdale and Miami during the 1970s and 1980s while authorities prosecuted at least two other men for Moseley's crimes (like Moseley, both were black). Authorities knew about Moseley but for a variety of reasons were disinclined to focus on him.

References

ABA. 1983. *Standards for Criminal Justice: Prosecution and Defense Functions.* Washington, D.C.: American Bar Association.

Abrams, Kathryn. 1999. "From Autonomy to Agency: Feminist Perspectives on Self-Direction." *William and Mary Law Review* 40: 805–846.

Ackerman, Bruce. 1998. *We the People,* Vol. 2: *Transformations.* Cambridge, Mass.: Harvard University Press.

Alapo, Lola. 2003. "Youths Get Jobs Instead of Jail,, Knox Program Lets Teens Do Chores to Pay Community." *Knoxville News-Sentinel,* March 6.

Alfieri, Anthony V. 2002. "Community Prosecutors." *California Law Review* 90: 1465–1512.

Anderson, Benjamin.1983. *Imaginary Communities: Reflections on the Origin and Spread of Nationalism.* London: Verso.

Anderson, Paul. 1994. *Janet Reno: Doing the Right Thing.* New York: John Wiley & Sons.

Anderson, Totton J., and Eugene C. Lee. 1967. "The 1966 Election in California." *Western Political Quarterly* 20: 535–54.

Armstrong v. Harris, 773 So.2d 7, Supreme Court of Florida (2000).

Aylward, Michael F. 1998. "Does Crime Pay? Insurance for Criminal Acts." *Defense Counsel Journal* 65 (April): 185–99.

Baker, Nancy V. 1992. *Conflicting Loyalties: Law and Politics in the Attorney General's Office, 1789–1990.* Lawrence: University Press of Kansas.

Baker, Tom. 1996. "On the Genealogy of Moral Hazard." *Texas Law Review* 75: 237–92.

Baker, Tom, and Jonathan Simon. 2002. "Embracing Risk." In *Embracing Risk: The Changing Culture of Insurance and Responsibility,* ed. Tom Baker and Jonathan Simon. Chicago: University of Chicago Press.

Banfield, Edward. 1970. *The Unheavenly City: The Nature and Future of Our Urban Crisis.* Boston: Little Brown.

Banner, Stuart. 2002. *The Death Penalty: An American History*. Cambridge: Cambridge University Press.

Barry, Dan. 2001. "As September 11 Widows Unite, Grief Finds a Political Voice." *New York Times*, November 25, A1, B7.

Baum, Dan. 1996. *Smoke and Mirrors: The War on Drugs and the Politics of Failure*. Boston: Back Bay Books.

Beccaria, Cesare. 1775/1992. *An Essay on Crimes and Punishments*, 2nd ed. Boston, MA: International Pocket Library.

Beck, Allen J. 2000. "Prisoners in 1999." *Bureau of Justice Statistics Bulletin*. Washington, D.C.: U.S. Department of Justice, August.

———. 2001. "Prisoners in 2000." *Bureau of Justice Statistics Bulletin*. Washington, D.C.: U.S. Department of Justice, August.

Beck, Ulrich. 1992. *Risk Society: Towards a New Modernity*. London: Sage Publications.

Beckett, Katherine. 1997. *Making Crime Pay: Law and Order in Contemporary American Politics*. New York: Oxford University Press.

Beckett, Katherine, and Bruce Western. 2001. "Governing Social Marginality: Welfare, Incarceration, and the Transformation of State Policy." In *Mass Incarceration: Social Causes and Consequences*, ed. David Garland. London: Sage.

Berger, Raul. 1977. Government by Judicary: The Transformation of the Fourteenth Amendment. Cambridge, MA: Harvard University Press.

Beschloss, Michael. 2001. *Reaching for Glory: Lyndon Johnson's Secret White House Tapes, 1964–1965*. New York: Simon & Schuster.

Bilionis, Louis D. 2005. "Conservative Reformation, Popularization, and the Lessons of Reading Criminal Justice as Constitutional Law." *UCLA Law Review* 52: 979–1060.

Black, Earl. 1976. *Southern Governors and Civil Rights: Racial Segregation as a Campaign Issue in the Second Reconstruction*. Cambridge, Mass.: Harvard University Press.

Black's Law Dictionary, 8th ed. 2004. Bryan A. Garner, editor in chief. St. Paul, Minn.: Thomson/West.

Blakely, Edward J., and Mary Gail Snyder. 1997. *Fortress America: Gated Communities in the United States*. Washington, D.C.: Brookings Institution Press 1997.

Blomberg, Thomas. 1987. "Criminal Justice Reform and Social Control: Are We Becoming a Minimum Security Society?" In *Transcarceration: Essays in the Sociology of Social Control*, ed. John Lowman, Robert Menzies, and T. S. Palys, pp. 218–226. London: Gower.

Bonczar, Thomas. 2003. "Prevalence of Imprisonment in the U.S. Population, 1974–2001." *Bureau of Justice Statistics, Special Report 197976*. Washington, D.C.: Bureau of Justice Statistics.

Bradsher, Keith. 2000. "Was Freud a Minivan or S.U.V. Kind of Guy?" *New York Times*, July 17, A1, A16.

Bright, Charles. 1996. *The Powers That Punish: Prison and Politics in the Era of the "Big House," 1920–1955: Law, Meaning, and Violence*. Ann Arbor: University of Michigan Press.

Bright, Steven B., and Patrick J. Keenan. 1995. "Judges and the Politics of Death: Deciding between the Bill of Rights and the Next Election in Capital Cases." *Boston University Law Review* 75: 759–835.

Brinkely, Alan. 1989. "The New Deal and the Idea of the State." In *The Rise and Fall of the New Deal Order, 1930–1980*, ed. Steve Fraser and Gary Gerstle. Princeton, N.J.: Princeton University Press.

Brown, Wendy. 1995. *States of Injury: Power and Freedom in Late Modernity*. Princeton, N.J.: Princeton University Press.

Bryant v. Livigni, 619 N.E.2d 550 (Appellate court of Illinois, Fifth District 1993).

Bumiller, Kristin. 1988. *The Civil Rights Society: The Social Construction of Victims*. Baltimore: Johns Hopkins University Press.

Burrough, Bryan. 2004. *Public Enemies: America's Greatest Crime Wave and the Birth of the FBI, 1933–1934*. New York: Penguin Press.

Bush, George H. W. 1988. "Transcript of Bush Speech Accepting Nomination for President." *New York Times*, August 19, A14.

Caplow, Theodore, and Jonathan Simon. 1998. "Understanding Prison Policy and Population Trends." *Crime and Justice: Prisons* 26: 63–120.

Carson, Jamie L., and Benjamin A. Kleinerman. 2002. "A Switch in Time Saves Nine: Institutions, Strategic Actors, and FDR's Court-Packing Plan." *Public Choice* 113: 301–324.

Carson, Rachel. 1994 (1962). *Silent Spring*. Revised ed. Boston: Houghton-Mifflin.

Center for Families, Children, and the Courts. 1996. "Preparing Court-Based Child Custody Mediation Services for the Future." San Francisco: Administrative Office of the Courts, September, 6, 9.

Clark, Geoffrey. 2002. "Embracing Fatality through Life Insurance in Eighteenth Century England." In *Embracing Risk: The Changing Culture of Insurance and Responsibility*, ed. Tom Baker and Jonathan Simon, 80–96. Chicago: University of Chicago Press.

Clausewitz, Carl von. 1984 (1832). *On War*. Edited by Michael Howard and Peter Paret. Princeton, N.J.: Princeton University Press.

Clawson, Marion. 1968. *The Land System of the United States: An Introduction to the History and Practice of Land Use and Land Tenure*. Lincoln: University of Nebraska Press.

Clayton, Cornell W. 1992. *The Politics of Justice: The Attorney General and the Making of Legal Policy*. Armonk, NY: M.E. Sharpe.

Clear, Todd R., and Dina R. Rose. 1999. "When Neighbors Go to Jail: Impact on Attitudes about Formal and Informal Social Control." *National Institute of Justice Research Preview* 1.

Cody v. Cigna Healthcare of St. Louis, Inc., 139 F.3d 595 (U.S. Court of Appeals for the 8th Circuit 1998).

Coen, Mark. 2001. "Prosecutors Sharpen Focus on Hate Crimes, Victims to Get Closer Attention." *Chicago Tribune*, December 1.

Cohen, Lizabeth. 2003. *A Consumers Republic: The Politics of Mass Consumption in Postwar America*. New York: Knopf.

Cohen, Stanley. 1985. *Visions of Social Control: Crime, Punishment, and Classification*. Cambridge, UK: Polity Press.

Coker, Donna. 2001. "Crime Control and Feminist Law Reform in Domestic Violence Law: A Critical Review." *Buffalo Criminal Law Review* 4: 801.

Cole, David. 2003. Enemy Aliens: Double Standards and Constitutional Freedoms in the War on Terror. New York: New Press.

Cooter, Robert. 1984. "Prices and Sanctions." *Columbia Law Review* 84: 1523–1560.

Cover, Robert. 1986. "Violence and the Word." *Yale Law Journal*. 95: 1601–1630.

Culver, John H. 1999. "Capital Punishment Politics and Policies in the States, 1977–1997." *Crime, Law, and Social Change* 32, 287: 291–92.

Cummins, Eric. 1994. *The Rise and Fall of California's Radical Prison Movement*. Stanford, CA: Stanford University Press.

Dahl, Robert. 1961. *Who Governs? Power in an American City*. New Haven, Conn.: Yale University Press.

Dallek, Robert. 1998. *Flawed Giant: Lyndon B. Johnson 1960–1973*. New York: Oxford University Press.

Daly, Kathy. 1994a. "Comment: Men's Violence, Victim Advocacy, and Feminist Redress." *Law and Society Review* 28: 77–86.

———. 1994b. Gender, Crime, and Punishment. New Haven, Conn.: Yale University Press.

Davies, Thomas Y. 1983. "A Hard Look at What We Know (And Still Need to Learn) about the 'Costs' of the Exclusionary Rule: The NIJ Study and Other Studies of 'Lost' Arrests." *American Bar Foundation Research Journal* 8: 611–69.

Davis, Angela J. 1999. "Prosecution and Race: The Power and Privilege of Discretion." *Fordham Law Review* 67: 13, 20.

Davis, Mike. 1990. *City of Quartz: Excavating the Future in LA*. London: Verso.

———. 1998. *Ecology of Fear: Los Angeles and the Imagination of Disaster*. New York: Metropolitan Books.

Decker, Scott H. 2000. "Increasing School Safety through Juvenile Accountability Programs." *Juvenile Accountability Incentive Block Grants Program Bulletin.* Washington D.C.: U.S. Department of Justice, Office of Justice Programs, Office of Juvenile Justice and Delinquency Prevention, December.

Department of Housing and Urban Development v. Rucker, et. al. 122 S.Ct. 1230 (2002).

Devine, John. 1996. *Maximum Security: The Culture of Violence in Inner-City Schools*. Chicago: University of Chicago Press.

Devoe, Jill F., Katherine Peter, Phillip Kaufmann, Amand Miller, Margaret Noonan, Thomas D. Snyder, and Katrina Baum. 2004. *Indicators of School Crime and Safety*: 2004. NCES 2005-002/NCJ 205290. U.S. Departments of Education and Justice. Washington: U.S. Government Printing Office.

DiLorenzo, Louis P., and Darren J. Carroll. 1995. "The Growing Menace: Violence in the Workplace." *New York State Bar Journal* 67, 24.

Dimond, Paul R. 1985. *Beyond Busing: Inside the Challenge to Urban Segregation.* Ann Arbor: University of Michigan Press.

Dinsmore, Alyson. 2002. "Clemency in Capital Cases: The Need to Assure Meaningful Review." *University of California Los Angeles Law Review* 49: 1825–58.

Dionne, E. J. 1991. *Why Americans Hate Politics.* New York: Simon and Schuster.

Dobash, R. Emerson, and Russell P. Dobash. 1992. *Women, Violence, and Social Change.* London: Routledge.

Donzelot, Jacques. 1979. *The Policing of Families.* Translated by Robert Hurley. New York: Pantheon.

Douglas, Mary, and Aaron Wildavsky. 1982. *Risk and Culture: An Essay on Risk Selection.* Berkeley: University of California Press.

Douglas, Thomas J. 2001. "Discipline and Punish? Cambodian Refugees Learning Parenting from the Police." *APLA Newsletter*, February.

Downey, Mike. 1998. "It's Debatable: Are We Seeing Lincoln-Douglas?" *Los Angeles Times,* August 2, A3.

Duany, Andres, Elizabeth Plater-Zyberk, and Jeff Speck. 2000. *Suburban Nation: The Rise of Sprawl and the Decline of the American Dream.* New York: North Point Press.

Dubber, Markus. 2002. *Victims in the War on Crime: The Use and Abuse of Victims Rights.* New York. New York University Press.

Dumm, Thomas. 1987. *Democracy and Discipline: Disciplinary Origins of the United States.* Madison: University of Wisconsin Press.

Dwyer, Jim, Peter Neufeld, and Barry Scheck.2000. *Actual Innocence: Five days to execution and other dispatches from the wrongly convicted.* New York: Doubleday.

Eckland, T. Nikki. 1999. "The Safe Schools Act: Legal and ADR Responses to Violence in Schools." *Urban Lawyer* 31 (spring): 309–28.

Edelman, Murray J. 1985 (1964). *The Symbolic Uses of Politics.* 2nd ed. Chicago: University of Illinois Press.

Eggen, Dan. 2002. "Ashcroft Aggressively Pursues Death Penalty." *Washington Post*, July 1, A1.Ehrenreich, Barbara. 2003. *Nickel and Dimed: On (Not) Getting By in America.* New York: Metropolitan Books.

Ely, John Hart. 1980. *Democracy and Distrust: A Theory of Judicial Review.* Cambridge, Mass.: Harvard University Press.

Emsellem, Maurice. 2005. *Memorandum: Congress Mandates Labor Input on AG's Criminal Background Check Proposal.* Oakland, Calif.: National Employment Law Project.

Epp, Charles. 1998. *The Rights Revolution: Lawyers, Activists, and Supreme Courts in Comparative Perspective.* Chicago: University of Chicago Press.

Erickson, Christopher L., Catherine L. Fisk, Ruth Milkman, Daniel J. B. Mitchell, and Kent Wong. 2002. "Justice for Janitors in Los Angeles: Lessons from

Three Rounds of Negotiations." *British Journal of Industrial Relations* 40: 543–567.

Ewing v. California, 538 U.S. 11 (2003).

Fass, Paula. 1993. "Making and Remaking an Event: The Leopold and Loeb Case in American Culture." *Journal of American History* 80: 919–951.

Feeley, Malcolm M., and Edward Rubin. 1998. *Judicial Policy Making in the Modern State: How the Courts Reformed America's Prisons*. Cambridge: Cambridge University Press.

Feely, Malcolm M., and Austin D. Sarat. 1980. *The Policy Dilemma: Federal Crime Policy and the Law Enforcement Assistance Administration, 1968–1978*. Minneapolis: University of Minnesota.

Feeley, Malcolm M., and Jonathan Simon. 1992. "The New Penology: Notes on the Emerging Strategy of Corrections and Its Implication." *Criminology* 30: 449–74.

Feld, Barry. 1999. *Bad Kids: Race and the Transformation of the Juvenile Court*. New York: Oxford University Press.

Felman, Shoshana, and Dori Laub. 1992. *Testimony: Crises of Witnessing in Literature, Psychoanalysis, and History*. New York: Routledge.

Ferguson, Ann Arnett. 2000. *Bad Boys: Public Schools in the Making of Black Masculinity*. Ann Arbor: University of Michigan Press.

Filosa, Gwen. 2003. "Jordan's Office Hoping to Get a Bit of Brooklyn Bite; Prosecutor visits N.O. to Give a Bit of Advice." *Times-Picayune*, March 20.

Fineman, Martha A. 1995. *The Neutered Mother, the Sexual Family, and Other Twentieth Century Tragedies*. New York: Routledge.

Finnegan, William. 1999. *Cold New World: Growing Up in a Harder Country*. New York: Modern Library.

Foner, Eric. 1989. *Reconstruction: America's Unfinished Revolution*. New York: Harper Collins.

Ford, David A., and Mary Jean Regoli. 1993. "The Criminal Prosecution of Wife Assaulters: Process, Problems, and Effects." In *The Impact of Police Laying Charges in Legal Responses to Wife Assault: Current Trends and Evaluation*, ed. N. Zoe Hilton. Newbury Park, CA: Sage.

Foucault, Michel. 1977. *Discipline and Punish: The Birth of the Prison*. New York: Pantheon.

———. 1978. *The History of Sexuality*. Vol. 1: *An Introduction*. Translated by Robert Hurley. New York: Random House.

———. 1985. *The Uses of Pleasure: The History of Sexuality*. Vol. 2. Translated by Robert Hurley. New York: Pantheon.

———. 1991. "Governmentality." in *The Foucault Effect, Studies in Governmentality*, ed. Graham Burchell, Peter Miller, and Collin Gordon, pp. 87–104. Chicago: University of Chicago Press.

———. 2000. "The Subject and Power." In *Essential Works of Foucault, 1954–1984*. Vol. 3: *Power*, ed. James D. Faubion. New York: New York Press.

Franklin, Richard H. 1998. "Assessing Supermax Operations." *Corrections Today*, July: 126.

Fraser, Steve, and Gary Gerstle. 1989. *The Rise and Fall of the New Deal Order, 1930–1980*. Princeton, N.J.: Princeton University Press.

Frisbie, Thomas, and Randy Garrett. 1998. *Victims of Justice: The True Story of Two Innocent Men Condemned to Die and a Prosecution Out of Control*. New York: Avon.

Furman v. Georgia. 408 U.S. 238 (1972).

Garland, David. 1996. "The Limits of the Sovereign State: Strategies of Crime Control in Contemporary Society." *British Journal of Criminology*, 36: 445–471.

Garland, David. 2001a. *The Culture of Control: Crime and Social Order in a Contemporary Society*. Chicago: University of Chicago Press.

———, ed. 2001b. *Mass Imprisonment: Social Causes and Consequences*. New York: Sage.

Garreau, Joel. 1991. *Edge Cities: Life on the New Frontier*. New York: Doubleday.

Gavey, Nicola. 1999. " 'I Wasn't Raped, but . . .': Revisiting Definitional Problems in Sexual Victimization." In *New Versions of Victims: Feminists Struggle with the Concept*, ed. Sharon Lamb, 57–81. New York: New York University Press.

Gelman, Andrew, James Liebman, Valerie West and Alexander Kiss. 2004. "A Broken System: The Persistent Patterns of Reversals of Death Sentences in the United States." *Journal of Empirical Legal Studies* 1: 209–61.

Geoghegan, Thomas. 1991. *Which Side Are You On? Trying to Be for Labor When It's Flat on its Back*. New York: Faffar, Straus & Giroux.

Gilliom, John. 1994. *Surveillance, Privacy, and the Law: Employee Drug Testing and the Politics of Social Control*. Ann Arbor: University of Michigan Press.

Giroux, Henry A. 2003. *Abandoned Generation: Democracy Beyond the Culture of Fear*. London: Palsgrave MacMillan.

Glassner, Barry. 1999. *The Culture of Fear: Why Americans Are Afraid of the Wrong Things*. New York: Basic Books.

Gleason, Christy. 2001. "Presence, Perspectives and Power: Gender and the Rationale Differences in the Debate over the Violence Against Women Act." *Women's Law Reporter* 23: 1–19.

Goldkamp, John S., Michael R. Gottfredson, Peter R. Jones, and Doris Weiland. 1995. *Personal Liberty and Community Safety: Pretrial Release in the Criminal Court*. New York: Plenum Press.

Gordon, Colin 1999. "Governmental Rationality: An Introduction" in *The Foucault Effect, Studies in Governmentality*, ed. Graham Burchell, Peter Miller, and Collin Gordon, pp. 1–52. Chicago: University of Chicago Press.

Gordon, Diana R. 1994. *The Return of the Dangerous Classes: Drug Prohibition and Policy Politics*. New York: Norton.

Gottschalk, Marie. 2006. *The Prison and the Gallows: The Politics of Mass Incarceration in America*. New York: Cambridge University Press.

Greenholtz v. Inmates of Nebraska Penal and Correctional Institutions, 443 U.S. 1 (1979).

Gronlund, Laurie E. 1993. "Understanding the National Goals," ERIC Digest. Available at www.ed.gov/databases/ERIC_ Digests/ed358581.htn.

Gruber, Aya. 2006. "Feminist War on Crime," *Iowa Law Review* forthcoming.

H.R. No. 1385, 83rd Cong., 2d Sess., 5 (1954); S. Rep. No. 1635, 83rd Cong., 2d Sess., 4 (1954).

Habermas, Jürgen. 1996. *Between Facts and Norms: Contributions to a Discourse Theory of Law and Democracy.* Translated by William Rehg. Cambridge: MIT Press.

Hacking, Ian. 1986. "Making Up People." In *Reconstructing Individualism: Autonomy, Individuality, and the Self in Western Thought,* ed. Thomas Heller, Morton Sosna, and David E. Wellbery, pp. 222–236. Stanford, Calif.: Stanford University Press.

———. 1990. *The Taming of Chance.* Cambridge: Cambridge University Press.

Hall, Darrien. 2001. *Gangster Dreams.* New York: Milligan Books.

Hall, Stuart, Charles Critcher, Tony Jefferson, John Clarke, and Brian Robert. 1978. *Policing the Crisis.* London: Macmillan.

Hamdi v. Rumsfeld. 542 U.S. 587 (2004).

Haney, Craig. 2003. "Mental Health Issues in Long-Term Solitary and 'Supermax' Confinement." *Crime & Delinquency* 49: 124–156.

Hanna, Cheryl. 1996. "No Right to Choose: Mandated Victim Participation in Domestic Violence Prosecutions." *Harvard Law Review* 109: 1849.

Harris, Louis. 1959. Why the Odds Are Against a Governor Becoming President. *Public Opinion Quarterly* 23: 361–70.

Harris, Richard. 1969. *Fear of Crime.* New York: Praeger.

Harrison, Paige M., and Allen J. Beck. 2002. *Prisoners in 2001.* Bureau of Justice Statistics Bulletin. NCJ 195189.

Hartman, Laura P., and Gabriella Bucci. 2001. "The Economic and Ethical Implications of the New Technology on Privacy in the Workplace." *Business and Society Review* 102/103: 1–24.

Hay, Douglas. 1975. "Property, Authority, and the Criminal Law." In *Albion's Fatal Tree: Crime and Society in 18th Century England,* ed. Douglas Hay, Peter Linebaugh, and E. P. Thompson. New York: Pantheon.

Hays, Samuel P. 1987. *Beauty, Health, and Permanence: Environmental Politics in the United States, 1955–1985.* New York: Cambridge University Press.

Heimer, Carol. 2002. "Insuring More, Ensuring Less: The Costs and Benefits of Private Regulation through Insurance." In *Embracing Risk: The Changing Culture of Insurance and Responsibility,* ed. Tom Baker and Jonathan Simon, pp. 116–135. Chicago: University of Chicago Press.

Heller, Robert. 1997. "Selective Prosecution and the Federalization of Criminal Law: The Need for Meaningful Judicial Review of Prosecutorial Discretion." University of Pennsylvania Law Review 145, 1309, 1326.

Herbers, John. 1970. "Democrats Shift to Right, in Line with G.O.P. on Crime Issues." *New York Times,* October 12.

Hermer, Joe, and Alan Hunt. 1996. "Official Graffiti of the Everyday." *Law and Society Review* 30: 231–57.

Herszenhorn, David M. 2000. "It's 'Not in My Backyard' for Anything: Affluent Neighbors Now Feud over Schools and Nature Trails." *New York Times*, April 16, A29.

Herzog, Don. 1989. *Happy Slaves: A Critique of Consent Theory*. Chicago: University of Chicago Press.

Hickman, Mathew H., and Brian A. Reaves. 2001. "Community Policing in Local Police Departments, 1997 and 1999." *Bureau of Justice Statistics Special Report*. Washington, D.C., Department of Justice, February.

Higham, Scott, Joe Stephens, and Margot Williams. 2004. "Guantanamo—A Holding Cell in War on Terror: Prison Represents a Problem That's Tough to Get Out Of," *Washington Post*, May 2, A01.

Hill, Judy. 1994. "Zero Tolerance for Violence Gains Support." *Tampa Tribune*, December 1, 1.

Hirschman, Albert O. 1977. *The Passions and the Interests*. Princeton, N.J.: Princeton University Press.

Hochschild, Arlie. 1997. *Timebind: When Work Becomes Home and Home Becomes Work*. New York: Metropolitan Books.

Hoffman, Sharona. 2001. "Preplacement Examinations and Job-Relatedness: How to Enhance Privacy and Diminish Discrimination in the Workplace." *University of Kansas Law Review* 49: 517.

Hollwitz, John. 1998. "Investigations of a Structural Interview for Pre-employment Integrity Screening." Ph.D. diss., psychology dept.,University of Nebraska.

Holmes, Oliver W. 1881. *The Common Law*. Boston: Little, Brown.

Hood, Roger. 2001. "Capital Punishment: A Global Perspective." *Punishment and Society* 3: 331–54.

Horn, David. 2003. *The Criminal Body: Lombroso and the Anatomy of Deviance*. London: Routledge.

Human Rights Watch. 2004. "No Second Chance: People with Criminal Records Denied Access to Public Housing." New York: Human Rights Watch.

Humes, Edward. 1999. *Mean Justice: A Town's Terror, A Prosecutor's Power, A Betrayal of Innocence*. New York: Simon & Schuster.

Huston, Luther A. 1967. *The Department of Justice*. New York: Praeger.

In re Rosenkranz, 80 Cal. App. 4th 409 (2000) 414, 419, 421, 428.

Inglehart, Ronald. 1981. "Post-Materialism in an Environment of Insecurity." *American Political Science Review* 75: 880–900.

Jacobs, James B., and Kimberly Potter. 1998. *Hate Crimes: Criminal Law and Identity Politics*. New York: Oxford University Press.

Jacoby, Joan. 1980. *The American Prosecutor: A Search for Identity*. Lexington, Mass: Lexington Books.

Jenness, Valerie, and Kendal Broad. 1997. *Hate Crimes: New Social Movements and the Politics of Violence*. New York: Walter de Gruyter.

Johnson, Lyndon B. 1968. *Public Papers of the President,* 725–78. Washington, D.C.: Government Printing Office.

Kahan, Dan. 1996. "What do Alternative Sanctions Mean?" *University of Chicago law Review* 63: 630–63.

Kalven, James. 1999. *Working with Available Light: A Family's World after Violence.* New York: Norton.

Kaminer, Wendy. 1995. *It's All the Rage: Crime and Culture.* Reading, Mass.: Addison-Wesley.

Kamisar, Yale. 2005. "How Earl Warren's 22 Years in Law Enforcement Affected His Work as Chief Justice." Earl Warren and the Warren Court: The Legacy in American and Foreign Law. Berkeley, CA: Institute for Governmental Studies, University of California.

Kantorowicz, Ernst. 1957. *The King's Two Bodies: A Study in Medieval Political Theology.* Princeton, N.J.: Princeton University Press.

Katz, Jesse. 1998. "Taking Zero Tolerance to the Limit," *Los Angeles Times,* home ed., March 1, A1.

Kay, Herma Hill. 1987. "Equality and Difference: A Perspective on No-Fault Divorce and Its Aftermath." *University of Cincinnati Law Review* 56: 1–88.

Kay, Herma Hill. 2002–2003. "No-Fault Divorce and Child Custody: Chilling out the Gender Wars." *Family Law Quarterly* 36: 27–48.

Kelling, George L., and James Q. Wilson. 1982. "Broken Windows," *Atlantic Monthly* 249: 29–38.

Kennedy, David J. 1995. "Residential Associations as State Actors: Regulating the Impact of Gated Communities on Nonmembers." *Yale Law Journal* 105: 761–793.

Kennedy, Joseph. 2001. "Monstrous Offenders and the Search for Solidarity through Modern Punishment." *Hastings Law Journal* 51: 829, 829–908.

Kenworthy E. W. 1968. "Nixon Scores 'Indulgence.' " *New York Times,* November 3.

Kessler, Michelle. 2003. "Companies Must add Rising Security Costs to Bottom Line," *USA Today,* March 28, 1B.

Kirp, David L. 1982. *Just Schools: The Idea of Racial Equality in American Education.* Berkeley: University of California Press.

Koons v. United States 530 U.S. 1278 (1996).

Kousser, J. Morgan. 1999. *Minority Voting Rights and the Undoing of the Second Reconstruction.* Chapel Hill: University of North Carolina Press.

Kracke, Kristen. 2001a. "Children's Exposure to Violence: The Safe Start Initiative." Fact sheet. Washington, D.C.: U.S. Department of Justice, Office of Justice Programs, Office of Juvenile Justice and Delinquency Prevention, April.

———. 2001b. "The 'Green Book' Demonstration." Fact sheet. Washington, D.C.: U.S. Department of Justice, Office of Justice Programs, Office of Juvenile Justice and Delinquency Prevention, May.

Kubik, Jeffrey, and John R. Moran. 2001. "Lethal Elections: Gubernatorial Politics and the Timing of Executions." Department of Economics and Center for Policy Research, Syracuse University, September.

Kurtz, Michael L. 1982. *Crime of the Century: The Kennedy Assassination from a Historian's Perspective*. Knoxville: University of Tennessee Press.

Lacayo, Richard. 1988. "A New Mission Impractical; Zero Tolerance for Users." *Time*, May 30, 18.

Laden, Vicki A., and Gregory Schwartz. 2000. "Psychiatric Disabilities, the Americans with Disabilities Act, and the New Workplace Violence Account." *Berkeley Journal of Employment and Labor Law* 21: 246–269.

Lakoff, George and Mark Johnson. 1980. *Metaphors We Live By*. Chicago: University of Chicago Press.

Lamb, Sharon. 1996. *The Trouble with Blame: Victims, Perpetrators, and Responsibility*. Cambridge, Mass.: Harvard University Press, 1996.

Lasch, Christopher. 1977. *Haven in a Heartless World: The Family Besieged*. New York: Basic Books.

Lederman, Cindy S., and Eileen N. Brown. 2000. "Entangled in the Shadows: Girls in the Juvenile Justice System." *Buffalo Law Review* 48, 909.

Lewin, Tamar. 2001. "Zero-Tolerance Policy Is Challenged: A Matter of Domestic Violence and Housing Ends Up in Court." *New York Times*, national ed., July 11, A10.

Liebman, James S. 2000. "The Over Production of Death." *Columbia Law Review* 100: 2030.

Lifton, Robert J., and Greg Mitchell. 2000. *Who Owns Death: Capital Punishment, the American Conscience, and the End of Executions*. New York: Morrow.

Litwak, Robert S. 2001. " 'Rogue State,' a Policy-Stifling Term." *Miami Herald*, May 9, 7B.

Locke, John. 1968. "Some Thoughts Concerning Education." *The Educational Writings of John Locke*.Cambridge: Cambridge University Press.

Lowi, Theodore J., ed. 1964. *Robert F. Kennedy: The Pursuit of Justice*. New York: Harper & Row.

Lyons, William, and Julie Drew. 2006. *Punishing Schools: Fear and Citizenship in American Public Education*. Ann Arbor: University of Michigan Press.

Madriz, Esther. 1997. *Nothing Bad Happens to Good Girls: Fear of Crime in Women's Lives*. Berkeley: University of California Press.

Mahoney, Martha R. 1994. "Victimization or Oppression? Women's Lives, Violence, and Agency." In *The Public Nature of Private Violence: The Discovery of Domestic Abuse*, ed. Martha Fineman and Roxanne Mykitiuk, pp. 59–92. New York: Routledge.

Marable, Manning. 1991. *Race, Reform, and Rebellion: The Second Reconstruction in Black America, 1945–1990*. Jackson: University Press of Mississippi.

Marion, Nancy E. 1993. *A History of Federal Crime Control Initiatives, 1960–1993*. Westport, Conn.: Praeger.

Mauer, Marc. 2002. *Invisible Punishment: The Collateral Consequences of Mass Imprisonment*. New York: New Press.

———. 1999. *Race to Incarcerate*: New York: New Press.

McCleskey v. Kemp. 481 U.S. 279 (1987).

McCluskey, Martha. 1998. "The Illusion of Efficiency in Workers' Compensation Reform," *Rutgers Law Review* 50: 657–941.

———. 2002. "The Rhetoric of Risk and the Redistribution of Social Insurance." In *Embracing Risk: The Changing Culture of Insurance and Responsibility,* ed. Tom Baker and Jonathan Simon. Chicago: University of Chicago Press.

McConnell, Darci. 2000. "Latest Senate Race Fight: Who's Softer on Crime?" *Detroit News,* October 31, 1.

McCurdy, Patrick P. 1975. "The PVC Puzzle: Some Pieces Are Still Missing." *Chemical Week,* September 24, 5.

McKenzie, Evan. 1994. *Privatopia.* New Haven, Conn.: Yale University Press.

Meranze, Michael. 1996. *Laboratories of Virtue: Punishment, Revolution, and Authority in Philadelphia, 1780–1835.* Chapel Hill: University of North Carolina Press.

Meyerson, Harold. 1994. *The American Prospect Reader in American Politics.* Chatham, N.J.: Chatham House.

Miller, Jerome. 1996. *Search and Destroy: African-American Males in the Criminal Justice System.* Cambridge: Cambridge University Press.

Miller, Lisa. 2001. *The Politics of Community Crime Prevention: Implementing Operation Weed and Seed in Seattle.* Burlington, Vt.: Ashgate, Dartmouth.

Miller, Marc. 2004. "Domination and Dissatisfaction: Prosecutors as Sentencers." *Stanford Law Review* 56: 1211–1269.

Mills, Linda G. 1997. *The Heart of Intimate Abuse: New Interventions in Child Welfare, Criminal Justice, and Health Settings.* New York: Springer.

———. 1999. "Killing Her Softly: Intimate Abuse and the Violence of State Intervention." *Harvard Law Review* 113, 550.

———. 2003. *Insult to Injury: Rethinking Our Responses to Intimate Abuse.* Princeton, N.J.: Princeton University Press.

Minow, Martha. 1993. "Surviving Victim Talk." *UCLA Law Review* 40, 1411.

Mnookin, Robert H., and Lewis Kornhauser. 1979. "Bargaining in the Shadow of the Law: The Case of Divorce." *Yale Law Journal* 88: 950–997.

Moran, Greg. 2000. "Chances Rare for Life-Term Prisoners: Davis, Parole Board Stand Firm on Issue." *San Diego Union-Tribune,* May 6, A1, A12.

Navasky, Victor. 1971. *Kennedy Justice.* New York: Atheneum.

Neely, Richard. 1981. *How Courts Govern America.* New Haven, Conn.: Yale University Press.

Neptune Fireworks, Inc. v. State Fire Marshall's Office, et. al., Memorandum Opinion and Order, No. 89 C 5074, United States District Court for the Northern District of Illinois, December 28, 1994. 1994 W. L. 721194.

New Jersey v. T.L.O., 469 U.S. 325 (1985).

Nixon, Richard. 1971. Annual Message to Congress on the State of the Union. The American Presidency Project, http://www.presidency.ucsb.edu/ws/index.php?pid=3110.

O'Malley, Pat. 1999. "Volatile and Contradictory Punishment." *Theoretical Criminology* 3: 175–196.

Packer, Herbert L. 1968. *The Limits of the Criminal Sanction*. Stanford, Cal.: Stanford University Press.

Padilla v. Rumseld. 542 U.S. 426 (2004).

Parenti, Christian. 1998. *Lockdown America: Police and Prisons in the Age of Crisis*. London: Verso, 1998.

Park, Robert, and Ernest W. Burgess. 1925. *The City*. Chicago: University of Chicago Press.

Patterson, James T. 1987. *The Dread Disease: Cancer and Modern American Culture*. Cambridge, Mass.: Harvard University Press.

Payne v. Tennessee. 501 U.S. 808 (1991).

Pence, Ellen and Melanie Shepard, eds. 1999. *Coordinating Community Responses to Domestic Violence: Lessons from Duluth and Beyond*. London: Sage.

Peter D. Hart Research Associates, Inc. 2002. "Changing Public Attitudes toward the Criminal Justice System: Summary of Findings." New York: Open Society Institute, February.

Peterson, Bill. 1988. "Bush Vows to Fight Pollution, Install 'Conservation Ethic'; Speech Distances Candidate from Reagan." *Washington Post,* September 1, A1.

Philbrick, Jane H., Marcia R. Sparks, Marsha E. Hass, and Steven Arsenault. 2003. "Workplace Violence: The Legal Costs Can Kill You." *American Business Review* 21.

Phillips, Ann E. 1996. Violence in the Workplace: Reevaluating the Employer's Role." *Buffalo Law Review* 44: 139.

Pierson, Paul. 1993. "When Effect Become Cause: Policy Feedback and Political Change." *World Politics* 45: 595–628.

Podair, Jerald E. 2002. *The Strike that Changed New York: Blacks, Whites and the Ocean Hill-Brownsville Crisis*. New Haven, CT: Yale University Press.

Potter, Clair Bond. 1998. *War on Crime: Bandits, G-Men, and the Politics of Mass Culture*. New Brunswick, N.J.: Rutgers University Press.

Pound, Roscoe. 1913. "The Administration of Justice in the Modern City." *Harvard Law Review* 26: 302–328.

Prejean, Sister Helen. 2005. "Death in Texas." *New York Review of Books* 52, 1 (January).

Rabin, Robert. 1986. "A History of Regulatory Models." *Stanford Law Review* 37, 1273.

Random House College Dictionary. 1975. Rev. ed. New York: Random House.

Raphael, Stephen and Jens Ludwig. 2002. "Do Prison Enhancements Reduce Gun Crime: The Case of Project Exile." in *Evaluating Gun Policy: Effects on Crime and Violence*. Washington, D.C.: Brookings Institution Press.

Rasul v. Bush. 542 U.S. 466 (2004).

Reisman, W. Michael. 2004. "*Rasul v. Bush*: A Failure to Apply International Law." *Journal of International Criminal Justice* 2: 973–987.

Renzetti, Claire M. 2001. " 'One Strike and You're Out', Implications of a Federal Crime Control Policy for Battered Women." *Violence Against Women* 7: 685–98.

Ricciardulli, Alex. 2002. "The Broken Safety Valve: Judicial Discretion's Failure to Ameliorate Punishment under California's Three Strikes Law." *Duquesne Law Review* 41: 1–67.

Richman, Daniel. 2001. " 'Project Exile' and the Allocation of Federal Law Enforcement Authority," *Arizona Law Review.* 43: 369–411.

Roberts, Paul. 2001. "Bad Sports or: How We Learned to Stop Worrying and Love the SUV." Harper's, April, 69.

Roosevelt, Franklin. 1934. "Address" in the Proceedings of the Attorney General's Conference on Crime. Washington, D.C.

Rose, Nikolas. 1999. *The Powers of Freedom: Reframing Political Thought.* Cambridge: Cambridge University Press, 1999.

Rosenberg, Charles E. 1987. *The Care of Strangers: The Rise of the American Hospital System.* New York: Basic Books.

Rosenberg, Gerald. 1991. *The Hollow Hope.* Chicago: University of Chicago Press.

Rothman, David J. 1971. *The Discovery of the Asylum: Order and Disorder in the New Republic.* Boston: Little, Brown.

———. 1980. *Conscience and Convenience: The Asylum and Its Alternatives in Progressive America.* Boston: Little, Brown.

Rothstein, Richard. 2001. "Of Schools and Crimes, and Gross Exaggeration." *New York Times,* national ed., February 7, 57.

Saguy, Abigail S. 2003. *What Is Sexual Harassment: From Capital Hill to the Sorbonne.* Berkeley: University of California Press.

Samuel, Terence. 1999. "Ashcroft Will Target Crime, Drugs in State." *St. Louis Post-Dispatch,* March 12, 1.

Sams, Jim. 2000. "Davis Saying No to Paroles." *San Diego Union-Tribune,* February 12, A1, A11.

Sanger, David E. 2001. "The New Administration: The Plan; Bush Pushes Ambitious Education Plan." *New York Times,* national ed., January 24, A1.

Sarat, Austin. 2001. *When the State Kills: Capital Punishment and the American Condition.* Princeton, N.J.: Princeton University Press.

Scammons, Richard, and Ben J. Wattenberg. 1969. *The Real Majority.* New York: Coward-McCann.

Schecter, Susan. 1982. *Women and Male Violence: The Vision and Struggle of the Battered Women's Movement.* Boston: South End Press.

Scheingold, Stuart A. 1984. *The Politics of Law and Order: Street Crime and Public Policy.* New York: Longman.

———. 1991. *The Politics of Street Crime: Criminal Process and Cultural Obsession.* Philadelphia: Temple University Press.

Scheingold, Stuart A., Toska Olson, and Jana Pershing. 1994. Republican Criminology and Victim Advocacy. Sexual Violence, Victim Advocacy, and Republican Criminology: Washington State's Community Protection Act." *Law & Society Review* 28: 729–764.

Scheck, Barry, Peter Neufield, and Jim Dwyer. 2001. *Actual Innocence: When Justice Goes Wrong and How to Make It Right.* New York: Signet.

Schmitt, Carl. 1996 (1923). *The Crisis of Parliamentary Democracy.* Translated by Ellen Kennedy. Cambridge: MIT Press.

Schneider, Elizabeth M. 1992. "Particularity and Generality: Challenges of Feminist Theory and Practice in Work on Woman-Abuse." *New York University Law Review* 67: 520.

———. 2001. "Battered Women and Feminist Lawmaking." *Women's Law Reporter* 23: 243–47.

Schrag, Peter. 1998. *Paradise Lost: California's Experience, America's Future.* Berkeley: University of California Press.

Schultz, Vicki. 1998. "Reconceptualizing Sexual Harassment." *Yale Law Journal* 107: 1683.

Seelye, Katharine Q. 2003. "For Gray Davis, Great Fall from Highest Height," *New York Times*, October 8, A27.

Shafro, Joan. 2001. "Note: Should These Marriages Have Been Saved?: Extreme Cruelty as a Cause of Action for Divorce in New Jersey 1950–1960." *Women's Rights Law Reporter* 23: 79–92.

Shapiro, Bruce. 1997. "Victims and Vengeance." *The Nation,* February 10, 11.

Shearing, Clifford, and Philip Stenning. 1984. From the Panopticon to Disney World: The Development of Discipline. Toronto: University of Toronto Press.

Sheley, Joseph F. 2000. "Controlling Violence: What Schools Are Doing, Preventing School Violence." *NIJ Research Forum.* Washington, D.C.: U.S. Department of Justice, 37.

Sherman, Lawrence W., and Richard A. Berk. 1984. "The Specific Deterrent Effects of Arrest for Domestic Assault." *American Sociological Review* 49: 261–72.

Sherman, Lawrence W., et al. 1992. "Crime, Punishment, and Stake in Conformity: Legal and Informal Control of Domestic Violence." *American Sociological Review* 57: 680, 686.

Shils, Edward. 1982. "Centre and Periphery." In E. Shils, *The Constitution of Society*, pp. 93–109. Chicago: University of Chicago Press.

Siegel, Reva B. 1996. " 'The Rule of Love': Wife Beating as Prerogative and Privacy." *Yale Law Journal* 105: 2117–2207.

Simon, Jonathan. 1988. "The Ideological Effects of Actuarial Practices," *Law & Society Review* 22: 801–30.

———. 1993. *Poor Discipline: Parole and the Social Control of the Underclass 1890–1990.* Chicago: University of Chicago Press.

———. 1995. "Power without Parents: Juvenile Justice in a Postmodern Society." *Carodozo Law Review* 16: 1363.

———. 1998a. "Driving Governmentality: Automobile Accidents, Insurance, and the Challenge to Social Order in the Inter-War Years, 1919–1941." *Connecticut Insurance Law Journal* 4: 522–88.

———. 1998b. "Ghosts of the Disciplinary Machine: Lee Harvey Oswald, Life-History, and the Truth of Crime." *Yale Journal of Law and the Humanities* 10: 113.

———. 2004. "Fearless Speech In the Killing State: The Power of Capital Crime Victim Speech." *North Carolina Law Review* 82: 1377–1413.

———. 2005. "Parrhesiastic Accountability: Investigatory Commissions and Executive Power in an Age of Terror." *Yale Law Journal* 114: 1419–57.

Simon, Jonathan, and Christina Spaulding. 1998. "Tokens of Our Esteem: Aggravating Factors in the Era of Deregulated Death Penalties." In *The Killing State: Capital Punishment in Law, Politics, and Culture*, ed. Austin Sarat. New York: Oxford University Press, 1998.

Smith, William French. 1991. *Law and Justice in the Reagan Administration: Memoirs of an Attorney General*. Stanford, Calif.: Hoover Institute Press.

Statement of the National Association of Secondary School Principals on Civil Rights Implications of Zero Tolerance Programs, presented before the United States Commission on Civil Rights, February 18.

St. Clair, Katy. 2004. "Striking Back at Bullies." *East Bay Express*, June 16–22, 1.

Steiker, Carol. 2002. "Things Fall Apart, but the Center Holds: The Supreme Court and the Death Penalty." *New York University Law Review* 77: 1475.

Stephenson, Bryant. 2002. "The Politics of Fear and Death: Successive Problems in Capital Federal Habeas Corpus Cases." *New York University Law Review* 77: 699.

Stith, Kate, and Jose A. Cabranes. 1998. *Fear of Judging: Sentencing Guidelines in the Federal Courts*. Chicago: University of Chicago Press.

Stuntz, William J. 2001. "The Pathological Politics of Criminal Law." *Michigan Law Review* 100: 505.

———. 2006. "The Political Constitution of Criminal Justice." *Harvard Law Review* 119: 780.

Sudnow, David. 1965. "Normal Crimes: Sociological Features of the Penal Code in a Public Defender Office." *Social Problems* 12: 255–276.

Sugrue, Thomas J. 1996. *The Origins of the Urban Crisis: Race and Inequality in Postwar Detroit*. Princeton, N.J.: Princeton University Press.

Terry v. Ohio. 392 US 1 (1968).

Thompson, E. P. 1975. *Whigs and Hunters: The Origins of the Black Act*. New York: Pantheon.

Tilly, Charles. 1985. "The State as Organized Crime," pp. 169–191 in *Bringing the State Back In*, ed. Peter Evans, Dietrich Rueschemeyer, and Theda Skocpol. Cambridge: Cambridge University Press.

Travis, Jeremy, and Amy Wahl. 2001. "Returning Home: Re-entry from Prison." Washington: Urban Institute.

Tribe, Lawrence. 1988. *American Constitutional Law*, 2nd Ed. Mineola, Minn.: Foundation Press.

Tyler, Tom. 1997. *Social Justice in a Diverse Society*. Boulder, Colo.: Westview Press.

Uchitelle, Louis. 2002. " 'Broken System? Tweak It. They Say,' (quoting George Akerlof)." *New York Times*, July 28, 3–12.

U.S. Department of Justice, F.B.I. 2002. "Crime in the United States 2001: Uniform Crime Report," October 28. Washington, D.C.: US Department of Justice.

United States v. Booker, 125 S.Ct. 738 (2005).

United States v. Fraguela, 1998 W.L. 560352 (E.D. La. Aug. 27, 1998).

United States v. Lowery, 15 F.Supp.2d 1348 (S.D.Fla. 1998).

United States v. Lowery, 166 F.3d 1119 (11th Cir. 1999).

United States v. Singleton, 165 F.3d 1297 (10th Cir. En Banc 1999).

United States v. Ware, 161 F.3d 414, 421 (6th Cir. 1998).

Uviller, H. Richard, and William G. Merkel. 2002. *The Militia and Right to Arms, or, How the Second Amendment Fell Silent.* Durham, N.C.: Duke University Press.

Vernonia School District 47J v. Acton, 515 U.S. 646 (1995).

Von Drehle, David. 1995. *Among the Lowest of the Dead.* New York: Times Books.

Wacquant, Loic. 2000a. "Deadly Symbiosis: When Ghetto and Prison Meet and Mesh." In *Mass Imprisonment: Social Causes and Consequences,* ed. David Garland. New York: Sage.

———. 2000b. "The New 'Peculiar Institution': On the Prison as Surrogate Ghetto." *Theoretical Criminology* 4: 377.

Walker, Lenore. 1984. *The Battered Woman Syndrome.* New York: Springer.

Walker, Samuel. 1980. *Popular Justice: A History of American Criminal Justice.* New York: Oxford University Press.

Weiler, Paul. 1990. *Governing the Work Place.* Cambridge, Mass.: Harvard University Press.

Weisberg, Robert. 1983. "Deregulating Death." *Supreme Court Review* 1983: 305–395.

Westley, William. 1953. "Violence and the Police." *American Journal of Sociology* 59: 34–51.

White, Theodore. 1998. *Making of the President.* New York: Buccaneer Books.

White House. 2004. "President Discusses Job Training and the Economy in Ohio" http://www.whitehouse.gov/news/releases/2004/01/20040121-2.html.

Whitman, James Q. 2003. *Harsh Justice: Criminal Punishment and the Widening Divide between America and Europe.* New York: Oxford University Press.

Williams v. New York, 337 U.S. 241 (1949).

Williamson, Oliver E. 1996. *The Mechanisms of Governance.* New York: Oxford University Press.

Willrich, Michael. 2003. City of Courts: Socializing Justice in Progressive Era Chicago. Cambridge, UK: Cambridge University Press.

Wilson, Michael. "Walking Tall on Hallway Beat: Growing Stature for Officers who Patrol the schools." *The New York Times,* National Edition, January 9, 2004, A17.

Wilson, Woodrow. 2002 (1900). *Congressional Government.* New Brunswick, N.J.: Transaction Books.

Winnick, Bruce. 2000. "Applying the Law Therapeutically in Domestic Violence Cases." *University of Missouri at Kansas City Law Review* 69: 33.

Woodward, Bob. 1999. *Shadowed: Five Presidents and the Legacy of Watergate, 1974–1999.* New York: Simon and Schuster.

Zernike, Kate. 2001a. "Antidrug Program Says It Will Adopt a New Strategy." *New York Times*, February 15, A17.

———. 2001b. "A Second Look: Charting the Charter Schools." *New York Times*, Week in Review, March 23, 3.

Zimring, Franklin E. 2002. "The Common Thread: Diversion in the Jurisprudence of Juvenile Courts." In *A Century of Juvenile Justice*, ed. Margaret Rosenheim, Franklin E. Zimring, David S. Tanenhaus, and Bernardine Dohrn. Chicago: University of Chicago Press.

———. 2004. *The Contradictions of American Capital Punishment*. New York: Oxford University Press.

Zimring, Franklin, and Gordon Hawkins. 1986. *Capital Punishment and the American Agenda*. Cambridge: Cambridge University Press.

Zimring, Franklin, and Gordon Hawkins. 1997. *Crime is Not the Problem: Lethal Violence in America*. New York: Oxford University Press.

Zimring, Franklin, Gordon Hawkins, and Sam Kamin. 2001. Punishment and Democracy: Three-Strikes and You're Out in California. New York: Oxford University Press.